UNIFICATION OF A
SLAVE STATE

UNIFICATION OF A
SLAVE STATE

The Rise of the Planter Class in the
South Carolina Backcountry, 1760–1808

Rachel N. Klein

Published for
The Institute of Early American History and Culture,
Williamsburg, Virginia,
by The University of North Carolina Press,
Chapel Hill and London

The Institute of Early American History and Culture
is sponsored jointly by the College of William and Mary
and the Colonial Williamsburg Foundation.

Library of Congress Cataloging-in-Publication Data

Klein, Rachel N.
Unification of a slave state : the rise of the planter class in
the South Carolina backcountry, 1760–1808 / Rachel N. Klein.
p. cm.
"This book began as a dissertation"
—Acknowledgments. Includes bibliographical references.
ISBN 0-8078-1899-2 (alk. paper)
1. South Carolina—Politics and government—Colonial period, ca. 1600–1775.
2. South Carolina—Politics and government—1775–1865. 3. Plantation owners
—South Carolina—History—18th century. 4. Plantation owners—South Carolina
—History—19th century. 5. Slavery—South Carolina—History—18th century.
6. Slavery—South Carolina—History—19th century. I. Title.
F272.K56 1990 975.7'02—dc20 89-16684 CIP

The paper in this book meets the guidelines for permanence
and durability of the Committee on Production Guidelines
for Book Longevity of the Council on Library Resources.

Manufactured in the United States of America

94 93 92 91 90 5 4 3 2 1

This volume received indirect support from an unrestricted book
publications grant awarded to the Institute by the L. J. Skaggs
and Mary C. Skaggs Foundation of Oakland, California.

Preliminary versions of Chapters 2 and 3 appeared in the following publications:
"Ordering the Backcountry: The South Carolina Regulation," *William and Mary
Quarterly*, 3d Ser., XXXVIII (1981), 661–680; and "Frontier Planters and the
American Revolution: The South Carolina Backcountry, 1775–1783" in Ronald
Hoffman *et al.*, eds., *An Uncivil War: The Southern Backcountry during the
American Revolution* (Charlottesville, Va., 1985), 37–69, reprinted by
permission of the University Press of Virginia.

For Bessie Boris Klein,
Robert S. Westman,
and in memory of
George S. Klein

Acknowledgments

Having spent more years with this project than I like to acknowledge, it is a pleasure, finally, to thank the many people who helped me bring it into being. This book began as a dissertation under the direction of Edmund S. Morgan, whose advice and example meant more to me than he knows. For their careful readings of the dissertation, I am also grateful to David Brion Davis and C. Vann Woodward. Over the years, George C. Rogers, Jr., has provided invaluable help and encouragement.

Without the assistance of archivists, this project could not have been completed. Alan Stokes and the staff of the South Caroliniana Library have been more than generous with their time and consideration. Alexia Helsley and the research room staff of the South Carolina Department of Archives and History also provided patient assistance, as did the archivists at the South Carolina Historical Society and the Charleston Library Society. For their help I also thank the staffs at the Historical Society of Pennsylvania, the Duke University Library, and the Southern Historical Collection, University of North Carolina, Chapel Hill.

Many friends helped to shape my understanding of the South Carolina backcountry. This project grew out of conversations with then fellow graduate students Barbara Weinstein, Rosario Perez, Steven Stern, and Florencia Mallon. It was my good fortune to be working at the Archives in Columbia while Alison Carl, David Carlton, Peter Coclanis, Lacy Ford, and John Scott Strickland were doing their own research. The friendly and intellectually stimulating atmosphere that they and others created made my stay in South Carolina an exceptionally happy one. For their kindness and help during my stay in Columbia and Charleston, I am especially grateful to George C. Terry, Carol Bleser, Scott Wilds, and Nan Woodruff.

A fellowship at the Institute of Early American History and Culture made it possible for me to continue my research. Thad Tate, Director of the Institute, offered support and encouragement. Cynthia Carter Ayres also made the Institute a pleasant place in which to work, as did William Breiten-bach and Thomas Doerflinger. Philip Morgan provided careful and perceptive editorial and substantive suggestions. Ann Hofstra Grogg did a meticulous job of copyediting, and Gil Kelly provided incomparable assistance in the final stages of the editing. I am thankful to Lewis Bateman for his consistently kind support.

This work has benefited from a number of careful readings. Steven Hahn must have seen nearly as many versions as I have. From the outset he encouraged me in the project, and as a colleague he has continued to be a generous critic and friend. Comments by Thomas Dublin, Michael P. Johnson, and James P. Whittenburg were also much appreciated. Eugene D. Genovese's generous reading saved me from serious embarrassments. Stephanie McCurry offered invaluable comments on the entire manuscript. I am particularly grateful for her stimulating critique of my earlier discussion of proslavery Christianity. Julie Saville patiently read my eleventh-hour revisions and made it possible for me to send the manuscript off.

I am grateful to my mother, Bessie Boris Klein, for having faith that my involvement in the South Carolina backcountry would eventually come to an end. Finally, let me thank Robert Westman for everything else.

Contents

Maps and Tables

UNIFICATION OF A
SLAVE STATE

Abbreviations

BPL	Boston Public Library, Boston
CHS	Connecticut Historical Society, Hartford
DUL	Duke University Library, Durham, N.C.
HSP	Historical Society of Pennsylvania, Philadelphia
LC	Library of Congress, Washington, D.C.
MHS	Maryland Historical Society, Baltimore
NA	National Archives, Washington, D.C.
NYHS	New-York Historical Society, New York
NYPL	New York Public Library, New York
PRO	Public Record Office, London
SCDAH	South Carolina Department of Archives and History, Columbia, S.C.
SCHM	*South Carolina Historical Magazine*; until January 1952, *South Carolina Historical and Genealogical Magazine*
SCHS	South Carolina Historical Society, Columbia, S.C.
SCL	South Caroliniana Library, Columbia, S.C.
SHC	Southern Historical Collection, University of North Carolina, Chapel Hill
SHSW	State Historical Society of Wisconsin, Madison
WPA Abs.	Work Projects Administration Abstracts
WPA Trans.	Work Projects Administration Transcripts
WMQ	*William and Mary Quarterly*

Introduction

In March 1769 a group of armed men marched more than one hundred miles from the western backcountry of South Carolina to the coastal parish of Prince William to elect their leader, Patrick Calhoun, to the colonial assembly. The men, who were protesting their region's lack of representation in the colonial government, undoubtedly followed the old Indian trading path that linked the rolling hills of their piedmont settlement to the coastal plain, or lowcountry. They chose Prince William, as the most accessible coastal parish that allowed frontiersmen to vote. Calhoun, a deputy surveyor and justice of the peace, was already in the process of accumulating the approximately thirty-one slaves that he held at the end of his life, but most of the men who traveled with him must have been nonslaveholders.[1] Many of Calhoun's followers, having migrated to the South Carolina frontier from Virginia and North Carolina, were probably surprised by the dramatic changes they observed as they approached the luxuriant swamplands of the coastal parishes. From a settlement of small farms and few slaves, they entered a region dominated by wealthy rice and indigo planters and characterized by a substantial slave majority.

Although Calhoun's men succeeded in electing their leader to the assembly, it took another forty years for the backcountry's fledgling leadership to win for itself an acceptable system of apportionment in South Carolina's

1. [John C. Calhoun], *Life of John C. Calhoun: Presenting a Condensed History of Political Events from 1811 to 1843* (New York, 1843), 4; Walter B. Edgar *et al.*, eds., *Biographical Directory of the South Carolina House of Representatives* (Columbia, S.C., 1974–1984), II, 133–135; U.S., Bureau of the Census, *Heads of Families at the First Census of the United States Taken in the Year 1790: South Carolina* (Washington, D.C., 1908). For a discussion of Patrick Calhoun's early backcountry settlement and his activities as a surveyor, see Robert L. Meriwether, *The Expansion of South Carolina, 1729–1765* (Kingsport, Tenn., 1940), 133–135, 246, 252–253.

legislature. Patrick Calhoun's son, John Caldwell Calhoun, far surpassed his father as a political figure, but Patrick himself served regularly as a state representative and senator and achieved considerable renown among planters of his own day.[2] Although he did not live to see the reform of the state constitution that signaled the political unification of South Carolina, he was among those backcountry leaders who initiated the process of consolidation and defined the boundaries of political equality in an emerging slave society.

Planters of Patrick Calhoun's region and generation were involved in a dual struggle: As they pressed for political parity with their coastal counterparts, they also strove for local power and legitimacy. Indeed, the protracted sectional debate over legislative apportionment cannot be understood independently of persistent class tensions and accommodations within the backcountry itself. More or less chronologically, this study explores the formation of South Carolina's backcountry planter class by tracing sectional conflicts and interregional alliances in the context of local struggles for power and authority. The year 1808 forms an end point to this story because in that year representatives from all parts of the state agreed to a new system of legislative apportionment that finally terminated the dispute over representation and thereby ended the sectional conflict as it had been defined over the preceding half-century.

Historians of South Carolina, recognizing the exceptional social and political unity of the state's antebellum planter class, have pointed to the years between 1790 and 1810 as the critical period of class and state unification. Their argument has become a truism: the spread of cotton through the western part of the state transformed the region from a yeoman frontier into a plantation area dominated by wealthy slaveowners. Not only did cotton promote a vast increase in the number of backcountry slaves; it also prompted lowcountry planters to settle in the developing areas. As inland planters acquired more slaves and came into contact with their more established coastal counterparts, sections of South Carolina began to resemble one another. The spread of a boom crop transformed crusty backcountry yeomen into a wealthy planter leadership. The constitutional reform of 1808, which provided for a substantial increase in backcountry representation, was, according to this argument, the direct result of economic and social unification brought on by the rise of cotton.[3]

2. Edgar *et al.*, eds., *Biographical Directory of the House*, II, 133–135.
3. William A. Schaper, *Sectionalism and Representation in South Carolina* (New York, 1968 [orig. publ. Washington, D.C., 1901]); William W. Freehling, *Prelude to Civil War: The Nullification Controversy in South Carolina, 1816–1836* (New York, 1966), 17–19;

Although there is much of value in this interpretation, political histories have constructed a mechanical relationship between cotton expansion and the emergence of a planter class. By pointing to the era of the cotton boom as the critical period of state unification, they have tended to homogenize the eighteenth-century backcountry. In their portrayal of frontier South Carolina as a yeoman area, they have not sufficiently recognized regional variations within the backcountry and the distinct social and political impact of an inland elite that developed within the context of a nonplantation society. Even before the spread of cotton, backcountry leaders had established economic and political ties to their coastal counterparts. The most prominent backcountry names of the early nineteenth century were also visible before 1790. Many of the wealthiest and most politically active backcountry families of the antebellum decades had acquired slaves before the Revolution. Frontier planters had begun to shape their society before cotton made its mark.

This study devotes considerable attention to the backcountry planters' aggressively acquisitive activities, but it does not suggest that planters were capitalists or that they were creating a capitalist South. Leading backcountrymen were, before the Revolution, acquiring slaves for the production of staple crops. As merchants, millers, distillers, and surveyors, they also stood at the center of a lively and often contentious network of local exchange. In various ways and to different degrees they were, along with their yeomen neighbors, involved in commercial activities. They did not, however, draw the relations of production into the marketplace. From the period under consideration up to the Civil War, the household was the primary context of production in the backcountry and throughout the southern states. Looked at from this perspective, the planter class was precapitalist—or noncapitalist—in two senses. First, slavery embodied, in an extreme form, the dependency relationships that defined production in the household economy as a whole. Second, planters, by their very attachment to slavery, inhibited the

---

James M. Banner, Jr., "The Problem of South Carolina," in Stanley Elkins and Eric McKitrick, eds., *The Hofstadter Aegis: A Memorial* (New York, 1974), 60–93. Richard Maxwell Brown's study of the South Carolina Regulators points to the development of an inland elite before the expansion of cotton culture, but Brown does not place his findings in the context of class formation. See Brown, *The South Carolina Regulators* (Cambridge, Mass., 1963). Jerome J. Nadelhaft recognizes the prevalence of indigo production in the middlecountry before the Revolution and the expansion of backcountry tobacco production during the 1780s. However, in his treatment of colonial and state politics during the Revolutionary era, he tends to portray the backcountry as a homogeneous yeoman area. See Nadelhaft, *The Disorders of War: The Revolution in South Carolina* (Orono, Maine, 1981), 22, 134–135.

development of a labor market. In the process, they insulated the majority
of southern households from the sort of market penetration that transformed northern society and culture during the half-century before the Civil
War.[4] In short, the story of southern regional distinctiveness can be most
usefully understood in the context of the halting and tumultuous development of capitalist relationships in the antebellum North.[5]

In the end, this characterization of evolving regional distinctions is more
an interpretive than an evidential matter, but it is essential to an understanding of South Carolina during the Revolutionary and Early National
periods. Something more than common or competing interests, narrowly
defined, mediated relations between yeomen and planters within the back-

4. Several important theoretical discussions attest to the value of defining capitalism as
a particular relationship of production from which the majority of southerners were
insulated before the Civil War. Barbara Jeanne Fields, "The Nineteenth-Century Ameri-
can South: History and Theory," *Plantation Society in the Americas*, II (1983), 7–27;
Eugene D. Genovese, *The Political Economy of Slavery: Studies in the Economy and
Society of the Slave South* (New York, 1965); Genovese and Elizabeth Fox-Genovese,
*Fruits of Merchant Capital: Slavery and Bourgeois Property in the Rise and Expansion of
Capitalism* (New York, 1983), 34–60; Steven Hahn, *The Roots of Southern Populism:
Yeoman Farmers and the Transformation of the Georgia Upcountry, 1850–1890* (New
York, 1983), 1–133 *passim*; Hahn, "The Problem of Class Formation and the Rural
South's Transition to Capitalism," paper presented at the Annual Meeting of the Organi-
zation of American Historians, Los Angeles, 1984.

5. A vast literature has explored the process of capitalist transformation in the antebellum North. For a study of the transformation of artisan production and the emergence of
a working class in New York City, see Sean Wilentz, *Chants Democratic: New York City
and the Rise of the American Working Class, 1788–1850* (New York, 1984). For a
discussion of evolving notions of character and self-discipline, see Paul E. Johnson, *A
Shopkeeper's Millennium: Society and Revivals in Rochester, New York, 1815–1837*
(New York, 1978); Ronald G. Walters, *The Antislavery Appeal: American Abolitionism
after 1830* (Baltimore, 1976); Eric Foner, *Free Soil, Free Labor, Free Men: The Ideology
of the Republican Party before the Civil War* (New York, 1970); Foner, "The Causes of
the American Civil War: Recent Interpretations and New Directions," in Foner, *Politics
and Ideology in the Age of the Civil War* (New York, 1980), 15–33; Karen Halttunen,
*Confidence Men and Painted Women: A Study of Middle-Class Culture in America,
1830–1870* (New Haven, Conn., 1983). On the creation of middle-class households and
the rise of domestic ideology, see Kathryn Kish Sklar, *Catharine Beecher: A Study in
American Domesticity* (New Haven, Conn., 1973); Mary P. Ryan, *Cradle of the Middle
Class: The Family in Oneida County, New York, 1790–1865* (Cambridge, 1981). The
impact of market penetration on rural households is explored in Thomas Dublin, *Women
at Work: The Transformation of Work and Community in Lowell, Massachusetts, 1826–
1860* (New York, 1979); Jonathan Prude, *The Coming of Industrial Order: Town and
Factory Life in Rural Massachusetts, 1800–1860* (Cambridge, 1983); Christopher Frederic Clark, "Household, Market, and Capital: The Process of Economic Change in the
Connecticut Valley of Massachusetts, 1800–1860" (Ph.D. diss., Harvard University,
1982).

country. Frontier planters rose to wealth and power within a household economy by providing a variety of essential services to their less prosperous neighbors. The resulting bonds of interdependency influenced the pattern of allegiances during the Revolution and contributed to the political standing of the backcountry's leading men. At the same time, yeomen and rising planters were able to identify with each other as property holders presiding over dependent households. During the 1760s, that common identification pitted them against others who lived differently, and, throughout the period under consideration, it gave meaning to their republican political language. Finally, backcountry yeomen and rising planters shared in the assumption that the family or household, not the individual, was the fundamental unit of social order and that relations within the family were necessarily characterized by some degree of dependence and inequality. That shared sense of family order gave shape to a Christian vision that sanctioned, even celebrated, slavery.[6]

Ideological differences, grounded in the divergent experiences of regional elites, defined many of the political tensions that divided coastal and backcountry leaders throughout much of the period under consideration. Although yeomen and planters throughout the state shared in the republican assumption that household dependents should be excluded from political participation, they differed markedly in their notion of the acceptable extent of political equality among independent men. Backcountry planters, who were bound to their yeomen neighbors by complex ties of accommodation and eager for entry into the state's political establishment, adhered to a democratic version of republican thought. Their anti-elitist style gave them some credibility among yeomen neighbors and constituents, but it was threatening to coastal leaders, who feared that the push for greater political equality among independent men would harm the interests of substantial planters throughout the state. Acutely sensitive to the presence of the backcountry's nonslaveholding white majority, coastal conservatives believed that reapportionment would render slavery itself insecure. The strength of the Federalist faction on the South Carolina coast derived, in large measure,

6. For exceptionally useful discussions of patron-client relationships, see John Duncan Powell, "Peasant Society and Clientelist Politics," *American Political Science Review*, LXIV (1970), 411–425; Eric J. Hobsbawm, "Peasants and Politics," *Journal of Peasant Studies*, I (1973–1974), 3–22; on southern households, see Elizabeth Fox-Genovese, "Antebellum Southern Households: A New Perspective on a Familiar Question," *Review*, VII (1983–1984), 215–253; Stephanie McCurry, "Defense of Their World: Class, Gender, and the Yeomanry of the South Carolina Lowcountry, 1820–1861" (Ph.D. diss., State University of New York, Binghamton, 1988). For a discussion of southern evangelicalism see Chapter 8.

from widespread concern that the backcountry's democratic-republican tendencies might get out of control.

Slavery was never a matter of dispute among political leaders in any part of the state, but coastal planters and merchants had reason to fear the backcountry's struggle for political parity. Although backcountry yeomen generally accepted the prerogative of their slaveholding neighbors and representatives, they did so only conditionally. From the Revolutionary era on, they gave evidence of considerable hostility toward planters, and coastal leaders knew that such anti-elitist inclinations might erupt into a further-reaching critique of planter power. That the backcountry became the primary scene of social unrest during the post-Revolutionary debtor crisis, and the source of the most radical proposals for the alleviation of debtor distress, intensified such concerns. Particularly alarming to the state's political establishment was the willingness of backcountry settlers and representatives to celebrate the French Revolution even in the wake of the revolution in Saint Domingue. For many lowcountry planters and merchants, the French Revolution served as an ominous reminder that democratic-republicanism might, given the extent of class and regional tensions, have dangerous implications at home.

Such concerns were not confined exclusively to the coast. Within the backcountry, planters and political leaders struggled, on various fronts, to establish class prerogative without alienating the region's yeoman majority. Even as representatives disputed the matter of representation, prominent backcountry planters and political figures sought to contain democratizing forces within their own region. Such men formed a bridge between the backcountry and coastal leadership and set the terms of an ideological compromise. Most notable among them were Patrick Calhoun, his nephew John Ewing Colhoun, Andrew Pickens, John Anderson, Wade Hampton, and, to a lesser extent, Thomas Sumter. All were key figures in an interregional Republican coalition spearheaded by the wealthy coastal planter Pierce Butler. They receive special attention in this study not only because they illustrate the experience of this emerging political leadership but because they played a central role in the political and ideological unification of the state's planter class.

The expansion of cotton culture fostered the process of unification, not by creating a class of backcountry planters, but by reassuring coastal leaders that backcountry republicanism would not develop into an assault on slavery. By lifting farmers and planters out of the post-Revolutionary debtor crisis, the cotton boom helped to assuage class and regional tensions. More important, it drew large areas of the backcountry into what would later be known as the Black Belt. The spread of slavery through the inland reaches of the state substantially reduced the number and proportion of nonslaveholding households and made it more difficult for the backcountry's yeoman majority to avoid direct involvement in the slave system.

The study of South Carolina's backcountry planters involves several problems of definition, most having to do with the designation of regions. During the eighteenth century, South Carolinians used the term *backcountry* in both a geographic and a political sense. For them *backcountry* meant the entire area beyond the nineteen coastal parishes, the most recent of which (Prince Frederick) had been created in 1734. Until 1768, that entire area included only one vaguely defined parish, which sent one representative to the colonial assembly. I have used the term *backcountry* interchangeably with *inland areas* to designate the region beyond the coastal parishes that remained virtually without political representation before the Revolution.

By the 1760s, substantial planters and slaves were more heavily concentrated in the lower backcountry than in the region above the fall line, but not until the 1790s did South Carolinians begin using the terms *middlecountry* and *upcountry* to distinguish broad regional differences within the backcountry. For convenience, I have used these area designations in reference to the pre-Revolutionary period, but it is important to remember that political tensions between regions within the backcountry did not emerge before the end of the eighteenth century. County and district names and boundaries changed during the period under consideration. (Appendix 1 and the maps of counties and districts will help clarify those area designations.)

The term *planter* presents somewhat thornier problems. In the absence of pre-Revolutionary backcountry tax and census records, it is generally impossible to be precise in tracing individual slaveholdings during the earlier period, but the conventional definition of a planter as an owner of at least twenty slaves has little meaning in the context of the eighteenth-century backcountry. The small group of leading planters and political figures on whom I have focused throughout this study held fewer than twenty slaves during the 1760s, but acquired at least that number by the first decade of the nineteenth century. What characterized them as an elite was not only their wealth relative to the region's white majority but their relative freedom from farm labor and hence their ability to involve themselves in a variety of alternative activities.

In fact, these backcountry South Carolinians were part of a process that recurred many times as frontier parvenus throughout the antebellum South forged relationships with their respective yeoman majorities and struggled for political parity with their eastern counterparts. Nowhere else did planters achieve the same degree of power and ideological unity, but similar struggles shaped politics and ideology throughout the southern states. For that reason, the story of South Carolina's unification speaks to a larger issue: the early formation and evolving political character of the southern planter class.[7]

7. For the classic account of the transformation of frontier farmers into planters, see W. J. Cash, *The Mind of the South* (New York, 1941). See, in particular, Eugene D. Genovese's reconsideration of Cash's discussion, in *The World the Slaveholders Made: Two Essays in Interpretation* (New York, 1969), esp. 137–150.

Settling the Backcountry:
The Emergence of the Planters

i

By the mid-1760s, South Carolina's extensive backcountry was no longer an unoccupied frontier. In addition to the Cherokee and Catawba Indians, the region contained about thirty-five thousand settlers—fully three-fourths of the colony's white population.[1] Clusters of settlement, bound by religious, ethnic, and familial ties, dotted the inland terrain. Throughout the backcountry, prosperous farmers, storekeepers, and millers were already struggling to increase their holdings in land and slaves. These inland entrepreneurs were the core of what would later become a backcountry planter class.

On the eve of the Revolution, South Carolina's colonial government and administration were confined to the coastal region. The area, extending about sixty miles inland, contained rich swampland ideally suited to rice cultivation and higher ground that planters used for indigo. The nineteen coastal parishes had been settled over the preceding century by English, Barbadian, and French immigrants. Although the region contained less than one-fourth of the colony's white population, its residents, by 1768, held about 86 percent of the colony's taxable wealth and more than 90 percent of its slaves. Coastal planters depended upon a slave majority that outnumbered whites in some parishes by seven or eight to one. The wealthiest of these planters owned hundreds of slaves and were among the richest men in Britain's American colonies.[2]

1. For an explanation of population figures, see n. 2, below.

2. Robert M. Weir, *Colonial South Carolina: A History* (Millwood, N.Y., 1983), 171–172, 213–218; U.S., Bureau of the Census, *Heads of Families at the First Census of the United States Taken in the Year 1790: South Carolina* (Washington, D.C., 1908) (hereaf-

By midcentury, a number of conditions coalesced to unify South Carolina's political and economic elite and to minimize tensions among the coastal parishes. Economic prosperity and mobility following King George's War reduced the sources of competition and conflict. At the same time, growing familial ties between merchants and planters fostered political bonds. By the second half of the eighteenth century, many of Charleston's wealthiest merchants owned plantations. Even in 1790, most parishes had fewer than two hundred white families, and their small numbers made possible a high degree of personal interaction. At the same time, the need for constant vigilance over the region's slave majority drew whites together. Persistent fears of conflict with the Indians had a similar effect. The result, as Robert M. Weir has pointed out, was that coastal planters and merchants were able to create a remarkably homogeneous polity that enjoyed virtually unchallenged rule until the backcountry made its bid for political parity in the late 1760s.[3]

Beyond the coastal parishes, swamplands rose into a pine-belt, sandhill, and red-clay region that rose still further into a fertile piedmont plateau. Connected with the coast by several great river systems, South Carolina's extensive backcountry remained forbidding to Europeans until the colonial victory in the Yamasee War of 1715–1717. By that time, white hunters and Indian traders were making their way to the inland reaches of the colony, but settlement did not really begin until the early 1730s. In 1731, Governor Robert Johnson won acceptance of a township plan that called for the establishment of eleven inland settlements from the Savannah River to the North Carolina line. The plan provided that bounties and fifty-acre head-right grants be given to white Protestants who settled in the new townships. Governor Johnson hoped thereby to promote the rise of a prosperous inland yeomanry that would serve as protection to coastal settlers in the event of a slave insurrection or Indian war. Only nine of the original townships came into being, although the council established three piedmont townships during the 1760s. Johnson's vision was never fully realized, but the induce-

---

ter cited as *Heads of Families, 1790*); Public Treasurer, General Tax Receipts and Payments, 1761–1769, Account of the General Tax Collected for the Charges of the Government, 1769 (for the year 1768), SCDAH.

3. Robert M. Weir, " 'The Harmony We Were Famous For': An Interpretation of Pre-Revolutionary South Carolina Politics," *WMQ*, 3d Ser., XXVI (1969), 473–501; Weir, *Colonial South Carolina*, 122–140. For a rich exploration of the development of the pre-Revolutionary lowcountry, see Peter A. Coclanis, "Economy and Society in the Early Modern South: Charleston and the Evolution of the South Carolina Low Country" (Ph.D. diss., Columbia University, 1984).

ments offered by the royal government did succeed in attracting a steady stream of European immigrants, and these people formed the first layer of backcountry settlement.[4]

Four of the early townships were sufficiently close to the coast to be absorbed relatively quickly into the political and economic life of the low-country. Purrysburg, initially settled by Swiss immigrants and French Huguenot refugees, was located southwest of Charleston, about thirty miles from the ocean. In 1746, it was designated St. Peter Parish and, the following year, sent a representative to the colonial assembly. Governor Johnson also planned for three northeastern townships (Kingston, Queensborough, and Williamsburg) within fifty miles of the coast. Of these, Williamsburg, located on the Black River, had the most fertile lands and became the most prosperous. During the early 1730s, the settlement drew Scotch-Irish immigrants from Belfast, but it also attracted absentee owners from the coast. After settlers acquired the basic provisions necessary for the production of indigo, they were able to do very well. Several of South Carolina's wealthiest eighteenth-century families were part of the early migration to Williamsburg.[5]

Extending further inland was a settlement that came to be known as Welsh Tract. Bounded on its south side by Queensborough, the region spanned eight miles on both sides of the Pee Dee River to the North Carolina line. The council did not designate Welsh Tract as a township, but it did grant the territory to a group of Welsh Baptists from Pennsylvania who hoped to grow "Hemp, flax, Wheat, Barley etc." They clustered in the northernmost part of their territory and established a Baptist church at Welsh Neck that continued to be a focal point of the community throughout the eighteenth century.[6]

West of Welsh Tract, the township of Fredericksburg formed the core of what would later become a thriving inland settlement. Surveyed in 1734,

4. Edward McCrady, *The History of South Carolina under the Royal Government, 1719–1776* (New York, 1969 [orig. publ. New York, 1899]), 121–138; Robert L. Meriwether, *The Expansion of South Carolina, 1729–1765* (Kingsport, Tenn., 1940), 17–30.

5. Arlin Charles Migliazzo, "Ethnic Diversity on the Southern Frontier: A Social History of Purrysburgh, South Carolina, 1732–1792" (Ph.D. diss., Washington State University, 1983), 31–67; McCrady, *History of South Carolina, 1719–1776*, 121–135, 138; Meriwether, *Expansion of South Carolina*, 34–41, 79–88; George C. Rogers, Jr., *The History of Georgetown County, South Carolina* (Columbia, S.C., 1970), 26–27. For an excellent overview of backcountry settlement, see Weir, *Colonial South Carolina*, 207–213.

6. Meriwether, *Expansion of South Carolina*, 90–93. Welsh Tract was not a township;

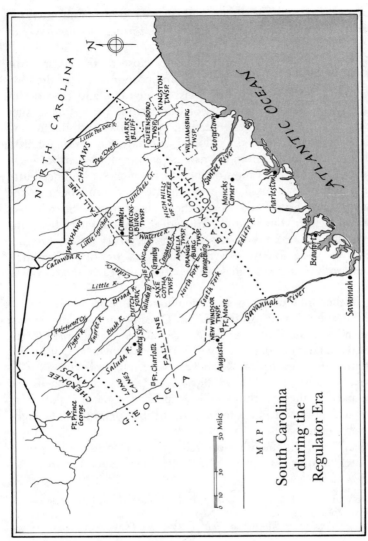

Map 1. South Carolina during the Regulator Era. After Guide Maps to the Development of South Carolina Parishes, Districts, and Counties, compiled by the South Carolina Department of Archives and History; Richard Maxwell Brown, The South Carolina Regulators (Cambridge, Mass., 1963); Lester J. Cappon et. al., eds., Atlas of Early American History: The Revolutionary Era, 1760–1790 (Princeton, N.J., 1976), 6. Drawn by Richard Stinely

Fredericksburg was set on the east side of the Wateree River at the mouth of Pine Tree Creek, with access to water transport as well as to the old Catawba Indian path. Initially the region attracted middling settlers from the coastal parishes. During the 1750s, a group of Irish Quakers also made their way to the Wateree area. With additional migrants from Virginia and North Carolina, the settlement at Fredericksburg rapidly extended up the Wateree River through an area called Rocky Mount. By 1767, the Anglican minister Charles Woodmason observed that people in that region were "already crowded together as thick as in England."[7]

The council located the township of New Windsor on the east bank of the Savannah River near Fort Moore in order to provide a defense against the Cherokee and Creek Indians. Initially settled by Swiss immigrants as well as Indian traders, New Windsor had a population of about three hundred by 1738. In 1754, the merchant John Tobler referred to that village as "one of the best trading towns in this province."[8]

Farther inland, between the Santee and Edisto rivers, the council established three township sites in order to protect the old Indian trading path that ran from the coast into the western piedmont. Set on the west bank of the Congaree and Santee rivers, the area designated Amelia Township had already attracted migrants from the coast and was developing as a plantation region. For this reason, when 250 Swiss immigrants arrived in South Carolina in July 1735, the council was more interested in their settling an unsettled area to the west. This township, called Orangeburg, attracted a steady stream of German settlers. Laid out in the Congaree Valley above Amelia, the township of Saxe Gotha also drew Swiss and German immigrants. By 1754, both Orangeburg and Saxe Gotha were, according to John Tobler, "densely" settled.[9]

Migrants from Pennsylvania, Virginia, and North Carolina had been making their way to South Carolina's inland communities throughout the 1740s, but it was not until the third quarter of the eighteenth century that the great southward migration brought waves of settlement to the pied-

it was located within the township of Queensborough. See Robert K. Ackerman, *South Carolina Colonial Land Policies* (Columbia, S.C., 1977), 86–87.

7. Meriwether, *Expansion of South Carolina*, 99–115; Charles Woodmason, *The Carolina Backcountry on the Eve of the Revolution: The Journal and Other Writings of Charles Woodmason, Anglican Itinerant*, ed. Richard Hooker (Chapel Hill, N.C., 1953), 22–23.

8. Meriwether, *Expansion of South Carolina*, 66–68; Walter L. Robbins, trans. and ed., "John Tobler's Description of South Carolina (1753)," *SCHM*, LXXI (1970), 149.

9. Meriwether, *Expansion of South Carolina*, 42–65; Robbins, trans. and ed., "Tobler's Description of South Carolina," *SCHM*, LXXI (1970), 154.

mont. Attracted by South Carolina's generous headright system and pressured by terror of Indians after General Edward Braddock's defeat in 1755, migrants from Pennsylvania and Virginia did their best to recreate the communities they had left behind. By 1760, these predominantly Scotch-Irish settlers were already spilling over onto Cherokee lands, and, in 1771, a traveler could write of South Carolina, though with considerable exaggeration: "Only a small portion remains King's property. . . . All lands . . . upon and between navigable streams and rivers are occupied."[10]

The Calhoun family of Augusta County, Virginia, was in many ways typical of the more prosperous families that joined the great migration through the Shenandoah Valley into the backcountry of the Carolinas. Born in 1727, Patrick Calhoun immigrated with his parents from their home in County Donegal, Ireland, to Bucks County, Pennsylvania, during the 1730s. From there the family moved to Virginia, where Patrick's father accumulated more than three thousand acres of rich bottomland in Augusta County. Although Patrick and his three brothers appear to have prospered, they decided, in 1756, to move with their recently widowed mother to the inland region of South Carolina. Years later, John C. Calhoun, Patrick's son, wrote that his family had left Virginia after Braddock's defeat, but fear of Indian attack was probably not their only reason for leaving.[11] Along with thousands of farmers, the Calhouns may well have been attracted by South Carolina's offer of a free fifty-acre headright grant for each household member, including slaves. Many Shenandoah Valley families, tempted by this promise of free and abundant land, simply sold their Virginia property at a profit to migrants who were arriving from the more densely populated northern colonies.

The Calhouns were among the approximately twenty-two hundred settlers who moved southward through the Shenandoah Valley each year between 1740 and 1760. Some ended their journey in North Carolina, but, for those who could afford to move farther, South Carolina was in many ways preferable. Backcountry North Carolinians lacked an accessible port in their own colony, and they had to market cash crops in Virginia or South Carolina. In addition, North Carolina's corrupt and chaotic land system left many titles to inland farms uncertain. Whatever its limitations, South Carolina's headright plan promised greater security. At the same time, the colo-

10. William Gerard De Brahm, "Philosophico-Historico-Hydrogeography of South Carolina, Georgia, and East Florida," in Plowden Charles Jennett Weston, ed., *Documents Connected with the History of South Carolina* (London, 1856), 170.

11. [John C. Calhoun], *Life of John C. Calhoun: Presenting a Condensed History of Political Events from 1811 to 1843* (New York, 1843), 3–4.

ny's extensive river system and well-established Indian trading paths enabled frontier settlers to carry on a lively, if cumbersome, trade with the coast.[12]

Trained as a surveyor, Patrick Calhoun was in a good position to find excellent land for himself and his family. He chose a fertile spot near an offshoot of the Savannah River called Long Cane Creek. Generally, neighbors and relations resettled close to one another, and the Calhouns were no exception. Joining them at Long Canes were members of the related Anderson, Pickens, and Noble families who had also made the trip from Augusta County. Along with other migrants, the Calhouns were commercially oriented and looked for a place that had access to a store and a market. Long Canes was situated not far from Robert Goudey's old Indian trading store at Ninety Six, and settlers enjoyed access to the Cherokee trade route that joined the western frontier to the coast. This choice location helped to make Long Canes, in the words of one pre-Revolutionary observer, "by far the most fruitful of all the back settlements."[13]

Long Canes was one of the most prosperous of the backcountry communities, but it was not unique. By the 1760s, pockets of commercial settlement dotted the inland terrain. Clustering near rivers, stores, and trading paths, settlers struggled to overcome obstacles associated with frontier life and to enter the colonywide trade. With the advantage of a few inherited slaves, Patrick Calhoun and others like him were poised to profit from opportunities offered by South Carolina's backcountry.

ii

In the decades before the Revolution, frontiersmen like Calhoun were acquiring and using slaves for the production of commercial crops. The colony's extensive river system and the influx of merchants who provided credit and marketing facilities encouraged the early development of staple agricul-

12. Robert D. Mitchell, *Commercialism and Frontier: Perspectives on the Early Shenandoah Valley* (Charlottesville, Va., 1977), 46, 59–84; A. Roger Ekirch, *"Poor Carolina": Politics and Society in Colonial North Carolina, 1729–1776* (Chapel Hill, N.C., 1981), 16–17, 126–143, 177–178; Ackerman, *S.C. Colonial Land Policies*, 94–114; James P. Whittenburg, "Colonial North Carolina's 'Burnt-over District': The Pattern of Back Country Settlement, 1740–1770," paper presented at the Annual Meeting of the Southern Historical Association, Charlotte, N.C., November 1986.

13. Meriwether, *Expansion of South Carolina*, 134–135; Frank A. Dickson, *Journeys into the Past: The Anderson Region's Heritage* (Anderson, S.C., 1975), 24–25; Alice Noble Waring, *The Fighting Elder: Andrew Pickens, 1739–1817* (Columbia, S.C., 1962), 1–5; *South-Carolina Gazette* (Charleston) Nov. 15, 1760.

ture in the backcountry. By the mid-1760s, indigo was already a leading backcountry commodity, particularly in the Pee Dee area and in the middle regions of the colony below the fall line. Only more prosperous settlers could afford the vats and other equipment required for indigo production, but those who managed the initial expense could expect rich returns. One well-informed traveler observed that a diligent planter with "one or two hundred acres" and "two or three negroes" might "in no long term of years become a man of handsome fortune."[14] Indigo and tobacco were not the only burgeoning backcountry crops. According to Lieutenant Governor William Bull, hemp production was also on the rise, and prosperous planters, particularly those below the fall line at the Wateree River swamps, were growing some rice for export.[15]

Frontier settlers were also producing some tobacco for market. In 1768, a Charlestonian noted that "several large quantities of excellent tobacco, made in the back settlements, have been brought to this market." Some farmers in the western piedmont sent tobacco to market in Augusta, Georgia, but, in 1769, petitioners requested that South Carolina establish inland tobacco inspection sites, and, that year, the crop appeared for the first time on the list of South Carolina exports. By 1770, Lieutenant Governor Bull informed Lord Hillsborough that "tobacco, tho' a bulky commodity, is planted from one hundred and fifty to two hundred miles from Charleston,

---

14. *American Husbandry, Containing an Account of the Soil, Climate, Production, and Agriculture of the British Colonies in North America and the West Indies*, I (London, 1775), 431. See also De Brahm, "Philosophico-Historico-Hydrogeography," in Weston, ed., *Documents Connected with South Carolina*, 169–170; Johann David Schoepf, *Travels in the Confederation [1783–1784]*, trans. and ed. Alfred J. Morison (Philadelphia, 1911), II, 160; Meriwether, *Expansion of South Carolina*, 46, 74–75, 94, 106, 109, 131, 167; Leila Sellers, *Charleston Business on the Eve of the American Revolution* (Chapel Hill, N.C., 1934), 162. Evidence of indigo production appears in numerous pre-Revolutionary backcountry inventories. See Inventories of Estates, 1754–1774, bks. R(2)–&, SCDAH (hereafter cited as Inventories). It is not possible to determine the extent of backcountry contributions to South Carolina's indigo exports. See Charles Joseph Gayle, "The Nature and Volume of Exports from Charleston, 1724–1774," South Carolina Historical Association, *Proceedings*, 1937, 29.

15. William Bull to Lord Hillsborough, Dec. 17, 1765, Records of the Province of South Carolina, Sainsbury Transcripts from the British Public Record Office, XXX, 300, SCDAH (hereafter cited as PRO Trans.). See also Bull to Hillsborough, Nov. 30, 1770, PRO Trans., XXXII, 393–396. British bounties on hemp were designed to encourage hemp production in the backcountry, but, according to Meriwether, production of hemp declined during the 1750s and 1760s. See Meriwether, *Expansion of South Carolina*, 167 (and 56, 106, 109, 143); see also Lewis Cecil Gray, *History of Agriculture in the Southern United States to 1860* (Gloucester, Mass., 1958 [orig. publ. New York, 1941]), I, 274–275; and *S.-C. Gaz.*, Feb. 9, 1765.

Table 1. Holdings of Cattle, 1754–1774

Head of Cattle	No. of Households Owning, by Quintile of Wealth					Total	Share
	Top	Second	Third	Fourth	Fifth		
Upcountry							
Unknown	0	0	1	0	0	1	1%
0	4	4	1	1	4	14	17
1–4	0	0	1	2	3	6	7
5–9	4	5	6	10	9	34	41
20–49	6	7	8	4	1	26	31
50–99	2	0	0	0	0	2	2
100+	0	0	0	0	0	0	0
Overall	16	16	17	17	17	83	100
Middlecountry							
Unknown	1	1	0	0	1	3	1
0	2	3	4	6	11	26	12
1–4	0	2	2	4	3	11	5
5–9	4	16	14	17	22	73	33
20–49	16	10	16	12	8	62	28
50–99	12	7	4	4	0	27	12
100–199	3	5	4	1	0	13	6
200+	6	0	0	0	0	6	3
Overall	44	44	44	44	45	221	100

Sources: Inventories of Estates, bks. R(2)–&, 1754–1774, SCDAH.

where the Emigrants from Virginia find the weed meliorate as they come south; and they cultivate it now with great advantage notwithstanding the distance of carriage to market."[16]

The extent and size of backcountry holdings in cattle suggest that wealthy settlers, particularly those living below the fall line, were contribut-

16. *Boston Chronicle*, Nov. 14, 1768, in H. Roy Merrens, ed., *The Colonial South Carolina Scene: Contemporary Views, 1697–1774* (Columbia, S.C., 1977), 247; South Carolina Commons House of Assembly Journal, July 5, Nov. 28, 1769, Feb. 7, 1771, SCDAH (hereafter cited as Commons Jour.); Gayle, "Nature and Volume of Exports from Charleston," South Carolina Historical Association, *Proceedings*, 1937, p. 33; Bull to Hillsborough, Nov. 30, 1770, PRO Trans., XXXII, 393–396, 402–406. See also D. Huger Bacot, "The South Carolina Up Country at the End of the Eighteenth Century," *American Historical Review*, XXVIII (1922–1923), 693–698.

ing various livestock products to the colonywide trade. Inventories indicate that ownership of livestock was widespread and that some planters were raising cattle for commercial as well as subsistence purposes (see table 1). In addition, backcountry farmers may have contributed certain food crops to the roster of the colony's exports.[17]

Appearing on inventories throughout the backcountry, wheat may well have been the most widely cultivated of any inland crop besides corn. As early as 1753, John Tobler wrote that "the Negroes [in Saxe Gotha] plant much wheat" and that settlers had "good mills and take the flour to Charles-Town." The introduction, by 1760, of a store and mills in the village of Pine Tree Hill (later Camden) encouraged production in the Wateree River area. That year, the *South-Carolina Gazette* reported that "fine Carolina flour just arrived from *Pine-tree-Hill*" was available at the Charleston store of Ancrum, Lance and Loocock. Charleston bakers were using wheat produced in their own backcountry in addition to the finer but more costly Philadelphia product.[18] Noting a blight on the backcountry's wheat crop of 1766, a newspaper report pointed out that inland wheat planters formed "not an inconsiderable Number" and that most of them placed "their whole Dependence on the raising of that Grain." Despite the devastation, 1766 was the first year in which flour appeared on the roster of the colony's exports, and, by 1769, the value of flour exported from the colony exceeded that of any backcountry crop except indigo. By 1770, grand jurors in Charleston presented as a grievance the lack of "proper inspectors of flour," which, they observed, was becoming a "staple" commodity. That year, William Bull could exult that it was "a growing article in our exportation; above four thousand barrels are now exported when formerly we imported more."[19]

17. Inventories, 1754–1774, bks. R(2)–&; Meriwether, *Expansion of South Carolina*, 168; Gayle, "Nature and Volume of Exports from Charleston," South Carolina Historical Association, *Proceedings*, 1937, pp. 29–33; D. Huger Bacot, "The South Carolina Middle Country at the End of the Eighteenth Century," *South Atlantic Quarterly*, XXIII (1924), 50–60.

18. Inventories, 1754–1774, bks. R(2)–&; Robbins, trans. and ed., "Tobler's Description of South Carolina," *SCHM*, LXXI (1970), 154; *S.-C. Gaz.*, July 12, Aug. 30, 1760, Feb. 15, 1768; Meriwether, *Expansion of South Carolina*, 106. See also Joseph A. Ernst and H. Roy Merrens, " 'Camden's Turrets Pierce the Skies!': The Urban Process in the Southern Colonies during the Eighteenth Century," *WMQ*, 3d Ser., XXX (1973), 562–565.

19. *South-Carolina Gazette; and Country Journal* (Charleston), July 15, 1766; export figures on flour, in *South-Carolina and American General Gazette* (Charleston), 1766–1769; Account of the Quantity and Value of Goods Raised and Exported from the Province of South Carolina from 1 November 1768 to 1 November 1769, PRO Trans., XXXII, 124–126; Charleston Court of General Sessions, Journal, Jan. 18, 1770, 43,

South Carolina's backcountry settlers exhibited their growing interest in commercial agriculture in a number of ways. They located their farms near rivers and old trading paths that led to the market in Charleston, they called upon coastal leaders to pass tobacco and flour inspection laws, and they inundated the assembly with petitions for ferries and road improvements. During the 1750s, wagon traffic between Charleston and the frontier had grown to such an extent that a village—Moncks Corner—grew up on the primary trade route. Tavern keepers and storekeepers were able to profit from the influx of travelers. In December 1771, the *South-Carolina Gazette* reported "no less than 113 Waggons on the Road to Town, most of them loaded with two Hogsheads of Tobacco, besides Indico, Hemp, Butter, Tallow, Bees Wax and many other Articles; who all carry out on their Return, Rum, Sugar, Salt, and European Goods." An advertisement for lands to be sold near Pine Tree Hill suggests the variety of commercial and other crops that interested farmers in that region of the colony. According to the seller, all of the lands were "very suitable for the cultivation of hemp, wheat, corn, or Indigo, and also very convenient to the road and river."[20]

In order to expand production and enter the colonywide trade, a prosperous few were demanding greater numbers of slaves. During the 1760s, inland residents owned only a small fraction of the colony's slaves, but the number was growing rapidly.[21] By 1768, about one-twelfth of South Carolina's slaves lived in the backcountry, where they constituted about one-fifth of the population (see table 2).[22] Charleston's leading merchant, Henry

---

SCDAH; Bull to Hillsborough, Nov. 30, 1770, PRO Trans., XXXII, 393–396; Commons Jour., Nov. 28, 1769.

20. Commons Jour., July 6, 1759, May 21, 1762, Jan. 29, 1766, Mar. 4, 1767, Jan. 27, Mar. 15, 1768, July 5, Aug. 3, Dec. 6–8, 1769, Jan. 10, Feb. 15, 1770, Feb. 8, 1771, Feb. 2, July 10, 1775, Feb. 3, 1789; George David Terry, " 'Champaign Country': A Social History of an Eighteenth-Century Lowcountry Parish in South Carolina, St. Johns, Berkeley County" (Ph.D. diss., University of South Carolina, 1981), 206–208; S.-C. *Gaz.*, Dec. 5, 1771; S.-C. and Amer. Gen. Gaz., Aug. 7, 1767.

21. Aggregate tax records for the 1760s are the only backcountry tax records from the pre-Revolutionary period that have survived.

22. Using militia rolls for 1770 and multiplying by the conventional figure of five, Richard Maxwell Brown estimated the backcountry population at between 30,000 and 35,000 in 1765. Brown relied on Robert L. Meriwether's calculations in suggesting that slaves constituted about 10% of the total population. Because Meriwether was referring only to the piedmont, Brown's estimate of 10% is far too low. I have assumed that the total inland population was about 35,000 by the late 1760s, but I have used tax records to arrive at the slave population. See Brown, *The South Carolina Regulators* (Cambridge, Mass., 1963), 182; Meriwether, *Expansion of South Carolina*, 260; Public Treasurer, General Tax Receipts and Payments, Account of the General Tax Collected for the Charges of the Government, 1768 (for the year 1767), SCDAH.

Table 2. Slave Population, 1760–1768

Region	No. of Slaves, Proportion of Total			Increase: No., Rate	
	1760	1764	1768	1760–1764	1764–1768
Backcountry	2,417	4,791	6,548	2,374	1,751
	4%	*7%*	*8%*	*98%*	*37%*
Lowcountry	44,501	51,967	54,761	7,466	2,794
	77	*72*	*67*	*17*	*5*
Charleston in the Country[a]	10,944	15,811	20,419	4,867	4,608
	19	*22*	*25*	*44*	*29*
Overall	57,862	72,569	81,728	14,707	9,159
	100	*101*	*100*	*24*	*13*

Sources: Public Treasurer, General Tax Receipts and Payments, 1761–1769, Account of the General Tax Collected for the Charges of the Government, 1760 (for year 1759), 1764 (for year 1763), 1768 (for year 1767), SCDAH.

Note: Deviations in totals from 100% in tables are due to rounding.

[a] Most of the slaves designated by the tax records as "Charleston in the Country" were probably living on plantations in the Charleston area. But some probably worked on backcountry plantations owned by Charlestonians.

Laurens, wrote in 1763 of "a large field for Trade [in slaves] opening in these Colonies." He pointed to the "vast number of people seting down upon our frontier Lands" who would, "with a little management . . . take off almost insensibly a Cargo by one or two in a Lot." According to Laurens, it was "from such folks that we have always obtain'd the highest prices and hitherto we have had no reason to be discourag'd from dealing with them on Account of bad debts." About nine years later, a wealthy Charlestonian named Peter Manigault confirmed Laurens's observation.

> The great Planters have bought few Negroes within these two Years. Upwards of two thirds that have been imported have gone backwards. These people some of them come at the Distance of 300 miles from Chs Town, and will not go back without Negroes, let the Price be what it will. And indeed they can afford it, for it is no uncommon Thing among them to make 150 wt of Indigo to a Hand, and Even at the present price of Indigo and Hemp, as their Lands cost them little they can well afford to pay £450 for a Negro.

A quarter of a century before the expansion of cotton culture, backcountry settlers could not purchase as many slaves as they wanted or were able to buy.[23]

Purchase was not the only way to "take off" slaves. Lowcountry owners accused frontier settlers of being less than zealous in returning runaways. In 1763, James Parsons denounced a "pernicious custom" whereby "back-settlers when they meet with run away negroes, and . . . some of the magistrates and others in the back parts of the country when such negroes are brought to them [d]o publish purposely blind advertisements for a short time of them, and afterwards keep them at work for themselves." Three years later, a runaway notice declared it "a customary thing for the back-settlers of this province, to take up new Negroes, and keep them employed privately."[24]

Even before the Revolution, the backcountry's wealthiest slaveholders were concentrated below the fall line in the region that would later be described as the "middlecountry." Earlier settlement, easier access to market, and the migration of coastal residents brought more rapid commercial development to that area than to the piedmont. Backcountry inventories from the years 1754 to 1774 paint a picture of considerable regional variation. More than half of the piedmont inventories did not list slaves, as compared to only about one-fifth from the middlecountry. It is significant that the wealthiest fifth of piedmont estates included an average of only eight slaves, while the comparable group from the middlecountry included an average of nineteen (see table 3).[25]

23. Henry Laurens to Richard Oswald and Co., Feb. 15, 1763, in Philip M. Hamer *et al.*, eds., *The Papers of Henry Laurens* (Columbia, S.C., 1968–), III, 260; Peter Manigault to William Blake, n.d. [Dec. 1772?], in Maurice A. Crouse, ed., "The Letterbook of Peter Manigault, 1763–1773," *SCHM*, LXX (1969), 191. See also Patrick S. Brady, "The Slave Trade and Sectionalism in South Carolina, 1787–1808," *Journal of Southern History*, XXXVIII (1972), 601–620.

24. *S.-C. Gaz.*, Jan. 29, 1763; *S.-C. Gaz.; and Coun. Jour.*, June 17, 1766.

25. Inventories, 1754–1774, bks. R(2)–Z. Only 303 legible and identifiable backcountry inventories from 1754 to 1774 have survived. Inventories do not always specify the region in which the estate was located. Backcountry records can be identified by checking the names of the deceased, the executors, and the appraisers against jury lists, local histories, and the Index to Colonial Land Grants, SCDAH. Because all South Carolina probates had to be processed in Charleston—a long and costly trip for most settlers—the surviving inventories are weighted toward the wealthy more than comparable records from the coast or other colonies. Recording an inventory involved a number of costs. The estate had to pay appraisers for their various tasks. At least one appraiser had to travel to and from Charleston in order to record the inventory and pay the recording fee. Appraisers might also receive fees for tracking down a stray animal or organizing an estate sale. The total cost of administering the estate of William Turk of Ninety Six was £46, though his total property (excluding land and £68 in debts due) was valued at only £214 (Estate of William Turk, Nov. 13, 1773, Inventories, bk. &, 471–472). The average value of

Table 3. Distribution of Personal Property and Slaves, 1754–1774

Quintile	Value of All Estates[a]	Share of Total Value	Average No. of Slaves per Household	Share of All Slaves
Middlecountry (Estates: $N = 221$; Slaves: $N = 1,432$)				
Top	£274,103	56%	19	57%
Second	107,753	22	8	25
Third	60,918	12	4	12
Fourth	35,232	7	2	5
Fifth	10,865	3	0	0
Overall	488,871	100	6	100
Upcountry (Estates: $N = 83$; Slaves: $N = 177$)				
Top	50,412	57%	8	70%
Second	17,674	20	2	18
Third	10,128	11	1	9
Fourth	7,059	8	1	3
Fifth	3,378	4	0	0
Overall	88,651	100	2	100

Source: Inventories of Estates, bks. R(2)–&, 1754–1774, SCDAH.
[a]Real property, crops, and seeds are excluded because they were rarely included by appraisers of estates.

By the 1780s, much had changed in the backcountry, but tax lists from that decade provide a rough indication of the distribution of slaves and plantations during the 1760s. The most-developed plantation areas in the inland reaches of the colony may well have been the High Hills of Santee and the region around the township of Camden. A fragment of a 1783 tax return from High Hills points to a substantial concentration of wealthy slaveholders. With only 89 people mentioned on the return, the list cannot be taken as descriptive of the area as a whole, but it is significant that the wealthiest fifth of this small group held an average of 29 slaves. Only one-eighth of taxpayers in this High Hills neighborhood were nonslaveholders (see table 4). Farther inland, the area around Camden also spawned a planter elite. By 1787, the wealthiest fifth of the 185 recorded taxpayers held more than four-fifths of the wealth, more than four-fifths of the re-

estates in the bottom fifth of recorded inventories was £195. Given the expense, it is not difficult to understand the small number and skewed representation of backcountry inventories.

Table 4. Distribution of Total Wealth and Slaves:
Middlecountry, 1783, 1787

Decile	Total Assessed Value of Taxes	Share of Taxes Assessed	Average No. of Slaves Owned	Share of Slaves
High Hills of Santee, 1783 (Taxables: $N = 89$; Slaves: $N = 866$)				
Top	£125	42%	38	39%
Second	56	19	19	20
Third	34	11	12	13
Fourth	26	9	9	10
Fifth	20	7	6	6
Sixth	14	5	5	6
Seventh	10	3	3	3
Eighth	6	2	1	1
Ninth	4	1	1	1
Tenth	2	1	1	1
Overall	297	100	10	100
Camden Township, 1787 (Taxables: $N = 189$; Slaves: $N = 1,025$)[a]				
Top	580	68	34	59%
Second	134	16	13	22
Third	64	7	6	11
Fourth	31	4	2	5
Fifth	19	2	1	2
Sixth	10	1	1	1
Seventh	8	1	0	0
Eighth	5	1	0	0
Ninth	3	0	0	0
Tenth	2	0	0	0
Overall	856	100	5	100

Sources: Tax returns, 1783–1784, District Eastward of Wateree, box 1, 1783, no. 6, 1787–1793, District Eastward of Wateree, box 3, 1787, no. 9, SCDAH.
[a] Camden Township became part of Kershaw County in 1785.

gion's slaves, and an average of 24 slaves. However, half of these Camden-area taxpayers were entirely without slaves (table 4).[26]

Slaveholders in the piedmont operated on a smaller scale than their

26. Surviving backcountry tax records from the 1760s include only aggregate figures, not lists of individual holdings. The earliest surviving backcountry tax lists date from the

middlecountry counterparts. By the 1780s, the wealthiest fifth of taxpayers in the Long Canes area held about three-quarters of the taxable wealth and about nine-tenths of the area's slaves. But the average number of slaves held in these elite households was only five. The majority of taxpayers around Long Canes held no slaves at all. The region across the Savannah River from Augusta was more commercially developed, but there, too, small-scale slaveholders were the norm (see table 5). Throughout the backcountry, the majority of taxpayers held between one hundred and four hundred acres. Slightly more than one-tenth of taxpayers in the Long Canes area were landless, as were about a quarter of taxpayers around the High Hills of Santee, but a number of these landless settlers were also slaveholders and were probably renting improved acreage or awaiting grants to warranted land. Most of the landless taxpayers in the Camden area were owners of town lots.

Distance from market compelled farmers and aspiring planters to attain a high level of self-sufficiency or household independence. Along with their wealthy neighbors, the farm families that predominated in the backcountry shot their own game, grew cotton and flax for cloth, produced corn, grain, peas, and potatoes for their daily needs, and kept cattle and hogs for dairy products and meat. More than nine-tenths of upcountry and middlecountry estates included at least one horse, and nearly that many included cattle. Considerably more than half had hogs, and about half listed at least one gun used for hunting. Slightly fewer included a plow and at least one spinning wheel (see tables 6, 7).[27]

Typical of the backcountry's yeoman majority was William Purse, who lived in the middle region between the Broad and Saluda rivers. At his death in 1772, appraisers valued his personal estate at £234. On the basis of the inventories, Purse was among the least affluent fifth of the inland population. Nonetheless, his estate included three head of cattle, two horses, sev-

---

1780s, but, in the absence of other records, they shed some light on social structure and regional variations during the 1760s. That untold numbers of slaves fled during the Revolution means that the postwar returns may actually reflect some decline in slaveholdings from the earlier period. The opening of the state land office, followed by a burst of speculative activity during the 1780s, limits the usefulness of post-Revolutionary tax records as an index of pre-Revolutionary landholdings.

27. In fact, these figures understate the extent of ownership. Whereas appraisers almost always itemized slaves and livestock, they frequently mentioned "plantation tools" and "household goods" without specifying particular items. Plows and spinning wheels were undoubtedly included in these categories. That nearly one-third of backcountry inventories failed to mention clothing gives some indication of the underrepresentation resulting from generalized categories. Nor were appraisers consistent in listing crops or seed.

Table 5. Distribution of Total Wealth and Slaves: Upcountry, 1787

Decile	Total Assessed Value of Taxes	Share of Taxes Assessed	Average No. of Slaves Owned	Share of Slaves
Long Canes (Taxables: $N = 226$; Slaves: $N = 236$)[a]				
Top	£120	59%	8	74%
Second	29	14	2	14
Third	17	8	1	6
Fourth	12	6	0	3
Fifth	10	5	0	3
Sixth	6	3	0	0
Seventh	4	2	0	0
Eighth	3	1	0	0
Ninth	2	1	0	0
Tenth	1	1	0	0
Overall	204	100	1	100
Edgefield (Taxables: $N = 326$; Slaves: $N = 713$)[b]				
Top	220	46	11	51
Second	97	20	5	24
Third	60	13	3	14
Fourth	37	8	1	7
Fifth	22	4	1	2
Sixth	15	3	1	2
Seventh	11	2	0	0
Eighth	9	2	0	0
Ninth	5	1	0	0
Tenth	3	1	0	0
Overall	479	100	2	100

Sources: Tax Returns, 1787–1793, Ninety Six District, box 3, 1787, nos. 10, 11, SCDAH.
[a] Long Canes was part of county designated as Abbeville in 1785.
[b] Area that became part of Edgefield County in 1785.

eral hogs, some carpenter's tools, two plows, and a spinning wheel. At the time of his death, Purse left small quantities of corn, wheat, flax, and hemp in addition to several deerskins. His household goods were modest, including some pewter, kitchen utensils, and furniture that the appraisers did not bother to itemize. His clothing included "1 homemade jacket."[28]

28. Estate of William Purse, Aug. 11, 1772, Inventories, bk. &, 303.

Table 6. Elements of Production and Exchange in
Upcountry Inventories, 1754–1774

Item	No. of Items, by Quintile of Estates (N = 83)					Total	Share of Estates
	Top	Second	Third	Fourth	Fifth		
Horses	16	16	16	16	15	79	95%
Cattle	13	12	15	16	13	69	83
Hogs	10	14	10	10	9	53	64
Wagons	7	9	7	6	1	30	36
Boats	2	0	0	0	0	2	2
Canoes	1	0	0	0	0	1	1
Plows	7	8	9	8	5	37	45
Cooper's tools	3	2	0	2	1	8	10
Shoemaker's tools	1	2	1	1	1	6	7
Turner's tools (pottery)	0	0	1	0	0	1	1
Tanning, saddler's tools	0	0	0	0	0	0	0
Blacksmith's tools	1	1	0	1	0	3	4
Guns	10	10	7	9	7	43	52
Stills	6	5	1	0	0	12	14
Spinning wheels	8	10	6	9	1	34	41
Debts due in notes/book accounts	6	9	6	4	5	30	36
Cash	4	2	1	1	1	9	11

Source: Inventories of Estates, bks. R(2)–&, 1754–1774, SCDAH.

The self-sufficiency of men like William Purse did not mean that farming households were independent of one another. Indeed, the struggle for
household independence drew settlers into the world of local exchange.
Farmers depended on millers to grind their wheat and corn; they probably
purchased liquor from more prosperous neighbors who could afford the

Table 7. Elements of Production and Exchange in
Middlecountry Inventories, 1754–1774

| Item | No. of Items, by Quintile of Estates (N = 221) | | | | | Total | Share of Estates |
	Top	Second	Third	Fourth	Fifth		
Horses	43	42	38	39	39	201	91%
Cattle	43	40	39	38	32	192	87
Hogs	33	35	35	29	22	154	70
Wagons	12	9	15	14	3	53	24
Boats	6	0	1	1	0	8	4
Canoes	5	4	1	4	2	16	7
Plows	24	19	27	24	11	105	48
Cooper's tools	6	9	4	2	0	21	10
Shoemaker's tools	2	7	3	4	5	21	10
Turner's tools (pottery)	0	0	0	0	2	2	1
Tanning, saddler's tools	1	1	1	1	0	4	2
Blacksmith's tools	2	4	0	4	4	14	6
Guns	31	30	26	29	16	132	60
Stills	2	3	2	5	0	12	5
Spinning wheels	21	23	27	17	13	101	46
Debts due in notes/book accounts	23	16	12	12	11	74	33
Cash	8	5	5	5	6	29	13

Source: Inventories of Estates, bks. R(2)–&, 1754–1774, SCDAH.

costly distilling equipment; they depended on local craftsmen for ironware, shoes, saddles, barrels, and various other goods. In a pinch, they probably supplemented the family's crop with purchases from neighbors.[29] William

29. Several studies of rural areas in the 19th-century United States explore the net-

Williamson, a wealthy planter in the western piedmont, grew corn, hemp, flax, cotton, and rice in addition to "Fruits of all sorts." In 1766, his peach orchard "yielded near three Thousand Bushel Baskets," which, according to a traveler, "proved of great use to the poor young inhabitants of that part of the province."[30] Planters of Williamson's great wealth were not the only ones to engage in local exchange. That settlers on virtually all levels of backcountry society died with debts due to them in book accounts suggests the extent of interdependency (tables 6, 7).

Some backcountry farmers were also becoming involved in the wider market that tied their region to the coast. About one-third of the piedmont and one-fourth of the middlecountry inventories included a wagon or boat capable of transporting goods to the coast. Even settlers who could not afford the cost of a vehicle could market produce with local merchants who hired boatmen or wagoners to make the lengthy trip. Inventories indicate that some farmers were becoming interested in the production of staple crops. John Inabnit of Orangeburg is a case in point. He died in 1773 with one slave and a total estate valued at nearly £1,000. With three spinning wheels, a loom, five cows, seven horses, twenty-three hogs, and a number of chickens, the Inabnit household was clearly capable of providing for many of its own needs. At the same time, Inabnit was commercially oriented. In addition to quantities of corn, peas, and flour, his estate included indigo and indigo seed valued at more than £200.[31]

There were various routes by which the backcountry's fledgling elite became differentiated from the yeomanry. Like the Calhouns, many of the migrants who emerged as leading slaveholders probably brought a few slaves with them to South Carolina, but even such prosperous families could not rely exclusively on farming. Difficulties associated with transpor-

works of local exchange that bound household economies. They go beyond the debate over farmer "self-sufficiency" by arguing that limited market involvement and reciprocal exchange relationships could, in certain contexts, serve the goal of household independence. See Steven H. Hahn, *The Roots of Southern Populism: Yeoman Farmers and the Transformation of the Georgia Upcountry, 1850–1890* (New York, 1983), 1–85; Christopher Frederic Clark, "Household, Market, and Capital: The Process of Economic Change in the Connecticut Valley of Massachusetts, 1800–1860" (Ph.D. diss., Harvard University, 1982), 60–85; Michael Merrill, "Cash Is Good to Eat: Self-Sufficiency and Exchange in the Rural Economy of the United States," *Radical History Review*, III (1977), 42–66. See also James A. Henretta, "Families and Farms: *Mentalité* in Pre-Industrial America," *WMQ*, 3d Ser., XXXV (1978), 3–32; David P. Szatsmary, *Shays' Rebellion: The Making of an Agrarian Insurrection* (Amherst, Mass., 1980); Gregory H. Nobles, *Divisions throughout the Whole: Politics and Society in Hampshire County Massachusetts, 1740–1775* (New York, 1983).

30. Thomas Griffith, Journal, fall 1767, SHC typescript.
31. Estate of John Inabnit, Nov. 17, 1773, Inventories, bk. Z, 447–450.

tation, land clearance, and labor shortage limited farm profits. Those who sought to expand commercial production by increasing the size of their slave labor force turned to multiple economic pursuits. Local exchange offered enterprising men additional avenues to economic advancement.

In making his claims as a loyalist refugee, George Platt, a planter on the Wateree River, illustrates the sort of activities that were typical of the backcountry's slaveholding elite. Before the Revolution, Platt had purchased a wagon, not with notes or currency, but with "pork and cows." On his first three-hundred-acre tract he had a gristmill, "which had constant work in grinding corn." According to a friend, it was "a valuable property," as Platt received a "10th bushel for grinding." In addition, Platt sold some corn to his neighbors and carried their flour to market. He requested compensation for carpenter's tools, and the £30 claimed as "debts due by sundry people" may have included payments owed for carpenter's work. Of his three-hundred-acre home plantation, Platt had only "30 or 40 acres under Tillage." It was probably by providing goods and sevices for neighboring farmers that Platt had been able to acquire his four slaves. These, in turn, enabled him to grow substantial commercial produce. Among the crops abandoned when Platt fled South Carolina was "2000 wt. of tobacco."[32]

Well-situated farmers such as George Platt could prosper and provide security for their families by building mills sufficient not only for household use but for the use of neighboring settlers as well. Alexander Burnside's claims as a loyalist refugee offer a rare glimpse into the moneymaking activities of another enterprising frontiersman. After immigrating from Ireland on the eve of the Revolution, Burnside had established two mills on the Catawba River. Of his 1,500 acres, only 110 were cleared by the time he fled the state. Burnside claimed compensation for fifty-one head of cattle, twenty-five horses, thirty-five sheep, and two hundred hogs. He had also been involved in commercial agriculture. Upon abandoning his plantation, Burnside left 250 pounds of indigo, a large quantity of flour, 115 bushels of oats, and 246 bushels of Indian corn. In addition to the mills, he owned indigo vats and two wagons. According to an acquaintance, Burnside had a "very good business in Milling, Malting and Brewing. He had the character of being a man who made money very fast and was an Honest and Industrious man."[33]

32. Claim of George Platt, in Great Britain, Audit Office, Transcripts of the Manuscript Books and Papers of the Commission of Enquiry into the Losses and Services of the American Loyalists Held under the Acts of Parliament of 23, 25, 26, 28, and 29 of George III, Preserved amongst the Audit Office Records in the Public Record Office of England, 1783–1790, LII, 156–164, NYPL microfilm (hereafter cited as Loyalist Claims).

33. Claim of Alexander Burnside, Loyalist Claims, LII, 414–426.

For those with the necessary coastal connections and capital, store ownership offered another avenue to economic advancement. Although most
purchases involved small sums for supplies that supplemented or sustained
household production, local merchants could count on a lively business.
Settlers bought such things as salt, rum, spices, tools, flints, utensils, and
padlocks. Local stores also carried books, buttons, buckles, hats, and even
cloth.[34] Traveling through South Carolina during the 1760s, a Rhode Island merchant gave clear testimony to the importance of inland stores. He
wrote that "the greatest advantages" he ever saw were "to be made in the
Country where settlements are located on some of the many rivers of the
Colony, where 50 per cent is the least advance." Apparently such wealthy
Charleston merchants as Henry Laurens and Ancrum, Lance and Loocock
made similar observations, for they were quick to establish their own stores
in the backcountry.[35] Charles Woodmason, an itinerant Anglican minister
and former storekeeper, recognized the mercantile activities of the region's
elite when he wrote, with some exaggeration, that most backcountry justices owned stores or taverns.[36]

Inventories make it clear that merchants were prominent among the
wealthiest backcountry slaveholders. The largest ten estates of the eighty-
three piedmont inventories recorded before 1775 include at least four merchants. William Harrison died in 1774 with the largest estate recorded in
the piedmont before the Revolution. In addition to twenty-eight slaves and
large stocks of cattle, hogs, horses, and sheep, Harrison's property included
stock in trade valued at more than £200. Harrison, whose descendants
would remain wealthy upcountry planters, was exceptional among piedmont planters, but other members of the upcountry elite were also operating as merchants on a smaller scale. At the time of his death in 1774, John

34. The only surviving backcountry account book from the colonial period is from the
Kershaw store. See Joseph Kershaw, Account Book, 1774–1775, SHSW microfilm. Store
goods are also listed in the estate inventory of John Lewis Gilbert, a merchant at Long
Canes (Estate of John Lewis Gilbert, Mar. 12, 1774, Inventories, bk. Z, 511–514).

35. Moses Lopez to Aaron Lopez, May 8, 1764, in Thomas J. Tobias, ed., "Charleston
in 1764," *SCHM*, LXVII (1966), 67; Meriwether, *Expansion of South Carolina*, 94–95;
Sellers, *Charleston Business*, 89–90; Laurens, Invoice, Jan. 9, Aug. 30, 1760, in Hamer
et al., eds., *Papers of Laurens*, 21–22, 44.

36. Woodmason, *Carolina Backcountry*, ed. Hooker, 97. Among those backcountry
magistrates who were involved in mercantile activities were Wood Furman, LeRoy Hammond, Moses Kirkland, John Lewis Gervais, James Mayson, John Tobler, Samuel Wyly,
and William Wofford. Walter B. Edgar *et al.*, eds., *Biographical Directory of the South
Carolina House of Representatives* (Columbia, S.C., 1974–1984), III, 301–302, 490–
491, 785–786; Brown, *S.C. Regulators*, 128–130, 184, 204, 209; Richard M. Brown,
"Prosopography of the Regulators," MS, 77–89, 113, 165–167; Meriwether, *Expansion
of South Carolina*, 67–68, 104, 170.

Lewis Gilbert was a storekeeper at Long Canes. As the owner of nine slaves, fifty-eight head of cattle, some horses, and a stock of hogs, Gilbert was one of the wealthiest men of his region.[37]

Owning more slaves and living closer to the coast, members of the middlecountry elite were better able to profit from planting, but they, too, included a number of merchants. When Samuel Wyly, who had been part of the early Quaker migration to the Camden area, died in 1768, he was one of the most prosperous men of his region. A successful storekeeper, he also owned a distillery and at least twenty-five slaves, whom he apparently used primarily for wheat, corn, and possibly indigo production. Unlike the great majority of backcountry settlers, Wyly had a small library. A merchant of New Windsor Township, Daniel Nail died with forty slaves in 1773. He, too, was growing corn, wheat, and peas, and his estate included small quantities of cottonseed, flax, and tobacco as well.[38]

The career of Joseph Kershaw, if in many ways exceptional, illustrates the way in which merchants were able to encourage and reap rewards from the expansion of commercial agriculture even within the context of a nonplantation, semisubsistence society. Arriving in Charleston from England during the 1750s, Kershaw was distinguished from the majority of inland settlers by his English birth, Anglican religion, and useful business connections. He was able to secure a position as clerk in Henry Laurens's firm, and, by 1758, he was a partner in the firm of Ancrum, Lance and Loocock, operating a store at Pine Tree Hill.[39]

Kershaw's various mercantile ventures rapidly made him a leading man of his region. His account book for the years 1774–1775 lists a preponderance of small debts owed for such items as thread, buttons, flints, hoes, and various iron tools. The most popular store goods were rum and salt, but people were also buying certain luxury items. Purchases included some sugar, allspice, silk, velvet, and ribbon in addition to linen and broadcloth. Apparently, Kershaw was also profiting from his mills. After the Revolution, he estimated that his gristmills and sawmills, "if properly attended bring in a clear income of eight hundred to one thousand pounds sterling per annum." He also had indigo works, a distillery, and a tobacco ware-

37. Estate of William Harrison, July 14, 1774, Inventories, bk. &, 417; estate of John Lewis Gilbert, 1774, Inventories, bk. Z, 511–514; Federal Population Census, South Carolina, 1810, NA microfilm. See also estate of William Howell, July 26, 1757, Inventories, bk. S, 178; estate of Elizabeth Shirea, Dec. 6, 1773, Inventories, bk. &, 367.

38. Estate of Samuel Wyly, July 20, 1768, Inventories, bk. X, 373; estate of Daniel Nail, n.d. [probably 1773], Inventories, bk. &, 206.

39. Thomas J. Kirkland and Robert M. Kennedy, *Historic Camden*, pt. I, *Colonial and Revolutionary* (Columbia, S.C., 1905), 87–89, 375–383; Edgar *et al.*, eds., *Biographical Directory of the House*, II, 374–377.

house. As a backcountry representative to South Carolina's colonial assembly, Kershaw, according to one acquaintance, "besides being one of the most popular Men in the Government, will probably be one of the richest." In 1776, a visitor to Camden referred to Kershaw as the man who "originally planned and was the Proprietor of Camden." Three years later, another traveler observed that Camden "commanded a valuable internal trade in tobacco, flour, deer-skins."[40]

Wade Hampton, termed by some observers the wealthiest man in the South at the time of his death in 1835, was also involved in an extensive mercantile operation. His father, Anthony Hampton, was a migrant from Virginia who increased his family fortunes as a small-scale land speculator in North Carolina. Before departing for South Carolina's backcountry with his wife and sons, Anthony won an election to North Carolina's assembly. Whether he owned slaves is not known, but he was a man of some means. Along with other members of South Carolina's backcountry elite, Wade Hampton began with certain advantages, but he was also quick to recognize the profits to be won through trade. Having arrived in South Carolina during the early 1770s, he and his brothers established an inland store. Before the end of the decade, they also had a base of operation in Charleston that was probably an outlet for backcountry produce. The business flourished during the Revolution and provided the foundation for Wade Hampton's extensive acquisitions of land and slaves.[41]

The story of Thomas Sumter, among the liveliest personalities and political figures of inland South Carolina, is similar in crucial respects. He was born in the backcountry of Virginia in 1734, but his early years remain something of a mystery. Acquaintances claimed that embarrassment about humble origins kept Sumter from discussing his youth. More is known of his service in the Seven Years' War, as he achieved sufficient prominence to accompany a Cherokee chief on an official trip to London. Returning to America in 1762, he stopped in South Carolina's Cherokee country, where

40. Joseph Kershaw, Account Book; will of Joseph Kershaw, 1815 [written 1788], County Wills, WPA Trans., Kershaw County, vol. I, bk. C, 13–18, SCDAH; *Gazette of the State of South-Carolina* (Charleston), Mar. 4, 1784; A. S. Salley, ed., "Diary of William Dillwyn during a Visit to Charles Town in 1772," *SCHM*, XXXVI (1935), 34; Dr. James Clitherall, quoted in Joseph A. Ernst and H. Roy Merrens, "The South Carolina Economy of the Middle Eighteenth Century: A View from Philadelphia," *West Georgia College Studies in the Social Sciences*, XIII (June 1973), 24; Elkanah Watson, *Men and Times of the Revolution; or, Memoirs of Elkanah Watson* (New York, 1857), 297.

41. Ronald Edward Bridwell, "The South's Wealthiest Planter: Wade Hampton I of South Carolina, 1754–1835" (Ph.D. diss., University of South Carolina, 1980), 7–41, 77–97; Charles E. Cauthen, ed., *Family Letters of the Three Wade Hamptons, 1782–1901* (Columbia, S.C., 1953), introduction; Court of Common Pleas, Judgment Rolls, July 18, 1766, box 68A, roll 212A, SCDAH (hereafter cited as Judgment Rolls).

he probably hoped to profit from the Indian trade. Upon his arrival in Virginia, he was jailed for indebtedness, but he escaped and fled to Long Canes. Tensions between settlers and Indians probably induced him to move to Eutaw Springs, about twenty miles above Moncks Corner. Using payment received from the trip to England, Sumter established a store and tavern, where he drew travelers making their way from Camden or Congarees to the coast. By 1766, he was a slaveholder and a self-described "merchant." Whereas most prosperous backcountry migrants tended to marry women from similar family backgrounds, Sumter managed to improve his fortunes by marrying Mary Cantey, a wealthy widow with a large plantation at the High Hills of Santee. The marriage took place in 1767, and Sumter moved to his wife's plantation, where he opened another store and operated mills and, eventually, a ferry. During the Revolution he became a prominent backcountry leader, and he later rose from a position in the new state legislature to a seat in the United States Senate. Sumter was one of those prosperous frontiersmen whose backcountry identification and growing ties to the coast helped to make him an important political figure in his region and state.[42]

Other backcountry merchants began as Indian traders and shifted operations with the advance of settlement. Meanwhile, crossroads of the Indian trade became centers of exchange for settlers. Robert Goudey, one of the largest slaveholders of the pre-Revolutionary backcountry, is a case in point. He began his career as a Cherokee trader at Ninety Six in what would later be Abbeville County. When he died, probably in 1774, Goudey had numerous settlers in his debt for small sums. Ninety Six, an outpost of the Indian trade, became a market center and the site of the region's first circuit court. LeRoy Hammond, later a substantial slaveholder and prominent political figure, migrated from Virginia during the 1760s. After a brief stopover in Augusta, he established an Indian trading post in South Carolina on the Savannah River. By the time of his death in 1790, Hammond was a storekeeper, tobacco planter, and official tobacco inspector, with a warehouse and ferry at his home plantation. Referred to as "merchant" rather than "trader," he was probably gearing his operations to settlers rather than to Indians. Alexander McIntosh, a leading planter of the upper Welsh Tract, followed a similar route.[43]

42. Anne King Gregorie, *Thomas Sumter* (Columbia, S.C., 1931), esp. 1–33; Edgar *et al.*, eds., *Biographical Directory of the House*, III, 693–697; Judgment Rolls, July 18, Sept. 10, 1766, box 68A, roll 212A, box 67A, roll 280A.

43. Estate of Robert Goudey, Nov. 13, 1776, Inventories, bk. A(2), 195–208; *Columbian Herald* (Charleston), Feb. 28, 1794; South Carolina Council Journal, Feb. 26, 1761, SCDAH (hereafter cited as Council Jour.); Meriwether, *Expansion of South Carolina*,

Andrew Pickens, who eventually became a United States congressman and whose son became the first South Carolina governor from the back-country, offers another glimpse at the early activities of the new planter elite. Pickens was part of the migration from Augusta County to Long Canes. Like his brother-in-law Patrick Calhoun, Pickens was the son of a prosperous landowner. In fact, the elder Pickens held several local offices, though he did not leave his son with any slaves. Nonetheless, Andrew Pickens held at least two slaves by 1773, whom he put up as security for a substantial loan. He used the funds to establish an Indian trading business, and he was listed on an early deed as a member of Andrew Pickens and Co. After the Revolution, Pickens expanded his operation in partnership with two Charleston lawyers who had held planting interests in the Long Canes area.[44]

Surveying was another lucrative occupation for ambitious backcountry-men who could afford the expense of surveying equipment.[45] In the words of one prosperous Camden-area resident, the surveyor had "the greatest opportunity to procure lands for himself, as also much benefit arising therefrom by surveying for other people." For years, Patrick Calhoun held a virtual monopoly over surveying in the fertile region of Long Canes. The occupation undoubtedly contributed to his rise in political prominence. Calhoun's appointment to the position of deputy surveyor was also profit-able. The one court case in which he appeared before the Revolution involved a debt of £131 15s. owed him for surveying work. Not coinciden-tally, a number of early backcountry planters and political figures, including Richard Richardson, Robert Anderson, and Edward Hampton (the brother of Wade Hampton), began their careers as surveyors.[46]

63, 132, 169; John H. Chapman, *History of Edgefield from the Earliest Settlements to 1897* (Newberry, S.C., 1897), 130–133, 140; Edgar *et al.*, eds., *Biographical Directory of the House*, III, 301–303, 458–459. For a reference to Alexander McIntosh as a trader, see Thomas Cooper and David J. McCord, eds., *The Statutes at Large of South Carolina* (Columbia, S.C., 1836–1841), IV, 685.

44. Clyde R. Ferguson, "General Andrew Pickens" (Ph.D. diss., Duke University, 1960), 3–15, 298–299; deed of Jan. 26, 1773, County Deeds, WPA Abs., Anderson County, no. 26 (MS, 115–117), SCDAH; Waring, *Fighting Elder*, 1–6.

45. An appraisement made in 1768 valued surveyor's tools at £50—more than the value of two fine horses and about one-sixth the value of a healthy male slave. Estate of Wyly, July 20, 1768, Inventories, bk. X, 373.

46. Claim of William Fortune, Loyalist Claims, LII, 106; Judgment Rolls, Oct. 14, 1766, box 67A, roll 284A. Richard Richardson is identified as having been a surveyor in Brown, *S.C. Regulators*, 26. Robert Anderson is identified as having been a surveyor in South Carolina Senate Journal, Dec. 20, 1793, SCDAH (hereafter cited as Senate Jour.). See also Dickson, *Journeys into the Past*, 23–28. Edward Hampton is identified as a

These various routes to economic advancement led finally to land and slaves. Although prosperous backcountrymen were eager to involve themselves in commercial activities, they regarded planting as the more desirable and respectable occupation. Laurens described the prevailing attitude when he advised his associates to establish themselves as planters before opening a frontier store. To enter immediately into retail trade would, he observed, "be mean, would Lessen them in the esteem of people whose respect they must endeavour to attract." Only after they were "set down in a Creditable manner as Planters" could Laurens's partners "carry on the Sale of many specie of European and West Indian goods to some advantages and with a good grace."[47]

Leading backcountry merchants made planting their goal. All the merchants whose estates were inventoried in the twenty years before the Revolution were, by the standards of their region, substantial slaveholders, and those who survived into the last years of the eighteenth century became planters. While Joseph Kershaw established himself in merchandising, he also acquired thousands of acres and considerably more than 100 slaves. James Mayson, a leading backcountry slaveholder and magistrate, was referred to on an early mortgage as "mcht. of Glasgow Plantation." Nonetheless, when writing his will in 1796, Mayson neglected to designate his occupation.[48] John Chesnut, whose son and grandson continued as prominent Camden-area planters, began his career as a clerk in Joseph Kershaw's store. As he rose to partnership in the enterprise, Chesnut acquired a huge planting interest. In 1790, he owned 135 slaves, and, by 1791, he was calling himself a "planter." Despite Thomas Sumter's extensive mercantile activities, an early deed also referred to him as a "planter."[49] Although Andrew Pickens was deeply involved in the Indian trade, an autobiographical sketch made no mention of such activities. Pickens recalled simply that

---

deputy surveyor in Miscellaneous Records, LVIIA, pt. I, 409, SCDAH (hereafter cited as Misc. Records).

47. Laurens to Oswald, July 7, 1764, in Hamer *et al.*, eds., *Papers of Laurens*, IV, 338.

48. Index to Colonial Plats, SCDAH; *Heads of Families, 1790*; deed of Mar. 28, 1768, Charleston Deeds, WPA Abs., no. 204, D-3 (MS, 337), SCDAH; will of James Mayson, 1796, County Wills, WPA Trans., Abbeville County, I, 261–264.

49. Deed of Mar. 31, 1791, County Deeds, WPA Trans., Kershaw County, no. 577A (MS, 13); Index to Colonial Land Grants; *Heads of Families, 1790*; Edgar *et al.*, eds., *Biographical Directory of the House*, III, 138–140; Kirkland and Kennedy, *Historic Camden*, pt. I, 366–368. Thomas Sumter was referred to as "merchant" on a 1784 deed, though he was already the owner of a large planting interest. By 1803, he was referring to himself as a "planter." Deeds of July 24, 1784, Oct. 22, 1803, County Deeds, WPA Abs., Sumter County, no. 841A (MS, 346, 349).

he "was a farmer . . . at the commencement of our revolutionary war."[50] The backcountry leaders who rose to wealth and prominence during the Revolutionary era were beginning to see themselves as planters, and that self-perception was already inseparable from ownership of slaves.

iii

If South Carolina's backcountry offered rich opportunities, frontier life was also fraught with difficulties. The colony's extensive river system and generous land-grant policy attracted settlers, but transportation was nonetheless expensive, time-consuming, and often hazardous. The trip from Long Canes to Charleston and back took from ten days to two weeks even under the best of circumstances; traveling with wagons took even longer. Travel and lodging for two people cost approximately £17 currency—more than most settlers could easily afford. For the same price, an inland farmer might have purchased several cows, a silver watch, or several luxurious featherbeds.[51] Clearly, the situation was more difficult for yeoman families, who needed their men for farm labor.

Colonial administration made matters worse for inland settlers. All courts and administrative offices were located in Charleston, and settlers had to process their land grants, deeds, and estate records in the coastal city. In 1770, backcountry petitioners protested the lack of regional land offices by observing that prospective grantees generally had to make two or three trips to Charleston at a total cost of about £40. Some migrants dealt with the situation by settling and clearing land before even applying for a warrant, and some never bothered to take out grants on their surveys. That the royal government charged quitrents on granted acreage gave settlers further incentive not to secure their titles.[52]

In fact, South Carolina's system of land administration gave an advantage to prosperous men with coastal connections. Conflict erupted as early as 1749, when land rioters in the fertile area of Rocky Mount protested ef-

50. Andrew Pickens to Henry Lee, Aug. 28, 1811, Andrew Pickens Papers, SCL. An early deed refers to a land conveyance of 1789 in which acreage was sold to "Andrew Pickens & Company." See deed of Jan. 25, 26, 1793, County Deeds, WPA Abs., Anderson County, no. 26 (MS, 115–117).

51. The two administrators of the estate of Archibald Wood charged £35 for their 14-day journey from Long Canes to Charleston. The administrator of William Turk's upcountry estate charged £19 for an 18-day trip to town. See estate of Archibald Wood, Dec. 13, 1769, Inventories, bk. Y, 162; estate of Turk, Nov. 13, 1773, Inventories, bk. &, 471–472. See also Brown, *S.C. Regulators*, 14, 181 n.

52. Ackerman, *S.C. Colonial Land Policies*, 96–97, 106–107.

forts to dispossess poorer settlers who took longer to obtain warrants and grants. The rioters achieved their goals, but tensions persisted. In 1767 and 1768, numerous prospective grantees brought caveats against competing claims before the council. Backcountry settlers challenged inland grants to Charleston residents who had the advantage of living close to the center of land administration. At the same time, backcountrymen challenged each other. Poorer settlers, unable to afford the granting and caveat procedure, may well have fallen victim to more prosperous competitors.[53]

Backcountry farmers had reason to resent members of their own local elite, but frontier hardships also drew farmers and rising planters together and sparked resentment against the coastal elite. Although struggling farmers were most vulnerable to the system of land administration, the situation was annoying to wealthy settlers as well. It is significant that several prominent men, including Joseph Kershaw, led the call for local land offices. Indeed, the result of South Carolina's centralized system of administration was that yeomen depended on wealthier men not only for marketing but for other services. Joseph Kershaw was probably not alone in taking his neighbors' land warrants to town for processing.[54]

Nothing did more to draw yeomen and rising planters together than a brutal war with the Cherokee Indians that broke out in 1760. The war lasted for only one year, but its devastating effects influenced South Carolina politics and society throughout the decade. Relations between British authorities and the Cherokees had disintegrated during the late 1750s, as Indians expressed growing resentment at encroachments on their hunting grounds in the western piedmont of South Carolina. Despite efforts by Governor William Henry Lyttleton and certain Cherokee chiefs to secure a treaty, settlers refused to respect Indian boundary lines. The Cherokees attacked South Carolina's Fort Prince George in January 1760, and, the following month, they ambushed a wagon train of 250 settlers who were fleeing their homes to escape an expected attack. About 50 people were killed or captured.[55]

During the following year, fighting on both sides created chaos throughout the backcountry. Settlers fled their homes and suffered the loss of their crops. One newspaper reported orphans found wandering through the woods and whole families starving as they sought refuge in frontier forts

53. Meriwether, *Expansion of South Carolina*, 107; *S.-C. and Amer. Gen. Gaz.*, May 1, Nov. 6, 1767, July 15, 1768; Council Jour., Mar. 19, 1770.

54. Council Jour., Mar. 19, 1770; Kershaw, Account of Sundrys paid in Charlestown, May 19, 1772, Joseph Kershaw Papers, SHC.

55. For an account of the war's impact on the backcountry, see Brown, *S.C. Regula-*

that were already "filled with most wretched people, destitute of every thing." In June, a backcountry militia captain informed the council that women and children who were hiding at Fort William Henry were "destitute of cloathing and every other necessary." Although the war came to an official end with a British victory in 1761, the Long Canes area, dubiously purchased from the Cherokees in the first place, was the scene of continuing conflict. In 1763, Creek Indians attacked settlers in the area and killed about fourteen people. Patrick Calhoun, whose mother had been killed during the early ambush of 1760, raised a company of rangers to protect the western part of the colony, but, as late as 1767, he claimed to have shouldered personally much of the cost because the assembly provided insufficient funds.[56]

Even during the Cherokee War, coastal representatives were grudging in their provision for frontier forts and payment of inland militiamen, and, as the assembly became more involved in the struggle with Parliament, it paid even less attention to inland defense. Henry Laurens, whose extensive holdings in the Long Canes area undoubtedly contributed to his firm support for backcountry interests, criticized the Charleston radical Christopher Gadsden for declaring "in full Assembly that he would rather submit to the destruction of one half of the Country than to give up the point in dispute with the Governor." Settlers at Long Canes were angered by coastal representatives who were more interested in opposing the British Stamp Act than in securing the frontier against the Cherokee. Such resentments may have contributed to the formation of the Loyal Frontier Friends Club around Ninety Six in the midst of the Stamp Act crisis.[57]

The Cherokee War was the dominant concern in the backcountry during the early 1760s, but settlers suffered from other difficulties as well. Of special annoyance was the centralization of criminal courts and jails in the port city. Suspected criminals had to be transported to Charleston, where judges frequently dismissed cases because witnesses had failed to appear. Even those found guilty frequently received judicial pardons. As a result, backcountry South Carolina became a haven for wandering bandits. From the 1760s through the following decade, settlers complained repeatedly

tors, 1–12. See also Meriwether, *Expansion of South Carolina*, 213–240. For an account of the ambush at Long Canes, see *S.-C. Gaz.*, Feb. 16, 1760.

56. *S.-C. Gaz.*, Feb. 16, 1760; Council Jour., June 18, 1760, Dec. 28, 1763, Aug. 8, 1764; Commons Jour., Jan. 7, 1764, Mar. 5, 1767. See also Brown, *S.C. Regulators*, 1–12.

57. Henry Laurens to Christopher Rowe, Feb. 8, 1764, Laurens to John Lewis Gervais, Jan. 29, 1766, in Hamer *et al.*, eds., *Papers of Laurens*, IV, 164–165, V, 53.

about the danger to their lives and property, and that complaint defined a common bond between yeomen and rising planters.[58]

Although the assembly appointed inland justices of the peace to consider debt cases involving less than £20, all other civil suits required plaintiffs and defendants to appear in the Charleston court. As a result, backcountry merchants found themselves in an awkward situation. Liable to suit by their creditors on the coast, at the same time they had trouble collecting sums owed by backcountry debtors. Robert Goudey's book accounts illustrate this dilemma. At the time of his death in the early 1770s, Goudey had debts due from nearly four hundred people. Some had been dead for many years. For backcountry creditors, the Charleston court offered little help. Joseph Kershaw brought only one suit for debt before the institution of circuit courts in 1769, and Dennis Hayes, also a backcountry merchant, appeared in only one court case as a defendant in a suit brought by a Charleston firm.[59] For merchants, the problems arising from South Carolina's centralized court system were obvious. Although the situation may have reduced resentment against local merchants, as they could not practically sue their neighbors to collect debts, it also intensified friction between the coast and the frontier.

The absence of local civil courts created problems for backcountry farmers as well as merchants, because the complex network of local exchange gave farmers experience as creditors. Of necessity, exchange relationships were flexible in order to accommodate seasonal requirements, neighborly ties, and a chronic shortage of cash, but backcountry farmers as well as merchants lacked a last resort for the collection of substantial outstanding debts.[60] The estate of Dennis Crosby offers an example. Crosby was a settler in the region between the Broad and Catawba rivers. He died in 1772 without slaves, and his estate, which totaled £1,124, was among the least affluent half of those recorded. Crosby's most valuable possessions were his four horses and two featherbeds, worth £43 and £55, respectively.

58. Brown, *S.C. Regulators*, 13–37; M. Eugene Sirmans, *Colonial South Carolina: A Political History, 1663–1763* (Chapel Hill, N.C., 1966), 250–251. See also Chapter 2. There is considerable evidence confirming accusations that the Charleston courts were lenient in meting out punishment for convicted criminals. See, for example, pardons of William Lee (1763), Richard Jackson (1764), Sabastian King (1765), James Walsh (1766), Anthony Distoe [Duesto] (1767), John Ryan (1767), James Ray (1767), Misc. Records, bk. MM, 1763–1767, LI, pt. I, 20, 85, 345, 365, pt. II, 586–587.

59. William A. Schaper, *Sectionalism and Representation in South Carolina* (New York, 1968 [orig. publ. Washington, D.C., 1901]), 324–345; estate of Robert Goudey, Nov. 13, 1776, Inventories, bk. A(2), 195–208; Meriwether, *Expansion of South Carolina*, 132; Index to Judgment Rolls, 96–97, 127, SCDAH.

60. See n. 29.

But Crosby also had about £128 due to him in book accounts. He may have been doing cooper's work for neighbors. John McKinley of Long Canes died in 1771 without slaves. His inventory suggests that his was among the least affluent two-fifths of backcountry households. McKinley owned eight horses, twenty-five head of cattle, twenty-seven hogs, some furniture, a few books, plantation tools, and about £150 due in book accounts and notes. Of this debt, £102 was due from "solvent debtors," but the appraisers did not "expect ever to get" the remainder. Another farmer near Ninety Six, William Turk, died in 1773 without slaves. He was among the least affluent fifth of backcountry settlers. Nonetheless, his estate included £68 in debts due. Unfortunately for Turk's heirs, the primary debtor had "absconded himself" and could not be found.[61] Such men as Crosby, McKinley, and Turk can hardly be ranked as members of the backcountry elite, but they probably shared an interest in the establishment of inland courts.

The colony's skewed tax policy did nothing to reduce sectional resentments. Throughout the 1760s, inland settlers expressed dissatisfaction with the existing system, which assessed land at a flat rate and thereby favored landowners from the enormously wealthy rice-producing parishes. Complaining that they were forced to pay more than their fair share, inland settlers urged the colony to adopt a tax policy that would take land value into account.[62]

In the absence of all but the most rudimentary forms of local organization, magistrates and militia officers, many of whom were slaveholders, storekeepers, and aspiring planters, were the primary agents of civil authority. Appointed by the governor, justices of the peace performed a variety of important functions in addition to their judicial role. They certified appraisements, advertised to find the owners of stray livestock, and sold unclaimed stock for the benefit of the public. Justices were also responsible for issuing "warrants of hue and cry," which meant calling communities together to hunt for suspected criminals. It was the justices who took depositions, though constables often took suspects to jail. Finally, justices issued certificates that made it possible for killers of "wild beasts" to collect bounty payments. The very absence of local government that plagued the local elite could provide those appointed as justices with opportunities for extending their influence. In at least one case, a local magistrate assumed other informal responsibilities that gave him added prestige as a neighbor-

61. Estate of Dennis Crosby, Jan. 1, 1772, Inventories, bk. &, 4–5; estate of John McKinley, Jan. 8, 1772, Inventories, bk. Z, 199–200; estate of Turk, Nov. 13, 1773, Inventories, bk. &, 471–472.

62. Brown, *S.C. Regulators*, 17, 139–140.

hood leader. Richard Richardson, an early migrant from Virginia and a wealthy slaveholder and militia colonel of the upper Santee settlement, was able to extend his duties as magistrate by holding a court at his residence. According to tradition, Richardson acted as "the judge and arbiter of most . . . feuds, bickerings and dissensions, and possessed an equity jurisdiction from the Santee to the North-Carolina boundary."[63]

Militia musters, held at least six times each year, and meetings of local justices became the occasion of neighborhood get-togethers. Charles Woodmason disapproved of the rowdy behavior associated with these events, but his description shows how the necessities of exchange and administration fostered a degree of community order while permitting justices and officers to display their authority: "Magistrates have their Sittings—Militia Officers their Musters—Merchants their Vendues—Planters their Sales. . . . Is their any Shooting, Dancing, Revelling, Drinking Matches carrying on? It is all begun on Saturday." These "Court Days," he continued, became "a Sort of Fair."[64]

If ambitious backcountrymen found ways to enhance their local influence, they were almost entirely without avenues to colonywide power. Created in 1757 to accommodate the spread of population, the vaguely defined parish of St. Mark remained the only backcountry parish in 1765. Although the backcountry as a whole contained about three-fourths of the colony's white population, its only representatives were the two allotted to St. Mark. The extreme inequity of backcountry representation derived from deep suspicions, but the failure of coastal leaders to make even limited concessions resulted from a royal prohibition that sought to limit the size and power of the assembly by disallowing the creation of new parishes. When, in 1765, the colonial government attempted to mollify the backcountry by creating a new parish called St. Matthew from the townships of Amelia and Orangeburg, British authorities refused to approve the act, because it would have added two additional representatives to the assembly. Any increase in the number of inland representatives would be permitted only if coastal residents forfeited an equal number of their own.[65]

63. W. Roy Smith, *South Carolina as a Royal Province, 1719–1776* (New York, 1903), 142; William Simpson, *The Practical Justice of the Peace and Parish-Officer, of His Majesty's Province of South-Carolina* (Charleston, S.C., 1761); Joseph Johnson, *Traditions and Reminiscences, Chiefly of the American Revolution in the South* (Charleston, S.C., 1851), 158–160.

64. Woodmason, *Carolina Backcountry*, ed. Hooker, 96–97, 127.

65. Edgar *et al.*, eds., *Biographical Directory of the House*, I, 4–5, 47. In 1768, the crown allowed the creation of St. Matthew and St. David parishes.

iv

Backcountry settlers did their best to create communities in religion despite the weakness of institutional structures. Before 1769, the only Anglican church in the backcountry was located in the lower part of St. Mark Parish—a region that drew migrants from the coastal parishes. Charles Woodmason, having been ordained in England, became the first rector of the church in 1766. He was also responsible for encouraging the spread of Anglicanism throughout the vast and vaguely defined inland parish. Woodmason's repeated complaints about irreligion in the backcountry should not be taken literally, since he gave little or no credence to dissenting sects. The interest he claimed to have elicited in the course of his travels testifies to considerable religious sentiment in the backcountry despite the paucity of ministers and churches. On various occasions, Woodmason said, he preached to groups of several hundred people. Much to his dismay, however, dissenting groups met together privately to socialize and sing hymns even in the absence of organized churches. Lieutenant Governor Bull acknowledged, "The good disposition of the generality of these people [backcountry settlers] toward their religious concerns appears by their . . . attendance on such persons who assume the Character of Preachers, tho' generally very enthusiastic or ignorant of such matters."[66]

Although only two backcountry Presbyterian churches had ministers in 1768, twenty-one had already been established. Most were located in the piedmont, where Scotch-Irish migrants predominated. A missionary sent by the New York and Philadelphia synods during the late 1760s believed that about fifteen hundred families belonged to the backcountry's scattered Presbyterian churches. Despite the lack of a minister, the congregation at Long Canes included five hundred families, among them the Calhouns and Pickenses.[67]

Methodism did not become widespread in South Carolina before the Revolution, but Baptists were already winning converts throughout the backcountry. The first to arrive were the migrants from Pennsylvania, who formed the backcountry's first Baptist church at Welsh Neck. By the late 1760s, at least five additional or branch congregations had appeared in the Pee Dee area. The membership included several of the wealthiest planters in

66. Patricia U. Bonomi and Peter R. Eisenstadt, "Church Adherence in the Eighteenth-Century British American Colonies," *WMQ*, 3d Ser., XXXIX (1982), 262–267; Woodmason, *Carolina Backcountry*, ed. Hooker, 97–98; Bull to the earl of Dartmouth, May 15, 1773, PRO Trans., XXXIII, 264.

67. George Howe, *History of the Presbyterian Church in South Carolina*, I (Columbia, S.C., 1870), 363; Brown, *S.C. Regulators*, 20–21.

that region. When the Charleston Association formed in 1751, the Welsh Neck Baptist Church became a member. Throughout the 1760s, Pee Dee Baptists were in correspondence with their coastal counterparts.[68]

Distinct from the Pee Dee Regulars were the New Light Baptists, or Separate Baptists, who migrated first to North Carolina from Connecticut in 1754 under the leadership of Shubal Stearns. Located at Sandy Creek in Orange County (in an area that later became Guilford County), the community sought to create a pure church consisting of those who had experienced conversion acknowledged through the ritual of adult rather than infant baptism. By 1758, there were six additional New Light churches in North Carolina, and, one year later, the sect was making inroads farther south. Together with a preacher named Philip Mulkey, several families moved southward from Sandy Creek in 1759 or 1760 and formed a church at Fairforest Creek in South Carolina. Influenced by Mulkey and his converts, branch congregations multiplied rapidly. Woodmason's furious assaults on the New Lights give some indication of their growing strength. He blamed "a Gang of Baptists or New Lights over the River" for the small size of his own audience at Pine Tree Hill and testified to the influence of one New Light preacher by asking, "What Man amongst all the Beaus and fine Gentlemen of the Land has such Influence over the Women as *Joseph Reez?*" Woodmason reserved his angriest attack for Mulkey himself. "Would any Mortal," exclaimed Woodmason, "have dreamd or imagin'd that such a Person as the infamous *Mulchey*, who came here lately in Rags, hungry, and bare foot can now, at his beck, or Nod, or Motion of his finger lead out four hundred Men into the Wilderness."[69]

If Woodmason had been alone in attacking Baptist itinerants, we could dismiss his comments as the ravings of an intensely partisan and frequently frustrated Anglican, but, in fact, evangelical itinerants were the subject of more widespread concern. In 1766, two wealthy middlecountry planters and militia officers wrote to the council of "a number of illiterate people in or about the Congarees in St. Marks parish [who] had set up for Preachers and performed other ministerial offices without Licenses and drew together

68. Leah Townsend, *South Carolina Baptists, 1670–1805* (Florence, S.C., 1935), 61–113; David Benedict, *A General History of the Baptist Denomination in America, and Other Parts of the World* (Freeport, N.Y., 1971 [orig. publ. New York, 1813]), II, 130–135.

69. Floyd Mulkey, "Rev. Philip Mulkey, Pioneer Baptist Preacher in Upper South Carolina," Southern Historical Association, *Proceedings*, 1945, p. 13; Townsend, *S.C. Baptists*, 122–175; Benedict, *General History of the Baptist Denomination*, II, 119–120, 137, 366–368; Donald G. Mathews, *Religion in the Old South* (Chicago, 1977), 23–24; Loulie (Latimer) Owens, *Saints of Clay: The Shaping of South Carolina Baptists* (Columbia, S.C., 1971), 43–45; Woodmason, *Carolina Backcountry*, ed. Hooker, 20–21, 112.

multitudes of weak and deluded people to whom they propagated the most erroneous pernicious and dangerous doctrines." The same year, Lieutenant Governor Bull complained of "those Baptist vagrants . . . who continually endeavour to Subvert all order, and make the Minds of the people Giddy with that which neither they nor their teachers understand." Even Woodmason was willing to distinguish among dissenting sects by urging Presbyterians and Anglicans to unite in opposition to the New Lights.[70]

It is difficult to reconstruct the substance of the New Lights' "dangerous doctrines," but tensions between Mulkey's church and the Regular Baptist churches at Pee Dee offer a clue. Such rituals of humility as the kiss of charity, the washing of feet, and the offer of the right hand of fellowship may have offended the sensibilities of the slaveholding Baptists of Welsh Neck and branch congregations. As Donald G. Mathews has observed, the very physicality of these rituals could, in certain contexts, challenge the traditional social hierarchy. In any case, so long as the New Light churches adhered to the full range of these practices and pressed regular Baptists to join them, they were refused membership in the Charleston Association.[71]

That Separate Baptists transgressed traditional gender hierarchy by allowing women to serve as elders and deacons may also have offended the Regulars. Nicholas Bedgegood, minister at Welsh Neck, made his own opinions perfectly clear when he declared that he "held no fellowship" with the New Lights, in part because they allowed "women to pray in public."[72]

Of particular concern to Woodmason and others were itinerant New Light preachers who, by their lack of education and their ability to attract the "lower Class," made the "Situation of any Gentleman extremely uneasy, vexatious, and disagreeable." Bedgegood condemned the New Lights for "permitting every ignorant Man to preach that chose." A North Carolinian also wrote that "the most illiterate" among the Separates "are their Teachers." Charleston's grand jurors were probably thinking of the New Lights when, in referring to the backcountry, they protested "the want of a law to hinder unqualified people preaching through the province," and, in 1775, Charleston's Regular Baptist minister admonished member churches of the association to "discountenance all disorderly Presumers on the Ministry; encourage none but such as have proper credentials."[73]

70. Council Jour., May 1, 1766; Bull, quoted in Townsend, *S.C. Baptists*, 124; Woodmason, *Carolina Backcountry*, ed. Hooker, 94 n.

71. Mathews, *Religion in the Old South*, 26; Owens, *Saints of Clay*, 42–43; Townsend, *S.C. Baptists*, 122–124, 174–175.

72. Townsend, *S.C. Baptists*, 123–124, quotation from Nicholas Bedgegood on 125.

73. Woodmason, *Carolina Backcountry*, ed. Hooker, 42; Bedgegood, quoted in Town-

It would be a mistake to join with Woodmason and Lieutenant Governor Bull in perceiving New Lights as subverters of order. If they were anything like their counterparts in North Carolina or their post-Revolutionary descendants, Mulkey's followers adhered to a church discipline that militated against many of the disorders that Woodmason himself found so obnoxious. The likelihood is that New Lights were no different from Regulars in admonishing their fellows against fighting, adultery, drunkenness, and covetousness. But the hostility engendered by the New Lights is significant because it suggests that the backcountry's fledgling elite was already sensitive to potential challenges from within its own region and already forming cultural identifications with the coastal elite. Tensions between Regulars and New Lights deepened during the Revolution, as the former stood firmly with the Whigs while the latter chose the path of nonresistance.

v

In sum, backcountry planters were beginning to establish their authority and class identity before the Revolution. Throughout the backcountry, a wealthy minority of settlers held most of the region's slaves. Involved in a variety of economic activities, they were oriented toward slave acquisition and commercial agriculture. Justices of the peace and militia officers—the primary sources of civil authority—were drawn from their ranks, and shared grievances against coastal authorities probably bolstered their standing among the yeomanry.

By the 1760s, relations between the backcountry and the coast tugged in two directions. On the one hand, sectional resentment ran high among inland settlers. Resentment against the colony's neglectful assembly and centralized system of administration united farmers and rising planters in a struggle that would explode at the end of the decade. But powerful forces also drew wealthy backcountrymen into contact with their coastal counterparts. Joseph Kershaw, Wade Hampton, and Thomas Sumter were among a small but significant group of men who had business connections in Charleston before the Revolution. The development of commercial agriculture prompted a growing traffic between the regions, and the early spread of slavery into the backcountry was providing the foundation for future political alignments and ideological identifications. Already, the

send, *S.C. Baptists*, 125; William L. Saunders, ed., *The Colonial Records of North Carolina* (Raleigh, N.C., 1886–1890), VII, 164; *S.-C. Gaz.*, Feb. 1, 1768; *Minutes of the Charleston Association* (Charleston, S.C.), 1775, p. 4, SCL microfilm.

Regular Baptist churches of the middlecountry were linked to their Charleston counterparts in opposition to the New Lights. In other words, certain leading men and their ministers were beginning to define the limits of spiritual equality in an increasingly inegalitarian social order.

To recognize that the regional elite was establishing a degree of local authority and legitimacy—that sectional hostility mitigated tension between commercially oriented farmers and wealthier men—is not to suggest that the backcountry was free of social disorder or class struggle. In the absence of courts and jails, planters and yeomen were plagued by bandits who drew support from wandering hunters. In fact, the primary social conflict in the backcountry was not between leading men and yeomen, but between those who relied primarily on hunting for a subsistence and those who looked to planting as the most respectable occupation. The late 1760s witnessed a joint effort by planters and yeomen to discipline threatening groups. In the process, they defined a social and political agenda that reflected the interests and aspirations of the backcountry's planter class.

CHAPTER 2.

Ordering the Backcountry

i

In 1769, a group of South Carolina frontiersmen chained John Harvey to a tree and took turns administering five hundred lashes while members of the party beat drums and played a fiddle. Harvey, a "roguish and troublesome" man, was believed to have stolen a horse.[1] He was one of many such "troublesome" persons brought under the lash by men who called themselves "Regulators." Supported by thousands of inland settlers, Regulators acted from 1767 through 1769 as the primary enforcers of order in the backcountry. The leaders were precisely the sort of ambitious, commercially oriented slaveowners who composed the backcountry's fledgling elite. During the late 1760s, they struggled to establish control of their own region by suppressing threatening groups. Their actions and demands open a window onto the values, fears, and early experience of the emerging planter class.

Regulators banded together in response to a wave of crime that swept the backcountry during the mid-1760s. Newspapers abounded with accounts of violent robberies perpetrated by groups of wandering bandits, and settlers feared for their lives and property. Lacking local courts and jails and frustrated by the leniency of the Charleston criminal justice system, Regulators took the law into their own hands. They punished suspected robbers by whipping or house burning. Some they drove from the colony, and others they carried to the Charleston jail. Gradually broadening their activities, they whipped "whores" and forced the idle to work. Not until 1769, with

---

1. South Carolina Council Journal, Feb. 3, 1772, SCDAH (hereafter cited as Council Jour.). Regulators were engaging in an age-old European ritual in which groups would play music or make loud noise while publicly, and often brutally, punishing blatant offenders of community standards. See E. P. Thompson, " 'Rough Music': Le charivari anglais," *Annales: Économies, sociétés, civilisations*, XXVII (1972), 285–312.

the passage of South Carolina's Circuit Court Act, did the insurgents finally disperse.[2]

Impelled to action by the spread of banditry, Regulators also enumerated a series of smoldering backcountry grievances, which they presented in a lengthy remonstrance to the colonial assembly in 1767. Focusing on robbers and vagrants, they demanded local jails and other measures for suppressing crime. They complained of absconding debtors and excessive fees charged by Charleston lawyers, and they requested local courts, local mechanisms for processing land warrants, and greater representation in the assembly. Regulators revealed their commercial aspirations by calling for the establishment of premiums on their crops.[3]

Finally, Regulators took steps to win influence in the colonial administration by claiming the right to vote in parish elections. They insisted that the western boundaries of the coastal parishes south of the Santee River extended into the backcountry, and, during the election of 1768, hundreds of Regulators marched to three lowcountry polling places. In St. Bartholomew they were not permitted to vote, and in St. Paul they did not succeed in influencing the election, but at St. James, Goose Creek, Regulators managed to elect three of their candidates. In March of the following year, Patrick Calhoun, who was probably a Regulator, traveled to the polls at Prince William Parish with a group of armed men, who elected him to the assembly.[4]

In his excellent study of the Regulator Uprising, Richard M. Brown concluded that the most active insurgents were acquisitive men whose primary purpose was "to stamp out crime and chaos so that ambition and enterprise could gain their rewards." Brown described the frontier as a region divided between "two societies" and argued that Regulators represented respectable, hard-working settlers who were struggling to suppress the various "low," lawless, and disorderly segments of the inland population. He found that 30 of the 120 known Regulators were or would become justices of the

2. Richard Maxwell Brown, *The South Carolina Regulators* (Cambridge, Mass., 1963).

3. The remonstrance is reprinted in Charles Woodmason, *The Carolina Backcountry on the Eve of the Revolution: The Journal and Other Writings of Charles Woodmason, Anglican Itinerant*, ed. Richard J. Hooker (Chapel Hill, N.C., 1953), 213–246.

4. For a discussion of the election of 1768, see David R. Chesnutt, " 'Greedy Party Work': The South Carolina Election of 1768," in Patricia U. Bonomi, ed., *Party and Political Opposition in Revolutionary America* (Tarrytown, N.Y., 1980), 70–86; [John C. Calhoun], *Life of John C. Calhoun: Presenting a Condensed History of Political Events from 1811 to 1843* (New York, 1843), 4; Walter B. Edgar *et al.*, eds., *Biographical Directory of the South Carolina House of Representatives* (Columbia, S.C., 1974–1984), II, 133–135.

peace and that 21 were militia or ranger officers before the Revolution. At least 31 acquired slaves, and at least 17 eventually owned ten slaves or more. Almost all known Regulators were landowners, and 19 accumulated one thousand or more acres. Five later participated in the State Convention that ratified the United States Constitution. In addition, Regulators won support from the wealthiest and most widely respected men of the region. Brown minimized the extent of sectional conflict between coast and frontier. He argued that coastal leaders were far more alarmed by Regulator methods than by their demands and pointed out that the struggle with England, rather than any fundamental lack of sympathy, delayed response to key Regulator demands.[5]

Brown did not portray the Regulators as the vanguard of the planter class, but his evidence points in that direction. If the majority of known insurgents were the sort of middling farmers who predominated in the backcountry, leading Regulators represented those inland entrepreneurs who were in the process of acquiring land and slaves. Together with his sons, Moses Kirkland was a leading member of the insurgency. Samuel Boykin, whose sons and grandsons remained prominent Camden-area planters, was a partner in Joseph Kershaw's mercantile operation. By 1790, he had sixty-four slaves. Joshua Dinkins, owner of two slaves, had a tavern near Camden. A pre-Revolutionary deed listed Morris Murphy of the Pee Dee area as a "merchant." George Hicks and Claudius Pegues, also prosperous Pee Dee area residents, accumulated forty-two and sixty-three slaves, respectively. A large slaveholder and magistrate of Long Canes, James Mayson had a store, mills, and a distillery at his home plantation. Alexander McIntosh, a leading Welsh Neck slaveholder, began his career in the Indian trade. Charles Woodmason, the Anglican minister who became a major spokesman for the Regulator movement, was a former storekeeper and owner of eighteen slaves. Ownership or control of toll roads and ferries offered additional commercial advantages. Although the toll itself was generally insubstantial, the location could afford excellent opportunities for a store or tavern. Five Regulators operated ferries. In addition, at least two leading Regulators—Benjamin Farrar and Tacitus Gaillard—were surveyors.[6]

5. Brown, *S.C. Regulators*, esp. 113–134, 145–147, quotation on 134.

6. Brown, *S.C. Regulators*, 115–128; Richard M. Brown, "Prosopography of the Regulators," MS, 19, 30–31, 36, 47, 145–148; U.S., Bureau of the Census, *Heads of Families at the First Census of the United States Taken in the Year 1790: South Carolina* (Washington, D.C., 1908) (hereafter cited as *Heads of Families, 1790*). Samuel Boykin is identified as a partner in the Kershaw enterprise in Joseph Kershaw, memorandum, n.d. [probably 1778], Joseph Kershaw Papers, SHC. Morris Murphy and James Mayson are identified as merchants in deeds of Feb. 10, 1761, Mar. 28, 1765, Charleston Deeds,

Of all known Regulators, Moses Kirkland had the most complex commercial involvements. He probably brought several slaves with him from Virginia, for, when he took out his first South Carolina land warrant in 1752, he had seven people in his household and was thereby able to receive 350 acres. In addition to his work as a surveyor, Kirkland had the wherewithal to open a store and a tavern near Camden, where he was accused of harboring runaways and selling rum to the Catawba Indians. By 1765, he was operating a gristmill, a sawmill, a brewery, and a ferry at the lower fork of the Broad and Saluda rivers, and, by 1767, he had entered into a partnership with several wealthy lowcountrymen who planned to build sawmills on the Edisto River. That year he joined three other Regulators in presenting the remonstrance to the assembly. In 1770, Kirkland nearly succeeded in defrauding settlers in the township of Saxe Gotha of a portion of their commons land. As a loyalist refugee after the Revolution, he claimed compensation for 33 slaves, 152 head of cattle, 24 horses, and 255 hogs. Kirkland held more than 10,000 backcountry acres, including a 950-acre indigo plantation.[7]

Common concerns and grievances united farmers and planters of different ethnic, religious, and geographic origins. At least six known Regulators—all slaveholders—had ties to the Welsh Neck Baptist Church. Others belonged to the early Camden-area Quaker settlement. Germans from the Congaree River area participated in the Regulation, as did settlers from the neighborhood of Long Canes and Saluda. Several wealthy planters of the upper Santee area also joined the movement. Regulators shared frustration with South Carolina's centralized court and administrative system. Angered by the difficulty in bringing suits for debt, they complained in the remonstrance that "No Credit can be given among Us—for no *Writ* can be obtain'd without going to *Charlestown*—No *Attachment* can be su'd out,

---

WPA Abs., nos. 203, C–3, 204, D–3 (MS, 179, 337), SCDAH. See also Will of James Mayson, Mar. 3, 1800, County Wills, WPA Trans., Abbeville County, bk. I, 261–264, SCDAH.

7. Council Jour., Nov. 15, Dec. 16, 1752, May 7, 1754; South Carolina Commons House of Assembly Journal, Mar. 15, 1765, SCDAH (hereafter cited as Commons Jour.); Brown, *S.C. Regulators*, 128–130; Brown, "Prosopography of the Regulators," 77–89; Robert L. Meriwether, *The Expansion of South Carolina, 1729–1765* (Kingsport, Tenn., 1940), 136–137, 169; *South-Carolina Gazette; and Country Journal*, Oct. 23, 1770; claim of Moses Kirkland, in Great Britain, Audit Office, Transcripts of the Manuscript Books and Papers of the Commission of Enquiry into the Losses and Services of the American Loyalists Held under the Acts of Parliament of 23, 25, 26, 28, and 29 of George III, Preserved amongst the Audit Office Records in the Public Record Office of England, 1783–1790, LVII, 336–353, NYPL microfilm (hereafter cited as Loyalist Claims).

but in *Charlestown*—and while these are preparing, Your Debtor has taken flight and is quite out of Reach." A group of Pee Dee Regulators pledged to assist any creditor "doubtful of a debt due" by "procuring good security for what may be owing" or by delivering absconding debtors to the Charleston jail. Regulators were speaking first for more prosperous inland planters and planter-merchants, but many other frontier farmers—also involved in small-scale trade or artisanal activities—could identify with demands for credit security.[8]

Above all, the Regulator movement linked yeomen and aspiring planters as property holders who shared an interest in making the backcountry safe for planting. The insurgents' primary concern was the wandering bandits who roamed the countryside with little fear of capture, but they also struggled to suppress the many hunters who threatened, in various ways, the system of household order and the network of exchange relationships upon which yeomen and aspiring planters depended. Regulators were not, in other words, simply seeking to establish order. They sought to establish a particular type of order that was consistent with the needs of planters.

ii

Regulators were responding to a deeply rooted social conflict between those who relied primarily on hunting for a subsistence and those who did not. South Carolina leaders had expressed concern about the wandering or "strolling" hunters described by one observer as "little more than white Indians." In 1750, the speaker of the assembly told of the "many hundred men whom we know little of and are little the better, for they kill deer and live like Indians." Lieutenant Governor William Bull made a similar observation in 1769, when he wrote of those "back inhabitants who chuse to live rather by the wandering indolence of hunting than the more honest and domestic employment of planting." Regulators complained in their remonstrance of people who "range the Country with their Horse and Gun, without Home or Habitation."[9]

8. Brown, *S.C. Regulators*, 38–52, 112–134, 145–147, quotation from the *South-Carolina Gazette* (Charleston) on the Pee Dee Regulators on 52; Woodmason, *Carolina Backcountry*, ed. Hooker, 224. For a discussion of Baptist Regulators, see n. 44.

9. Council Jour., Apr. 1, 1751; Andrew Rutledge to James Crocket, June 6, 1750, Records of the Province of South Carolina, Sainsbury Transcripts from the British Public Record Office, XXIV, 36–41, SCDAH (hereafter cited as PRO Trans.); William Bull to Lord Hillsborough, Oct. 4, 1769, PRO Trans., XXXII, 108–110; Woodmason, *Carolina Backcountry*, ed. Hooker, 226. In 1786, a settler living in the upper piedmont referred to many "who depend wholly on hunting for a subsistence and have supplied nature's calls out of the forest without attending to cultivation." *Charleston Morning Post, and Daily*

It would be a mistake to imply that farmers and hunters were absolutely distinct groups, though contemporaries recognized the difference. Guns were frontier staples, and backcountry settlers of all types shot game for meat. Similarly, those who depended primarily upon hunting and foraging were not, in all cases, landless wanderers. The likelihood is that untold numbers of yeoman families, unable to surmount the hardships of frontier life, slipped into hunting and foraging for a subsistence. Members of households that lacked the labor necessary for participation in the farm economy were, of course, particularly vulnerable. In any case, whatever the origins of the hunting population, contemporaries recognized a distinction between farmers who hunted and hunters who supplemented their diet with foraging and only minimal planting. Charles Woodmason described a community of the latter sort during his travels near the Broad River. The settlers, he wrote, were "so burthen'd with Young children, that the Women cannot attend both House and Field—And many live by Hunting, and killing of Deer."[10]

The vagrancy law that finally passed the South Carolina House of Representatives in 1787 identified the nonplanting population that annoyed farmers and planters throughout the later eighteenth century. In defining "vagrant," the law referred not simply to wanderers but to "all persons (not following some handicraft trade or profession, or not having some known or visible means of livelihood,) who shall be able to work, and occupying or being in possession of some piece of land, shall not cultivate such a quantity thereof as shall be deemed . . . necessary for the maintenance of himself and his family." The first part of this definition derived directly from British precedent; the second, which identified vagrants as occupants or possessors of land who did not provide a subsistence, represented an adaptation to a particular American condition.[11]

Advertiser, July 3, 1786. See also S. F. Warren to Dr. [James] Warren, Jan. 22, 1766, in H. Roy Merrens, ed., *The Colonial South Carolina Scene: Contemporary Views, 1697–1774* (Columbia, S.C., 1977), 233–234.

10. Woodmason, *Carolina Backcountry*, ed. Hooker, 39.

11. Thomas Cooper and David J. McCord, eds., *The Statutes at Large of South Carolina* (Columbia, S.C., 1836–1841), V, 41–45. See also Great Britain, "An Acte for Punyshment of Rogues Vagabonds and Sturdy Beggars," 39 Eliz. C.4, 1597–1598, in *The Statutes of the Realm*, IV ([London], 1819), 899–902; Statute 12 Ann. C.23, s.v. "vagabonds," in Giles Jacob, *The Law-Dictionary: Explaining the Rise, Progress, and Present State of the English Law*, 2d ed., VI (London, 1809). The Revolution interrupted the implementation of several key Regulator demands, including the demand for a vagrancy law. Richard M. Brown suggests that the establishment of backcountry courts also "eased the pressure for such a law"; see Brown, *S.C. Regulators*, 217. Disruptions associated with the Revolution spurred renewed demands for a vagrancy act during the 1780s.

Conflicts between hunters and planters were not confined to South Carolina's frontier. In 1749, Moravians in the Shenandoah Valley of Virginia observed "a kind of white people . . . who live like savages. Hunting is their chief occupation." North Carolina's act of 1745 to "prevent killing Deer at Unreasonable Times" described the "Numbers of idle and disorderly Persons, who have no settled Habitation, nor visible Method of Supporting themselves." A Georgia statute of 1764 referred to people who had "no kind of Property or visible way of living or supporting themselves but by Hunting being People of loose disorderly Lives."[12]

Writing in 1786, Benjamin Rush of Pennsylvania gave clear expression to the social conflict that pervaded frontier society during the eighteenth century. He observed that the original type of settler was "nearly related to an Indian in his manners." Such hunters built rough cabins and fed their families on Indian corn, game, and fish. Their "exertions," according to Rush, "while they continue, are violent, but they are succeeded by long intervals of rest." Of a "second" type of settler Rush noted that "the Indian manners are more diluted," but it was, he insisted, "in the third species [of settler] only that we behold civilization completed." Rush portrayed the farmer as a "conqueror" whose "weapons . . . are the implements of husbandry" and whose guiding virtues were "industry and economy." The struggle between hunters and farmers was, according to Rush, "a new species of war."[13]

Settlers also issued repeated complaints against wandering hunters. In 1785, petitioners from the backcountry election district of Little River noted, "The late war having given some people habits of idleness and vice . . . we petition therefore that some mode of vagrant law may pass in order to curb idleness and vice." Two years later, the Edgefield County Grand Jury presented "as a great Grievance that a number of Strolling persons are allowed to pass unnoticed often to the great Injury of the Peaceable Inhabitants of this Country." The Camden Grand Jury issued a similar complaint in 1785. South Carolina House of Representatives Journal, Feb. 7, 1787, in Theodora J. Thompson *et al.*, eds., *Journals of the House of Representatives*, The State Records of South Carolina (Columbia, S.C., 1977–), *1787–1788*, 66; petition from Little River District, Petitions to the General Assembly, 1785, no. 105, SCDAH (hereafter cited as Petitions); presentment from Edgefield County Grand Jury, General Assembly, Grand Jury Presentments, County of Edgefield, 1787, SCDAH (hereafter cited as Grand Jury Presentments); *State Gazette of South-Carolina* (Charleston), Dec. 12, 1785.

12. Robert D. Mitchell, *Commercialism and Frontier: Perspectives on the Early Shenandoah Valley* (Charlottesville, Va., 1977), 134–135; Walter Clark, ed., *The State Records of North Carolina*, XXIII (Goldsboro, N.C., 1904), 218–219, 435–437, 656; Allen D. Candler, comp., *The Colonial Records of the State of Georgia . . .*, XVIII (Atlanta, Ga., 1910), 588.

13. Benjamin Rush to Thomas Percival, [Oct. 26, 1786], in L. H. Butterfield, ed., *Letters of Benjamin Rush* (Princeton, N.J., 1951), I, 400–405. After traveling through North America during the 1760s and 1770s, Crèvecoeur observed: "Our bad people are

The conflict became particularly acute in South Carolina. Distress and dislocation associated with the Cherokee War, coupled with severe droughts in 1759 and 1766, placed settlers in a precarious situation. Many probably turned to hunting and foraging, not to mention thievery, in order to survive. Confronted with exceptional hardships, those farm families that were operating at the margins had to find alternatives. In addition, Regulators insisted that their country was swarming "with Vagrants—Idlers—Gamblers, and the Outcasts of Virginia and North Carolina," and it may well be that the lack of a vagrancy law and the absence of local government drew hunters to South Carolina's frontier. Some hunters were tied to the deerskin trade, but others were probably members of farming households whose farms could no longer provide a subsistence.[14]

In various ways, this hunting population interfered with and offended the more settled members of frontier society. Many hunters lacked notions of respectability common among farmers and rising slaveowners. They were, wrote Woodmason,

> very Poor—owing to their extreme Indolence for they possess the finest Country in America, and could raise but ev'ry thing. They delight in their present low, lazy, sluttish, heathenish, hellish Life, and seem not desirous of changing it. Both Men and Women will do any thing to come at Liquor, Cloaths, furniture, etc. etc. rather than work for it—Hence their many Vices—their gross Licentiousness Wantonness, Lasciviousness, Rudeness, Lewdness, and Profligacy.

Whereas backcountry planters grew cotton for their clothes, hunting families went scantily clad. Of the Broad River community, Woodmason ob-

---

those who are half cultivators and half hunters; and the worst of them are those who have degenerated altogether into the hunting state. . . . If manners are not refined, at least they are rendered simple and inoffensive by tilling the earth; all our wants are supplied by it, our time is divided between labour and rest, and leaves none for the commission of great misdeeds. As hunters it is divided between the toil of the chase, the idleness of repose, or the indulgence of inebriation." See Crèvecoeur, *Letters from an American Farmer* (New York, 1904 [orig. publ. London, 1782]), 69. See also James Axtell, "The White Indians of Colonial America," *WMQ*, 3d Ser., XXXII (1975), 55–88.

14. The dislocation associated with the Cherokee War is described in Commons Jour., June 20, 30, 1760, July 23, 30, 1761; *S.-C. Gaz.*, Feb. 16, 1760. See also Brown, *S.C. Regulators*, 1–12. David Ramsay linked the Cherokee War to the conflicts of the Regulator era. See Ramsay, *History of South Carolina from Its First Settlement in 1670, to the Year 1808* (Newberry, S.C., 1858 [orig. publ. Charleston, S.C., 1809]), I, 119–120. References to droughts appear in *S.-C. Gaz.*, Sept. 29, 1759; *S.-C. Gaz.; and Coun. Jour.*, June 3, July 15, 1766; Woodmason, *Carolina Backcountry*, ed. Hooker, 7. Drought conditions also gave farmers problems in 1769. See *S.-C. Gaz.*, July 6, 1769. Regulators are quoted in Woodmason, *Carolina Backcountry*, ed. Hooker, 246.

served, "It is well if they can get some Body Linen, and some have not even that."[15]

Hunters did more than challenge the Regulators' standards of respectability. By hunting or squatting on Indian lands, the hunters exacerbated frontier tensions. In 1769, Bull complained of their "frequent intrusions on the Indian hunting grounds, and other injurious practices." Creek Indians in Georgia also pointed to those who "live chiefly by Hunting, wandering all over the Woods destroying our Game," and Georgia's vagrancy law suggested that hunters "frequently Tresspass on the Lands and Hunting Grounds of the Indians and Occasion Quarrels and Disturbances among them." In 1770, the Cherokees in South Carolina "expressed great Uneasiness on account of Encroachments on their Hunting Grounds. . . . They also complained of the Number of White Hunters who destroy their Game." By angering neighboring Indians, hunters also threatened planting communities.[16]

Particularly disturbing was night hunting, or fire-hunting. Adopted from the Indians, the practice enabled hunters to curtail the chase by blinding the deer with torchlight, but fire-hunters also endangered livestock and people. Fire-hunters easily mistook cattle and horses for deer and sometimes set fire to the woods in order to force out game for slaughter. In 1770, settlers on the Edisto River petitioned "on behalf of themselves and the rest of the Inhabitants living in the Interior parts of this Province" against those who "set fire to the woods" and thereby "destroy the range for Horses and Cattle." A South Carolina act of 1778 provided that any person convicted of fire-hunting was to be deemed a "vagrant." As late as 1786, Patrick Calhoun urged that wolves and other "noxious animals" be killed "by inducing such persons as were employed in fire hunting to turn themselves to killing wild beasts." It was, Calhoun added, "always best to let a thief catch a thief." Finally, in 1789, the legislature passed an additional Ordinance for the Preservation of Deer that prohibited the "practice of hunting with fire in the night time, whereby great numbers of deer are unnecessarily destroyed, and the cattle and other stock of the good citizens of this state are frequently injured."[17]

15. Woodmason, *Carolina Backcountry*, ed. Hooker, 39, 52.

16. Bull to Hillsborough, Oct. 4, 1769, PRO Trans., XXXII, 108–109; Candler, comp., *Colonial Records of Georgia*, VIII, 167, XVIII, 588; *South-Carolina and American General Gazette* (Charleston), Apr. 27, 1770.

17. Commons Jour., Jan. 24, 1770; Cooper and McCord, eds., *Statutes of South Carolina*, IV, 410–413, V, 124–126; *Chas. Morn. Post, and Daily Adv.*, Feb. 16, 1786. See also Council Jour., Oct. 30, 1773; *Columbian Herald* (Charleston), Apr. 16, 1789; Thomas J. Kirkland and Robert M. Kennedy, *Historic Camden*, pt. I, *Colonial and*

Hunters who sold fur and deerskins caused additional problems. An early frontier storekeeper wrote of "many people who avoid work and prefer to wander around in the woods . . . in order to catch in their traps beavers which they later sell to the hatters. They also shoot bears and deer, only for the skin and fat, although meat from the fat young bears is also used occasionally." Backcountry settlers complained about men who took skins, "leaving the flesh to rot, whereby wolves and other beasts of prey are brought among the stocks of cattle, hogs and sheep, to the great annoyance and damage of the owners thereof." Regulators demanded "that Hunters be put under some Restrictions, and oblig'd not to leave Carcasses unburied in the Woods."[18]

While hunters depended on an open range, farmers and rising planters hoped to establish their rights to private property. By the 1760s, the supply of game had noticeably diminished in the more populated areas, and settlers wanted to safeguard a supply for themselves. In 1769, the assembly responded to backcountry grievances by passing an act for the preservation of deer that protected private ranges by restricting hunters to areas within seven miles of their residence.[19]

Settlers insisted that hunters pilfered livestock, and, indeed, farmers made livestock theft relatively easy by branding rather than fencing their cattle and horses. Animals wandered freely over uncleared lands. Backcountry petitioners insisted that "numbers of Idle Vagrant Persons . . . after the season of hunting is over, Steal Cattle, Hogs and Horses." Georgia's vagrancy law made a similar connection by observing that hunters "do also Trafick much in Horses which there is great Reason to believe are frequently Stolen." In their remonstrance, Regulators told of "large Stocks of Cattel" that were "either stollen and destroy'd" and of "valuable Horses . . . carried off." They asked that cattle- and horse-stealing laws be made more effective.[20]

Revolutionary (Columbia, S.C., 1905), 96; Brown, *S.C. Regulators*, 47–48; presentment from Orangeburg District, Grand Jury Presentments, Orangeburg, 1783.

18. Walter L. Robbins, trans. and ed., "John Tobler's Description of South Carolina, 1753," *SCHM*, LXXI (1970), 159; Adelaide L. Fries, ed., *Records of the Moravians in North Carolina*, I (Raleigh, N.C., 1922), 50; Cooper and McCord, eds., *Statutes of South Carolina*, IV, 310–312; Woodmason, *Carolina Backcountry*, ed. Hooker, 231. See also Commons Jour., Jan. 7, 1768.

19. Cooper and McCord, eds., *Statutes of South Carolina*, IV, 310–312.

20. Commons Jour., Jan. 7, 1768; Candler, comp., *Colonial Records of Georgia*, XVIII, 588; Woodmason, *Carolina Backcountry*, ed. Hooker, 214. North Carolina's Act to Prevent Killing Dear at Unreasonable Times also made an explicit connection between hunters and horse stealers. See Clark, ed., *State Records of North Carolina*, XXIII, 218–

Prosperous frontiersmen had more to fear than theft of livestock. During the 1760s, organized gangs of inland bandits not only robbed families of cash and valuables but often inflicted torture on the victims. When a gang near Pine Tree Creek robbed a man named Charles Kitchen, they also "beat out one of his Wife's eyes, and then burned the poor Man Cruelly." Bandits in the same area "met with one Davis, whom they tied, and tortured with red hot Irons." After Davis revealed the location of his money, the gang "set fire to his House, and left the poor Man tied, to behold All in Flames." A group near Long Canes robbed a man named Michael Watson of "every thing worth carrying off." Afterward, they set fire to his house and crops.[21]

Most striking was the case of John ("Ready Money") Scott, a prosperous frontier entrepreneur. As a storekeeper, slaveowner, and magistrate living on the Savannah River across from Augusta, Scott acquired his nickname because he reportedly would accept only cash for payment. When bandits demanded that he deliver his valuables, Scott initially "offered them some half-pence." According to a newspaper report, the bandits then covered Mrs. Scott's head with an empty beehive, "tied her up in a blanket, ran a brand's end of fire into her face, filled her eyes with ashes, and then threw her into the chimney-corner." When Scott continued to resist, "they held him to the fire till his eyes were ready to start out of his head, burnt his toes almost off, heated irons and branded and burnt him . . . and then made him swear three times on the bible, that he had no more money."[22]

Frontier robbers also endangered travelers. Thomas Griffith, who visited Orangeburg in 1767, passed through "the place where five people had been Rob'd and murder'd but two days before by the Virginia Crackers and Rebells." The following day, he and a companion met two known murderers. Griffith and his companion were carrying firearms, which, they believed, must have scared the bandits off. The travelers arrived at "a small pleasant village," but the tavern was "frequently visited by thieves." Before

---

219. In 1773, the Cheraws District Grand Jury presented as a grievance "the Want of a Vagrant Act; the District being infested with many idle and disorderly Persons, who, having no visible Means of Subsistance, either plunder the industrious Inhabitants, or become chargeable to the Parish" (*S.-C. Gaz.*, May 31, 1773). See also Lewis Cecil Gray, *History of Agriculture in the Southern United States to 1860* (Gloucester, Mass., 1958 [orig. publ. New York, 1941]), I, 200–201; Harvey Toliver Cook, *Rambles in the Pee Dee Basin, South Carolina* (Columbia, S.C., 1926), 74; *American Husbandry*, I (London, 1775), 459–460.

21. *S.-C. Gaz.; and Coun. Jour.*, July 28, Aug. 4, 1767.

22. *S.-C. Gaz.*, Aug. 25, 1766; John A. Chapman, *History of Edgefield County from the Earliest Settlements to 1897* (Newberry, S.C., 1897), 386–392.

Regulators took the law into their own hands, conditions in the South Carolina backcountry gave wandering bandits free rein.[23]

Bandits probably acted in groups of no more than twenty, but separate gangs became part of a larger network. Opposition from the Regulators apparently strengthened the bandits' resolve to coordinate activities. A report from the backcountry in 1767 referred to "the gang of villains . . . who have for some years past, in small parties, under particular leaders, infested the back parts of the southern provinces." The correspondent suggested that the "villains" consisted "of more than 200, form a chain of communication with each other, and have places of general meeting, where (in imitation of councils of war) they form plans of operation and defense." Several months later, another report told of "banditti" who were "so powerful, as to cause magistrates, who have been active in bringing some of their gangs to justice, to be seized, carried before them, and tried by a jurisdiction of their own forming." Among these unfortunate magistrates was the Regulator James Mayson, who was taken from his house at night and "dragg'd, and insulted all the way, to about eighty miles distant." What happened at the ensuing "trial" remains unknown, but the event attests to the organization and power of Mayson's accusers.[24]

These violent robbers cannot simply be identified with South Carolina's hunting population. Several gang members who were mentioned by name in newspaper accounts and court records appear to have been typical and even prosperous farmers before they became criminals. For example, the several Moon and Black brothers, members of a brutal group of robbers, had been part of an early Quaker settlement at Camden. At his death in 1771, James Moon had three slaves and fifteen head of cattle. George Burns, executed for robbing a store, also appears to have been an unexceptional frontier farmer. His estate included fourteen head of cattle, four sheep, thirty-seven hogs, farm tools, and a "parcel [of] old books."[25]

The motives of such men remain obscure. Some were simply carrying to an extreme the acquisitive impulse that characterized many frontiersmen. In the absence of local courts and jails, banditry could be an easy way to quick

23. Thomas Griffith, Journal, summer 1767, p. 4, SHC typescript.

24. *S.-C. Gaz.*, Aug. 3, Oct. 19, 1767.

25. Brown, *S.C. Regulators*, 29–30; indenture between James Moon and Joseph Kershaw, Oct. 19, 1765, Chesnut-Miller-Manning Papers, SCHS; estate of James Moon, Feb. 21, 1772, Inventories of Estates, bk. &, 18, SCDAH (hereafter cited as Inventories); estate of George Burns, Oct. 17, 1771, Inventories, bk. &, 7; deed of May 21–22, 1756, Charleston Deeds, WPA Abs., no. 200, R-2 (MS, 369); plats of Aug. 21, 1756, June 14, 1766, July 1767, Colonial Plats, V, 465, XVIII, 325, X, 88, SCDAH; Kirkland and Kennedy, *Historic Camden*, pt. I, 74–75.

money. The "notorious" bandit Anthony Duesto was an affluent landowner who, before the Regulator Uprising, had made a substantial profit by small-scale land speculation.[26] For Duesto and men like him, banditry was but an extension of an earlier pursuit of gain.

But other landowning bandits had suffered hard times before their entry into lives of crime, and resentment born of misfortune may help to account for the gratuitous violence often perpetrated by frontier gangs. At least six "notorious" bandits had fought in the Cherokee War and doubtless suffered war-related disruptions; one was a deserter.[27] The droughts of 1759 and 1766 made it that much harder for struggling planters to recoup. At least one leading bandit had gone heavily into debt before he became a criminal. In 1761, six years after selling his entire 100-acre tract to the future Regulator William Boykin, Thomas Moon became indebted to the Camden merchant Joseph Kershaw for £640. Kershaw took Moon to court in 1765 and won his suit for the portion of the bond that was due. The same year, Thomas Moon's brother James sold his 131-acre plot to Kershaw. James had served in the Cherokee War and probably suffered losses as a result. Fellow bandits and half brothers of the Moons, George and Govee Black had similar experiences. They, too, were members of the early Quaker settlement at Fredericksburg who fell on hard times during the early 1760s. Govee Black sold his 100-acre inheritance to the merchants Joseph Kershaw and Samuel Wyly. In 1764 he sold an additional 131 acres to James Moon (the same property that Moon later transferred to Kershaw). There is no record that George Black ever held title to land, and the sales apparently left Govee Black landless as well.[28]

Whether or not their greed was reinforced by a sense of grievance, back-country bandits succeeded in winning support from hunters who had their own reasons for resenting respectable frontier society. Woodmason insisted that hunters gave their support to wandering bandits, thereby enabling rob-

26. Deeds of Dec. 21, 22, 1755, Feb. 8, Mar. 7, 8, 1763, Charleston Deeds, WPA Abs., nos. 200, Y-2, 202, B-3, (MS, 357, 367, 491).

27. The following bandits served in the militia during the Cherokee War: Isaac Edward Wells, George Underwood, Edward Walker, William Lee, James Moon, and Jeremiah Joyner. See Militia Rolls, Cherokee Expedition, 1759–1760, SCDAH.

28. Brown, *S.C. Regulators*, 29–30; indenture between Moon and Kershaw, Oct. 19, 1765; deeds of May 21–22, 1756, Jan. 28, 29, 1762, Charleston Deeds, WPA Abs., no. 200, R-2, Y-2 (MS, 369, 342, 404); Court of Common Pleas, Judgment Rolls, Oct. 17, 1765, box 62A, roll 119A, SCDAH (hereafter cited as Judgment Rolls). James Moon took out another warrant in 1767 for 150 acres, but Thomas Moon probably remained landless after he sold his acreage to William Boykin (plat of July 14, 1767, Colonial Plats, X, 88). The Moons and Blacks are identified as half-brothers in *S.-C. Gaz.; and Coun. Jour.*, Oct. 20, 1767.

bers to roam the country without fear of capture. In 1766, efforts to suppress a gang of horse thieves were obstructed because "most of the low
People around had Connexions with these Theives, [and] this gave them the
Alarm." The following year, a letter from Augusta told of "a gang of notorious horse thieves" that "consisted of upwards of twenty men, and had
settled a correspondence through the whole country with others that se-
cretly supported them."[29]

That some hunters became actively involved with bandit gangs suggests
that the groups overlapped. Benjamin Burgess, member of a large and violent horse-stealing ring, belonged to a hunting and trading community located between the Broad and Saluda rivers. In 1751, after stealing 331
deerskins from the Cherokees, he sought refuge with the Indian trader John
Vann. Some years later, Vann himself appeared in court on a charge of horse
stealing. Referring to Vann's settlement, one South Carolina official observed that "not three Families on Saludy would suffer any one of them to
remain four and twenty Hours on their Plantation." Nimrod Kilcrease, who
belonged to a gang accused of "robbing a dwelling house," was John Vann's
neighbor.[30]

An examination of bandit landholdings from 1767 to 1775 provides
further evidence of the association between hunters and bandits. Of approximately 166 backcountrymen referred to as horse stealers, robbers, or
bandits in court records or newspaper accounts, more than half never purchased land or applied for headright grants. Even under the headright system, land acquisition required considerable effort, but there is no indication
that settlers who wanted warrants, if not grants, to land were unable to get
them. Regulators and other backcountrymen demanded more convenient
mechanisms for processing grants and deeds, but the several impediments
to land acquisition did not prevent the insurgents from acquiring farms.
More than 90 percent of all known Regulators purchased land or received
headright grants. That more than half of all known horse stealers or bandits
failed to take advantage of the colony's free land-grant policy suggests not

29. Woodmason, *Carolina Backcountry*, ed. Hooker, 10; *S.-C. and Amer. Gen. Gaz.*,
June 5, 1767. Although bandits drew support from alienated members of the inland
population, there is no evidence to suggest that they behaved like European social bandits. See E. J. Hobsbawm, *Social Bandits and Primitive Rebels: Studies in Archaic Forms
of Social Movement in the Nineteenth and Twentieth Centuries* (Glencoe, Ill., 1959), 13–
29.

30. Meriwether, *Expansion of South Carolina*, 121–122, 143 n; Charleston Court of
General Sessions, Journal, Oct. 19, 1770, SCDAH; James Francis to James Glen, Apr.
14, 1752, in William L. McDowell, Jr., ed., *Documents Relating to Indian Affairs: May
21, 1750–August 7, 1754*, Colonial Records of South Carolina (Columbia, S.C., 1958),
250–251. See also Brown, *S.C. Regulators*, 30.

only that some were new arrivals but that they did not regard landowner-
ship and planting as primary goals (see Appendix 2).

iii

Strengthened by their ties to hunters, bandits posed a terrifying threat to
frontier settlements, and prosperous men, with cash on hand, naturally had
the most to fear. As the crime wave swept the backcountry, a correspondent
observed, "The lowest state of poverty is to be preferred to riches and
affluence, for the person who by his honest labour has earned 50l. and lays
it up for his future occasions, by this very step endangers his own life, and
his whole family." Regulators put the matter succinctly in their remonstrance. Frontier life, they insisted, provided

> not the least Encouragement for any Individual to be Industrious. . . . If
> We save a little Money for to bring down to Town Wherewith to pur-
> chase Slaves—Should it be known, Our Houses are beset, and Robbers
> plunder Us, even of our Cloaths. If we buy Liquor for to Retail, or for
> Hospitality, they will break into our dwellings, and consume it. . . .
> Should We raise Fat Cattle, or Prime Horses for the Market, they are
> constantly carried off tho' well Guarded.

The Regulators' call for local courts and jails was, above all, an effort to
make the backcountry safe for property holders. "Every Man of Property,"
declared an inland correspondent, "is a Regulator at Heart."[31]

Bandits evoked other, less obvious fears. By attracting women into their
ranks, they appeared to threaten the stability of farm households. Several
bandits were married, and some farm women apparently left their homes
to join in the plunder. In 1771, authorities arrested a young backcountry
woman for stealing seventeen horses, but, according to a correspondent,
"her beauty and elegant Figure joined to the native Innocence visible in
her Countenance" won the judge's sympathy and secured her acquittal. In
1781, a piedmont planter recalled his unfaithful wife in his will:

> And as I was Lawfully married to Angelica Elizabeth Boar . . . and she
> without Reason or provocation whatsoever hath eloped from my bed
> and boarding, and associated herself with one vagabond, to Rob me of
> all my effects . . . and being discovered, to avenge herself and satisfy her
> Lust and ambition, had come divers times with divers other vagabonds,
> Robed my house, and threatening my Life firing guns tourough my
> house in order to kill me.

31. *S.-C. and Amer. Gen. Gaz.*, Aug. 7, 1767; Woodmason, *Carolina Backcountry*, ed.
Hooker, 226–227; *S.-C. Gaz.; and Coun. Jour.*, Mar. 28, 1769.

Regulators whipped another "infamous" woman along with Anthony Duesto and several other bandits.[32]

Whatever the extent of female participation in criminal activity, Regulators perceived bandits as a threat to household order and gender hierarchy. In a sermon delivered before two companies of Regulator Rangers, Woodmason observed that many in the audience had "personally been injur'd by the Rogues. Some in their Wives—Others in their Sisters, or Daughters." He claimed "Women and Girls are very deep in the foulest of Crimes, and Deeds of darkness not to be mention'd—And that they have been very instrumental in aiding, abeting—Watching—Secreting—Trafficking and in ev'ry Manner supporting and assisting these Villains." Woodmason also claimed that a group led by the insurgents Moses Kirkland and Henry Hunter followed a gang of bandits into Virginia and retrieved much plunder, along with "Thirty fine y[oung] girls" whom they "brot back to their Families." In his later account of the uprising, Woodmason recalled that "whores were whipped and drove off."[33]

Bandits posed another, more direct threat to backcountry planters: they endangered the growing slave system. Commentators noted the interracial character of bandit gangs. In 1768, the *South-Carolina Gazette* reported that a group of Regulators had met near Lynches Creek after some of them had been "roughly used by a Gang of Banditti, consisting of Mulattoes—Free Negroes, and notorious Harbourers of run away Slaves." Woodmason thundered against the "Gangs of Rogues . . . composed of Runaway negroes, free mulattoes and other mix'd Blood." The thieves Winslow Driggers and Robert Prine were black, and newspapers described Edward Gibson as mulatto. An early observer wrote that the Indian trader John Vann had "no less than three Negroes, one Mulatto, and a half-bred Indian now living with him" in addition to the white bandit Benjamin Burgess. The

32. *S.-C. and Amer. Gen. Gaz.*, Feb. 5, 1771; will of John Eymerie, 1798 [written 1781], County Wills, WPA Trans., Abbeville County, I, 232; *S.-C. Gaz.*, June 13, 1768. James Moon's wife is mentioned in indenture between Moon and Kershaw, Oct. 19, 1765; and in deed of May 21–22, 1756, Charleston Deeds, WPA Abs., no. 200, R-2 (MS, 369). The wife of the bandit Benjamin Spurlock is mentioned in deed of Jan. 12, 1761, Charleston Deeds, WPA Abs., no. Q-3 (MS, 389). The wife of the bandit Charles Hutto is mentioned in deed of Jan. 5, 1755, Charleston Deeds, WPA Abs., no. S-3 (MS, 392). The wife of the bandit George Burns is mentioned in the inventory of her husband's estate. See estate of Burns, Oct. 17, 1771, Inventories, bk. &, 7. An early petition from settlers living near the Pee Dee River had complained of "Horse Stealers and other Felons, having made their escape from North Carolina and other parts—other cohabiting with their neighbors' wives and living in a most lascivious manner." Alexander Gregg, *History of the Old Cheraws . . .* (New York, 1867), 131–132.

33. Woodmason, *Carolina Backcountry*, ed. Hooker, 214; Charles Woodmason, Memorandum, in Woodmason, Sermon Book, IV, 20, NYHS.

mulatto had escaped from prison, and "one of the Negroes" had been "burnt in the Cheek for his Practices."[34]

Reports accused bandits of stealing slaves, but one suspects that some runaways voluntarily sought refuge with the gangs. Clearly, escaped slaves were making their way inland. During the 1760s, the *South-Carolina Gazette* reported 49 slaves captured in the backcountry. The number rose to 132 during the 1770s, or about 8 percent of all captured slaves. A runaway notice of 1767 offered £100 for a slave who had escaped from a Savannah River plantation "and was seen . . . on Savannah river, in company with Timothy Tyrrell, George Black, John Anderson, Anthony Distow [Duesto], Edward [Isaac] Wells, and others, all horse thieves." Several months later, Regulators captured two members of the same gang, along with four "stolen" slaves. In 1770, an inland planter advertised for a "very sensible and smart" young slave who was "supposed to be enticed away or stolen by some villain or villains."[35]

The problem was clear: slavery could not be made secure in a region where bandits captured or offered refuge to slaves. In his characteristically exaggerated style, Woodmason hit the main point. "The Lands," he wrote, "tho' the finest in the Province unoccupied, and rich Men afraid to set Slaves to work to clear them, lest they should become a Prey to the Banditti."[36]

Angered by the threat to their lives and property, Regulators not only called for local courts and jails but demanded other measures for the eradication of crime. They called for the establishment of public schools, the lack of which had enabled "A Great Multitude of Children" to grow up "in the Greatest Ignorance of ev'ry Thing, Save Vice . . . For, they having no Sort of Education, Naturally follow Hunting—Shooting—Racing—Drinking—Gaming, and ev'ry Species of Wickedness." Fifteen years later, a backcountry judge echoed Regulator demands for free schools by suggesting that the spread of "knowledge and learning thro' the Land w[ould] have this good effect, the Youth in our Back Country w[ould] become valuable useful men, instead of being, as they are at present, brought up deer-hunters and horse thieves, for want of Education." Patrick Calhoun, along with other promi-

---

34. *S.-C. Gaz.*, July 25, 1768; Woodmason, Memorandum, in Woodmason, Sermon Book, IV, 22; Woodmason, *Carolina Backcountry*, ed. Hooker, 277; *S.-C. and Amer. Gen. Gaz.*, Dec. 12, 1766; Francis to Glen, Apr. 14, 1752, in McDowell, ed., *Documents Relating to Indian Affairs: 1750–1754*, 250–251; Meriwether, *Expansion of South Carolina*, 120–122.

35. *S.-C. Gaz.*, Oct. 26, 1767; *S.-C. Gaz.; and Coun. Jour.*, Mar. 8, 1768, Aug. 28, 1770. I am indebted to Philip D. Morgan for providing me with his analysis of runaway notices published in the *S.-C. Gaz.* before 1780.

36. Woodmason, *Carolina Backcountry*, ed. Hooker, 27.

nent backcountrymen, repeated Regulator demands for a vagrancy law, the want of which "hath sent such a gang among us, that it hath been in a great measure the Occasion of the Regulators laying themselves open to the Law." Reports from the backcountry in 1770 referred to a new influx of "Horse-Thieves and other Vagabonds, from whose Depredations and out-rages they fear, they can never be completely relieved, 'till a Vagrant-Act is passed."[37]

In the absence of such a law, Regulators tried to force hunters to plant. In 1768, a large meeting of "the most respectable people" of the backcoun-try adopted a *"Plan of Regulation"* and were, according to an inland cor-respondent, "every day excepting Sundays, employed in this *Regulation Work.*" They whipped and banished many of the "baser sort of people," but those they thought "reclaimable they are a little tender of; and those they task, giving them so many acres to attend in so many days, on pain of Flagellation, that they may not be reduced to poverty, and by that be led to steal from their industrious neighbours."[38] Farming was to be the founda-tion of social respectability and order.

The insurgents did not confine their attention to hunters and bandits; they also sought to enforce work discipline among fellow farmers. Accord-ing to tradition, the wife of a man named Bennet Dozier went to the Regula-tor Samuel Boykin to complain that her husband was a poor provider. Boykin and several of his friends obligingly visited the Dozier home and whipped the neglectful husband thirty-nine times. An early genealogist of the Boykin family insisted that Dozier led "a better life" from then on.[39]

iv

Beginning in 1766 and ending five years later, an uprising of an estimated six thousand settlers in backcountry North Carolina shared the name "Reg-ulator" with the insurgency to the south, but the two movements had far less in common than the obvious similarities suggest. Whereas South Caro-

---

37. *Ibid.*, 226; Aedanus Burke to Arthur Middleton, July 1782, in Joseph W. Barnwell, ed., "Correspondence of Hon. Arthur Middleton, Signer of the Declaration of Indepen-dence," *SCHM*, XXVI (1925), 204; Commons Jour., July 4, 1769; *S.-C. Gaz.*, Apr. 19, 1770. The Regulator remonstrance called for "Coercive Laws fram'd for the Punishment of Idleness and Vice, and for the lessening the Number of Vagrant and Indolent Persons, who now pray on the Industrious." Woodmason, *Carolina Backcountry*, ed. Hooker, 231.

38. *S.-C. and Amer. Gen. Gaz.*, Sept. 2, 1768.

39. Edward M. Boykin, *History of the Boykin Family, from Their First Settlement in Virginia 1685, and in South Carolina, Georgia, and Alabama, to the Present Time* (Cam-den, S.C., 1876), 1–9, 18.

lina Regulators sought to establish local courts and other forms of civil authority, North Carolina insurgents protested corruption in the existing local government. While South Carolina Regulators attacked bandits and complained of absconding debtors, North Carolina frontiersmen challenged corrupt officials and overzealous creditors.[40]

Although backcountry settlers in the neighboring colonies shared certain grievances, the North Carolinians suffered special hardships that gave a distinctive cast to their insurgency. Lacking an accessible port in their own colony, they had to bear the expense of marketing crops in South Carolina or Virginia. The situation was made no easier by the stringent credit policies of Scottish merchants who settled the inland reaches of the colony. As a result of competition among land speculators, the closing of the Granville land office, and boundary disputes with South Carolina, North Carolina farmers also had a more difficult time securing land titles than their counterparts to the south. Petitioners complained that absentee speculators received patents to the best lands, thereby forcing settlers onto acreage that was barely suitable for cultivation. Finally, North Carolina settlers found themselves victimized by local officeholders, who rivaled any in self-aggrandizement, and by a tax structure that one student of the uprising has termed "the most regressive and corrupt . . . in the Anglo-American trans-Atlantic community of the mid-eighteenth century."[41]

North Carolina insurgents were seeking to secure their property (farms

40. The North Carolina Regulators have been the subject of continuing debate. An early account portrayed the movement as an expression of sectional resentments. See John S. Bassett, "The Regulators of North Carolina, 1765–1771," American Historical Association, *Annual Report, 1894* (Washington, D.C., 1895), 141–212. Marvin L. Michael Kay has argued that Regulators were struggling against the elite of their own region. See Kay, "The North Carolina Regulation, 1766–1776: A Class Conflict," in Alfred F. Young, ed., *The American Revolution: Explorations in the History of American Radicalism* (De Kalb, Ill., 1976), 84–102. In an exceptionally interesting article, James P. Whittenburg suggested that Regulators, having suffered from the stringent credit policies of the Scottish merchants who were flocking to the North Carolina backcountry, were espousing a radical anticommercial ideology. See Whittenburg, "Planters, Merchants, and Lawyers: Social Change and the Origins of the North Carolina Regulation," *WMQ*, 3d Ser., XXXIV (1977), 215–238. A. Roger Ekirch portrays the Regulators as settlers whose hopes for profit were frustrated by conditions in the colony. He minimizes the ideological differences between Regulators and their opponents and suggests that the protesters were adapting "Country Ideology" to their struggle against the rampant corruption of local officials. See Ekirch, *"Poor Carolina": Politics and Society in Colonial North Carolina, 1729–1776* (Chapel Hill, N.C., 1981), 161–220. A later study of Herman Husband, upon which I have relied heavily, points to the fusion of Radical Whig and millennial themes in the movement. See Mark Haddon Jones, "Herman Husband: Millenarian, Carolina Regulator, and Whiskey Rebel" (Ph.D. diss., Northern Illinois University, 1983), 1–189.

41. Ekirch, *"Poor Carolina,"* 161–183; Jones, "Herman Husband," esp. 96–101.

and improvements) from corrupt officials, speculators, and regressive taxes, but that very effort impelled them to develop a deeper critique of colonial government and society than their counterparts to the south. North Carolina Regulators demanded not only a reform of the tax structure and a new system for securing land titles but the replacement of local officials with honest men who would ask no more than legally established fees for their services. They specifically requested that lawyers not be allowed to stand as candidates for the assembly and that secret ballots be used in order to diminish the influence of the local gentry in elections. North Carolina Regulators urged that roll call votes be recorded and sent to local justices of the peace so that freeholders could monitor their representatives, and they demanded an increase of currency through the mechanism of a land bank.[42]

Herman Husband, the leading spokesman for the North Carolina insurgents, fused millennial faith with radical whig themes. A compelling study argues effectively that Husband, who was deeply touched not only by the Great Awakening but by the colonial opposition to the Stamp Act, became convinced that a reform in civil government would usher in the millennium. He looked forward to a day when industrious, small-scale freeholders would control the government for the public good rather than for the selfish interest of corrupt officeholders. Husband translated the evangelical faith in the inner light into a more explicitly political attack on gentry power by arguing that farmers, who might be lacking in formal education, were the possessors of "right reason" and most in tune with God's will. Husband himself had Quaker and evangelical Presbyterian roots, but his message resonated among the New Light Baptists and other dissenters who played a prominent role in the movement. It is significant that the North Carolina Regulators included an even higher proportion of New Lights than the backcountry population as a whole.[43]

New Lights were less prominent and influential in the South Carolina insurgency. We know too little about the religious orientation of South Carolina Regulators to make adequate comparisons on that count, but the scant evidence that does exist points in interesting directions. Of the 120 known South Carolina Regulators, the only identifiable Baptists belonged to the Regular churches of Welsh Neck and Cashaway—churches that distinguished themselves from Separate or New Light practices. Evan Pugh,

42. Jones, "Herman Husband," 145–149.

43. *Ibid.*, esp. 160–163. Jones bases his claim concerning New Light participation in the movement on James P. Whittenburg, "God's Chosen in the Backcountry," paper presented at the Annual Meeting of the Southern Historical Association, Atlanta, Ga., November 1979. See also William L. Lumpkin, *Baptist Foundations in the South: Tracing through the Separates the Influence of the Great Awakening, 1754–1787* (Nashville, Tenn., 1961), 82–83.

owner of seventeen slaves and a minister at the Cashaway Baptist Church, was himself a Regulator.[44] Unknown New Lights may have participated in the South Carolina Regulation, but it is significant that Woodmason and the Regulator Tacitus Gaillard singled out the New Lights for special ridicule.[45] Unlike the North Carolinians, who challenged established government and local officials, the South Carolina insurgents pressed for the creation of local administration. It was not coincidental that the man who emerged as their spokesman was obsessively concerned about the maintenance of civil and household order and particularly hostile to a religious sect that appeared to celebrate the inner light over external forms of authority.

Like their South Carolina counterparts, North Carolina Regulators included prosperous men and slaveholders, but it is revealing of the movement that Husband's opposition to North Carolina's political elite led him to challenge slavery itself. In marked contrast to Charles Woodmason, Husband insisted that slavery was antithetical to social harmony. He believed that slaves, as human beings, would be discontented so long as they remained in bondage, and he feared that the system would make it impossible for deserving farmers to acquire desirable land.[46]

Judged by modern or suprahistorical standards, the North Carolina Regulators may have been something less than radical social critics, but their opponents had no difficulty in recognizing them as a profound threat to North Carolina's social and political order. It is significant that South Carolina insurgents received lenient treatment from coastal authorities, while North Carolina Regulators met with defeat in a battle that one historian has aptly termed "the largest single instance of collective violence in early American history." Lieutenant Governor Bull may have understood the distinction better than the insurgents themselves, for he was able to assure the

44. At least seven Regulators had close ties to the Regular Baptist churches of the Pee Dee region. In addition to Evan Pugh, Gideon Gibson and Morris Murphy belonged to the Cashaway Baptist Church. Alexander McIntosh and George Hicks were members of the Welsh Neck Baptist Church. Claudius Pegues was the brother-in-law of Nicholas Bedgegood, a minister at Welsh Neck. His second wife was a daughter of George Hicks. Philip Pledger had a relative who was a church member, and he may well have been a member himself. Welsh Neck Baptist Church, Minutes, 1731–1735, May 2, 1761, Mar. 8, 1776, May 8, 1777, WPA Trans., SCL; Brown, *S.C. Regulators*, 103, 147, 188; Leah Townsend, *South Carolina Baptists, 1670–1805* (Florence, S.C., 1935), 177–178, 276; Meriwether, *Expansion of South Carolina*, 96–97; Gregg, *History of the Old Cheraws*, 72 n, 95; James A. Rogers, *Richard Furman: Life and Legacy* (Macon, Ga., 1985), 21.

45. Woodmason, *Carolina Backcountry*, ed. Hooker, 20, 42, 94 n; Council Jour., May 1, 1766. See also Chapter 1.

46. Jones, "Herman Husband," 66–74. The property holdings of the Regulators are summarized in Ekirch, "*Poor Carolina*," 165–166.

English Lord Hillsborough that the South Carolina uprising "differs from the commotions in the neighboring colony."[47]

v

As protectors of property, slavery, and household order, Regulators initially won a sympathetic response from coastal authorities. Bull had been sensitive to backcountry grievances even before the uprising. As early as 1765 he had informed the Lords of Trade that "the inhabitants settled from 250 miles west from thence [Charleston] lie under great hardships for want of that protection of their persons and their property which the law affords." Bull was not alone in his sentiments, for, in November 1767, within a week of receiving the remonstrance, the assembly effectively legalized Regulator attacks upon bandits by establishing two backcountry ranger companies in which both captains and many of the men were already involved in the Regulation. During the same session, the assembly began work on the Circuit Court and vagrancy acts. The Charleston Grand Jury of 1768 demonstrated its agreement with at least one key Regulator demand by urging the establishment of "public schools in the back parts of this province, for the education and instruction of the children of poor people."[48]

As Richard M. Brown has shown, the struggle with England interrupted the coastal response to Regulator grievances. A dispute with Parliament concerning the tenure of judges delayed passage of the Circuit Court Act for nearly two years. Preoccupation with the growing colonial controversy also led the assembly to suspend action on the public school and vagrancy acts. Such neglect indicated that the backcountry was not a priority for the majority of assemblymen, but it did not signify antagonism toward Regulator demands. Bull cut to the heart of the matter when he observed that the insurgents were not "Idle vagabonds, the canaille, the mere dregs of mankind." He wrote, instead, that they were "in general an industrious hardy Race of men, each . . . master of one Horse, many of several, besides cattle and slaves." Regulators were men of property whose leaders held property in slaves. In their efforts to secure their possessions, they supported, rather than challenged, the interests of coastal planters and merchants.[49]

Not until the summer of 1768, following a violent confrontation between

47. Ekirch, "*Poor Carolina*," 161; Bull to Hillsborough, Sept. 10, 1768, PRO Trans., XXXII, 37–38.

48. Bull to Lords of Trade, Mar. 15, 1765, PRO Trans., XXX, 251; Brown, *S.C. Regulators*, 41–44; Commons Jour., Nov. 11, 1767; *S.-C. Gaz.*, Feb. 1, 1768.

49. Brown, *S.C. Regulators*, 64–82; Bull to Hillsborough, Sept. 10, 1768, PRO Trans., XXXII, 39–40.

Regulators and coastal authorities near Welsh Tract, did the assembly and council begin to see the Regulation as a threat to social order within the colony. The incident involved a prosperous Pee Dee Regulator named Gideon Gibson, who was himself both a mulatto and a slaveholder. His large plantation in a fertile area called Marrs Bluff was the scene of the conflict. The struggle at Marrs Bluff not only sheds light on coastal perceptions of the insurgents; it also speaks to the changing position of free blacks in an emerging slave society.[50]

Gideon Gibson led a group of Pee Dee Regulators who, in July 1768, took Joseph Holland, an anti-Regulator militia captain, into custody. George Thomson, a coastal militia captain and constable, led a company of men to Gibson's house in order to deliver a warrant ordering Holland's release. The meeting erupted into violence, with Regulators seriously wounding several of Thomson's party and administering fifty lashes to each of the others. William White, a member of the company, later described the Marrs Bluff Regulators as "a great number of People of different Colours, (viz.t) Whites, Blacks, and Mulattoes."[51]

The incident alarmed authorities in Charleston, who, three weeks later, sent Provost Marshal Roger Pinckney and about twenty-five militiamen to arrest Gideon Gibson. Colonel George Gabriel Powell, a Georgetown planter and political figure, accompanied Pinckney on the unsuccessful mission. Seeing that Gibson was "guarded by a large body of men," Pinckney and Powell requested aid from captains Philip Pledger, George Hicks, and Alexander McIntosh. But those men were themselves Regulators, and the three hundred men whom they brought "absolutely refused" to aid in the capture of Gibson, "as Gibson they said, was one of them (Regulators) and had applied to them for protection." They went on to restate their grievances "for the want of County Courts and the Exorbitant expense of the law." The authorities never managed to capture Gibson, and Powell, who recounted the story, resigned his militia commission in disillusionment.[52]

When, in August 1768, Lieutenant Governor Bull proclaimed a pardon for all Regulators on condition that they disperse, he was careful to exclude "the persons concerned in those outrageous and daring violences Committed by Gideon Gibson and others upon George Thomson a lawfull Consta-

---

50. Miscellaneous Records, bk. MM, 371, bk. RR, 400–401, SCDAH (hereafter cited as Misc. Records). Gideon Gibson's family came to South Carolina from Virginia during the 1730s. See Winthrop D. Jordan, *White over Black: American Attitudes toward the Negro, 1550–1812* (Chapel Hill, N.C., 1968), 171–174; Brown, "Prosopography of the Regulators," 51–56; Meriwether, *Expansion of South Carolina*, 90, 96.
51. Council Jour., Aug. 26, 1768; Commons Jour., Aug. 15, 1770.
52. Council Jour., Aug. 26, 1768.

ble and his party in the actual Execution of a legal Warrant." Governor
Lord Charles Greville Montagu later excluded Gibson from the general
Regulator pardons of 1771. One suspects that their concern arose as much
from Gibson's race as from his actions. Earlier that summer, several Little
River Regulators had assaulted John Wood, a deputy of Provost Marshal
Pinckney, who had been attempting to deliver some warrants. Although the
incident involved fewer people and less injury than the fight at Marrs Bluff,
Wood clearly had been violently stopped "in the actual Execution of a legal
Warrant." Yet Bull took no special action against the Little River Regu-
lators.[53]

An article published first in the *South-Carolina Gazette* and later in the
Boston Chronicle reveals the confusion and fears of many lowcountrymen
following the Marrs Bluff incident. Written in August 1768, the article
attempted to explain the "outrageous Opposition lately offered to the civil
Authority near Marr's Bluff," which was then "a general subject of Conversation." According to this report, the incident had been falsely attributed to
Regulators. Gibson, suggested the author, was actually a bandit.

> That there are *two* Parties so called, and the Proceedings of the One fre-
> quently confounded with those of the *other*. That the *first* (called the
> *Honest Party*) consists, in general, of People of good Principles, and
> Property, who have assembled . . . professedly with the View of driving
> all Horse-Thieves, with their Harbourers, Abettors, and other Vaga-
> bonds, from amongst them; and that the *other* (called the *Rogues* Party)
> are a Gang of Banditti, or numerous Collection of outcast Mulattoes,
> Mustees, free Negroes, all Horse-Thieves, etc., from the Borders of Vir-
> ginia and other Northern Colonies (the very People whom the *Regulators*
> would have *expelled* the Province, or brought to Justice) and have taken
> up Arms to carry on their Villainy with Impunity.

The report went on to confuse Gideon Gibson and his group with the
"latter" or "rogues party."

> The last Accounts we have received of both are, That the *former* on the
> 16th past, took one Charles Sparks, of infamous Character, on Pedee,
> and ordered him to receive 500 Lashes, and quit the Province. And of
> the *latter*, that an armed Company of them, headed by one Gideon Gib-
> son, on the 25th past, near Marrs Bluff, surrounded a Constable and
> twelve Men, who were sent to bring one of the Villains before a
> Magistrate.[54]

53. Council Jour., Aug. 5, 1768; *S.-C. and Amer. Gen. Gaz.*, Aug. 19, 1768. The
incident involving John Wood is described in Council Jour., July 29, 1768. The Regulator
pardons are recorded on June 29, Oct. 31, 1771, Misc. Records, bk. OO, 614–615, bk.
PP, 46–47, and discussed in Brown, *S.C. Regulators*, 144, 159–160.

54. *S.-C. Gaz.*, Aug. 15, 1768; *Boston Chronicle*, Oct. 10, 1768.

By identifying Gibson with the horse thieves, the article reveals the confusion of lowcountry authorities who found wealthy and "respectable" Pee Dee Regulators standing firm in their support of Gideon Gibson's interracial band.

The incident at Marrs Bluff prompted a lengthy discussion in both the council and the assembly. Colonel Powell spoke openly of his perplexity. Having heard that several Regulators were "men of good property," he believed that they might be "induced to admit that the method they were persuing was not the proper mode to bring their wished for purpose." To Powell's "astonishment," he "found all argument lost upon them," and he advised the council that, unless the uprising was speedily terminated, "the consequences will be very shocking." Though Powell did not mention Gibson's race in his statement, the assembly did discuss the issue. Some representatives wanted Gibson subjected to the "Negro Law," and years later Henry Laurens recalled his own part in the debate.

> Gideon Gibson escaped the penalties of the negro law by producing upon comparison more red and white in his face than could be discovered in the faces of half the descendants of the French refugees in our House of Assembly, including your old acquaintance the Speaker. I challenged them all to the trial. The children of this same Gideon, having passed through another stage of whitewash were of fairer complexion than their prosecutor George Gabriel [Powell].[55]

Although Gibson apparently passed the color test, his race (as understood by members of the coastal elite), and that of his companions, was cause for concern. Given the overwhelming black-white ratio near the coast, it is not surprising that lowcountry observers should have been particularly sensitive to the potential dangers of violence from the backcountry's nonwhite population. It is impossible to determine the extent to which Powell and others were reacting to the violence or the race of the Marrs Bluff Regulators, but they clearly found the combination intolerable.

The Regulator Uprising prompted a clearer definition of backcountry racial boundaries. When the Regulator Captain Philip Pledger and his "party" captured the bandit Winslow Driggers, they tried and hanged him under the "Negro Act." In order to crush a bandit gang, they resorted to a race law. Authorities also grew more vigilant in identifying free blacks. In 1767, when tax collectors assessed Welsh Tract (the region encompassing Marrs Bluff), they counted 938 slaves and 13 free blacks. One year later, following the Marrs Bluff incident, they counted 1,276 slaves and 88 free blacks. One doubts that the number of free blacks in the area could have

55. Council Jour., Aug. 26, 1768; Henry Laurens to William Drayton, Feb. 15, 1783, quoted in Jordan, *White over Black*, 173.

increased from 13 to 88 between 1767 and 1768. What the tax records do suggest is that assessors had grown more sensitive to their presence. Following the incident at Marrs Bluff, "free negroes" at Welsh Tract were defined as such.[56]

vi

However much the Marrs Bluff incident alarmed coastal leaders, the angriest anti-Regulator opposition came from within the backcountry itself. In March 1769, a newspaper reported, "A new sett of people who call themselves *Moderators* have appeared against the *Regulators*. These two parties mutually accuse each other." Moderators were similar to the Regulators in background. The leaders included slaveowners, magistrates, and local merchants.[57] The story of their opposition points yet again to the more fundamental social conflict that precipitated the Regulation in the first place.

The Moderator reaction arose as a result of Regulator attacks on men whom the insurgents accused of "harboring horse thieves." Woodmason insisted that some magistrates "not only winked at them [bandits], but enter'd into Leagues, Confederacies, and Association with them—The first by way of Self Defence—On Promise that their Property should be untouch'd if they'd let them alone—The 2d Class, went Snacks with them, and received Presents—The third not only favour'd—but harbour'd protected and assisted them." Woodmason's accusation may have been correct in the case of at least one prominent Moderator. Jacob Summerall, a large landowner on the Savannah River, was among those magistrates whom Regulators accused of encouraging bandits. He was, in fact, the brother and neighbor of a convicted horse stealer. Woodmason's charge was not, however, justified in all cases. Some Moderators had been involved in personal disputes with Regulators, and others appear to have been genuinely outraged by Regulator brutality. As magistrates, some may have come into conflict with Regulators when they tried to serve legal processes. Whatever the

56. *S.-C. Gaz.*, Oct. 3, 1771; Public Treasurer, General Tax Receipts and Payments, 1761–1769, Account of the General Tax Collected for the Charges of the Government, 1767, 1768 (for the Years 1766, 1767), SCDAH. The "Negro Act" mentioned in the newspaper report was probably a reference to the South Carolina act of May 10, 1740, "for the Better Ordering and Governing Negroes and other Slaves in this Province" (Cooper and McCord, eds., *Statutes of South Carolina*, VII, 397–417). Gibson lived in the original Welsh Tract, which was encompassed by Prince Frederick when the western boundary of that parish was set in 1757 (the parish had been created in 1734). The likelihood is that the Marrs Bluff settlement was included in the Welsh Tract rather than the Prince Frederick Tax District. See Meriwether, *Expansion of South Carolina*, 79, 90–98.

57. *S.-C. and Amer. Gen. Gaz.*, Mar. 27, 1769; Brown, *S.C. Regulators*, 83–95.

sources of the Regulator-Moderator dispute, it did not reflect a fundamental divergence of attitude or class interest.[58]

Moderators joined forces after Regulators attacked John Musgrove, a merchant, surveyor, and magistrate living between the Broad and Saluda rivers. They demanded that nine leading Regulators be stripped of their commissions as militia officers and magistrates. Having soured on the Regulators as a result of the Marrs Bluff affair, Charleston authorities were initially sympathetic to Moderator demands. The council deprived leading Regulators of their commissions and authorized the Moderators to launch an all-out challenge against the Regulators.[59]

John Musgrove and his friend Jonathan Gilbert chose a man named Joseph Coffel (also spelled Scoffel, Scovil, Scophol) to lead the anti-Regulator forces in serving warrants against the insurgents. Little is known of Coffel except that he probably came from the Orangeburg area and served as a constable for the region between the Broad and Saluda rivers. Removed from office in 1772 for being "guilty of evil Practices in the Execution of his Office, as well as in assuming greater Authority than a Constable has a Right to do," Coffel was convicted the following year on a charge of cattle stealing. The future governor William Moultrie referred to Coffel as "a man of some influence in the back country, but a stupid, ignorant, blockhead."[60]

Just why Musgrove and Gilbert fixed on Joseph Coffel is not entirely clear. Probably they wanted to find a leader who had influence among the sort of people whom the Regulators had been regulating, and, if that was their intent, they succeeded very well. The *South-Carolina Gazette* reported that Coffel and his party were impressing "provisions and horses wherever he pleases, leaving whole families destitute of both." Coffel, continued the report, had "many returned horsethieves and banditti in his retinue." An inland militia colonel informed the council that Coffel had the frontier population "under very great distress by imprisoning people Women and Children as well as men and Going from House to House taking away their provisions."[61]

58. Woodmason, *Carolina Backcountry*, ed. Hooker, 218 n; Brown, *S.C. Regulators*, 83–95. Henry Summerhill is identified as the older brother of Jacob Summerhill of Ninety Six in deed of Aug. 10, 1783, Charleston Deeds, WPA Abs., no. H-5 (MS, 160).

59. Council Jour., Feb. 22, Mar. 13, Mar. 15, 1769; *S.-C. and Amer. Gen. Gaz.*, Feb. 27, Mar. 13, Mar. 20, 1769; *S.-C. Gaz.*, Mar. 16, 1769.

60. *S.-C. Gaz; and Coun. Jour.*, May 12, 1772; *S.-C. Gaz.*, Dec. 20, 1773; William Moultrie, *Memoirs of the American Revolution, So Far As It Relates to the States of North and South Carolina, and Georgia* (New York, 1802), I, 109. See also Chapman, *History of Edgefield County*, 19; Brown, *S.C. Regulators*, 204–205.

61. *S.-C. Gaz.*, Mar. 23, Apr. 6, 1769; Council Jour., Mar. 22, 1769. See also *S.-C. Gaz.; and Coun. Jour.*, Mar. 28, 1769.

The Moderators were active for less than two weeks. The governor and council announced that "Coffells illegal and arbitrary proceedings were entirely without any authority from Government." On March 25, hundreds of Regulators and Moderators met at a plantation on the Saluda River with the intention of engaging in combat, but three widely respected men, including the planter and militia colonel Richard Richardson, intervened. The peacemakers informed the Moderators that they no longer had support from the coast, and they persuaded both groups to disperse.[62]

The Moderator movement is significant because it highlights the social position of the Regulators. In order to muster anti-Regulator forces, Moderators had to recruit from the nonplanting, "low," or bandit population. Leaders such as Musgrove and Gilbert were notable exceptions. Even those Charleston authorities who condemned Regulator excesses after Marrs Bluff and sympathized with men like Musgrove, who had been objects of Regulator abuse, ultimately opposed the Moderators. To have done otherwise would have been to support precisely that segment of the population that both they and the Regulators wished to suppress.

vii

By the time the Regulators disbanded, they had achieved considerable, if incomplete, success. The assembly's Circuit Court Act of 1769 established a system of courts, jails, and sheriffs in four newly created backcountry judicial districts. One year earlier, the Privy Council had finally consented to the creation of two backcountry parishes, St. David and St. Matthew, after the colonial administration reduced apportionment for St. Mark and St. James, Goose Creek. Also in 1768, Regulators had succeeded in electing six of their candidates to the colonial assembly, and, the following year, Patrick Calhoun and the Regulator Tacitus Gaillard won assembly seats from Prince William and St. Stephen, respectively. Finally, the colonial government adopted an Act for the Preservation of Deer that placed restrictions on hunters. In 1771, Governor Montagu issued general Regulator pardons.[63]

Hunters and bandits continued to annoy inland settlers, but, with the establishment of courts and jails, they could never again throw the region into chaos. Several of the most prominent bandits, including James Moon and Govee Black, had been executed. Others left the colony. In 1770, the *South-Carolina Gazette* reported the return of "a great number of Horse-

---

62. Brown, *S.C. Regulators*, 83–95, quotation on 94.
63. *Ibid.*, 60–82, 159–60; Cooper and McCord, eds., *Statutes of South Carolina*, IV, 298–302, 310–312; *S.-C. Gaz.*, Oct. 10, 1768; *S.-C. and Amer. Gen. Gaz.*, Sept. 28–30, 1768; [Calhoun], *Life of John C. Calhoun*, 4.

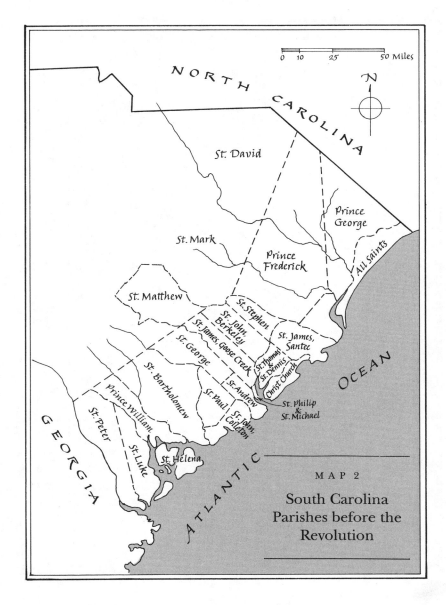

Map 2. South Carolina Parishes before the Revolution. *After Walter B. Edgar, ed., Biographical Directory of the South Carolina House of Representatives, I, Sessions Lists, 1692–1793 (Columbia, S.C., 1974), 46; Lester J. Cappon et al., eds., Atlas of Early American History: The Revolutionary Era, 1760–1790 (Princeton, N.J., 1976), 6. Drawn by Richard Stinely*

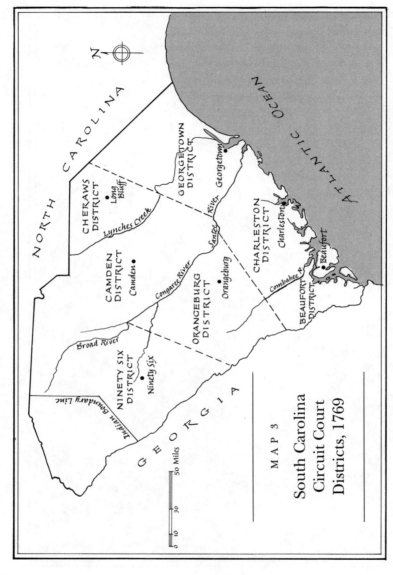

Map 3. South Carolina Circuit Court Districts, 1769. After *Historical Records Survey*, WPA, 1938; Lester J. Cappon et al., eds., *Atlas of Early American History: The Revolutionary Era, 1760–1790* (Princeton, N.J., 1976), 6, 42. Drawn by Richard Stinely

Thieves and other Banditti, who fled from the back parts of this and the neighbouring provinces . . . while the regulating scheme prevailed," but the author also observed that they would be "narrowly watched" and that they would probably "furnish the first business for our new Circuit-Courts."[64]

That Regulators succeeded as well as they did testifies to the growing bonds between South Carolina's regional elites. Coastal leaders shared the Regulators' concern for property rights, slavery, and household order. Meanwhile, prominent lowcountrymen were also extending business and planting interests to the frontier. Several Charlestonians held partnerships in backcountry stores, and such prominent merchants as Peter Manigault and Henry Laurens owned sizable inland plantations. Other wealthy low-countrymen, including Governor Montagu, owned large backcountry tracts, which they must have acquired for speculative purposes. Laurens was quick to see the advantage of circuit courts for his own substantial holdings. The acreage would, he suspected, "from an increase of inhabitants and from an expected establishment of Circuit Courts . . . become valuable very soon."[65]

This is not to minimize the deep suspicion that existed between the sections and dominated state politics until cotton transformed the frontier. Not until a greater proportion of inland settlers held a considerably larger number of slaves would coastal leaders give in to demands for a fundamental reapportionment of legislative representation, but contemporaries recognized that powerful interests already drew the regions together. Woodmason expressed the situation clearly when he admonished lowcountrymen "Who treat Us not as Brethren of the same Kindred—United in the same Interests—and Subjects of the same Prince, but as if we were of a different Species from themselves."[66] Regulators insisted that they were not a different species and that the leading men of both regions had basic concerns in common. The backcountry would not be a plantation society for years to come, but an emerging planter class had already begun to mold the frontier in its own image.

64. *S.-C. Gaz.*, Sept. 26, 1768, Apr. 5, 1770. See also *S.-C. and Amer. Gen. Gaz.*, May 6, 1768; Commons Jour., Feb. 28, 1770.

65. Index to Colonial Land Grants, SCDAH; Edgar *et al.*, eds., *Biographical Directory of the House*, II, 431–432; Henry Laurens to Richard Oswald, Apr. 27, 1768, in Philip M. Hamer *et al.*, eds., *The Papers of Henry Laurens*, (Columbia, S.C., 1968–), V, 665.

66. Woodmason, *Carolina Backcountry*, ed. Hooker, 222.

CHAPTER 3.

Inland Civil War

i

Eight months before the colonies declared their independence from Great Britain, the South Carolina backcountry was embroiled in a violent conflict between whigs and loyalists. Estimates of loyalist strength varied throughout the Revolutionary war, but several observers believed that the inhabitants of Ninety Six District were about evenly divided and that tories may have outnumbered whigs in the fork between the Broad and Saluda rivers. As early as 1774, coastal radicals were concerned about inland allegiances and struggled, with only mixed success, to win frontier support.[1] In September 1775 the British governor William Campbell wrote confidently, "The loyalty of those poor, honest, industrious people in the back part of

1. David Ramsay believed that loyalists outnumbered whigs only in the Broad and Saluda fork. According to the loyalist Colonel Robert Gray, tories in South Carolina composed about "one third of the whole," but he insisted that settlers in Ninety Six District were about evenly divided. The situation changed when British troops moved into the backcountry. In January 1781, General Nathanael Greene believed that whigs and loyalists were evenly divided in the Pee Dee area, and, in May, he despaired that the Camden-area loyalists were equal in number to their opponents. See David Ramsay, *History of South Carolina from Its First Settlement in 1670, to the Year 1808* (Newberry, S.C., 1858 [orig. publ. Charleston, S.C., 1809]), I, 144; "Colonel Robert Gray's Observations on the War in Carolina," *SCHM*, XI (1910), 140, 148; Greene to Chevalier de la Luzerne, Jan. 9, 1781, Nathanael Greene Papers, LC; Greene to Joseph Reed, May 14, 1781, Joseph Reed Papers, NYHS; Robert Woodward Barnwell, Jr., "Loyalism in South Carolina, 1765–1785" (Ph.D. diss., Duke University, 1941), 131–134; Edward McCrady, *The History of South Carolina in the Revolution, 1775–1780* (New York, 1901); David Duncan Wallace, *South Carolina: A Short History, 1520–1948* (Columbia, S.C., 1951),243–331. For a more comprehensive account of the process by which backcountry areas were drawn into the Revolutionary struggle, see David Ammerman, *In the Common Cause: American Response to the Coercive Acts of 1774* (Charlottesville, Va., 1974).

this and neighboring provinces discontents them [the Charleston whigs] greatly." By November 1775, the two sides had come to blows, and not until winter did whig forces finally gain the ascendancy by rounding up the "most leading and active" tories, whom they carried to jail in Charleston. Sporadic fighting persisted through the 1770s, and, in 1780, with the arrival of the British, the frontier exploded into a virtual civil war.[2]

In many ways, the Revolution in backcountry South Carolina was a continuation and intensification of struggles that erupted during the Regulation. Coastal whigs won support in the backcountry by identifying their cause with the interests and aspirations of the planters who had led the Regulator Uprising. At the same time, the British actually weakened their position by winning the support of various groups already alienated from the backcountry's leadership. Although social conflicts, deepened by the war, persisted throughout the 1780s, the whig victory also extended the local and statewide power of the backcountry's planter class.

Historians have generally recognized a connection between frontier loyalism and sectional hostilities. With only one seat allotted in the colonial assembly until 1768, and only three thereafter, backcountry settlers had ample reason to resent requests for support from Charleston rebels. By January 1766, several months after South Carolina's assembly joined the protest against the British Stamp Act, a group of backcountry settlers expressed their resentment against coastal radicals by forming the Loyal Frontier Friends Club. Despite Regulator successes, many backcountry demands had gone unanswered, largely because the broader colonial struggle had drawn legislative attention away from the frontier. When the Revolution came, many inland settlers regarded coastal radicals with suspicion.[3]

The sectional interpretation of backcountry loyalism is clearly insufficient. Precisely because resentment of coastal leaders was so pervasive, it cannot account for the many settlers who joined the whigs. Richard M. Brown's discovery that only 6 of the 120 known Regulators actively sup-

2. William Campbell to Lords of Trade, Sept. 19, 1775, Records of the Province of South Carolina, Sainsbury Transcripts from the British Public Record Office, XXXV, 252–253, SCDAH (hereafter cited as PRO Trans.); Richard Richardson to the Council of Safety, Jan. 2, 1776, in R. W. Gibbes, ed., *Documentary History of the American Revolution . . .* (New York, 1855–1857), I, 249–253; Lewis Pinckney Jones, *The South Carolina Civil War of 1775* (Lexington, S.C., 1975).

3. Wallace, *South Carolina*, 263; McCrady, *History of South Carolina, 1775–1780*, 33–35; Charles Woodmason, *The Carolina Backcountry on the Eve of the Revolution: The Journal and Other Writings of Charles Woodmason, Anglican Itinerant*, ed. Richard Hooker (Chapel Hill, N.C., 1953), 118–119. The Loyal Frontier Friends Club was mentioned by Henry Laurens in Laurens to John Lewis Gervais, Jan. 29, 1766, in Philip M. Hamer *et al.*, eds., *The Papers of Henry Laurens* (Columbia, S.C., 1968–), V, 53.

ported the loyalists, while 55 joined the whigs, virtually dispelled the sectional thesis. Brown's research demonstrated that the most outspoken proponents of frontier demands for courts, jails, schools, churches, and legislative representation tended to join the colonial opposition.[4] Regulators resented the neglectful assembly, but their concern for the protection of property, their growing involvement in slavery, and their increasing interest in commercial agriculture tied them in fundamental ways to the wealthier planters and merchants of the coast. That many Regulators managed to overcome their sectional animosity should not surprise us, but then the loyalty of so many other inland settlers remains unaccounted for.

Nor did ideology or political language distinguish backcountry whigs from loyalists. Frontier settlers had used Radical Whig principles to define their own grievances, and their identification of themselves as landed property holders gave particular meaning to the republican political language that resonated among them. Their charges against the government in Charleston were, in many ways, analogous to colonial grievances against Parliament. Regulators complained that their property was being arbitrarily taken, that they were taxed without adequate representation in the assembly, and that they suffered trial by distant juries. A Regulator sympathizer from the Pee Dee area urged the establishment of county and circuit courts so that backcountrymen "may enjoy by that means, the rights and privileges of British subjects, which they think themselves now deprived of." The Regulators' remonstrance reads much like colonial petitions to Parliament. "We are," declared the remonstrance, "*Free-Men*—British Subjects—Not Born *Slaves*." By their "Birth-Right, as *Britons*," Regulators claimed the right to trial by juries of their peers.[5]

Some backcountrymen applied the ideas and language of the remonstrance to support the patriot cause against Britain. In 1774, the grand juries of Camden, Ninety Six, and Cheraws—a group that included six former Regulators—presented as a grievance "*the most dangerous and alarming Nature*, the Power exercised by the Parliament, to Tax, and to make Laws to bind, the *American* Colonies, in all Cases whatsoever."[6] In their struggle for greater representation in the assembly, some frontiersmen may well have grown more sympathetic to the whig cause.

By contrast, Charles Woodmason, author of the remonstrance and one of the few known Regulators who became a staunch loyalist, drew what

4. Richard Maxwell Brown, *The South Carolina Regulators* (Cambridge, Mass., 1963), 123–125.

5. *South-Carolina and American General Gazette* (Charleston), Sept. 2, 1768; Woodmason, *Carolina Backcountry*, ed. Hooker, 215, 220.

6. *South-Carolina Gazette* (Charleston), Dec. 12, 1774.

would seem to have been the more logical conclusion. He demonstrated how easily republican rhetoric could be turned against the Charleston radicals. Woodmason admonished lowcountry rebels who made "such Noise about Liberty! Liberty! Freedom! Property! Rights! Priveleges! and what not; And at the same time keep half their fellow Subjects in a State of Slavery." Woodmason was not referring to black slaves, but to the thousands of white frontiersmen who remained all but unrepresented in the assembly. His denunciation of Charleston also sounded much like colonial charges against London. Woodmason contrasted the wealth and luxury of the coastal city with the virtue and simplicity claimed for the backcountry. "Such as have spent their whole Lives, in feasting and High Living" could not, he insisted, "bear the thoughts of keeping of Lent in the Back Country."[7] Inland and coastal leaders spoke the same political language, but, on the frontier, republican ideology could accommodate the loyalist at least as well as the whig position.

Finally, ethnic and simplistic economic explanations provide little additional help in distinguishing frontier whigs from tories. Foreign-born were more likely than native-born colonists to side with the loyalists, and contemporaries believed that the German origin of many settlers at the lower Broad and Saluda fork was largely responsible for loyalism in that region. But many Irish-born, English-born, and German-born South Carolinians joined the rebels. Similarly, Camden-area Quakers and New Light Baptists of what would later be Union County inclined to loyalism, while Regular Baptists of Charleston and Cheraws supported the whigs. Presbyterians, who probably formed the majority of the inland population, were divided, as were South Carolina's Anglicans. Neither wealth nor occupation explains the divisions on the frontier. Storekeepers, planters, slaveholders, and nonslaveholders were found in both rebel and loyalist camps. By October 1775, alliances were already so complex that one backcountry writer described the situation mysteriously as "a wheel within a wheel."[8]

Conflict within the Revolutionary backcountry may not have been a class struggle in any simple sense, but it did have an important class dimension. Although ambitious planters and merchants chose one side or the other, the whigs more consistently represented the broad class interests of rising back-

---

7. Woodmason, *Carolina Backcountry*, ed. Hooker, 262, 255.
8. Wallace Brown, *The King's Friends: The Composition and Motives of the American Loyalist Claimants* (Providence, R.I., 1965), 213–338; McCrady, *History of South Carolina, 1775–1780*, 32–52; Barnwell, "Loyalism in South Carolina," 2; Floyd Mulkey, "Rev. Philip Mulkey, Pioneer Baptist Preacher in South Carolina," Southern Historical Association, *Proceedings*, 1945, pp. 7–13; Edward Musgrove to William Henry Drayton, Oct. 14, 1775, in Gibbes, ed., *Documentary History*, I, 203.

country slaveowners. As much by default as by design, it was whigs rather than loyalists who, in the course of the Revolution, were best able to continue Regulator struggles. In so doing, they strengthened their position within a divided frontier and furthered the interests of aspiring inland planters. In the end, the whigs, not the loyalists, became the vanguard of an emerging planter class.

ii

Historians have generally divided South Carolina's Revolutionary experience into three phases.[9] The first, which lasted from 1774 to 1776, was characterized in large measure by a struggle for influence in the backcountry. Coastal whigs began opening opportunities for greater participation in the new state government. In July 1774, the backcountry sent delegates, including the former Regulators Moses Kirkland and Benjamin Farrar, to a general meeting in Charleston. After discussing the deepening crisis and debating the nonimportation and nonexportation agreements, the meeting selected a general committee that, in turn, called for the election of a provincial congress. Committee members determined apportionment at thirty delegates for Charleston, six for each parish, ten for each of four large inland districts, and three for the sparsely settled district between the Savannah River and the North Fork of the Edisto. The backcountry, including the parishes of St. David and St. Matthew, was to have 55 of 187 representatives in the new legislative body.[10]

Not only did coastal whigs include backcountry leaders in the Provincial Government; they also attempted to win inland support by appointing a committee, including about eighty-four inland representatives, to circulate the Continental Association through the backcountry. This document endorsed the nonimportation and nonexportation agreements and pledged

9. The following summary is based on a number of excellent accounts of the Revolution in South Carolina. See Ramsay, *History of South Carolina*, I, 124–274; McCrady, *History of South Carolina, 1775–1780*; McCrady, *The History of South Carolina in the Revolution, 1780–1783* (New York, 1902); Wallace, *South Carolina*, 243–331; Jones, *S.C. Civil War*; Russell F. Weigley, *The Partisan War: The South Carolina Campaign of 1780–82* (Columbia, S.C., 1970); Gary D. Olson, "Loyalists and the American Revolution: Thomas Brown and the South Carolina Backcountry, 1775–1776," *SCHM*, LXVIII (1967), 201–219, LXIX (1968), 44–58.

10. Walter B. Edgar *et al.*, eds., *Biographical Directory of the South Carolina House of Representatives* (Columbia, S.C., 1974–1977), I, 5, 164–165; Edward McCrady, *The History of South Carolina under the Royal Government, 1719–1776* (New York, 1969 [orig. publ. New York, 1899]), 733–742.

solidarity with Massachusetts, which was then suffering under the penalties of Parliament's Coercive Acts.[11]

In their effort to unify South Carolina behind the Revolutionary cause, coastal radicals encountered serious problems. By spring 1775, rumors were circulating in Charleston that several members of the Provincial Congress had defected to the loyalists. In July, the executive arm of the Provincial Congress, known as the Council of Safety, dispatched a three-man committee to the backcountry to win more signatures to the Continental Association and to counter the growing influence of prominent tories. The committee included the Reverend William Tennent, a Charleston Presbyterian; the Reverend Oliver Hart, South Carolina's leading Baptist; and William Henry Drayton, a prominent radical. Joseph Kershaw later joined their stump-speaking tour through loyalist strongholds.

The committee was only partly successful in achieving its mission. In Ninety Six District, and particularly in the fork between the Broad and Saluda rivers, committee members won few new signatures to the Continental Association. Tensions between whigs and loyalists mounted, and, in November 1775, the two parties came to blows. About nineteen hundred loyalist militiamen laid siege to Fort Ninety Six, which was defended by some six hundred whig recruits. Despite a twenty-one-day truce following the siege, the whig colonels William Thomson and Richard Richardson began mobilizing troops for their highly successful Snow Campaign through the loyalist areas of Ninety Six. Whig authorities freed most of the captured loyalists in 1776, after successfully repulsing an attempt by the British to take Charleston.

With the defeat of British forces off the Charleston coast and the near-destruction of the Cherokee Nation on the frontier, South Carolina entered the second phase of Revolutionary conflict. Between the summer of 1776 and January 1780, the state enjoyed a period of relative calm. Many leading loyalists fled to East Florida, where they formed themselves into a ranger company. Under the leadership of a Georgia merchant named Thomas Brown, they engaged in a series of pillaging raids into backcountry Georgia and South Carolina. Whig forces made two unsuccessful attempts, one in 1776 and the other in 1778, to crush British and loyalist armies operating out of East Florida.

The third phase of the Revolution in South Carolina began during the first weeks of 1780, when British troops, commanded by Major General Henry Clinton, attacked Charleston. That May, the Revolutionary General

11. Ammerman, *In the Common Cause*; *S.-C. Gaz.*, Jan. 30, 1775.

Benjamin Lincoln formally surrendered the city. Meanwhile, British troops had begun moving inland, giving new impetus to the loyalists. For more than twelve months, the backcountry was wracked by civil war. Writing from Camden in 1781, Nathanael Greene, commander of the Revolutionary southern armies, despaired that "the whigs and the Tories are butchering one another hourly." No people, he believed, had "suffered greater calamities."[12]

British strategy was based on the assumption that loyalist strength would be sufficient to hold posts taken by the invading army. Clinton and other commanders believed that they could move their troops northward through South Carolina, leaving the southern states securely in loyalist hands. The British plan simultaneously overestimated loyalist strength and underestimated the persistence and effectiveness of the whig militia. As the occupying army moved northward to face final defeat at Yorktown, whig forces succeeded in retaking backcountry areas once held by the loyalists.[13] By autumn 1781, the rebels had regained control of the backcountry, and, in December 1782, the British finally evacuated Charleston.

iii

To unravel the web of divisions that split the Carolina backcountry, we need to begin with the early struggle for control of the frontier. In their very effort to win the support of certain prominent "men of influence," leading rebels revealed one important dynamic of backcountry allegiances during the early phase of Revolutionary conflict: the tendency of neighborhoods or communities to coalesce around key individuals. Thomas Fletchall, for example, was a militia colonel for the area between the Broad and Saluda rivers. His defection to the loyalist side caused considerable alarm among coastal whigs. As one observer later wrote, Fletchall's position as colonel

12. Nathanael Greene to Joseph Reed, May 14, 1781, Reed Papers.

13. In two articles on the British southern strategy, John Shy points out that British commanders were torn between contradictory policies of conciliating and of terrorizing the backcountry population. Because the British were unable to win new allies or to make full use of existing loyalist strength, the whig militia repeatedly regained control of posts abandoned by the invading army. See Shy, "The American Revolution: The Military Conflict Considered as a Revolutionary War," in Stephen G. Kurtz and James H. Hutson, eds., *Essays on the American Revolution* (Chapel Hill, N.C., 1973), 121–156; Shy, "British Strategy for Pacifying the Southern Colonies, 1778–1781," in Jeffrey J. Crow and Larry E. Tise, eds., *The Southern Experience in the American Revolution* (Chapel Hill, N.C., 1978), 155–173. For an important overview of the British southern strategy, see Ira D. Gruber, "Britain's Southern Strategy," in W. Robert Higgins, ed., *The Revolutionary War in the South: Power, Conflict, and Leadership: Essays in Honor of John Richard Alden* (Durham, N.C., 1979), 205–238.

"of course gave him great influence in that part of the country." At a stump meeting held near Fairforest Creek, Oliver Hart observed "with sorrow . . . that Col. Fletchall has all those people at his beck, and reigns amongst them like a little King." Not coincidentally, those areas in which Drayton, Tennent, and Hart enjoyed greatest success were neighborhoods in which militia captains were sympathetic to the whig cause.[14]

There were other such loyalist men of influence living between the Broad and Saluda rivers who, along with Fletchall, helped to make that region a persistent problem for South Carolina whigs. Among the loyalists were two former Regulators, Moses Kirkland and Robert Cunningham. The whig militia general, Andrew Pickens, later testified to Cunningham's local prestige. "There would not have been," Pickens insisted, "so virulent an opposition to our cause in this country" had Cunningham joined the rebels. Evan McLaurin, a prosperous store owner at the lower Broad and Saluda fork, also attracted surrounding settlers to the loyalist cause. When Drayton visited the area in August 1775, he found that McLaurin was able to throw such "a damp on the people" that not a single person signed the Continental Association.[15]

The very term *man of influence*, so frequently used by contemporaries, is revealing. In communities where settlers depended upon stores and mills for a variety of services, store owners and millers, many of whom were also magistrates or militia officers, naturally wielded political influence. Drayton recognized the power of such men when, in the course of his journey, he declared that "no miller, who was a subscriber [to the Continental Association], should grind wheat or corn for any person who was a non-subscriber." It is no coincidence that such prominent backcountry loyalists as Cunningham, McLaurin, and Kirkland were all involved in local trade. Fletchall owned and operated large gristmills.[16]

14. John Drayton, *Memoirs of the American Revolution* . . . (Charleston, S.C., 1821), I, 312; Glenwood Clayton and Loulie Latimer Owens, eds., "Oliver Hart's Diary of the Journey to the Back-Country," *Journal of the South Carolina Baptist Historical Society*, I (1975), quotation on p. 21. See also "Fragment of a Journal Kept by the Reverend William Tennent . . . ," in Gibbes, ed., *Documentary History*, I, 225–238; Barnwell, "Loyalism in South Carolina," 141.

15. Andrew Pickens to Henry Lee, Aug. 28, 1811, Andrew Pickens Papers, SCL; John Drayton, *Memoirs*, I, 364; W. H. Drayton to Council of Safety, Aug. 16, 1775, in Gibbes, ed., *Documentary History*, I, 141.

16. W. H. Drayton to Council of Safety, Aug. 16, 21, 1775, in Gibbes, ed., *Documentary History*, I, 141, 150. See also John Drayton, *Memoirs*, I, 363. Evan McLaurin had a large store at Dutch Fork—the area in the lower Broad and Saluda fork—and a partner in Charleston. Robert Cunningham operated a ferry on the Saluda River. His claim to £1,000 due in book accounts suggests that he was involved in trade. Thomas Fletchall claimed compensation for 14 slaves, more than 1,000 acres, and gristmills at Fairforest

Influence could, and apparently did, work two ways. Thomas Fletchall, who lived on lands adjoining those of the pacifist and tory minister Philip Mulkey, presumably serviced the Mulkey community with his mills. One cannot help wondering the extent to which Mulkey and his followers influenced Fletchall. Similarly, Evan McLaurin operated his store in the lower Broad and Saluda fork, where Germans predominated. According to contemporary accounts, these "Dutch" settlers remained staunch loyalists because they feared that an independent American government would retract all royal land grants. Again, McLaurin's proximity to the German settlement may have encouraged him to remain loyal.[17]

Whatever the interaction between various inland areas and their leading men, it worked to divide the Revolutionary backcountry by neighborhood. When persuasion failed, communities had ways of enforcing—or trying to enforce—unanimity. One loyalist refugee from the Camden area admitted to taking the Rebel Oath, but, he explained, "The millers and blacksmiths would not work for any one who did not take the oath."[18] That families and common ethnic groups lived on adjoining lands only reinforced the tendency for clusters of settlement to act as whig or tory units. Following the British occupation, one loyalist officer observed, "The whole province resembled a piece of patch work, the inhabitants of every settlement when united in sentiment being in arms for the side they liked best and making continual inroads into one another's settlements."[19]

Creek. Moses Kirkland also had a gristmill and a sawmill in addition to his other extensive holdings. Brown, *S.C. Regulators*, 203; claims of Isabella McLaurin, Robert Cunningham, Thomas Fletchall, and Moses Kirkland, in Great Britain, Audit Office, Transcripts of the Manuscript Books and Papers of the Commission of Enquiry into the Losses and Services of the American Loyalists Held under the Acts of Parliament of 23, 25, 26, 28, and 29 of George III, Preserved amongst the Audit Office Records in the Public Record Office of England, 1783–1790, LIII, 320–332, LIV, 317–326, esp. 319, LVII, 223–239, 318–344, esp. 344, NYPL microfilm (hereafter cited as Loyalist Claims).

17. Bob Compton, "The Fairforest Church," *Jour. S.C. Baptist Hist. Soc.*, I (1975), 49; W. H. Drayton to Council of Safety, Aug. 16, 21, 1775, in Gibbes, ed., *Documentary History*, I, 141, 151; William Tennent to Laurens, Aug. 20, 1775, in Gibbes, ed., *Documentary History*, I, 141; John Drayton, *Memoirs*, I, 311–312, 325–326; John C. Hope to Lyman Draper, Jan. 1, 1873, Lyman C. Draper Manuscripts, Ser. DD, King's Mountain Papers, XIII, no. 86, SHSW (hereafter cited as Draper).

18. Claim of Robert McClelland, Loyalist Claims, LII, 464. Colonel William Bratton of the New Acquisition, in what would later be York County, commanded 125 men, "principally his neighbors." Proceedings of a Celebration of Huck's Defeat, Brattonsville, York District, S.C., July 12, 1839, Draper, Ser. DD, King's Mountain Papers, XIII, no. 50.

19. "Gray's Observations," *SCHM*, XI (1910), 153. Claims filed by loyalists from Ninety Six confirm the officer's picture of a region divided by neighborhood. Of more than 50 claimants, most lived in the region of Long Cane, Hard Labor, and Cuffeytown

Not surprisingly, the store owners, millers, magistrates, and officers most likely to wield local influence were also the people most likely to entertain statewide political and military ambition. For some, the decisive consideration in choosing or shifting sides during the spring and summer of 1775 was status. In January of that year, both Robert Cunningham and Moses Kirkland were, by all appearances, sympathetic to the whig cause. Yet by the following summer, the two men were among the staunchest opponents of the Provincial Government.[20] Many years later Andrew Pickens offered what seems a plausible explanation. When the Council of Safety established a backcountry regiment, the candidates for colonel were Cunningham, Kirkland, and James Mayson—all former Regulators. The position went to Mayson, an outcome that, according to Pickens, "so exasperated the others that they immediately took the other side of the Question." Pickens was not merely speaking ill of tory leaders, for he also pointed out that he "never had any doubt but that . . . [Cunningham] . . . would have made the best officer." The whig colonel, William Thomson, made a similar observation when he wrote "of their being a private [p]eak and great resentment between Mayson, Kirkland, and this Cunningham[.] the latter with some more of his Neighbours, think they have not been taken proper notice of." Henry Laurens, president of the Council of Safety, suspected that Thomas Fletchall had been motivated by similar concerns. "It has been said," wrote Laurens to Fletchall, "that you were in some measure disposed to unite with the friends of America, but that you were deterred, partly . . . by the dread of losing your commission of Colonel in the Militia, and your rank as a Justice of the Peace."[21]

---

creeks. Many had been neighbors or friends before the Revolution. All appear to have served in the militia regiment officered by Colonel John Hamilton. Loyalist Claims, XXVI.

20. Kirkland and Cunningham were among those appointed to the committee responsible for circulating the Continental Association. Kirkland was also a member of the grand jury of Ninety Six when that body protested the exercise of parliamentary power "to tax and bind the Americans in all Cases whatsoever." In June 1775, Kirkland accepted a commission as captain from the whig government in Charleston. *S.-C. Gaz.*, Dec. 12, 1774, Dec. 30, 1775; Barnwell, "Loyalism in South Carolina," 98–103; McCrady, *History of South Carolina, 1775–1780*, 14, 37–38; John Drayton, *Memoirs*, I, 321.

21. Pickens to Lee, Aug. 28, 1811, Pickens Papers; William Thomson to Henry Laurens, July 22, 1775, in A. S. Salley, Jr., *The History of Orangeburg County, South Carolina, from Its First Settlement to the Close of the Revolutionary War* (Orangeburg, S.C., 1898), 406; Henry Laurens to Thomas Fletchall, July 14, 1775, in "Journal of the Council of Safety for the Province of South-Carolina, 1775," South-Carolina Historical Society, *Collections*, II (Charleston, S.C., 1858), 40–43. See also Barnwell, "Loyalism in South Carolina," 97–98.

Settlers were also watchful of the positions granted to their local leaders. If recognition of leading men aided in winning the allegiance of whole communities, failure to do so could incur their animosity. When Andrew Williamson received an appointment to the rank of major rather than colonel, many settlers in the neighborhood of Long Canes were offended. Writing of the settlement in Williamson's area, a prominent backcountry whig observed, "If they join us at all (which I doubt), they will be very apt to prejudice the service by altercations about command."[22]

Recognizing both the ambition and local authority of backcountry men of influence, lowcountry whigs sought to win support by offering access to political and military positions. In July 1775, Henry Laurens was eager to prevent the defection of Captain George Whitfield to the loyalists. It occurred to Laurens "that Captain Whitfield however chearfully he may shew an inclination to serve the Colony by resignation, may not be content with a subcommand / if he is a man of spirit he will not." Laurens suggested that the captain petition the Council of Safety for a higher rank. Also in 1775, the Provincial Congress established three regular regiments, one of which was to consist of backcountry mounted rangers. The Revolutionary general William Moultrie later recalled, "It was thought not only useful, but political to raise them, because the most influential gentlemen in the back country were appointed officers, which interested them in the cause."[23]

As the Revolution progressed—as people lost friends and family in the conflict—the war assumed greater meaning for many of those involved. Some undoubtedly fought to preserve liberty as they conceived it. As one frontier officer wrote to his son from headquarters at Ninety Six:

> I feel myself distracted on both hands by this thought, that in my old age I should be obliged to take field in defence of my rights and liberties, and that of my children. God only knows that it is not of choice, but of necessity, and from the consideration that I had rather suffer anything than lose my birthright, and that of my children.[24]

Experience on the frontier may well have made some such men particularly sensitive to colonial complaints about Parliament.

Yet, during the early phase of the struggle, most backcountry settlers were less concerned about England than about their own local grievances and

22. Francis Salvadore to W. H. Drayton, July 18, 1776, in Gibbes, ed., *Documentary History,* II, 24–25.

23. Laurens to Fletchall, July 14, 1775, in Salley, *History of Orangeburg County,* 402–403; William Moultrie, *Memoirs of the American Revolution, So Far As It Relates to the States of North and South Carolina, and Georgia* (New York, 1802), I, 64.

24. James Williams to his son, June 12, 1779, in Gibbes, ed., *Documentary History,* II, 115–116.

aspirations. Coastal whigs were able to win inland support precisely because they recognized and helped to fulfill the political and military ambition of leading frontiersmen. In so doing, they extended the statewide political power of backcountry settlers and thereby furthered the political goals expressed by Regulators during the preceding decade. Following roughly on the system of apportionment established for the Provincial Congress, the South Carolina Constitution of 1776 allowed the backcountry 76 of 202 seats in the new General Assembly. Although the backcountry did not have anything approximating proportional representation, the new government did make possible increased political influence for inland settlers. For Moses Kirkland and Robert Cunningham, the whig offer was not good enough, but, for others with similar ambitions, opportunities opened by the Revolution must have been very welcome.[25]

iv

Like their whig counterparts, many backcountry loyalists were ambitious slaveholders, storekeepers, millowners, and rising planters, but, in their effort to attract followers, they played on widespread resentments against the wealthier planters and merchants on the coast. Writing of his unsuccessful labors between the Broad and Saluda rivers, the Reverend William Tennent insisted that leading loyalists "blind the people and fill them with bitterness against the gentlemen as they are called." Settlers believed that "no man that comes from below, and that no paper printed there can speak the truth." According to Oliver Hart, Fletchall addressed an audience near Fairforest Creek, intimating that "the people below wanted them to go down and assist them against the Negroes." Only a "Fool," suggested Fletchall, would agree to go. Another loyalist leader addressed a meeting in the same upper piedmont region by reading a "ministerial piece" similarly

25. The South Carolina Constitution of 1776 allowed 30 representatives for Charleston and 6 for each of the parishes. It added 15 backcountry representatives to the lower house of the legislature by apportioning 3 additional representatives to the District between the Savannah River and the North Fork of the Edisto, 10 representatives to the New Acquisition (later York County), and 2 additional representatives to the District between the Broad and Saluda Rivers. The latter was divided into 3 smaller districts, each of which was allowed 4 representatives. The lower house, which totaled 202 members, was to elect the upper house. The South Carolina Constitution of 1778 removed the governor's veto power, provided for direct election of state senators, and disestablished the Anglican church, but the system of apportionment remained essentially unchanged until 1790. Thomas Cooper and David J. McCord, eds., *The Statutes at Large of South Carolina* (Columbia, S.C., 1836–1841), I, 131–146; Wallace, *South Carolina*, 271–282; William A. Schaper, *Sectionalism and Representation in South Carolina* (New York, 1968 [orig. publ. Washington, D.C., 1901]), 367–369.

designed to tap sectional animosities. "It is hard," observed the author, "that the charge of our intending to enslave you, should come oftenest from the mouths of lawyers who in your Southern Provinces at least, have long made you slaves to themselves." After the reading, Hart wrote, "with sorrow," of the "Marks of approbation set almost on every Countenance." Backcountry settlers suffered particular hardship from a shortage of salt, and, during a meeting at Philip Mulkey's community, Hart overheard a man who "wish'd there was not a grain of Salt in any of the sea Coast Towns on the Continent." Some were, according to David Ramsay, South Carolina's first historian, "induced to believe that the whole was an artful deception, imposed upon them for interested purposes, by the gentlemen of fortune and ambition on the sea coast."[26]

Whig leaders struggled against these sectional and class hostilities. When the Regular Baptist minister Richard Furman wrote an open letter to settlers living between the Broad and Saluda rivers, he attempted to counter suspicions that wealthy coastal radicals were motivated by self-interest. "For what end," asked Furman, "should the People in the Lower Parts of the Province try to deceive you?" He insisted that in war "the Great Men are the Chief Losers." Not only were their coastal houses most vulnerable to bombs and cannon, but, "as they have the most in their Hands, the Taxes must be Heavier upon them." A circular letter to the backcountry revealed the same peculiar logic and made the same point. Suggesting that poor people had suffered most from the Stamp Act, the author observed that "the rich men of America" nonetheless made "such a resistance, that the cruel act was repealed." The letter admonished those "ill-disposed persons" who claimed that "this duty upon tea could not hurt the poor people who did not drink it."[27]

Although resentment against lowcountry planters proved to be a powerful weapon in the hands of backcountry loyalists, it also involved them in the first of a series of inconsistencies. Such prominent tories as Evan McLaurin, Moses Kirkland, and Robert Cunningham had various business connections with people on the coast. As slaveowners, they had important interests in common with the coastal elite. Kirkland, Cunningham, and

26. William Tennent to Henry Laurens, Aug. 20, 1775, in Gibbes, ed., *Documentary History*, I, 145; Clayton and Owens, eds., "Oliver Hart's Diary," *Jour. S.C. Baptist Hist. Soc.*, I (1975), 20–22; David Ramsay, *The History of the Revolution of South-Carolina, from a British Province to an Independent State* (Trenton, N.J., 1785), I, 79–80. The "ministerial piece" mentioned by Hart was probably Sir John Dalyrumple, "Address of the People of Great Britain to the Inhabitants of America," in Peter Force, ed., *American Archives*, 4th Ser. (Washington, D.C., 1837–1846), I, 1431.

27. Open letter from Richard Furman, Nov. 1775. Richard Furman Papers, SCL; *S.-C. Gaz.*, Sept. 7, 11, 1775.

others also had statewide political ambitions. By fueling antagonism toward the "gentlemen of fortune and ambition on the seacoast," loyalist leaders worked against the broad class interests of those wealthy inland settlers who were seeking greater participation in statewide political affairs. Many backcountry whigs also felt personally suspicious of seacoast gentlemen, but through their participation in the Revolutionary cause they accelerated the pre-Revolutionary trend toward political and economic association between the elites of both sections.

v

A greater advantage for South Carolina whigs was their inability to win support from the western Indians. That very failure served to strengthen their position among frontier settlers who lived in constant fear of Cherokee attack. Though inland men of influence were drawing their local communities toward one side or the other during the first months of Revolutionary conflict, many backcountry settlers were unwilling to become actively involved on either side. They were suspicious of coastal whigs, but, apart from those areas in which loyalist men of influence held sway, they tended not to join the tories. Some of these previously uninvolved people— particularly those living in the western piedmont—became sympathetic to the whig cause only after the broader colonial struggle became identified with a frontier war against the Cherokees.[28] During the summer and fall of 1775, many South Carolina frontiersmen were less concerned about the growing colonial crisis than about the threat from the western Indians. Both loyalists and whigs attempted to capitalize on the situation by accusing each other of trying to foment Indian war. The accusations were probably groundless on both sides, but the ensuing rumors caused great alarm among western settlers, who had borne the brunt of the Indian conflicts of the 1760s. Writing from Ninety Six District in July 1775, the American officer Andrew Williamson told of "a good deal of confusion . . . on account of the expected danger from the Cherokees."[29]

Although neither side wanted to instigate an Indian war, both whigs and

28. Many backcountry settlers were "disaffected" but not actively loyal. The subject is discussed in Ronald Hoffman, "The 'Disaffected' in the Revolutionary South," in Alfred F. Young, ed., *The American Revolution: Explorations in the History of American Radicalism* (De Kalb, Ill., 1976), 273–316.

29. Olson, "Loyalists and the American Revolution," *SCHM*, LXVIII (1967), 201–219, LXIX (1968), 44–58; James H. O'Donnell III, *Southern Indians in the American Revolution* (Knoxville, Tenn., 1973), 17–29; William Tennent from Long Canes, Sept. 1, 1775, in John Drayton, *Memoirs*, I, 383; Andrew Williamson to Council of Safety, July 1775, in "Journal of the Council of Safety," S.C. Hist. Soc., *Colls.*, II, 55.

tories were trying to win Cherokee allegiance, if only to prevent the Indians from joining the opposition. The British sent the deputy Indian agent Alexander Cameron to negotiate with the Cherokees, while the Council of Safety, in a last effort at conciliation, agreed to send a gift of ammunition. On November 3, a band of loyalists intercepted the shipment of powder and used it as evidence that whigs were, in fact, attempting to provoke a conflict. Andrew Williamson's militiamen were able to retake the ammunition, but, in late November, about nineteen hundred loyalist troops laid siege to Fort Ninety Six, where the powder was held. That Williamson had fewer than six hundred recruits for defense of the fort is itself testimony to the unpopularity of whig efforts at appeasement.[30]

Recognizing the seriousness of the situation, the Provincial Congress tried to defend its actions by issuing a public declaration. "Nothing could," proclaimed the declaration, "in the least degree satisfy them [the Cherokees] but a promise of some ammunition." Although the gift was "the only probable means of preserving the frontiers from the inroads of the Indians," it had been "by some non-associators made an instrument for the most diabolical purposes."[31] The whigs, by their very efforts to win the allegiance of the western Indians, were alienating backcountry settlers, particularly those in the vulnerable area of Ninety Six District.

What finally decided the question of Cherokee allegiance and brought on an Indian war had little to do with whig or loyalist efforts. Cherokees had good reason to be less suspicious of British officials than of the rebel government, for the British had at least attempted to restrict western migration into Indian territory. By spring 1776, Cherokees were on the brink of war with South Carolina settlers over the familiar problem, and, in April, they attacked a community in what would be York County, killing, among others, the parents of Wade Hampton.[32]

With the Cherokees leaning toward the British side, whig leaders abandoned their policy of conciliation and called for an all-out offensive against the Indians. This time, Williamson had no problem raising recruits. By July

30. Major Mayson to Colonel William Thomson, Nov. 24, 1775, in Gibbes, ed., *Documentary History*, I, 215. See also John Drayton, *Memoirs*, II, 64–65; McCrady, *History of South Carolina, 1775–1780*, 90–91.

31. "Declaration by Authority of Congress," Nov. 19, 1775, in Gibbes, ed., *Documentary History*, I, 211–212. Elias Ball, Jr., a wealthy planter from St. John, Berkeley, and member of the Provincial Congress, was troubled by news that loyalists had captured the powder. "This disturbance in the back parts," wrote Ball, "alarmes me moore than the men of war doe at present." Ball to Isaac Ball, Nov. 19, 1775, Elias Ball Family Papers, SCHS.

32. O'Donnell, *Southern Indians in the American Revolution*, 6–15; "Mr. Huger's" Recollection of a Conversation of 1819 with Wade Hampton, Draper, Ser. VV, Thomas Sumter Papers, VI, no. 193.

1776, he had approximately one thousand militiamen from Ninety Six District, who virtually burned their way through the Cherokee Nation. William Henry Drayton, who had negotiated the gift of ammunition to the Cherokees the previous year, now called for the total destruction of the western Indians. "It is expected," he wrote to a backcountry officer, that "you make smooth work as you go—that is, you cut up every Indian corn-field, and burn every Indian town."[33]

The whigs' decisive response to the Cherokee attack seemed to confirm rumors that British agents were trying to foment an Indian war. In July 1776, the governor received letters from various influential tories complaining of the king's allegedly "low and diabolical designs" and declaring that "they were now willing to do everything in their power to assist their brethren in America." According to a minister at Ninety Six, the indiscriminateness of Cherokee attacks "greatly alarmed" the loyalists, who realized that they were in danger along with the whigs.[34]

Once the lines were drawn, loyalists and Indians did begin to cooperate with one another. During the early years of the Revolution, whigs captured a number of white men who had joined with the Cherokees in attacks on backcountry settlements. In July 1776, an inland militia unit defeated a party consisting of "about ninety Indians, and 120 white men." According to the Reverend James Cresswell of Ninety Six, "Ten of the white Indians were made prisoners, nine of which were painted." Andrew Williamson also observed that four of the white men "were found painted as Indians." At a trial of tory prisoners held near Augusta, Georgia, in 1779, a man named Edmond Lyceums confessed "that he was with the Indians in arms against the United States." Years later, Andrew Pickens wrote that "some of the worst tories went to the Cherokees and were almost continually harassing and murdering the frontier inhabitants." He personally led an expedition against "a powerful tribe of Indians, aided by a banditti of desperadoes."[35]

33. James Creswell to W. H. Drayton, July 27, 1776, W. H. Drayton to Francis Salvadore, July 24, 1776, in Gibbes, ed., *Documentary History*, II, 31, 29.

34. Olson, "Loyalists and the American Revolution," *SCHM*, LXIX (1968), 54; extract of a letter from Charleston, July 21, 1776, in Force, ed., *American Archives*, 4th Ser., VI, 1230; James Creswell to W. H. Drayton, July 27, 1776, in Peter Force, ed., *American Archives*, 5th Ser. (Washington, D.C., 1848–1853), I, 610. A version of this letter is published in Gibbes, ed., *Documentary History*, II, 31.

35. Creswell to W. H. Drayton, July 27, 1776, Andrew Williamson to ———, July 22, 1776, in Gibbes, ed., *Documentary History*, II, 27, 31; Proceedings of a Court Held in 1779 by Order of General Williamson, Matthew Singleton Papers, SCL; Pickens to Lee, Aug. 28, 1811, Pickens Papers. See also John [Linn] to his wife, Apr. 1, 1779, Draper, Ser. VV, Thomas Sumter Papers, VI, no. 62; Ramsay, *History of South Carolina*, I, 123, 159, 258; Salvadore to W. H. Drayton, July 18, 1776, in Gibbes, ed., *Documentary History*, II, 26.

These "white Indians" were probably loyalist settlers forced from their homes by whig depredations, but some may have been drawn from the backcountry's hunting population. In any case, given the prevailing hostility toward hunters and marginal groups, one suspects that the association between loyalists and "white Indians" did little to popularize the British cause in the backcountry.

Though the whigs adopted an aggressive policy only after failing at conciliation, the new strategy was consistent with the experience and aspirations of backcountry settlers. Many, particularly in Ninety Six District, had lost friends and relatives during the Cherokee War and other clashes of the 1760s. The threat of Indian attack had been a perpetual source of terror. Years later, Wade Hampton put the matter succinctly. He recalled how he and his brothers had vowed to avenge the death of their parents by each killing an Indian. "We all," added Hampton, "kept our word, and a little over." That several active loyalists admitted to serving under Williamson during the summer of 1776 suggests the broad consensus that underlay the newly aggressive whig stance.[36]

Greed for land was not the immediate motive behind Williamson's Cherokee campaign, but the connection between land hunger and Indian war was obvious. Land hunger had been the source of the initial conflict. Even while Williamson was raising his troops, W. H. Drayton urged that the Cherokee Nation "be extirpated, and the lands become the property of the public." He promised never to support a treaty with the Indians "upon any other terms than their removal beyond the mountains." As it turned out, Drayton had his way. In the ensuing treaty, Cherokees ceded the entire territory of what would become Pendleton County. From those lands, South Carolina's militia and Continental soldiers received their bounty payments after the war.[37]

Within this context of deep antagonism toward the western Indians, a tenuous alliance with the Cherokees could not promote the British cause in the backcountry. Evan McLaurin, who by 1780 was a loyalist officer, inadvertently described the tory dilemma. "The Indians," he wrote with undisguised contempt, "God knows they are good for Little." At best he thought they could be used as a "Bug Bear" to annoy whig settlements and interrupt communications. For that purpose, McLaurin proposed building a frontier

36. "Mr. Huger's" Recollection of Hampton, Draper, Ser. VV, Thomas Sumter Papers, VI, no. 193; claims of Charles Bowers, John Dores, and Lawrence Marks, Loyalist Claims, XXVI, 39, 67, 136.

37. W. H. Drayton to Salvadore, July 24, 1776, in Gibbes, ed., *Documentary History*, II, 29; Wallace, *South Carolina*, 278.

fort designed to protect the Indians' northern townships.[38] In return for a negligible military advantage, McLaurin found himself advocating a measure that could only have antagonized western settlers. As objects of long-standing fear and hostility, the Cherokees were more useful to the whigs as enemies than as allies. The whigs, and not the loyalists, were thus in a position to continue the backcountry struggle for land and security begun during the preceding decade.

vi

Loyalists attracted others whose support proved to be a mixed advantage. If, as seems to have been the case, the whigs had best success in winning allegiance from former Regulators, loyalists had the misfortune of drawing support from individuals who had inspired Regulator wrath. Most important was Joseph Coffel himself. With the outbreak of the Revolution, this former leader of anti-Regulator forces reappeared in the backcountry as a British supporter. The Council of Safety was alarmed in July 1775 by the appearance of "one Coffel" at Fort Charlotte, and Henry Laurens ordered that the fort be immediately taken. Later that year, the Council of Safety received information that "the Scoffol lights were coming down from the back country in great force" to take public records and ammunition then held by whig forces at Dorchester. General Moultrie believed that, during the spring of the following year, Coffel recruited a band of South Carolinians who joined loyalist exiles in East Florida. From there, under the leadership of a Georgia merchant named Thomas Brown, loyalist rangers were engaged in a series of pillaging raids into backcountry Georgia and South Carolina. According to David Ramsay, "The names of Scouilites and regulators were insensibly exchanged for the appellation of tories and whigs, or the friends of the old and new order of things." Many, he thought, had actually followed Coffel, though the name "was applied to others as a term of reproach on the alleged similarity of their principles."[39]

By the close of the war, South Carolinians were using the term *scoffelite*

38. Evan McLaurin to Colonel [Nisbet] Balfour, Aug. 7, 1780, Emmet Collection, NYPL.

39. Henry Laurens to William Thomson, July 16, 1775, in "Journal of the Council of Safety," SCHS, *Colls.*, II, 44–45; Moultrie, *Memoirs*, I, 109, 203–204; Ramsay, *History of South Carolina*, I, 122–124. See also Lorenzo Sabine, *Biographical Sketches of Loyalists of the American Revolution with an Historical Essay* (Boston, 1864), II, 267; Wilbur Henry Siebert, *Loyalists in East Florida, 1774 to 1785: The Most Important Documents Pertaining Thereto, Edited with an Accompanying Narrative* (Boston, 1972 [orig. publ. Deland, Fla., 1929]), I, 54.

in order to designate and denigrate all former loyalists, but some early commentators made important distinctions between loyalists in general and Coffel's followers. An early historian of the Revolution in South Carolina noted that of frontiersmen who had "been marshalled by Schovel under the authority of the royal governor, most of them joined the tories," and General Moultrie referred to "scopholites" as "some of the tories who were led by one Col. Scophol, Col. of militia." Recalling the winter of 1775–1776, Major Henry Moore observed that backcountry loyalists were "called by the whigs, scoffolites—from their leader." David Ramsay was willing to distinguish between lowcountry tories, some of whom were "gentlemen of honor, principle and humanity," and backcountry tories, who included "a great proportion of . . . ignorant unprincipled banditti; to whom idleness, licentiousness and deeds of violence were familiar. Horse thieves and others whose crimes had exiled them from society attached themselves to the British." Even the loyalist Woodmason wrote that "the Rogues . . . called themselves Friends of Government."[40]

It is possible to trace more precise links. In the winter of 1775, when whig forces rounded up the leading loyalists of Ninety Six District, they designated 6 of the 136 prisoners as "scopholite." The Revolutionary General Richard Richardson termed 5 of the 6 men "scopholite Captain"—a title that set them apart from the others, whom he referred to simply as "militia captain." Like followers of Joseph Coffel, the group was interracial. Of the 5 scoffelite captains, 2 were nonwhite: "Capt. Jones of Ninety Six" was a "Colored Powder man," and William Hunt was listed as a "mulatto."[41] That Richardson distinguished the 6 from other prisoners is itself an indication that individuals with a specific connection to Coffel before the Revolution subsequently joined the tories.

Most notable among Richardson's list of scoffelite captains was the trader Richard Pearis, owner of twenty-six slaves and more than twenty thousand backcountry acres. If Pearis played an active role on either side during the Regulator struggles, it remains undiscovered, but he became an

40. Joseph Johnson, *Traditions and Reminiscences, Chiefly of the American Revolution in the South* (Charleston, S.C., 1851), 46; Moultrie, *Memoirs*, I, 203; Recollection of Major Henry Moore, Printed in the *Chester Reporter*, Aug. 14, 1870, Draper, Ser. DD, King's Mountain Papers, XIII, no. 118; Ramsay, *History of South Carolina*, I, 259; Charles Woodmason, Memorandum, in Woodmason, Sermon Book, IV, 12, NYHS. See also Aedanus Burke to Arthur Middleton, July 25, 1782, in Joseph W. Barnwell, ed., "Correspondence of Hon. Arthur Middleton, Signer of the Declaration of Independence," *SCHM*, XXVI (1925), 205; William Butler, *Memoirs of General William Butler* (Atlanta, Ga., 1885), 10.

41. Richard Richardson to Council of Safety, Jan. 2, 1776, in Gibbes, ed., *Documentary History*, I, 249–253.

object of concern for the council in 1772, when officials accused him of hiring Indians to "beat or kill" a man and "purchasing lands from and holding congresses with the Indians without the authority or consent of Government." Despite whig efforts to win his support, Pearis emerged in 1776 as a primary conduit between loyalists and the Cherokees. Precisely why Richardson chose to label Pearis as a "scopholite" remains unclear; perhaps Richardson was aware of a prior connection between Pearis and Coffel. The likelihood is that Richardson associated Pearis with the sort of people whom Regulators had tried to suppress. As a trader, Pearis necessarily maintained ties to backcountry hunters, and his marriage to an Indian woman probably helped to identify him with the backcountry's "white Indian" population. In July 1776 a backcountry whig informed Drayton that Pearis's home had been "a rendezvous for the Indians and Scopholites." Soon thereafter, in the course of his flight from South Carolina to East Florida, Pearis received food and protection from people he later called "my friendly Indians."[42]

The term *scoffelite* could refer broadly to the sort of people who had followed Joseph Coffel, but individual bandits of the 1760s also attached themselves to the British. Included on the list of Richardson's prisoners was James Burgess of Ninety Six District, described as "an old man, but bloody minded." He may have been related to the bandits Joseph and Benjamin Burgess, the latter a hunter in the loyalist-leaning region between the Broad and Saluda rivers, where James was captured. Several years later, a whig captain heard of a party of tories hiding out near Orangeburg. He set out to surprise them and captured a "disaffected man named Hutto." Two members of the Orangeburg Hutto family had been well-known bandits during the preceding decade.[43]

Most intriguing is the association between the loyalist leader William Cunningham and the bandit William Lee. The latter had been sentenced to death for horse and cattle stealing in 1763, but he was reprieved on grounds of insanity. Among the most widely feared of backcountry tories, William ("Bloody Bill") Cunningham was related to Robert, David, and Patrick Cunningham, all of whom were officers in the loyalist militia. William

42. Council Journal, Sept. 21, 26, 1772, SCDAH (hereafter cited as Council Jour.); Salvadore to W. H. Drayton, July 18, 1776, in Gibbes, ed., *Documentary History*, II, 25; claim of Richard Pearis, Loyalist Claims, XXVI, 362–385, esp. 370. See also John Drayton, *Memoirs*, II, 116.

43. "Prisoners Sent to Charles Town by Col. Richardson," in Gibbes, ed., *Documentary History*, II, 249–253; Joseph Johnson, *Traditions and Reminiscences, Chiefly of the American Revolution in the South* (Charleston, S.C., 1851), 548; Miscellaneous Records, bk. VVV, 164, SCDAH (hereafter cited as Misc. Records); *S.-C. and Amer. Gen. Gaz.*, May 6, 1768.

Cunningham began his Revolutionary career as a whig, but he switched sides after participating in Williamson's Cherokee campaign. According to tradition, Cunningham had helped the whig captain John Caldwell organize a militia company on condition that Caldwell promote him to lieutenant and allow his early retirement from the company. The captain not only reneged on his promise but had Cunningham court-martialed for insubordination. Despite his acquittal, Cunningham enlisted in the royal militia, rose to the rank of major, and sought revenge against his former allies.[44]

By 1783, William Lee was a member of Cunningham's party. When, in March of that year, the South Carolina Senate created a special company of rangers to "capture such notorious offenders who disturb the peace, tranquility and harmony of the country," both Lee and Cunningham received special mention. The House and Senate agreed to offer a reward for Cunningham, Lee, and several others, dead or alive. Lee was still active in 1785, when the legislature again offered a reward for his capture and termed him one of the "most noted of the banditti who have so long infested the district of Ninety-Six." Cunningham had fled to East Florida.[45]

The exceptional career of Daniel McGirt suggests how various alienated or lawless segments of the inland population gravitated to the loosely organized East Florida tories. The son of a prosperous merchant from the Camden area, he became a loyalist after a whig officer—who wanted McGirt's prize mare—placed him on trial and had him punished on trumped up charges. McGirt escaped to East Florida, where he joined the loyalist rangers and rose to the rank of lieutenant colonel. Perhaps McGirt's experience of injustice made him sensitive to others with grievances against the settled backcountry population, but, whatever his motives, by 1779 he had become a bandit leader whose "corps" resembled the gangs of the 1760s.[46]

Like his predecessors, McGirt had an ambiguous relationship with the black population. One backcountry woman reported that the gang would

44. Misc. Records, bk. MM, 21; McCrady, *History of South Carolina, 1775–1780,* 467–470; John A. Chapman, *History of Edgefield County from the Earliest Settlements to 1897* (Newberry, S.C., 1897), 70–71; Sabine, *Biographical Sketches of Loyalists,* I, 349; Ramsay, *History of South Carolina,* I, 257.

45. South Carolina Senate Journal, Mar. 6, 1783, SCDAH (hereafter cited as Senate Jour.); South Carolina House of Representatives Journal, Mar. 4, 1783, Mar. 7, 10, 1785, in Theodora J. Thompson *et al.,* eds., *Journals of the House of Representatives,* The State Records of South Carolina (Columbia, S.C., 1977–), *1783–1784,* 215, *1785–1786,* 198, 211; Joseph Byrne Lockey, ed., *East Florida, 1783–1785: A File of Documents Assembled and Many of Them Translated by Joseph Byrne Lockey,* ed. John Walton Caughey (Berkeley, Calif., 1949), 15–17.

46. Siebert, *Loyalists in East Florida,* II, 328–330; Thomas J. Kirkland and Robert M. Kennedy, *Historic Camden,* pt. I, *Colonial and Revolutionary* (Columbia, S.C., 1905), 114–115, 297–304; Johnson, *Traditions and Reminiscences,* 172–173.

"only take . . . clothes and negroes." Andrew Pickens recalled a skirmish in Georgia in which his men retook from "McGirt's party . . . a number of negroes taken from Carolina," and, at the end of the war, McGirt had in his possession "a number of negroes" belonging to the lowcountry Middleton family.[47] On at least one occasion, McGirt actually sold two slaves to a backcountry settler. However, it seems that the gang was interracial, and, despite accusations that it "stole" slaves, black Carolinians may have joined the group voluntarily. An article in the *South-Carolina Gazette* told of

> a large body of the most infamous banditti and horsethieves that perhaps ever were collected together anywhere, under the direction of McGirt (dignified with the title of colonel), a corps of Indians, with negro and white savages disguised like them, and about 1,500 of the most savage disaffected poor people, seduced from the back settlements of this State and North Carolina.

McGirt was still associated with the British in April 1780, when General Augustine Prevost considered using a corps of "McGirt's people" to attack whigs in Georgia.[48]

Association with bandits proved a risky business for British and loyalist leaders. During the confused period of joint British and Spanish rule in Florida, McGirt and others took advantage of the situation by plundering numerous wealthy loyalists. In 1784 Patrick Tonyn, the British governor of East Florida, proclaimed McGirt "an outlaw, the Head and support of a desperate Gang of high Way Robbers."[49]

Not coincidentally, contemporaries used the term *scoffelite* to identify those tories who fled to East Florida during and after 1775. Thomas Pinckney, while serving in General Robert Howe's unsuccessful expedition against

47. Backcountry woman, quoted in Alexander Garden, *Anecdotes of the American Revolution, Illustrative of the Talents and Virtues of the Heroes and Patriots, Who Acted the Most Conspicuous Parts Therein* (New York, 1865 [orig. publ. Charleston, S.C., 1828]), II, xxv; Deposition of Andrew Pickens, July 3, 1798, Pickens Family Papers, SCL; James Hume to Arthur Middleton, June 9, Aug. 12, 1783, Signers, Dreer Collection, HSP.

48. Claim of Charles Bowers, Loyalist Claims, XXVI, 40; *S.-C. Gaz.*, July 7, 1779, quoted in Kirkland and Kennedy, *Historic Camden*, pt. I, 300. Charles Bowers, a backcountry loyalist, claimed that McGirt had sold two stolen slaves. Other contemporaries accused McGirt of "stealing" slaves. See Patrick Tonyn to Vincente Manuel de Zespedes, Sept. 24, 1784, in Lockey, ed., *East Florida*, 360; [Augustine] Prevost, quoted in Siebert, *Loyalists in East Florida*, II, 329–330.

49. Siebert, *Loyalists in East Florida*, II, 44, 48, 66–67, 181, 230, 234; Patrick Tonyn to Vincente Manuel de Zespedes, July 5, 1784, in Lockey, ed., *East Florida*, 214. See also *S.-C. Gaz.*, May 12, June 12, 1784, quoted in Kirkland and Kennedy, *Historic Camden*, pt. I, 304.

the East Florida loyalists, spoke to a captured "lieut. of Scoffieldites," who informed him that "Brown whose Party amounts to 150 men has been reinforced by 200 Regulars under a Major Bovost [Prevost] and 200 Scoffieldites." Another member of the same expedition received news that Brown had about three hundred men at Fort Tonyn in East Florida and about "500 Scopholites and a few Red Coats" between the fort and St. Johns River. Rumors circulated among the whig forces that General Augustine Prevost intended to march through the middle settlements of Georgia, where he would be joined "by a number of Scophilites supposed to Amount to 1000 or 1200 disaffected Insurgents from the back parts of S. Carolina, N. Carolina and Georgia."[50] Obviously, the East Florida tories did not consist completely or primarily of Coffel's followers, but, given the behavior of the rangers and the presence of McGirt and Coffel among them, it is not difficult to understand how whigs drew the connection.

The British made matters worse by participating in plundering raids. Despite early efforts to conciliate the backcountry population, British commanders moved toward a systematic plan of plunder and intimidation as their situation became more desperate. Banastre Tarleton, whose Loyal Legion moved into the backcountry during the spring of 1780, became infamous among backcountry settlers for his pillaging raids. In May 1781, as the British abandoned Camden, they burned the mill, jail, and "many private houses." Writing to his cousin in 1782, a settler from Ninety Six District described his personal experience of the British occupation in the following terms:

> Our own true Colonels and head officers fled into the North State and a grat many of the young men went also. We being left like sheep among wolves, were obliged to give up to them our Arms and take purtection. But no sooner we had yielded to them but set to Rob us taking all our livings, horses, Cows, Sheep, Clothing, of all Sorts, money pewter, tins, knives, in fine Everything that sooted them. Untill we were Stript Naked.[51]

Even a loyalist officer recognized that "the abuses of the [British] Army in taking peoples Horses, Cattle and provisions in many cases without

50. Thomas Pinckney to his brother, July 1, 1778, in Jack L. Cross, ed., "Letters of Thomas Pinckney, 1775–1780," *SCHM*, LVIII (1957), 157; John Fauchereaud Grimké, "Journal of the Campaign to the Southward: May 9 to July 14, 1778," *SCHM*, XII (1911), 63–64, 128. See also Thomas Pinckney to Harriott Pinckney, Apr. 7, 1778, in Cross, ed., "Letters of Pinckney," 148–149.

51. Maj. [Nathaniel] Pendleton to Gen. Francis Marion, May 10, 1781, Nathanael Greene to Samuel Huntington, May 14, 1781, in Gibbes, ed., *Documentary History*, III, 69–70; George Park to Arthur Park, July 23, 1782, Private Papers, Sumter Family, gift box 1, SCDAH. See also McCrady, *History of South Carolina, 1780–1783*, 225–248.

paying for them, abuses perhaps inseparable from a Military Government, disgusted the inhabitants." A wealthy Georgetown planter made essentially the same point:

> The British Commanders, and Officers in South Carolina, who with every wish, (I may safely do them that justice) of promoting the entire reduction of the Country, have done every thing, that could keep it ours. . . . The horror of war should have been softened, and the returning beams of Royal government would have gladdened the heart of many a now determined foe.[52]

Despite complaints of plundered backcountrymen, General Charles Cornwallis was less than sympathetic to the problems of frontier settlers. Writing from a backcountry post in November 1780, he observed, "If those who say they are our friends will not stir, I cannot defend every man's house from being plundered; and I must say that when I see a whole settlement running away from twenty or thirty robbers, I think they deserve to be robbed." The following month, Nathanael Greene wrote that many tories were giving themselves up to the whigs, "being tired of such a wretched life and not finding the Support, Respect or attention which they expected from the British army."[53]

The British compounded their problems by issuing a series of orders that further alienated active backcountry whigs. General Henry Clinton's Proclamation of June 3, 1780, stated that all paroled prisoners, excepting those who had been in Charleston or Fort Moultrie at the time the city surrendered, were subject to British military service. In Camden, the British adjutant general, Lieutenant Colonel Francis Rawdon, attempted to enforce the order by imprisoning about 160 people, including John Chesnut and Joseph Kershaw, for refusing to join the royal militia. The result of this rigid policy was that many whig officers resumed active opposition to the invading army. To make matters worse, in August 1780, Cornwallis ordered that the property of anyone refusing to take up arms with the British be confiscated. According to Charles Cotesworth Pinckney, it was "notorious that he [Cornwallis] has no abilities as a politician, or he would have endeavoured to conciliate the affections of those whom he has subdued." General Greene understood what the British could never quite grasp: that the country

52. "Gray's Observations," *SCHM*, XI (1910), 141; Francis Kinloch to Thomas Boone, Oct. 1, 1782, in Felix Gilbert, ed., "Letters of Francis Kinloch to Thomas Boone, 1782–1788," *Journal of Southern History*, VIII (1942), 91.

53. Charles Cornwallis to Moses Kirkland, Nov. 13, 1780, in Charles Ross, ed., *Correspondence of Charles, First Marquis Cornwallis* (London, 1859), I, 69; Nathanael Greene to President of Congress, Dec. 28, 1780, Greene Papers.

would be "inevitably ruined" and the inhabitants "universally disgusted, if, instead of protection, they are exposed to the ravages of every party."[54]

Given the notoriety of British behavior among the backcountry population, the British association with Joseph Coffel and other known bandits could only have damaged the loyalist cause. It is impossible to gauge the extent of the stigma, but David Ramsay stated the obvious connection. Referring to "horse thieves" and other "banditti" who "attached themselves to parties of the British," he observed, "The necessity which their indiscriminate plundering imposed on all good men of defending themselves, did infinitely more damage to the royal cause than was compensated by all the advantages resulting from their friendship."[55]

Ramsay probably overstated the case. Early ties between loyalists and Coffel and other known bandits may well have stigmatized the British and influenced early alignments in the backcountry, but the behavior of inland whigs diminished whatever advantages they won as a result of these loyalist associations. Despite the inevitable bias of surviving records, one does not have to look far to find evidence of plundering and savagery perpetrated by the whigs. By the later years of the Revolution, South Carolina rebels and tories were, with considerable justification, accusing each other of behaving like bandits. In December 1780, General Greene was concerned that his own militia had "almost laid waste the country and so corrupted the Principles of the People that they think of nothing but plundering one another." Through their repeated injunctions against plundering, Nathanael Greene, his generals, and Governor John Rutledge suggest that the practice was widespread.[56]

The chronic shortage of supplies and the desperate condition of backcountry recruits blurred the line between indiscriminate plunder and legiti-

54. Ramsay, *History of South Carolina*, I, 193–194, 210–211; McCrady, *History of South Carolina, 1775–1780*, 618–619, 706–710; Charles Cotesworth Pinckney to the Delegates from South Carolina in Philadelphia, Jan. 5, 1782, in Barnwell, ed., "Correspondence of Middleton," *SCHM*, XXVI (1926), 58; Shy, "British Strategy," in Crow and Tise, eds., *Southern Experience in the American Revolution*, 168–169; Nathanael Greene to Thomas Sumter, Aug. 1, 1781, Thomas Sumter Papers, II, LC.

55. Ramsay, *History of South Carolina*, I, 259.

56. Nathanael Greene to Robert Howe, Dec. 29, 1780, Greene Papers. See also Col. W. R. Davies Account of the Battle of Hanging Rock, Aug. 6, 1780, Draper, Ser. VV, Thomas Sumter Papers, V, no. 175; John Rutledge to Thomas Sumter, Oct. 6, 1780, Jan. 1781, Draper, Ser. VV, Thomas Sumter Papers, VII, nos. 105, 178–179; Thomas Sumter to Francis Marion, Feb. 20, 1781, Andrew Pickens to William Butler, Aug. 21, 1782, in Gibbes, ed., *Documentary History*, II, 210–211, III, 23; Greene to Sumter, Aug. 1, 1781, Sumter Papers, II, LC.

mate modes of raising supplies.[57] Writing from his camp on the Pee Dee River, Greene despaired that he had "but the Shadow of an Army without Clothing, Tents and Provisions except what is provided by daily Collections." By the following month, more than half his troops were "naked." Many had "not any clothes on them, except a little piece of blanket in the Indian form worn round their waists." Given the situation, it is not surprising that the army had become "so addicted to plundering, that the utmost exertions of the Officers" could not put an end to the practice. Whigs, like loyalists, were tempted to take what they could get. Governor Rutledge, despite his repeated injunctions against plundering raids, seems to have recognized the limited impact of official orders. "Everything in my power," he wrote in January 1781, "shall be done to restrain plundering, tho' I fear nothing so effectual as I could wish can be till the courts of Justice can be opened."[58]

In fact, Revolutionary generals did not always condemn plundering raids if the victims were loyalists. Thomas Sumter, who solemnly urged the whig general Francis Marion to "suppress every specie of plundering," personally took the entire library of a wealthy backcountry loyalist. In the spring of 1781, General Greene, by his own admission a "great Enemy of plundering," argued that the need for a superior cavalry justified taking horses from inhabitants "within the enemy's lines."[59] Ultimately, the establishment of slave bounty payments for militia and Continental troops made robbery from loyalists official policy and tempted numerous militiamen to rob from whigs as well.

Whigs perpetrated their share of atrocities. A group of about one hundred backcountry Georgians transformed Thomas Brown into a committed loyalist by beating him to unconsciousness and placing burning torches on his feet when he refused to sign the Continental Association. After the battle of King's Mountain, whig victors beat a surgeon who attempted to dress the wound of a vanquished loyalist. According to the *Royal South-*

57. For an excellent discussion of plundering by whigs and loyalists that changed my perspective on the problem, see Robert M. Weir, "'The Violent Spirit': The Reestablishment of Order and the Continuity of Leadership in Post-Revolutionary South Carolina," in Ronald Hoffman *et al.*, eds., *An Uncivil War: The Southern Backcountry during the American Revolution* (Charlottesville, Va., 1985), 70–77.

58. Nathanael Greene to Robert Howe, Dec. 29, 1780, Greene Papers; Nathanael Greene to Thomas Sumter, Jan. 15, 1781, Sumter Papers, I, LC; Rutledge to Sumter, Jan. 1781, Draper, Ser. VV, Thomas Sumter Papers, VII, nos. 178–179.

59. Sumter to Francis Marion, in Gibbes, ed., *Documentary History*, III, 23; claim of James Carey, Loyalist Claims, XXVI, 89; Greene to Sumter, Apr. 15, 1781, Draper, Ser. VV, Thomas Sumter Papers, VII, no. 246.

Carolina Gazette, they frequently went "among the prisoners, and with their swords cut . . . the prisoners with the most remorseless barbarity." General Marion was distressed that one of his own colonels insisted upon burning "a great number of houses on Little Peedee," and, by August 1780, Cornwallis complained that "every friend of Government [between the Pee Dee and Santee rivers] has been carried off, and his plantation destroyed." The following year a British colonel accused whig militiamen of burning the homes of "desolate widows."[60]

By the end of the war, the backcountry was ravaged by parties from both sides, and many settlers, having fled their homes, lived like the hunters and bandits of the preceding decades. Throughout the backcountry, according to Colonel Robert Gray, people "dared not sleep in their Houses." Parties of men hid out in the swamps and lived by pillaging surrounding settlements. In January 1781, General Greene despaired that the backcountry was "full of little armed parties, who follow their resentments with little less than savage fury." Four months later, he declared that the "Whigs and the Tories are butchering one another hourly."[61]

Revolutionary leaders, most notably Governor Rutledge and General Greene, were more sensitive than the British to the dangers of indiscriminate plundering. Their injunctions probably had a restraining influence, but there was only so much they could do so long as the state remained at war. During the spring of 1781, the governor issued a proclamation ordering an end to plunder and appointing magistrates in all parts of the state recovered from the British. The following year, the legislature passed a militia law establishing severe penalties for officers and men found guilty of plundering.[62] The problem was that by the end of the war intense resentments between whigs and loyalists had a life of their own, and the hope of plunder taken from tories was the only way that the government could attract and retain recruits.

vii

Plundering and savagery may well have lost the whigs much of what they gained from the association between loyalists and Coffel's people, but whigs

60. Olson, "Loyalists and the American Revolution," *SCHM*, LXVIII (1967), 207–208; *Royal South-Carolina Gazette* (Charleston), Dec. 19, 1780; Francis Marion to Horatio Gates, Oct. 4, 1780, Draper, Ser. VV, Thomas Sumter Papers, VII, no. 67; Cornwallis to Sir Henry Clinton, Aug. 6, 1780, in Ross, ed., *Correspondence of Cornwallis*, I, 54; John Watson to Francis Marion, Mar. 9, 1781, in Gibbes, ed., *Documentary History*, III, 34.

61. "Gray's Observations," *SCHM*, XI (1910), 145, 153–154; Greene to Chevalier de la Luzerne, Jan. 9, 1781, Greene Papers; Greene to Reed, May 14, 1781, Reed Papers.

62. Ramsay, *History of South Carolina*, I, 256; Senate Jour., Feb. 10, 1782; Cooper and McCord, eds., *Statutes of South Carolina*, IX, 684.

won a more significant advantage when the British attracted a substantial following among South Carolina slaves. In June 1780, General Clinton issued a proclamation promising freedom to all rebel-owned slaves on the condition that they agree to serve the British throughout the war. Thousands of slaves followed Clinton's troops in the belief that the invading army was an army of liberation. Many died in disease-ridden camps or were shipped to the West Indies for sale. But some made their way to East Florida, and others became foragers, spies, workmen, or even soldiers for the British. Toward the close of the war, the whig major Henry Hampton attacked a black British regiment in the backcountry, and, in 1782, British commanders created a black cavalry unit.[63]

The problem for British and loyalist forces was obvious. By using slaves as soldiers with the promise of freedom in payment, they simultaneously threatened the slave system and evoked the specter of insurrection. In so doing, the British could only have alienated people from whose support they might have benefited. Writing to General Marion from a backcountry whig encampment, Sumter observed: "The enemy oblige the negroes they have to make frequent sallies. This circumstance alone is sufficient to rouse and fix the resentment and detestation of every American who possesses common feelings."[64]

Had the British been a true army of liberation for South Carolina slaves, they might have gained considerable military advantage from their natural allies. The irony was that British leaders could not wholeheartedly embrace the notion of having large numbers of armed slave recruits. The former lieutenant governor and prominent loyalist William Bull was alarmed even by the small black cavalry unit that, he insisted, was committing the sort of "outrages" to which "their savage nature prompts them." In 1781, British commanders rejected or ignored proposals for the creation of two black regiments. Instead, they followed a halfhearted policy. Clinton encouraged slaves to follow his armies, and he used some runaways as soldiers.[65] Ultimately, however, leading loyalists were as dependent on slavery as their whig opponents. They could not, without threatening their own interests,

---

63. Benjamin Quarles, *The Negro in the American Revolution* (Chapel Hill, N.C., 1961), 138, 149; Ira Berlin, "The Revolution in Black Life," in Young, ed., *American Revolution*, 352–354; Recollections of Thomas McDill (n.d.), Draper, Ser. VV, Thomas Sumter Papers, XI, 341. For an excellent discussion of the role of Virginia slaves in the Revolution, see Sylvia R. Frey, "Between Slavery and Freedom: Virginia Blacks in the American Revolution," *Journal of Southern History*, XLIX (1983), 375–398.

64. Sumter to Marion, Feb. 20, 1781, in Gibbes, ed., *Documentary History*, III, 23.

65. William Bull, quoted in Quarles, *Negro in the American Revolution*, 149; see, generally, 111–157.

exploit the potential military strength of the thousands of slaves who flocked to their camps.

By contrast, whig policies were consistent with the interests and attitudes of both actual and aspiring slaveowners. Despite a serious problem in raising recruits, South Carolina's leadership persistently resisted attempts to employ slaves as soldiers. In 1779, the legislature decisively rejected a proposal by the Continental Congress to recruit slave troops. According to David Ramsay, the plan was "received with horror by the planters [in the House], who figured to themselves terrible consequences." Subsequent efforts by Nathanael Greene and others to use slaves as soldiers fared no better in the legislature.[66] Instead, the whig government chose to deal with the recruitment problem by appealing to the burgeoning backcountry demand for slaves.

That greed for slaves could become a motive for Revolutionary service was apparent as early as 1776, when Andrew Williamson asked the legislature whether he might tell his men that "such of those Indians as should be taken Prisoners would become slaves and the Property of the Captors." According to Governor Rutledge, that expectation already "prevailed in his [Williamson's] Camp insomuch that an Indian woman who had been taken prisoner was sold as a slave." William Drayton probably helped to encourage the notion by suggesting that "every Indian taken shall be the slave and property of the taker." The assembly refused to grant Williamson's request, insisting that Indians should be regarded as prisoners of war because enslavement might "give the Indians a precedent which may be fatal to our own people who may unfortunately fall into their Hands." Williamson's men had to settle for indents issued in return for Indian scalps.[67]

When it came to black slaves, South Carolina's legislature had no such

66. David Ramsay to W. H. Drayton, Sept. 1, 1779, in Gibbes, ed., *Documentary History*, II, 121; McCrady, *History of South Carolina, 1775–1780*, 312–314. In February 1782, Edward Rutledge observed that the House had had "another hard Battle on the Subject of arming the Blacks." He believed that the motion was supported by "12 or 15" members and was opposed by "about 100." Rutledge to Arthur Middleton, Feb. 6, 1782, in Barnwell, ed., "Correspondence of Middleton," *SCHM*, XXVII (1926), 4. See also Quarles, *Negro in the American Revolution*, 60–67; M. Foster Farley, "The South Carolina Negro in the American Revolution, 1775–1783," *SCHM*, LXXIX (1978), 80–82. Revolutionary leaders in the Upper South were somewhat less wary of using black recruits. See Ira Berlin, *Slaves without Masters: The Free Negro in the Antebellum South* (New York, 1974), 16–19; Berlin, "Revolution in Black Life," in Young, ed., *American Revolution*, 354–355.

67. South Carolina General Assembly Journal, Sept. 25, 27, 1776, in William Edwin Hemphill *et al.*, eds., *Journals of the General Assembly and House of Representatives, 1776–1780*, The State Records of South Carolina (Columbia, S.C., 1970), 95–96, 103; W. H. Drayton to Salvadore, July 24, 1776, in Gibbes, ed., *Documentary History*, II, 29.

reservations. Members sanctioned efforts by militia generals to raise recruits by providing a bounty payment not only in land but in slaves taken from loyalist estates. Thomas Sumter set a precedent for other generals when, in April 1781, he sought to raise six regiments by offering a slave bonus to each militiaman who would serve for ten months. Even privates were to receive "one grown negro," and the numbers increased with rank. Sumter promised each lieutenant colonel "three large and one small negro." Other militia generals followed suit, with slight variations in their pay scales. The legislature also established a slave bonus for Continental troops.[68]

So great was the demand for slaves among backcountry troops that Greene and others had considerable difficulty preventing soldiers and officers from taking slaves, without discrimination, from whigs and loyalists alike. After the war, numerous petitions requested that slaves taken by troops led by Pickens and Sumter be returned or that compensation be provided by the state.[69]

Once again, the British acted in opposition to the broad class interest of South Carolina's planters without incurring to themselves any significant military advantage. By serving as a magnet for runaway slaves, and by using such slaves as armed fighters, the British could hardly have endeared themselves to slaveowners. Meanwhile, whigs not only avoided the contradictions of British policy; they also exploited and encouraged a growing backcountry demand for slaves.

viii

The Revolution in South Carolina's backcountry cannot be termed a class struggle in any simplistic sense. Rather than wealth or occupation, it was neighborhood affiliation, reinforced by ethnic, religious, and familial ties, that influenced the initial division between whigs and loyalists. Consider-

68. Richard Hampton to John Hampton, Apr. 2, 1781, Draper, Ser. VV, Thomas Sumter Papers, VI, nos. 22–23; South Carolina House of Representatives Journal, Feb. 13, 1782, SCDAH (hereafter cited as House Jour.); Senate Jour., Feb. 3, 1782; Quarles, *Negro in the American Revolution*, 108–109; Cooper and McCord, *Statutes of South Carolina*, IV, 513–515.

69. See for example, Senate Jour., Feb. 8, Mar. 11, 13, 1783; House Jour., Mar. 4, 1785, in Thompson *et al.*, eds., *Journals of the House, 1785–1786*, 185; House Jour. Nov. 30, 1792, Dec. 12, 1793, Dec. 8, 1797. The legislature ordered the return of slaves taken from whigs, but in 1784 it passed measures to indemnify Andrew Pickens, Thomas Sumter, and their men from "vexatious suits" arising from actions taken during the British occupation. The legislature noted that 22 slaves taken by Pickens's troops from "friends" had been restored. Cooper and McCord, eds., *Statutes of South Carolina*, IV, 598–600.

ations of status, more than ideological disagreements, moved many leading men to choose one side or the other during the early phase of Revolutionary conflict. But while whig and loyalist forces failed to divide along clear-cut class lines, the British did attract groups that had fundamental grievances against the elites of both sections. Cherokees, bandits, and slaves all gravitated to the British in opposition to an emerging social order more clearly represented by the whigs. Had the British been fully able to accept their "disaffected" allies, those groups might have done them considerable military service. As it was, leading loyalists were involved in a series of contradictions. By their various associations, they alienated potential supporters and sealed the fate of the British war effort in the South.

It was the whigs who were best able to represent the interests and aspirations previously represented in the Regulator movement. The Revolution had forced lowcountry whigs to make political concessions to their inland counterparts. By joining the whig cause, leading frontiersmen could pursue their struggle for greater access to statewide political affairs. In fighting the war, whigs were also continuing a pre-Revolutionary struggle for Indian lands and for security from Indian attack. By opposing backcountry loyalists, they were working to suppress Joseph Coffel and others previously opposed by the Regulators. And while South Carolina whigs may not have fought for anything so abstract as American slavery in general, many did, particularly in the backcountry, fight the Revolution for slaves.

CHAPTER 4.

Containing the Revolution: 1782–1790

Looking back on the postwar decade, David Ramsay observed, "The eight years of war in Carolina were followed by eight years of disorganization, which produced such an amount of civil distress as diminished with some their respect for liberty and independence."[1] Ramsay might have been referring to any one of a number of disorders in the backcountry, for, if the Revolution deepened the region's commitment to slavery and gave new political influence to inland leaders, it also created severe social disruption. The period after the war witnessed a new wave of crime and vagrancy, a threatened return to the form of summary justice that had prevailed during the Regulation, and a debtor crisis that sparked opposition to the courts. The State Constitutional Convention at the end of the decade was the culmination of a successful effort by the coast-dominated government to legitimate its own authority in the midst of mounting challenges. This legislative triumph derived not only from the willingness of coastal leaders to conciliate their backcountry counterparts but from the interregional alliances that prevented postwar conflicts from polarizing the state.

i

Although the distinction between the backcountry and the coastal parishes continued to be the dominant political and social division in South Carolina after the Revolution, political alignments of the 1780s (and 1790s) make no sense without consideration of regional variations within each of the state's two sections.[2] The basic distinction among the inland settlements was be-

---

1. David Ramsay, *History of South Carolina from Its First Settlement in 1670, to the Year 1808* (Newberry, S.C., 1855; reprint, Spartanburg, S.C., 1959 [orig. publ. Charleston, S.C., 1809]), II, 238.

2. In his careful analysis of politics in post-Revolutionary South Carolina, Jerome J.

tween the lower backcountry (or middlecountry), where slavery had made the deepest inroads, and the upcountry (or piedmont). The lowcountry included four socially and politically significant areas: the city of Charleston (St. Philip and St. Michael parishes), the eleven additional parishes of Charleston Judicial District, the northern coastal parishes that composed the judicial district of Georgetown, and the southern coastal parishes that formed the judicial district of Beaufort.

Whereas parishes remained the primary administrative and political unit in the lowcountry throughout the Revolutionary and Early National periods, the backcountry's administrative subdivisions and political districts changed several times during the later eighteenth century, and not until the constitutional reform of 1790 did they begin to mirror one another. In 1785, the legislature responded to long-standing backcountry demands by dividing the old circuit court districts into counties. The first federal census (1790) reflected the persistence of parish organization on the coast but used the new county system as the basis of its returns for most of the backcountry. (Census takers made no subdivisions in the middlecountry court district of Cheraws, and they divided the middlecountry court district of Orangeburg only into northern and southern parts.) Those census units must be the basis for any overview of South Carolina's population at the end of the eighteenth century (see Appendix 1 and map 3).

The first census of South Carolina's population highlights the social distinction between the lower and upper backcountry. In 1790, the upper piedmont remained a region of small farms and few slaves. Slaves in the eleven upcountry counties composed less than 15 percent of that area's population. By contrast, large areas within the middlecountry, which extended from the coastal parishes to the lower piedmont, were already transitional. Slaves and free blacks in Claremont County, a region that included the town of Camden and the settlement formerly known as the High Hills of Santee, composed about 46 percent of the population.[3] The northern part of Orangeburg District was only 60 percent free, and, in Richland County, which included the settlement known as the Congarees, slaves

---

Nadelhaft recognized the need to distinguish between regions within the lowcountry. My understanding of this period draws heavily on his work. See Nadelhaft, *The Disorders of War: The Revolution in South Carolina* (Orono, Maine, 1981), esp. 21–23. For an exceptionally perceptive analysis of political affairs in South Carolina during the late 18th century that emphasizes interregional alliances, see Raymond Gale Starr, "The Conservative Revolution: South Carolina Public Affairs, 1775–1790" (Ph.D. diss., University of Texas at Austin, 1964).

3. In 1791, the legislature created Kershaw County from the northern part of Claremont, the eastern part of Richland, and the southern part of Lancaster. The new county, which did not appear on the census of 1790, included the town of Camden.

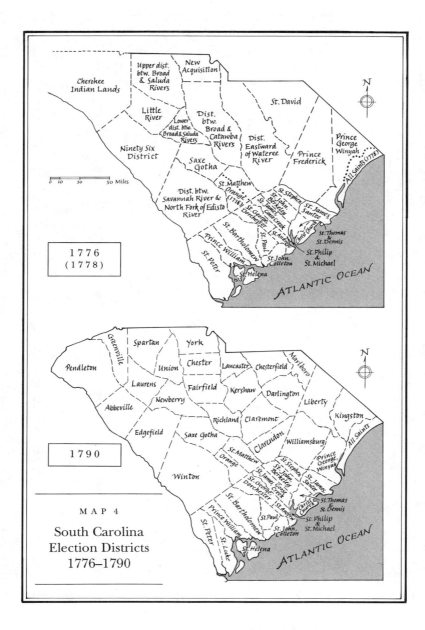

Map 4. South Carolina Election Districts, 1775–1790. *After Walter B. Edgar, ed.,* Biographical Directory of the South Carolina House of Representatives, *I, Sessions* Lists, 1692–1793 *(Columbia, S.C., 1974), 150, 164. Drawn by Richard Stinely*

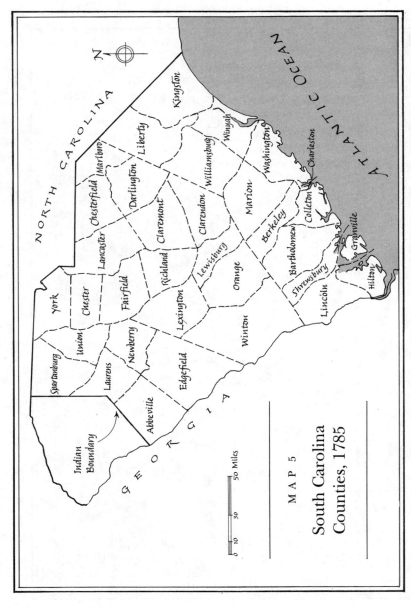

Map 5. South Carolina Counties, 1785. *After Historical Records Survey, WPA, 1938; Lester J. Cappon et al., eds., Atlas of Early American History: The Revolutionary Era, 1760–1790 (Princeton, N.J., 1976), 73. Drawn by Richard Stinely*

M A P 5

South Carolina
Counties, 1785

composed about 36 percent of the whole. Slavery had not made great inroads into the region around the Little Pee Dee River of Cheraws District, but wealthy planters located near the Great Pee Dee brought slaves into the area, with the result that slaves composed about 30 percent of Cheraws's total population in 1790.[4]

Throughout the backcountry, yeoman households predominated, but slaveholders and substantial planters were more heavily concentrated in several middlecountry counties. In most inland areas more than 70 percent of all households did not hold slaves, but, in Claremont County of lower Camden District, only 58 percent of all households were nonslaveholders. About 3 percent of all middlecountry households included at least twenty slaves, as compared to less than 1 percent of all households in the upcountry.[5]

Social and political divisions within the lowcountry were as complex as variations among inland regions. Charleston, where slaves composed nearly half of the population, remained the state's only urban center and the hub of mercantile activity. Artisans were a conspicuous presence in the city, but merchants exercised the most powerful political voice. They were socially and economically tied to the wealthy rice and indigo planters of the neighboring coastal parishes, where more than 70 percent of all households held slaves and more than 30 percent of all households included at least twenty slaves. Together, the merchants and planters of Charleston and the neighboring parishes came close to controlling the new state legislature. With only 11 percent of the state's white population, Charleston District elected 47 percent of the House of Representatives and thirteen of the twenty-nine state senators.[6]

The coastal parishes to the north and south of Charleston District resembled the middlecountry in certain respects. With a slave population that composed more than three-fourths of the whole, the southern parishes of Beaufort District were solidly within the Black Belt, but slaves were less widely distributed than in the Charleston area; nonslaveholders in the southern coastal parishes constituted about 40 percent of all households. The northern parishes of Georgetown District came closer to resembling the middlecountry. Prince Frederick and Prince George, Winyah, parishes had a

4. U.S., Bureau of the Census, *Heads of Families at the First Census of the United States Taken in the Year 1790: South Carolina* (Washington, D.C., 1908) (hereafter cited as *Heads of Families, 1790*).

5. *Ibid.*

6. *Ibid.*; Walter B. Edgar *et al.*, eds., *Biographical Directory of the South Carolina House of Representatives* (Columbia, S.C., 1974–1984), I, 166; Thomas Cooper and David J. McCord, eds., *The Statutes at Large of South Carolina* (Columbia, S.C., 1836–1841), I, 137–146; Nadelhaft, *Disorders of War*, 209.

slave population that composed nearly 57 percent of the whole, but the nonslaveholding population constituted more than 50 percent of all households. The narrow coastal parish of All Saints was the only one of the three northern parishes that mirrored the social composition of Charleston District.[7]

Relative to their counterparts in the backcountry, the voters of Georgetown and Beaufort were well represented, but they were at a clear disadvantage in comparison to voters in Charleston District. With only 3 percent of South Carolina's white population, Beaufort elected eighteen representatives (nearly 9 percent of the House) and three senators (10 percent of the Senate). The three parishes of Georgetown District included 6 percent of the state's white population and elected twelve (about 6 percent) of the state representatives, along with two senators.[8]

On every important legislative issue from 1787 through the first decade of the nineteenth century, the principal division was between backcountry and lowcountry representatives, with Charleston and the upcountry as the principal antagonists. The ideological sources of these disputes will be explored in the next chapter, but for now it is important to recognize that, during the economic crisis of the middle and later 1780s, complex alliances across sections succeeded in weakening the Charleston contingent and promoting constitutional reform. By 1790, it was apparent that powerful interests bound planters across regional lines.

ii

After eight years of war and nearly three years of British occupation in South Carolina, the end of hostilities did not effect an end to disruptions. War had interrupted foreign trade and drained specie from the colonies. Having lost thousands of slaves—David Ramsay estimated twenty-five thousand—South Carolina planters had no hope of restoring earlier production levels without going into debt for labor. Exports of rice during the 1780s fell far below prewar levels, a decline that undoubtedly reflected the departure of many slaves. Planters also suffered from the constriction of markets for South Carolina products. New British duties on imported tobacco and the formation of a single French purchasing agency caused tobacco prices to fall during the 1780s. At the same time, the French government was seeking to establish indigo as a leading crop in French colonies, while Portugal was encouraging rice production in Brazil. The result was

7. *Heads of Families, 1790.*
8. *Ibid.*; Edgar *et al.*, eds., *Biographical Directory of the House*, I, 166; Cooper and McCord, eds., *Statutes of South Carolina*, I, 137–146; Nadelhaft, *Disorders of War*, 209.

that, in 1783, South Carolina planters lost markets in Portugal and the West Indies. Despite the loss of the British bounty, indigo planters continued to send their crop to Great Britain, but the loss of the West Indian market, coupled with two crop failures during the 1780s, placed them in a particularly vulnerable position.[9]

Writing to his father in March 1785, Elias Ball, Jr., a planter of St. John, Berkeley, was probably not far off the mark in suggesting that "half the people" in South Carolina had failed to pay the state's new land tax. The historian Jerome J. Nadelhaft found that the coastal parishes other than Charleston paid only £7,100 of the approximately £37,000 they owed, and he suggests that backcountry tax collectors confronted comparable problems. A 1783 return from a segment of Claremont County (part of the tax and election district known as the District Eastward of Wateree) recorded only £120 paid toward a total of £177 owed, including Thomas Sumter, who, in September 1785, still owed all of his 1783 taxes on sixty-seven hundred acres and thirty-nine slaves. By July 1787, residents in a section of the tax and election district known as the District between the Broad and Catawba Rivers had paid about £155 of the £238 they owed for the year 1784, and, in 1788, residents from a section of Ninety Six District still owed £55 on a total assessment of £202 for the preceding year.[10]

Although the war had provoked disruptions throughout the state, Georgetown, Beaufort, and particularly the backcountry experienced the most severe distress. Those areas saw the most savage fighting between whigs and loyalists and the most extensive physical destruction. Years of burning and pillaging had made the backcountry a wasteland. Much of Camden, including the Kershaw mills, had been leveled, and observers described other settled areas as barren.

In fact, the inland civil war created conditions comparable to those that had provoked the Regulator Uprising nearly twenty years earlier, and they prompted the renewal of key Regulator demands. Dislocation and deepening poverty forced untold numbers into marginality and sparked demands for a vagrancy law. In 1784 the Georgetown Grand Jury attributed the insecurity of property to "the ignorance, idleness, and excessive corruption of manners" particularly prevalent in the northern part of the district. The jurors claimed that the district jail was "scarce ever free from wretches,

9. David Ramsay, *The History of the Revolution in South Carolina* (Trenton, N.J., 1785), II, 384; Nadelhaft, *Disorders of War*, 145–157.
10. Elias Ball, Jr., to Elias Ball, Mar. 10, 1785, Elias Ball Family Papers, SCHS; Nadelhaft, *Disorders of War*, 157–158; Tax Returns, 1783–1784, District Eastward of Wateree, 1783, box 1, no. 6, District between the Broad and Catawba Rivers, 1784, box 1, no. 8, 1787–1793, Ninety Six District, 1787, box 3, no. 10, SCDAH.

who, for theft, must be continually made victims to our laws." The following year, the Camden Grand Jury complained that "idleness is a great cause of many becoming, not only useless to themselves, but a nuisance to society." Also in 1785, petitioners from the Little River District expressed concern that the war had given "some people habits of idleness and vice." They asked that "some mode of a vagrant law may pass in order to curb idleness and vice." Edgefield grand jurors were distressed by the "number of strolling persons" who were "allowed to pass unnoticed often to the great injury of the peaceable inhabitants." In 1786, a resident of Spartanburg County complained of people "who depend wholly on hunting for a subsistence, and have supplied nature's calls out of the forest without attending to cultivation."[11]

Although the connection between war and banditry cannot be measured, war-related distress and dislocations no doubt promoted the criminal activities that became the subject of widespread complaint during the 1780s. In 1784, residents of Orangeburg District requested a company of rangers to suppress "men of bad Character lurking in that Neighborhood." One year later, residents of the Little River District asked that a reward be granted for "the Heads" of "a desperate set of Outlaws who have done much damage." The same year, Aedanus Burke, the Charleston lawyer and representative who became a backcountry circuit court judge, wrote that people in Ninety Six District were "worried and half ruined by a sett of horse thieves and outlying Banditti that constantly beset the roads, rob the inhabitants and plunder their dwellings." He observed that robbers had put an end to trade within the district, since "a wagon cannot come to market in safety if they have anything of a good horse." Wagoners traveling inland from Charleston could expect to meet with robbers as soon as they crossed the Saluda River. William Bratton, a representative from the upcountry election district of the New Acquisition (York County), suggested that settlers in that area suffered from similar conditions.[12]

11. *South-Carolina Gazette and General Advertiser* (Charleston), May 11, 1784; *State Gazette of South-Carolina* (Charleston), Dec. 12, 1785; petition from Little River District, Petitions to the General Assembly, 1785, no. 105, SCDAH (hereafter cited as Petitions); presentments from Edgefield County Grand Jury, General Assembly, Grand Jury Presentments, County of Edgefield, 1786, 1787, SCDAH (hereafter cited as Grand Jury Presentments); *Charleston Morning Post and Daily Advertiser*, July 3, 1786. See also South Carolina House of Representatives Journal, Mar. 7, 1785, in Theodora J. Thompson *et al.*, eds., *Journals of the House of Representatives*, The State Records of South Carolina (Columbia, S.C., 1977–), 1785–1786, 196.

12. Senate Journal, Mar. 1, 1784, SCDAH (hereafter cited as Senate Jour.); petition from Little River District, Petitions, 1785, no. 105; House Jour., Mar. 7, 1785, in Thompson *et al.*, eds., *Journals of the House, 1785–1786*, 196; Aedanus Burke to Benjamin Guerard, Dec. 14, 1784, William Bratton to Benjamin Guerard, Feb. 13, 1784,

Given the extent of wartime plundering, it is not surprising that the practice persisted after the British departure. Bands of whigs and tories continued to live as "out-lyers" by pillaging surrounding settlements. Writing in the spring of 1782, Aedanus Burke observed that the country was "ravaged by small armed parties, who retiring in swamps, make cruel excursions on the inhabitants." With news that the House would "not listen to a pardon," one such group "became more desperate" and killed, among others, a representative from Ninety Six.[13]

Whatever their wartime affiliation, bandits of the 1780s found strength in numbers. In 1786, Andrew Pickens lost the contents of four wagons to six robbers. Another gang included Tobias and Ambrosius Sikes, who may have been related to the brothers Arthur and Solomon Sikes, notorious bandits of the 1760s. Organization among thieves made it difficult to secure backcountry jails. In 1785, the House ordered that a brick wall be built around the jail at Ninety Six, "as the number of Criminals" there was "considerable and their Escapes have hitherto been frequent." In 1786, seven men attempted to rescue prisoners at Cheraws District. Two years later, in the midst of a fire at Cambridge jail, two men accused of horse stealing and cattle stealing succeeded in escaping. The governor suspected that the fire had been "intentionally set . . . by some evil disposed persons" who intended to free the prisoners.[14]

As war in the backcountry gave rise to criminality and vagrancy, it threatened to provoke a return to a system of summary justice reminiscent of the Regulation.[15] Not until 1783 did circuit courts reopen, and, then, the insecurity of jails and the intensity of resentment between wartime enemies promoted extralegal actions against accused or suspected criminals. Having

---

General Assembly Papers, Governors' Messages, SCDAH. See also Jerome Nadelhaft, "The 'Havoc of War' and Its Aftermath in Revolutionary South Carolina," *Histoire sociale*, XII (1979), 115.

13. Aedanus Burke to Arthur Middleton, May 14, 1782, in Joseph W. Barnwell, ed., "Correspondence of Hon. Arthur Middleton, Signer of the Declaration of Independence," *SCHM*, XXVI (1925), 201.

14. Judge William Drayton, Warrants for Arrest, May 1, 1789, Thomas Kirkland Papers, box 1, SCL; *South-Carolina Weekly Gazette* (Charleston), Feb. 22, 1783, Feb. 13, 1784; House Jour., Mar. 7, 1785, in Thompson *et al.*, eds., *Journals of the House, 1785–1786*, 198; *Chas. Morn. Post, and Daily Adv.*, Jan. 4, 1787; *St. Gaz. of South-Carolina*, Apr. 16, 1789. See also Joseph Johnson, *Traditions and Reminiscences, Chiefly of the American Revolution in the South* (Charleston, S.C., 1851), 396–402.

15. For an analysis of the threatened return to summary justice following the Revolution, see Robert M. Weir, " 'The Violent Spirit,' the Reestablishment of Order, and the Continuity of Leadership in Post-Revolutionary South Carolina," in Ronald Hoffman *et al.*, eds., *An Uncivil War: The Southern Backcountry during the American Revolution* (Charlottesville, Va., 1985), 70–98.

been the primary enforcers of order (and disorder) during the war, militia officers and men assumed responsibility for meting out justice in the post-war backcountry. Colonel Benjamin Cleveland settled in the old Indian territory (later Pendleton County) after the war. According to tradition, he was accompanied by a number of his militiamen, and he established a "patriarchal government" among them. Rather than transporting accused criminals to the nearest, but still distant, jail in Abbeville, Cleveland adjudicated criminal cases and presided over executions at his plantation.[16]

Even after the reopening of backcountry circuit courts in 1783, hostility toward former loyalists threatened to undermine civil authority. Writing in May 1782, Aedanus Burke admitted that he would have "a difficult card to play, with regard to holding Courts," and expressed his feeling of "exquisite misery to be in a situation, that exposed m[e] to be a tool to gratify the fierce revenge of the people." Several representatives and others from the backcountry warned him against allowing lawyers to argue on behalf of loyalists. They were, wrote Burke, "ready to devour me with their looks, on my telling them, 'that there would be one spot of neutral ground in Court, where I sat, where no distinction of Whig or Tory should be admitted.'" All of Burke's best efforts could not prevent angry whigs from taking the law into their own hands. After Burke's court decided to free a former loyalist and accused horse stealer for lack of evidence, a group of men led by General William Butler carried the man from the court and hanged him in the courtyard.[17]

iii

The new state government acted quickly to reestablish order and legitimate its own authority by making backcountry militia officers responsible for suppressing the region's most troublesome bandits and "out-lying" loyalists. In March 1783, the legislature granted Andrew Pickens's request for a company of rangers to suppress banditry. Noting that "some troublesome persons" had appeared in the backcountry, the governor urged that ammunition be purchased for backcountry regiments. During the same session, the legislature established two companies of rangers, under the respective commands of captains William Butler and Jacob Rumph, to hunt down

16. Johnson, *Traditions and Reminiscences*, 401; House Jour., Nov. 4, 1788, in Thompson *et al.*, eds., *Journals of the House, 1787–1788*, 628.

17. Burke to Middleton, May 14, July 6, 1782 in Barnwell, ed., "Correspondence of Middleton," *SCHM*, XXVI (1925), 201, 205; Johnson, *Traditions and Reminiscences*, 420–421; John Belton O'Neall, *Biographical Sketches of the Bench and Bar of South Carolina* (Charleston, S.C., 1859), II, 36.

William Cunningham and his band and protect the populace from other "notorious offenders." Given Butler's apparent willingness to engage in vigilante action against former loyalists, one suspects that this legislative appointment gave official sanction to power that he would have assumed anyway. One year later, the legislature responded to a petition from residents of Orangeburg by establishing a special company of rangers to bring "to justice Men of bad Character lurking in that Neighbourhood."[18]

As Burke feared, the newly opened circuit courts served the interest of revenge, but they also served to bolster the authority of the new government. Criminal executions were public events that demonstrated the power of the law before the assembled onlookers. In describing one execution, a minister of Cheraws District suggested the symbolic importance of the proceedings. In December 1786, the minister accompanied two accused horse stealers named Pettis and Ginn to the place of execution. He recalled never having seen "such a concourse of people collected in this district before, who all of them behaved with solemnity suitable to the awful occasion." Pettis "in a very few words, exhorted parents to be careful in the bringing up of their children, and advised all to avoid bad company, and to take timely warning by his shameful end." The minister thought that "both the unhappy criminals appeared penitent" before they were "launched to Eternity." It seems unlikely that all doomed prisoners were as obliging as Pettis, but public executions gave the assembled onlookers an immediate display of civil authority. Nine years later, another backcountry minister was even more explicit in suggesting the symbolic significance of public executions. Writing from Union County, he observed that nearly two thousand spectators watched the prisoners, who were guarded "by a large body of horse and foot: who, if any attempt had been made to rescue the criminals— appeared determined to have the laws of their country, put into execution."[19]

Finally, the legislature passed a series of acts designed to curb criminality, facilitate the administration of justice, and assuage long-standing backcountry grievances. An act of 1784 strengthened the law against horse and cattle stealing. In 1785, the state provided for the creation of county courts and jails, and, two years later, the legislature adopted its first vagrancy law. An ordinance passed in 1789 sought to protect deer and cattle by imposing penalties on the "many idle and disorderly persons" who made a "practice

18. Andrew Pickens to William Butler, Aug. 21, 1782, in R. W. Gibbes, ed., *Documentary History of the American Revolution . . .* (New York, 1855–1857), II, 210; House Jour., Feb. 17, Mar. 4, 1783, in Thompson *et al.*, eds., *Journals of the House, 1783–1784*, 152, 214–215; Senate Jour., Mar. 6, 1783, Mar. 1, 1784.

19. *Chas. Morn. Post, and Daily Adv.*, Jan. 4, 1787; *South-Carolina State-Gazette* (Charleston), Nov. 30, 1795.

of hunting with fire in the night time." The Revolution in the backcountry had reflected divisions and aspirations already apparent during the Regulation; now, in the aftermath of war, key Regulator demands were finally met.[20]

Backcountry courts, public displays of justice, and tougher laws did not put an end to criminal activities. Scattered newspaper accounts and surviving judicial records give ample testimony to the persistence of the full spectrum of criminal behavior.[21] Nonetheless, backcountry complaints about criminality dropped off by the end of the decade, as did instances of summary justice. If the Revolution created conditions comparable to those that had prevailed during the 1760s, the reopening of inland courts probably helped to prevent a second regulation.

iv

Formulating a state policy toward former loyalists was a thornier problem for the new government than controlling the bandits and marginal people who had long been subjects of complaint in the backcountry. The problem was that backcountry whigs clamored for vengeance while prominent coastal whigs sought conciliation. With the exception of the northern part of Georgetown District, the coast had not experienced the ferocious fighting that had characterized the Revolution in the backcountry. Moreover, many prominent coastal whigs had family and friends who had accepted British protection or remained sympathetic to the crown. As Robert M. Weir has effectively pointed out, a blanket amnesty might have served the interest of reconciliation, but it would also have provoked more widespread vigilantism by angry backcountry whigs.[22]

Governor John Rutledge dealt with the problem by "applying the stick while offering a carrot to the loyalists." In September 1781, he issued a pardon to all British supporters who appeared before a militia general within thirty days and who agreed to serve in the militia for six months. In November, Rutledge extended the terms of the pardon, with the result that

20. Cooper and McCord, eds., *Statutes of South Carolina*, IV, 622, 719–720, V, 41–44, 124–126.
21. See, for example, Camden District, Journal of the Court of General Sessions, 1786–1798, SCDAH; Kershaw County, Court of Common Pleas, Minute Book, 1791–1799, WPA Trans., SCDAH.
22. George C. Rogers, Jr., *Evolution of a Federalist: William Loughton Smith of Charleston (1758–1812)* (Columbia, S.C., 1962), 124–134; Weir, " 'The Violent Spirit,' " in Hoffman *et al.*, eds., *Uncivil War*. See also Marvin R. Zahniser, *Charles Cotesworth Pinckney, Founding Father* (Chapel Hill, N.C., 1967), 71–74.

hundreds of loyalists sought protection with the whigs. At the same time, the government adopted punitive legislation. In January 1782, Rutledge convened the legislature at Jacksonboro, a village located about thirty-five miles southeast of the still-occupied capital. In his opening address, he pointed to South Carolina's "extraordinary Lenity" in dealing with the loyalists and reminded legislators that "other States have thought it just and expedient to appropriate the property of British Subjects to determine whether the forfeiture and Appropriation of the Property should now take place."[23] Rutledge may well have intended the threat of confiscation to encourage potential victims of the acts to take advantage of the pardon.

In any case, the legislature enthusiastically followed through on the governor's suggestion by passing the Confiscation Act, which called for the banishment of about 375 loyalists and the confiscation of their estates. Another measure, known as the Amercement Act, passed during the same session and established a 12 percent tax on nearly 50 additional loyalist estates. Most of the people identified on the first confiscation list were lowcountrymen, but, in 1783, the legislature passed another act confiscating the estates of all loyalists who had departed the state. Backcountry militia captains drew up lists naming about 700 loyalists of this sort. The legislature did not record roll calls until 1787, but a vote taken that year on a proposal to repeal the Confiscation and Amercement acts suggests the extent of backcountry support for punitive legislation. While coastal representatives split their vote, with fifty-five supporting and thirty-nine opposing the proposal, the backcountry contingent opposed repeal by a vote of fifty-eight to six.[24]

The story of these acts has already been well told, but, for purposes here, it is important to remember that in practice the state's policy toward former loyalists was more lenient than it appeared. The coast-dominated legislature responded sympathetically to numerous petitions by individual victims of the Jacksonboro acts. In 1783 and 1784, about 130 petitioners were either moved from the confiscation to the amercement list or freed from punishment altogether. Indeed, the Confiscation Act of 1783 may well have been intended to pacify backcountry settlers who resented the retreat from the original punitive acts.[25]

23. John Rutledge, quoted in Senate Jour., Jan. 18, 1782; Weir, " 'The Violent Spirit,' " in Hoffman *et al.*, eds., *Uncivil War*, esp. 81–82.

24. Cooper and McCord, eds., *Statutes of South Carolina*, IV, 516–525, 568–570, VI, 629–633; Nadelhaft, *Disorders of War*, 81–84, 96–97; Weir, " 'The Violent Sprit,' " in Hoffman *et al.*, eds., *Uncivil War*, 79; House Jour., Feb. 21, 1787, in Thompson *et al.*, eds., *Journals of the House, 1787–1788*, 124–126.

25. For detailed accounts of the Jacksonboro Acts and the subsequent retreat from punitive measures, see Edward McCrady, *History of South Carolina in the Revolution*,

The state's increasingly lenient policy toward former loyalists did spark opposition in the backcountry. In March 1783, about 270 settlers from Ninety Six District urged the legislature to adhere to punishments described in the Jacksonboro measures. William Butler and his men were not the only angry whigs to administer punishment in defiance of civil authority. In April 1784, a newspaper reported that a group of "true-whigs" at High Hills had chased and whipped a returning loyalist named William Reese, whose estate had been removed from the confiscation list. Thomas Sumter probably led the attackers.[26]

Opposition persisted into 1785, when the Ninety Six Grand Jury complained, "Men who have been inimical to the liberties of the United States, are permitted to hold places of trust and honor in this State." The same year, petitioners from the Little River District—part of the deeply divided region between the Broad and Saluda rivers—deplored the returning "British refugees . . . whose characters were obnoxious." They urged the House of Representatives to prohibit former loyalists from voting or holding office.[27]

As Weir has suggested, the Confiscation and Amercement acts may well have prevented sporadic violence against backcountry loyalists from exploding out of control. Had the legislature failed to demonstrate its willingness to punish former tories, the likelihood is that backcountry militiamen would have been more than willing to deal with the situation on their own.[28]

Patrick Cunningham was among the few prominent backcountry loyalists who returned to the state and regained a semblance of their former stature, and his story is testimony to the success of the state's apparently contradictory loyalist policy. Along with his brother William, Patrick Cunningham petitioned successfully to be moved from the confiscation to the amercement lists, and he may have become a candidate for the House of Representatives in 1786. That year, election managers in the Little River District reported that a mob of angry whigs had grabbed the ballot box when it appeared that former loyalists would be elected. On that occasion, the whigs prevailed, but Cunningham did serve in the House from 1792 to 1794. Apparently he resented the "paltriness" of his committee assignments

1780–1783 (New York, 1902), 555–588; Nadelhaft, *Disorders of War*, 71–85, 96–97, 109; Weir, " 'The Violent Spirit,' " in Hoffman *et al.*, eds., *Uncivil War*.

26. House Jour., Mar. 10, 1783, in Thompson *et al.*, eds., *Journals of the House, 1783–1784*, 242–243; *Gazette of the State of South-Carolina* (Charleston), Apr. 29, 1784; Anne King Gregorie, *Thomas Sumter* (Columbia, S.C., 1931), 207–209.

27. *Gaz. of the State of South-Carolina*, Dec. 20, 1784; House Jour., Mar. 7, 1785, in Thompson *et al.*, eds., *Journals of the House, 1785–1786*, 195.

28. Weir, " 'The Violent Spirit,' " in Hoffman *et al.*, eds., *Uncivil War*.

and refused to run for a second term, but in retrospect the fact that he was able to serve at all seems more significant. He also served as a district surveyor in 1793.[29]

If more leading backcountry loyalists had attempted to return to their homes and avoid the penalties of confiscation, the state's modified punitive measures might not have been sufficient to quell backcountry disturbances. As it was, such leading backcountry loyalists as Thomas Fletchall, Moses Kirkland, and Richard Pearis fled the state along with hundreds of their fellows. Those who remained were accepted with less opposition than one might have expected. Punitive measures helped to satisfy the resentment of backcountry whigs while leniency served the interest of conciliation not only on the coast but in the long-divided region between the Broad and Saluda rivers.

v

By the mid-1780s, outspoken opposition to former loyalists had become intertwined with a growing opposition to South Carolina's resident British merchants, whom planters throughout the state blamed for a deepening debtor crisis. The British merchants had flocked to Charleston soon after the whig surrender of that city in 1780. Occupying forces required native merchants and artisans to accept British protection in order to be granted the right to work. Many, in desperation, complied with this demand, but others did not, and British merchants were delighted to take advantage of the situation by filling the vacuum. In the summer of 1782, with the departure of the British Army imminent, the merchants requested permission to stay in South Carolina for an additional eighteen months to sell their remaining goods and collect outstanding debts. Assuming the governorship in January 1782, John Mathews was less concerned than his predecessor with ameliorating the rage of inland whigs. Closely identified with the coastal planters who desperately wanted goods quickly on credit, he granted the merchants' request.[30]

Throughout the 1780s and 1790s there developed in Charleston a social and political network consisting of British merchants, American merchants with British connections, and such politically prominent lawyers as William L. Smith, Jacob Read, John Julius Pringle, and Governor John Mathews, all

29. Edgar *et al.*, eds., *Biographical Directory of the House*, IV, 139–140; House Jour., Jan. 6, 1783, Feb. 21, 1784, Jan. 23, Feb. 23, 1787, in Thompson *et al.*, eds., *Journals of the House, 1783–1784*, 58, 480, *1787–1788*, 11, 45–46 (see also xxiii–xxix).

30. Nadelhaft, *Disorders of War*, 143–172; Rogers, *Evolution of a Federalist*, 97–111; Starr, "Conservative Revolution," 155–157; McCrady, *History of South Carolina, 1780–1783*, 657–658.

educated at the Inns of Court. Powerful beyond their numbers because of the state's skewed apportionment system, the group was politically identified with the legislative contingent from Goose Creek. They helped to elect Ralph Izard and his son-in-law, William L. Smith, to the First United States Congress.[31]

Wealthy planters initially welcomed the merchants. Eager to recoup wartime losses in slaves, crops, equipment, and luxury goods, they made extensive purchases on credit. According to the Charleston lawyer Timothy Ford, "The planters impelled by their necessities to procure slaves eagerly grasped at the first opportunities that offered; and unable to pay down the cash supplied themselves on credit, at whatever rate the british Merchants were pleased to fix." Some South Carolinians made overtures to French and Dutch traders, but they were unable to win the same liberal credit arrangements provided by the British. With native merchants unable to compete, the British, who were already accustomed to South Carolina, shortly "became the creditors of a great part of the state." Everybody, according to John Lewis Gervais, "was in want of necessities and made purchases at any price on credit without considering how they could make payments."[32]

Native artisans and merchants mounted the first protest against the British traders. Finding it difficult to compete, they became enraged by Mathews's agreement, which gave trade advantages to the state's former enemies. Initially led by the merchant Christopher Gadsden, opposition to the British rapidly developed into a more widespread protest against loyalists and a broadened critique of Charleston-area planters, many of whom were politically and socially tied to the British traders. Although leaders of the protest included prosperous merchants and professionals, the movement won support from less prosperous artisans as well. As the protest broadened in scope and membership, Christopher Gadsden turned against his former friends, and Alexander Gillon, a merchant and member of the House of Representatives whose estate had been taken and wife expelled during the British occupation, became leader of the Marine Anti-Britannic Society, an organization dedicated to the expulsion of foreign traders.[33]

Initially, the artisans found some support in the backcountry, where hostility to British sympathizers ran high. Indeed, one suspects a degree of coordination or mutual admiration between Charleston protesters and

31. Rogers, *Evolution of a Federalist*, 97–134.

32. Joseph W. Barnwell, ed., "Diary of Timothy Ford, 1785–1786," *SCHM*, XIII (1912), 192–193; John Lewis Gervais to Leonard De Neufville, Apr. 13, 1786, John Lewis Gervais Papers, SCL.

33. For a discussion of the artisan protest, see Nadelhaft, *Disorders of War*, 87–124; Richard Walsh, *Charleston's Sons of Liberty: A Study of the Artisans, 1763–1789* (Columbia, S.C., 1959), 92–124; Starr, "Conservative Revolution," 154–175.

backcountry opponents of legislative leniency toward former loyalists. It is no coincidence that the *Gazette of the State of South-Carolina*, a newspaper that had been sympathetic to the Charleston opposition movement, reported the attack on the backcountry loyalist William Reese. Probably written by Thomas Sumter, an accompanying letter complimented the *Gazette* as the "*only free* and *uninfluenced* (by *mock Nobility*) Press, this Commonwealth can boast of." One week later, the same newspaper reported that backcountry whigs had killed eight tories who had returned to their plantations at Fishing Creek. Four others had been allowed to escape "to tell the news to their brother Tories." The report may have been exaggerated for the benefit of Charleston protesters, who, in June of the same year, assembled at Gadsden's wharf and hanged a man named James Cook in effigy after Cook's estate was moved from the confiscation to the amercement list.[34] Christopher Gadsden was probably correct in sensing a connection between Charleston and backcountry protesters. Writing after the attack on William Reese, he suggested that "the Champions of the town" were "again probably to strike some notable stroke for the admiration of the Country party."[35]

Nonetheless, Gillon's group achieved, at best, a very limited victory. In the summer of 1783, a poorly attended session of the legislature passed an act incorporating the city of Charleston that facilitated the prosecution of protesters by giving extensive power to city wardens. Gillon's group was decisively defeated in the local election of 1784. In fact, its only political accomplishment was the election of several wealthy artisans to Charleston's legislative contingent.[36] By 1785, protest against the merchants had moved from city artisans to planters throughout the state, and artisan representatives found themselves aligned with British merchants in opposition to debtor legislation.

The problem for planters came when the merchants began calling in their loans. With their own establishments in a precarious situation, the merchants "insisted rigidly upon the punctual fulfillment of their contracts," and, according to Timothy Ford, there ensued in South Carolina "an universal alarm." In 1786, John Lewis Gervais bemoaned the presence of those "British Merchants which were suffered to remain here at the evacuation of

34. *Gaz. of the State of South-Carolina*, Apr. 29, May 6, 1784. Nadelhaft points out that the report of the Fishing Creek incident may have been written to "stir up anti-Tory and anti-British sentiment in Charleston." See Nadelhaft, "The 'Havoc of War,'" *Histoire sociale*, XII (1979), 120; Nadelhaft, *Disorders of War*, 109.

35. *Gaz. of the State of South-Carolina*, May 6, July 26, 1784. The author is identified as Gadsden in Richard Walsh, ed., *The Writings of Christopher Gadsden, 1746–1805* (Columbia, S.C., 1966), 195–196.

36. Nadelhaft, *Disorders of War*, 99–103, 119.

Charleston with goods perhaps to the value of five hundred Thousand pounds sterling which they sold at an amazing advance." Patrick Calhoun spoke sarcastically of the "negro merchants . . . [who] had the goodness to come amongst us" and who, having been "received . . . with Kindness . . . in return exerted their best endeavors to carry every shilling out of the country." According to Aedanus Burke, a "standing army of merchants, factors, clerks, agents, and emissaries . . . came here, monopolized our trade, speculated on our necessities, and holding out every object of temptation, plunged us into a debt."[37]

Wealthy coastal planters were the foremost beneficiaries of British bounty and the first victims of indebtedness, but the debtor crisis extended to the backcountry as well. The Revolution left backcountry planters eager for credit. Thomas Sumter, who became heavily indebted to a British firm, was a notable example. Joseph Kershaw, whose Camden mills were burned by the British, never managed to recoup. He died in 1787, insolvent and deeply in debt. James Lincoln, a backcountry representative from Ninety Six and a delegate to the State Convention that ratified the United States Constitution, died in 1792 with a mortgage on all of his thirty-three slaves. Writing in support of extended debtor legislation in 1788, one observer suggested that the debtor crisis had caused a chain reaction.

> A owes B in England ten thousand pounds for goods, which A has sold in this state, on credit, to two hundred different persons; each of whom may have five debtors, and every one of those two a piece. B commences an action against A, who of course is compelled to do the same to his debtors, *they* then in self defense must follow the example and *theirs* are likewise obliged to pursue a similar plan: so that two thousand persons will be sued on account of the debt owing B.[38]

Leading backcountry planters may well have become directly dependent on British credit, but many others were indirectly drawn into the web of indebtedness.

37. Barnwell, ed., "Diary of Ford," *SCHM*, XIII (1912), 193; Gervais to Neufville, Apr. 13, 1786, Gervais Papers; *Chas. Morn. Post, and Daily Adv.*, Mar. 16, 1786; [Aedanus Burke], *A Few Salutary Hints, Pointing out the Policy and Consequences of Admitting British Subjects to Engross Our Trade and Become Our Citizens* (Charleston, S.C., 1786), 4. See also George C. Rogers, "Aedanus Burke, Nathanael Greene, Anthony Wayne, and the British Merchants of Charleston," *SCHM*, LXVII (1966), 75–83.

38. Kate Furman, "General Sumter and His Neighbors," Southern History Association, *Publications*, VI (1902), 383; *Gaz. of the State of South-Carolina*, Mar. 4, 1784; *William Ancrum Esq. v. John Chesnut Esq.*, Sept. 18, 1801, Joseph Kershaw Papers, SCH; *St. Gaz. of South Carolina*, Mar. 15, 18, 1790; estate of James Lincoln and account of estate sale, Aug. 15, 1793, Abbeville Inventories, WPA Trans., I, 114–115, 144, SCDAH.

By 1784, farmers and planters throughout the state were clamoring for debtor legislation and protesting against the courts. The latter, according to Timothy Ford, "being the resort of one became the terror and hatred of the other." Protests erupted throughout the state. Late in 1784, Camden's Colonel Hezekiah Mayham, "being served by the sheriff with a writ, obliged him to eat it." The following spring, planters in Camden forcibly closed the district court and prevented the sheriff from serving notices. When Judge John Faucheraud Grimké expressed his desire to follow the rioters, the grand jurors dissuaded him, "alledging that altho' they were ready and willing to support the Dignity of the court, that they were sensible they would be overpowered by numbers." In October 1785, the *Columbian Herald* reported, "THE EMPIRE OF THE LAWS IS SUBVERTED throughout the state, except within the city of Charleston, and its environs: as, beyond that, no officer of justice 'dare serve a writ, or levy an execution.' "[39]

Each year from 1782 through 1784, the legislature passed acts allowing debtors to postpone payment of certain obligations, but not until 1785 did state representatives adopt radical measures. In September of that year Governor William Moultrie called a special session of the legislature at which he expressed concern that it was "in the Power of the Law if allowed to Opperate forcibly to transfer the whole Property of a large part of your Own Citizens, into the Hands of Aliens, and this at much under its real worth."[40]

The legislature responded to the emergency by passing two acts in 1785 and another act in 1787 designed to ease the plight of indebted planters. The first was a valuation bill that most contemporaries referred to as the Sheriffs' Sale or Pine Barren Act. Written so as to dissuade creditors from bringing debtors to court, it provided that any person facing suit for debt could offer the creditor "such part of his property, real or personal, as he shall think proper." The only qualification was that three-fourths of the appraised value of the property be equal to the debt. The special session also passed a paper money, or currency, act that provided for the issue of £100,000 to be based on mortgages of land, gold, or silver. The currency was not a legal tender, but creditors who refused to accept the paper risked receiving less valuable property under the terms of the Sheriffs' Sale Act. A third proposal, calling for an end to slave imports until South Carolina's

39. Barnwell, ed., "Diary of Ford," *SCHM*, XIII (1912), 193; Robert A. Becker, ed., "John F. Grimke's Eyewitness Account of the Camden Court Riot, April 27–28, 1785," *SCHM*, LXXXVIII (1983), 209–213; *Columbian Herald* (Charleston), Oct. 26, 1785.

40. Cooper and McCord, eds., *Statutes of South Carolina*, IV, 513, 640–641, VI, 627–628; House Jour., Sept. 26, 1785, in Thompson *et al.*, eds., *Journals of the House, 1785–1786*, 314; *Charleston Evening Gazette*, Sept. 26, 1785.

economic crisis eased, did not pass the special session. The legislature did not renew the Sheriffs' Sale Act in 1787, but it did adopt an Act to Regulate the Recovery and Payment of Debts, which provided that all debts contracted before 1787 could be paid in installments. Widely known as the Installment Act, the measure included a three-year ban on slave imports designed to halt the purchases that were widely perceived as a primary cause of the planters' problems.[41]

The year 1788 brought renewed trouble to South Carolina planters. Again many British firms were on the brink of collapse, and merchants had little choice but to press for payment. Meanwhile, with the first installment on past debts due in March, a new spate of petitions requested legislative interference on behalf of debtors. This time backcountry settlers were in the vanguard of the call for debtor relief. Settlers from Fairfield echoed complaints from other inland counties when they referred to "distressing Scenes frequently exhibited in our Vicinity, as well as through the State at large, by the rigorous enforcing the payment of debts, at this critical Juncture."[42]

Compounding the difficulty was the perennial shortage of currency, a problem that had not been resolved by the conservative issue of paper money in 1785. During the fall of 1788, backcountry petitions flooded the House of Representatives. Residents of Orangeburg declared:

> In Consiquence of the ravages and Depredations of the late War, on the property of your petitioners, they have not only been renderd incapable of discharging those debts which they Contracted before the War, and Since the Conclusion of peace, with the fairest prospect of Satisfying, but were Necessiated at the Close of the Contest, to Contract New engagements, for the resettlement of their pillaged famlies, and Desolated Farms.

They claimed that an "Enormous Interest," a series of crop failures, and "a Want of Sufficient Circulating Medium" were causing property sold at sheriffs' sales to bring in "one third of its Intrinsick Value and in Manny not one Sixth." Settlers from Ninety Six insisted that property sold under execution was yielding less than one-tenth of its "real value" as a result of the currency shortage. Similarly, petitioners from Newberry pointed to the "Great Distress the Law in its Opperations, has upon the People of this Country at this Time, all which Proceeds from the s[c]arcity of Circulateing Medium

41. Cooper and McCord, *Statutes of South Carolina*, IV, 710–716, V, 36–38. For clear explanations of these acts, see Starr, "Conservative Revolution," 223–241; Nadelhaft, *Disorders of War*, 155–168; Robert A. Becker, "Salus Populi Suprema Lex: Public and South Carolina Debtor Relief Laws, 1783–1788," *SCHM*, LXXX (1979), 65–75.

42. Nadelhaft, *Disorders of War*, 194–200; House Jour., Oct. 20, 1788, in Thompson *et al.*, eds., *Journals of the House, 1787–1788*, 575; petition from Fairfield County, Petitions, 1788, no. 9.

that is in this state at Present, The Unsertainty of Market for our Produce, and the Unrelenting Disposition of our Creditors." Similar complaints issued from Camden District. That year a group of settlers from Cheraws District attempted to prevent all sales for cash, claiming that cash could not be "procured even by the most eminent planters for any merchantable produce." Major Pierce Butler, a planter of Prince William Parish, believed that new measures were necessary in order to prevent "the ruin of the country" and to offset the danger of civil war. Responding to the mounting protest, the legislature agreed to extend the Installment Act of 1787.[43] But it did not pass another valuation act, nor did it provide for a reissue of paper currency.

Along with Butler, a number of South Carolina leaders saw debtor legislation as a necessary antidote to mounting social unrest. Invoking thoughts of the debtor rebellion that swept western Massachusetts in 1786, Aedanus Burke urged extension of the Sheriffs' Sale Act by suggesting that "5000 troops the best in America or Europe" would be unable to "enforce obedience to the common pleas" if the legislature failed to pass the measure. Robert Goodloe Harper, a Charleston lawyer who later became a United States congressman from Ninety Six, wrote that debtor legislation had been necessary in order to cool "the heats and political animosities which possessed the minds of the people for some time subsequent to the peace." These, he continued, "ran so high that it required the spirited interposition and firmness of the most respectable part of the community to prevent them from breaking out into the most dangerous tumults." Reflecting on the relative calm of South Carolina by comparison with the more turbulent North, the Charleston representative David Ramsay observed, "Much of our quiet arises from the temporising of the legislatures in refusing legal protection to the prosecution of the just rights of creditors."[44]

Without denying that South Carolina's debtor measures served to ameliorate social conflict in the backcountry and throughout the state, historians have pointed out that legislation was geared to the needs of wealthy coastal planters rather than to the less affluent debtors of the inland counties. The Sheriffs' Sale Act of 1785 was a boon to debtors with sizable landholdings, for it allowed them to offer worthless land as payment. Creditors had no choice but to accept the property or extend the loan. The act establishing a

43. House Jour., Oct. 14, 15, 20, 21, Nov. 2, 4, 1788, in Thompson *et al.*, eds., *Journals of the House, 1787–1788*, xvi, 555–556, 561, 574–575, 578, 614–617, 630; *City Gazette, and the Daily Advertiser* (Charleston), Feb. 9, Oct. 16, 1788.

44. *Chas. Morn. Post, and Daily Adv.*, Feb. 22, 1786; *St. Gaz. of South-Carolina*, Feb. 8, 1787; David Ramsay to Thomas Jefferson, Apr. 7, 1787, in Julian P. Boyd *et al.*, eds., *The Papers of Thomas Jefferson* (Princeton, N.J., 1950–), XI, 279.

paper medium enabled people to borrow currency valued at between £30 and £250, so long as they mortgaged land equaling three times the amount of the loan or gold or silver plate equaling twice the amount of the loan. Those provisions limited direct beneficiaries of the act to prosperous planters. Such prominent backcountrymen as John Chesnut, Andrew Pickens, and Wade Hampton were able to take out mortgages on the paper medium, but the struggling farmers who predominated in the backcountry found the measure of little use. As petitioners from Chester County put it, the act establishing a paper medium failed to "Alleviate the Wants and distresses of the middle and lower class." In any case, by 1788, rice production was recovering, and coastal planters were more divided on issues involving debtor legislation. As a result, backcountry representatives failed to win a valuation act and a reissue of paper currency. The extension of the Installment Act, with its ban on slave imports, that passed the House in 1787 was a compromise measure favored by merchants as the lesser of various possible evils.[45]

There is no question that the coast-dominated legislature failed to pass the debtor laws favored by the majority of inland representatives in 1788 and 1789, but disputes over debtor legislation did not follow clear sectional lines. Indeed, the debtor crisis of the 1780s promoted allegiances across sections that belie simple assumptions about sectional conflict. Throughout the 1780s, powerful interests continued to link planters across the state in opposition to Charleston's merchant contingent, and a significant minority within the backcountry opposed radical measures favored by the majority of piedmont representatives. These interregional links helped to contain conflict and limit the extent of reform.

Backcountry representatives were far from unanimous in their attitude toward particular debtor measures. Disputes arose not only from regional differences within the backcountry but from the complexity of credit relations in the inland counties. Farmers indebted for small sums to local merchants were burdened by the lack of currency and had an obvious interest in winning concessions on debts involving small sums. The problem was that many backcountry farmers and planters were also creditors who had reason to oppose legislation that might make it more difficult to collect small sums owed for local transactions.

A 1787 House vote on whether to exclude debts of less than £10 from the benefits of the Installment Act illustrates the complexity of sectional align-

45. Nadelhaft, *Disorders of War*, 155–172, 194–200; Starr, "Conservative Revolution"; Plats and Appraisements, Mortgages to the Commissioners of the Paper Medium Loan, 1785, SCDAH; House Jour., Feb. 20, 1786, in Thompson *et al.*, eds., *Journals of the House, 1785–1786*, 440–441.

ments on the debtor question. By a vote of sixty-four to fifty-seven, the House decided against the exemption. Not surprisingly, Charleston representatives, by a vote of twenty to two, opposed the small debtors, but the coastal parishes split their vote, with twenty-three supporting and twenty-seven opposing the Charleston contingent. Thirty-five backcountry representatives (71 percent) voted against the exemption. They probably agreed with Benjamin Cudworth of the District Eastward of Wateree, who pointed out that the exception for small debts "would subject the country people . . . many of whom might be distressed for £5 whilst the rich man that owed £5000 was secured."[46]

But backcountry representatives were divided in their attitude toward small-scale debtors. John Hunter, a planter from Laurens County in the Little River District, went so far as to suggest that all debts for sums under £20 be excluded from the benefits of the Installment Act. He pointed out that the law "was not intended to relieve the poor, they were not in debt; it was to save from ruin the rich, or those who had great property." James Lincoln, a representative from Ninety Six District, also favored the exemption; he believed it was necessary to protect the many small-scale creditors who predominated in the backcountry. Lincoln "mentioned an instance of a man that had run a piece of land, and in order to take up the grant, sold a horse, the person that bought it sheltered himself under the laws that screened debtors, and the poor man lost both his horse and land."[47] Such reasoning probably influenced the fourteen backcountry representatives who joined the unsuccessful Charleston contingent in an effort to limit benefits of the Installment Act to larger debts.

Backcountry representatives also differed among themselves concerning the prohibition on slave imports. Initially proposed by Ralph Izard in 1785, the temporary ban was seen by many wealthy planters and merchants as the least objectionable way of easing South Carolina's economic woes. Efforts to institute the plan failed in 1785, but in 1787 the legislature adopted the ban, and the vote that year attests to the extent of interregional links. As the House debated the installment bill, a motion was made to strike the clause prohibiting the importation of slaves into the state. The seventy-three negative votes included twenty from Charleston, thirty-three from the other coastal parishes, and twenty from the backcountry. The fifty-six representatives who favored eliminating the temporary ban included only four from Charleston, nineteen from the other coastal parishes, and thirty-three from

46. House Jour., Mar. 22, 1787, in Thompson *et al.*, eds., *Journals of the House, 1787–1788*, 250–251; *Chas. Morn. Post, and Daily Adv.*, Feb. 22, 1787.
47. *Chas. Morn. Post, and Daily Adv.*, Feb. 22, 1787.

the backcountry.[48] Overall, the upper piedmont districts, where representatives and voters held fewer slaves, were most united in opposition to the ban. Rather than representing the interests of impoverished farmers, upcountry representatives who opposed Charleston acted on behalf of the region's aspiring planters.

Nor was the backcountry united on the subject of the Sheriffs' Sale Act. Adopted at the height of the debtor crisis in 1785, the act had been allowed to lapse in the wake of numerous complaints that wealthy debtors were taking advantage of the measure by paying creditors with worthless pine barrens. Leading the opposition to renewal were Charleston merchants and representatives such as Thomas Bee, who believed that "it had been common for people to purchase grants of pine barren" for the express purpose of paying creditors who had no choice but to accept. But opposition came from the backcountry as well. The Camden Grand Jury objected that the Sheriffs' Sale Act, "though it was intended for very salutary purposes, has been so much abused by some artful and designing debtors as to become very detrimental to many honest and indulgent creditors." In 1787, settlers in Ninety Six District petitioned against renewal of the Sheriffs' Sale Act, insisting that it had been "productive of the most pernicious Consequences." Their reasoning is of particular interest because it points to the presence of merchants and planters in the western piedmont who were turning away from the prevailing backcountry call for more radical measures. Observing that "the well being of all commercial Countries, in a great Measure depends on the Support of Credit," the petitioners argued that it had always "been the Maxim of Wise Governments to promote a proper degree of Credit; by compelling Persons who enter into pecuniary Engagements, Strictly to comply with them."[49]

A proposal for a new valuation act also promoted controversy among the backcountry legislative contingent. In the midst of the debtor crisis that persisted into 1788, hundreds of backcountry petitioners requested a new valuation act in order to prevent property sold at sheriffs' sales from bringing in only a fraction of its "true worth." The failure of the legislature to pass a new paper currency act gave added importance to the valuation measure. Pierce Butler of Prince William Parish in Beaufort District proposed a bill requiring that property paid to creditors be transferred at a minimum of three-fourths the value established by district appraisers. Again,

48. *Chas. Even. Gaz.*, Sept. 28, 29, Oct. 1, 1785; House Jour., Oct. 6, 1785, Mar. 22, 1787, in Thompson *et al.*, eds., *Journals of the House, 1785–1786*, 336, *1787–1788*, 252–253; Senate Jour., Mar. 11, 1785.

49. *Chas. Morn. Post, and Daily Adv.*, Feb. 22, Dec. 13, 1786; House Jour., Feb. 9, 1787, in Thompson *et al.*, eds., *Journals of the House, 1787–1788*, 76–78.

the backcountry was more divided than the coastal contingent. The Charlestonians cast all of their twenty-seven votes in opposition to Butler's proposal. Joining them were forty-five representatives from the other coastal parishes and seventeen backcountrymen. The minority who favored the new valuation act included nineteen coastal representatives and twenty-five backcountrymen. The inland group did not divide according to region. Both upcountry and middlecountry representatives split on the issue of valuation.[50] Inland opponents of the bill probably shared coastal fears that it bore too close a resemblance to the Sheriffs' Sale Act and would make creditors vulnerable to the decisions of local appraisers. In any case, the vote demonstrated not only that backcountry representatives were the prime movers behind the valuation proposal but that 40 percent of the inland contingent shared coastal concerns about the interest of creditors.

Backcountry representatives may have differed among themselves concerning particular debtor measures, but they were almost completely united with coastal planters on the need to extend the Installment Act. In 1788, the House, by a vote of ninety-five to thirty-seven, decided to continue legislative interference on behalf of debtors. The negative votes included twenty-one from Charleston, twelve from the neighboring coastal parishes, and only four from the backcountry. Five Charlestonians supported the extension, probably with the thought that creditors had less reason to oppose the Installment Act than other proposed debtor measures. They were joined by forty representatives from the other parishes of Charleston District, fourteen representatives from the more distant coastal parishes, and thirty-six backcountrymen.[51] The vote testifies to a broad consensus among planters of all regions on specific debtor relief measures.

Currency shortage remained the primary problem, according to the hundreds of backcountry settlers who petitioned the legislature in 1788, but, even on this subject, a substantial segment of the inland contingent voted with the majority from the coast. Although Thomas Sumter pledged to bring in a bill for the emission of £300,000 in notes, the House ignored repeated demands until early 1789, when members, by a vote of 110 to 48, decided against a further emission of paper money. Joining all of Charleston's twenty-seven representatives in opposition to the proposal were fifty-nine from the coastal parishes and twenty-four backcountrymen. Among the minority that supported the paper currency bill were six coastal repre-

50. Petitions, 1788, nos. 5, 9, 24, 69, 72, 96; House Jour., Oct. 14, 15, 18, 21, 23, 27, 1788, in Thompson *et al.*, eds., *Journals of the House, 1787–1788*, 555–557, 560–562, 570–571, 578–580, 588–589, 595–596; *City Gaz., and Daily Adv.*, Nov. 5, 1788.

51. House Jour., Oct. 21, 1788, in Thompson *et al.*, eds., *Journals of the House, 1787–1788*, 583–584.

sentatives and forty-two backcountrymen. Whereas the upcountry districts supported paper currency by a vote of thirty to twelve, the middlecountry's twenty-four representatives divided evenly. That Charleston opposed the currency bill is hardly surprising. Nor, given the widespread complaints about currency shortage, is it surprising that the majority of piedmont representatives supported the measure. Why the majority of parish and middlecountry representatives joined the Charlestonians is somewhat more difficult to explain. Clearly, wealthier rice and indigo planters were beginning to recoup and were no longer desperate for currency. One historian has suggested that wealthier planters may have been opposing a provision that would have prevented people who had borrowed under the Currency Act of 1785 from taking advantage of the new measure.[52] In any case, the effect of such considerations was to divide the inland contingent and promote allegiances across sectional lines.

Voting alignments on debtor legislation suggest sectional patterns. In the first place, the Charleston contingent was almost completely isolated in its opposition to all forms of legislative interference on behalf of debtors. In other words, representatives from the rest of the state were more or less united behind the most conservative form of legislative interference on behalf of debtors, namely, continuation of the Installment Act of 1787. Second, on the more controversial measures of exemption for small debts, valuation, paper currency, and the ban on slave imports, representatives from the coastal parishes cast the majority of their votes with the city. On those four issues, the parishes neighboring Charleston cast 67 percent of their votes with the majority of city representatives. Representatives from the northern and southern coastal parishes cast about 67 and 54 percent of their votes, respectively, with the city.[53]

Finally, in the backcountry, piedmont representatives were more consistent in opposing Charleston than were their counterparts in the middle region of the state. They were more interested in protecting small-scale debtors, more reluctant to end slave imports, more supportive of valuation, and more eager for paper currency than any other group. Whereas representatives from the predominantly middlecountry districts cast 43 percent of their votes with Charleston, only 31 percent of the upcountry vote went with city and neighboring coastal parishes.[54]

52. *City Gaz., and Daily Adv.*, Feb. 20, 1788; South Carolina House of Representatives Journal, Feb. 20, 1789, SCDAH (hereafter cited as House Jour.); Nadelhaft, *Disorders of War*, 198–199.
53. House Jour., Mar. 22, Oct. 21, 23, 1788, in Thompson *et al.*, eds., *Journals of the House, 1787–1788*, 250–253, 583–584, 588–589.
54. *Ibid.*

Even within the piedmont, there was considerable division. A contingent of representatives from Ninety Six and the Little River District voted consistently with Charleston and the coastal parishes. On the four measures mentioned above, representatives from those districts cast 64 percent of their votes with the city and neighboring coastal parishes. The remaining four upcountry districts cast only 16 percent of their votes with Charleston. Among the most consistent supporters of the Charlestonians were Robert Anderson, Patrick Calhoun, and John Hunter of Laurens, whose support for the Charlestonians was not confined to issues involving debt. Anderson and Calhoun were among the six backcountrymen who, in 1787, favored coastal efforts to repeal the Confiscation and Amercement acts.[55] On a variety of important issues, key upcountry representatives were developing political identifications with their coastal counterparts. Patrick Calhoun died in 1792, but it is no coincidence that Anderson and Hunter, together with Andrew Pickens, came to the fore during the 1790s as leaders of an interregional Republican political coalition.

In sum, the debtor crisis of the 1780s prompted planters throughout the state to unify in opposition to the merchants, whose interests were represented by the Charleston contingent. At the same time, allegiances across regions limited the extent of debtor legislation to measures favored by the state's wealthier planters. The result was the passage of debtor laws sufficient to contain conflict without meeting the full spectrum of debtor demands.

vi

The establishment of county courts in the midst of the debtor crisis contributed to the maintenance of civil authority in the backcountry and strengthened the position of the region's political and economic elite. As one might expect, the new system came under attack during the late 1780s and early 1790s, but rioting erupted in only one county and only after ratification of the United States Constitution put an end to debtor laws. Despite the shortage of currency, most local courts functioned smoothly and without public opposition. The new system contributed to the reestablishment of civil authority in the backcountry and the local standing of the region's leading men.

The Court Act of 1785 created thirty-four counties, each of which was to hold quarterly courts. Consisting of seven justices appointed by the legislature, each court had jurisdiction in debt cases in which damages did not

---

55. *Ibid.*; House Jour., Feb. 21, 1787, *ibid.*, 124–126; House Jour., Feb. 20, 1789.

exceed £20 and other civil cases in which damages did not exceed £50. Criminal cases that did not involve the possibility of corporal punishment also came under the auspices of the new courts. In addition, county courts had jurisdiction in boundary disputes and bore the responsibility for appointing sheriffs, licensing taverns, fixing whiskey prices, levying local taxes, recording deeds, and overseeing roads, bridges, and ferries. The act gave individual justices power in civil cases involving up to 20s. and allowed participants to appeal from individual justices to the county courts, and from there to one of the seven district courts, whose jurisdiction was based on the old circuit court boundaries established in 1769. Apparently residents of Charleston and Georgetown districts never established the new local courts, but county courts functioned in the backcountry until 1799, when South Carolina overhauled its judicial system.[56]

At the apex of the county government were the judges. Appointed by the legislature, they were drawn largely from the backcountry's economic and political elite. Five of Abbeville's first seven judges were or became state representatives. Among these were Robert Anderson, Patrick Calhoun, and Andrew Pickens. (Pickens and Anderson subsequently moved to Pendleton, where they served on that county court.) Fairfield's first court included four current or future state representatives, among whom were such men as the former Regulator William Kirkland and the merchant James Craig, who, by 1790, owned ten and seven slaves, respectively. Spartanburg's first court included two state representatives. Among these was James Jordan, who, with thirteen slaves in 1790, was one of the eight wealthiest planters in Spartanburg. Baylis Earle, another Spartanburg judge, held only four slaves in 1790, but he had already been a state senator and was serving as a state representative at the time of his appointment as a county judge. Baylis's brother, Elias Earle, was a substantial planter and upcountry gunmaker who became a United States congressman. The first county court in York included five current or future state representatives and several of the wealthiest men in that county. Newberry's first court also included five state representatives. Among these was Wade Hampton's brother John, who held twelve slaves in 1790. Serving with him was the former Regulator James Mayson. The merchant and former Regulator Samuel Boykin served on Claremont's court, together with his brother Francis. They held seventy-six and ten slaves, respectively.[57]

56. Cooper and McCord, eds., *Statutes of South Carolina*, VII, 211–242; David Duncan Wallace, *South Carolina: A Short History, 1520–1948* (Columbia, S.C., 1951), 337.

57. House Jour., Mar. 21, 1785, in Thompson *et al.*, eds., *Journals of the House, 1785–1786*, 272–274; Edgar *et al.*, eds., *Biographical Directory of the House*, III, 30–31, 39–40, 80–81, 132–133, 161–162, 197–198, 208–209, 281–282, 304–306, 339–

Despite long-standing backcountry demands for local courts, the new county courts met with protest within two years of their formation. Given the extent of debtor distress, the inexperience of county judges, and the inconvenience associated with frequent sessions, such opposition hardly seems surprising. In 1787, local petitioners demanded the abolition of courts in Winton and Orange counties of Orangeburg District and in Lincoln County in Beaufort District in the lowcountry. The following year, petitioners protested the courts in Claremont and Clarendon, and, in 1791, the Fairfield court became the object of organized opposition. By 1792, Newberry settlers were demanding the abolition of their court as well.[58]

In Winton County, protest erupted into violence. Frustrated by the shortage of currency and by the failure of their own anticourt petitioners, rioters forcibly closed the court during the opening session of 1791. According to the official record, John Weekley (Wickley), a militia captain, "declared there should be no more County Courts" and "tore down from the Court House all the Sheriff's Advertisements for Sales as levied for Executions . . . and openly declared there should be no more Sales of Property in this County." He and his followers then pulled down the justices' and jurymen's benches and "took the Clerks Table, opened the Drawer and threw [it] out in the Rain." The next morning they set fire to the building.[59]

The rioters were not impoverished farmers, but their leaders were suffering from indebtedness. Weekley himself owned three slaves in 1790, and he had sufficient property to mortgage land for the state's paper currency under the Currency Act of 1785. Weekley's neighbor and fellow rioter Charles Brown owned twenty slaves. Colonel William Davis, who "aided and abetted" the insurgents, owned twenty-five. The three remaining rioters did not own slaves. Both Weekley and his accomplice, John Redd, had property advertised for sale in execution during the February court. Weekley's problems were already apparent in 1788, when he signed a Winton County petition requesting a new issue of paper currency and fell into arrears on interest payments for the paper medium.[60]

340, 388, 407, 424–425, 490–491, 505–506, 552–553, 620–621, 626–627; *Heads of Families, 1790.*

58. House Jour., Feb. 1, 22, Mar. 26, 1787, Jan. 19, 22, 30, Feb. 18, Oct. 16, 1788, Jan. 13, 18, 28, Dec. 13, 1791, in Thompson *et al.*, eds., *Journals of the House, 1787–1788*, 32–33, 130, 283, 329, 341, 374, 459, 565, 1791, 25–26, 62, 92–94, 150, 384–386; Petition from Newberry County, Petitions, 1792, no. 29.

59. Barnwell County, Clerk of Court, Winton Court, Minute Book, 1786–1791, WPA Trans., no. 31, SCDAH.

60. *Heads of Families, 1790; St. Gaz. of South-Carolina*, Mar. 31, 1788; petitions from Winton County, Petitions, 1788, nos. 72, 74.

Debtor distress prompted the Winton riot and exacerbated opposition to other controversial courts, but it was not the only source of anticourt sentiment in the backcountry. Orangeburg petitioners noted the "astonishing" increase of litigation and complained, "Those petty quarrels and trifling disputes which were heretofore settled by a reference to friends or subsided of themselves when men had time to cool and reflect are now constantly brought into court." A traveler through the backcountry confirmed this observation, suggesting that lawsuits had "been multiplied beyond all former knowledge" since the establishment of county courts. As a result, settlers were inconvenienced by frequent and lengthy court sessions. Newberry residents complained that militia musters, patrol duty, and attendance at court as jurors or witnesses kept some people from their "daily Employment as Farmers, Planters, etc. at least twenty-five or thirty days in the year." Opponents of the courts complained further about the cost of building courthouses and jails and about the lawyers who profited "from the Follies and Distress of the People which, it becomes their interest to promote."[61]

County judges also met with opposition. Petitioners from Fairfield, Newberry, and Orangeburg insisted that the justices, not being "proper judges of the law," were simply incompetent. Two former Regulators became the objects of public criticism. Newberry residents challenged James Mayson for sitting on their court even though he resided in Edgefield, and, in 1790, a man named Robert Dumville insisted that Andrew Baskin had been guilty of extortion and neglect of duties while serving as a Lancaster County justice. The attorney general refused to prosecute, however.[62]

Apparently settlers in the seven counties with controversial courts suffered from a variety of local hardships that made the courts particularly burdensome. Residents of Winton and Orange lived in a region that was more sparsely settled than other areas of the backcountry. The results, as anticourt petitioners complained, were that residents were called repeatedly as jurors and witnesses and that cases were frequently postponed because of

61. Petition from Orangeburg District, Petitions, 1788, no. 99; William Winterbotham, *An Historical, Geographical, Commercial, and Philosophical View of the American United States and of the European Settlements* . . . (London, 1795), III, 261; petition from Newberry County, Petitions, 1792, no. 29 (oversize). See also petition from Clarendon County, Petitions, 1789, no. 114; petitions from Fairfield County, Orange County, Winton County, Petitions, 1791, nos. 16, 50, 63.

62. Petitions from Orangeburg District, Fairfield County, Newberry County, Petitions, 1788, no. 99, 1791, no. 16, 1792, no. 29 (oversize); Edgar *et al.*, eds., *Biographical Directory of the House*, III, 56; Newberry County, Clerk of Court, Minute Book, Jan. 1791, WPA Trans., 159 [MS, 432], SCDAH; Richard Maxwell Brown, *The South Carolina Regulators* (Cambridge, Mass., 1963), 128.

absenteeism. The situation in Claremont, Clarendon, and Lincoln counties was probably similar. Troubled at finding their "property handled by a few designing men as they see cause," anticourt petitioners in Fairfield may have been expressing resentment at the brothers Richard, John, and Minor Winn. The three were local merchants and frequent litigants. Richard and John were also county justices who, not coincidentally, signed at the top of Fairfield's procourt petition. Thomas S. Parrot, one of the first signers on the anticourt document, had been a defendant in a suit brought by Evans, Winn, and Company.[63]

In any case, with the possible exception of Fairfield, the petition campaign does not reveal a clear class distinction between proponents and opponents of the new system. For the most part, signers of petitions supporting and opposing the controversial courts were drawn from comparable social backgrounds. Nonslaveholders predominated in both groups, and many signed with a mark. More affluent men also joined both groups. Anticourt petitioners from Orange County included Lewis Golsan, Henry Patrick, and Samuel Rowe, who owned twenty-one, nineteen, and seventeen slaves, respectively. Opponents of the Clarendon court also included several of that county's wealthiest and most prominent residents.[64]

That the majority of the new courts remained, to all appearances, trouble-free requires some explanation. Proponents of the new system articulated one likely explanation for its success. To many settlers, who could not afford the cost of transport and legal fees required by the district court, the county courts offered an obvious advantage. Residents of Newberry explained that there were "numbers of inhabitants in this county, whom if sued by litigious persons, would not be able to attend at Cambridge." And residents of Chester later observed that backcountry settlers who were "generally possessed of small fortunes and scarce of cash, a natural consequence of their remote situation from Market . . . [were] not able to pay the expense of a suit in the Superior Court for every trifling dispute that was above the jurisdiction of a justice of the peace." In other words, although the county courts exacerbated social conflicts in several counties, they also helped to contain tension in others by making the law more widely accessi-

---

63. Petition from Orangeburg District, Petitions, 1788, no. 99; petition from Fairfield County, Petitions, 1791, no. 16; Edgar *et al.*, eds., *Biographical Directory of the House*, III, 777–781; Clerk of Court, Fairfield County, Common Pleas and General Sessions, Dockets, 1786–1789, Aug. 1788, SCDAH.

64. Petition from Orange County, Petitions, 1791, no. 50; petition from Clarendon County, Petitions, 1789, no. 114; *Heads of Families, 1790*. See also petitions from Fairfield County, Orange County, Petitions, 1791, nos. 16, 20, 45, 50; petition from Winton County, Petitions, 1791, no. 63; petitions from Newberry County, Petitions, 1792, nos. 28 and 29 (oversize).

ble. As defenders pointed out, the county court system made litigation more affordable for people with small claims and small debts.[65]

That county courts to some extent formalized and extended the local authority already exercised by the region's leading men also contributed to the courts' success. Before the Revolution, Richard Richardson had arbitrated many feuds in his region and, according to one early commentator, had exercised equity jurisdiction from his High Hills plantation to the North Carolina line. His son became one of the first justices for Claremont County. Similarly, Colonel Benjamin Cleveland of Greenville, who had established what the same writer called "a patriarchal government" over his neighborhood before the formation of local courts, subsequently received an appointment as a county judge.[66] Like Richardson and Cleveland, many of the county justices were also militia officers during the Revolution. That six former Regulators became county judges is a further indication of continuity between the new system of local justice and pre-Revolutionary backcountry leadership.[67]

County involvement in criminal cases may have added to the popularity of local courts. Although the Court Act of 1785 limited county jurisdiction to cases that did not involve corporal punishment, justices erected pillories, whipping posts, and stocks. Fairfield judges were probably not alone in calling for use of the whip when they meted out punishment. Although district judges continued to preside over the most serious criminal cases, the county system provided a mechanism for controlling the petty crimes that had been the subject of long-standing complaint in the backcountry.[68]

It was probably for these reasons that backcountry representatives were favorably disposed to the new courts and generally reluctant to dismantle the system even in areas where the courts provoked opposition. They may

65. Petition from Newberry County, Petitions, 1792, no. 28; petition from Chester County, Petitions, 1798, no. 24 (oversize). See also petitions from Fairfield County, Orange County, Petitions, 1791, nos. 20, 45.

66. Johnson, *Traditions and Reminiscences*, 158–160, 401; House Jour., Mar. 28, Nov. 4, 1788, in Thompson *et al.*, eds., *Journals of the House, 1787–1788*, 301, 628.

67. The following were among the militia officers appointed in 1785 as county judges: Robert Anderson, Andrew Hamilton, and Andrew Pickens in Abbeville; Leroy Hammond and Hugh Middleton in Edgefield; Henry Hampton and Richard Winn in Fairfield; Thomas Brandon, William Bratton, and William Hill in York. Edgar *et al.*, eds., *Biographical Directory of the House*, III, 39–40, 86–89, 298–299, 301–305, 339–340, 493–494, 552–553, 779–780. The six Regulators named as county judges were Andrew Baskins, Samual Boykin, George Hicks, Moses Kirkland, James Mayson, and Claudius Pegues. See House Jour., Mar. 21, 1785, in Thompson *et al.*, eds., *Journals of the House, 1785–1786*, 272–274.

68. *St. Gaz. of South-Carolina*, Jan. 18, 1787; Fairfield County, Clerk of Court, Minute Book, 1791–1799, WPA Trans., Jan. 1793, Jan. 1794, SCDAH.

have been fearful that abolition in several counties would pose an imminent danger in others. In February and March 1789, the House of Representatives voted to abolish the Winton and Orange county courts and nearly supported a move to discontinue courts in Claremont, Clarendon, and Lancaster counties. Although House efforts met with defeat in the Senate, the roll calls on abolition suggest the extent of backcountry support for the county court system. Representatives from the Orangeburg area voted solidly in favor of abolition in all five of the counties under consideration; the District Eastward of Wateree, which included Claremont, Clarendon, and Lancaster, was divided. But the rest of the backcountry opposed abolition and prevented the House from voting to discontinue courts in Clarendon, Claremont, and Lancaster counties.[69]

Coastal representatives generally favored abolition of the controversial courts, but they were notable primarily by their absence or abstention. Whereas backcountry attendance on the five court-related votes ranged from fifty-five to sixty-five of a possible seventy-six members, attendance or voting by the Charlestonians ranged from fourteen to twenty of thirty members. Representatives from the coastal parishes other than St. Philip and St. Michael also supported abolition, but their absenteeism was even more conspicuous. Of the ninety-six representatives from coastal parishes other than St. Philip and St. Michael, no more than thirty-four were present for any of the roll calls on the county court question.[70] Clearly, the coastal contingent remained only marginally interested in the issue. Those who favored abolition and bothered to vote may have been trying to avoid social unrest by assuaging grievances against the controversial courts, and Charlestonians may have been representing the city lawyers who had an interest in keeping the state's legal system and legal business highly centralized.

The very success of the new courts in most counties testified to the local prestige of the untrained judges who presided over them. No doubt many unnamed judges became the objects of private resentment, and one suspects that the Kershaw cabinetmaker who referred to the county court as a "court of buffoonery" was not alone.[71] But, in balance, it seems more significant that James Mayson and Andrew Baskin were the only judges who became targets of public ridicule. By instituting county courts, the new state government not only answered a long-standing backcountry grievance; it also strengthened civil authority by localizing it. In the process, it

69. House Jour., Feb. 21, 23, Mar. 3, 1789, in Thompson *et al.*, eds., *Journals of the House, 1789–1790*, 173–174, 178–180, 215–218.
70. *Ibid.*
71. Will of William Luyten, Kershaw Wills, WPA Trans., I, 37, SCDAH.

reinforced the power and prestige of the backcountry's political and economic elite.

vii

The first post-Revolutionary call for state constitutional reform reflected a
widespread effort to stabilize the new government by grounding it in a
popular representation more fundamental than that of the state legislature.
With the hostilities of war still simmering in the backcountry and artisan
radicals protesting the British influence in the city, political leaders hoped
that a government based on constitution by convention would be more
successful in creating social harmony. In 1784, Governor Moultrie urged
state repesentatives to "revise and perfect" the South Carolina Constitution, "the foundation and Stability of our prosperity; or, in vain will it be to
proceed with the Superstructure." That Christopher Gadsden, a leading
opponent of the Charleston opposition movement, introduced the convention bill suggests that the early proponents of reform included lowcountry
representatives who hoped that a new constitution would quell social disorder. Thomas Tudor Tucker, a leading lowcountry spokesman for constitutional reform, was explicit in suggesting that a new constitution would be
the only viable antidote to social unrest of the sort that swept Charleston
after the Revolution. A physician, planter, and representative from St.
George, Dorchester, he argued that a constitution grounded in a convention
"would be of all the most happy, and perhaps of all the most quiet and
orderly."[72]

By 1785, the backcountry was in the vanguard of the call for reform, and
the issue took on new meaning. Petitioners linked the call for constitutional
change to other issues, particularly demands for paper currency, debtor
laws, and the removal of the state capital to an inland location. Settlers
from the Little River District were careful to mention the need for reapportionment, noting that "the present representation being as we conceive very
unequal property being larger represented than the free white inhabitants."[73] By 1785, it was clear that the call for reform had become a chal-

72. Gordon S. Wood, *The Creation of the American Republic, 1776–1787* (Chapel
Hill, N.C., 1969), 328–343; House Jour., Jan. 31, Aug. 5, 1783, Feb. 2, Mar. 8, 23,
1784, in Thompson *et al.*, eds., *Journals of the House, 1783–1784*, 70, 327, 401, 529,
600; Senate Jour., Mar. 23, 1784; Philodemus [Thomas Tudor Tucker], *Conciliatory
Hints, Attempting, by a Fair State of Matters, to Remove Party-Prejudices . . . Submitted
to the Consideration of the Citizens of the Commonwealth of South-Carolina* (Charleston, S.C., 1784), 17.
73. Petition from Little River District, Petitions, 1785, no. 105. See also petition from
Camden District, Petitions, 1785, no. 104; House Jour., Jan. 27, Mar. 7, 1785, Feb. 20,

lenge to the Charleston contingent, the most consistent opponents of debtor legislation.

Demands for a new state capital also testified to the growing resentment against the Charleston contingent. Proponents of the move were obviously concerned about facilitating attendance by backcountry representatives, but they also hoped to weaken the power of Charleston's resident British merchants and the coastal leaders with whom they were associated. It is no coincidence that John Lewis Gervais, an outspoken opponent of the British community in Charleston who had represented both the city and Ninety Six District in the legislature, introduced a plan to place the capital at the center of the state, at a site that would soon become Columbia. In 1789, Pierce Butler cut to the heart of the matter when he supported the call for an inland capital not only because backcountry settlers "were thickly settled in places far distant" from Charleston and were "consequently ignorant of public transactions" but because merchants in the port city enjoyed "great influence and weight" in the legislature, "it being always in their power, by the assistance of those who fluctuated in opinion, to carry everything their own way."[74]

Although an interregional coalition supported reform, coastal leaders were far from unanimous in their support. In 1784, 1785, and 1787, the Senate defeated convention bills passed by the House. The vote on the last occasion reveals the sectional nature of the dispute. Of the eleven senators who favored the convention, eight were backcountrymen. The twelve senators who opposed the proposal included only one from the backcountry.[75]

Opponents of the convention feared that the delegates, presumably under backcountry influence, might abolish the Senate and radically alter the system of apportionment. In 1785, after the House voted in favor of a Camden convention, it "recommended in the Strongest terms, that the Delegates be not empowered to Vote for the Abolition of either Branch of the Legislature." Two years later, Ralph Izard was still "inimical to a convention because every thing must be thrown into a state of nature," leaving the delegates "unlimited authority to make whatever alterations they thought proper." David Ramsay suspected that the convention "might abrogate the

---

1786, Feb. 1, 1787, Jan. 14, 1788, in Thompson *et al.*, eds., *Journals of the House, 1785–1786,* 26–27, 194–195, 440–441, *1787–1788,* 33, 320; Senate Jour., Sept. 29, 1785.

74. *Chas. Even. Gaz.*, Mar. 7, 1786; *City Gaz., and Daily Adv.*, Jan. 26, 1789. Backcountry petitions requesting a new state capital appear in House Jour., Jan. 27, Mar. 7, Oct. 5, 1785, Feb. 22, 1786, in Thompson *et al.*, eds., *Journals of the House, 1785–1786,* 26–27, 195, 284–285, 330–331.

75. Senate Jour., Mar. 23, 1784, Feb. 25, Mar. 1, 1785, Mar. 21, 1787.

Senate, and equalize the representation." He thought it "folly to suppose" any recommendation from the legislature could restrain the delegates.[76]

Such concerns were not confined to the coast. Although backcountry representatives, for the most part, favored reapportionment, some feared that a convention might go too far. In 1786, Judge Henry Pendleton, representing Saxe Gotha, suggested that a convention was necessary in order to prevent a further-reaching popular revolt. He declared that persistent Senate opposition to reform would result in "a sort of convention he never wished to see, a convention of the people." That year Patrick Calhoun opposed a convention because "the general mass of people were so much bent for a democratical government, that . . . a convention would do more harm than good."[77] Apparently, Pendleton and Calhoun feared the democratizing tendencies within their own region.

The call for an inland capital was slower to win House approval, not only because coastal members resisted the plan but because backcountry speculators were in competition with one another. When Gervais presented his proposal in 1786, much of the objection in both houses centered, not on the principle, but on the precise location. Thomas Sumter attempted to establish the capital at Stateburg, where he, not coincidentally, owned substantial property. Others hoped that the inland site might be located closer to the coast.[78]

Presumably, lowcountry opponents were concerned about the inconvenience of the journey inland, but they also feared that the change would give the backcountry added influence over legislative transactions. As early as 1784, Ralph Izard informed Thomas Jefferson that a backcountry capital would increase backcountry influence by a ratio of four to one. Arguing for a lowcountry site, one senator reminded his fellows of recent inland disturbances by asking a series of pointed questions: "Had not the people in that part of the country hoisted the banner of defiance against the Laws? Was this then a place where new ones could be made with propriety? Certainly not." William L. Smith believed that an inland capital would "shed a malignant influence on all the proceedings of the Legislature."[79]

That the legislature finally supported the backcountry call for an inland capital suggests the extent of interregional political links. Despite consider-

76. House Jour., Feb. 24, 1785, in Thompson *et al.*, eds., *Journals of the House, 1785–1786*, 140; *Chas. Morn. Post, and Daily Adv.*, Mar. 16, 1787.
77. *Chas. Morn. Post, and Daily Adv.*, Feb. 4, 1786; *Chas. Even. Gaz.*, Feb. 21, 1786.
78. Johnson, *Traditions and Reminiscences*, 137–138; Nadelhaft, *Disorders of War*, 137; Gregorie, *Thomas Sumter*, 212–213.
79. Ralph Izard to Jefferson, Apr. 27, 1784, in Boyd *et al.*, eds., *Papers of Jefferson*, VII, 130; *Chas. Even. Gaz.*, Mar. 11, 1786; William L. Smith to Edward Rutledge, July 4, 1790, William Loughton Smith Papers, SCHS.

able opposition, Gervais's plan passed both houses of the legislature, along with his proposal that the new capital be called "Columbia." In 1788, after the state building burned in Charleston, the legislature became actively interested in the move. The following year, Arthur Simkins of Ninety Six moved that a committee be formed to bring in a bill for the removal of public records to Columbia. The House concurred only because twenty-one of ninety-three coastal representatives joined their unanimous backcountry colleagues. Only one Charlestonian supported the Columbia move, but the parishes of Beaufort and Georgetown split their votes, with seven supporting and eight opposing Simkins's proposal. When, in 1789, both houses finally agreed to a convention bill, nineteen of sixty-five coastal representatives (including only two from the city of Charleston) joined their backcountry colleagues in making Columbia the convention site.[80]

Backcountry representatives won support for a convention and an inland capital, but they did not succeed in gaining control of the reform process itself. Although the legislature voted to locate the convention in Columbia, it also provided that each parish and district could send only as many delegates as it had representatives and senators. The backcountry, in 1789, had been allotted six additional representatives and two senators for the new counties of Pendleton and Greenville, but apportionment at the convention placed the lowcountry firmly in control.[81]

The result was that the State Constitutional Convention of 1790 made markedly limited concessions to the backcountry contingent, which had pressed for reform. Coastal delegates succeeded in their efforts to reduce the size of the lower house from 202 members (or 208 in 1789) to 125. At the same time, they increased Senate membership from 29 (31 in 1789) to 37. By apportioning representation on a combination of wealth and population, the convention allotted the backcountry 54 seats in the lower house and 17 seats in the Senate. Delegates tried to guard against future democratic innovations by creating a cumbersome amendment procedure, failing to provide for reapportionment, and defeating backcountry efforts to make population the basis of representation. They also left property requirements for voting and officeholding unchanged. The only issue that "produced some warmth" was a move to establish Columbia as the new capital. Delegates approved the move by a margin of only four votes.[82]

80. Nadelhaft, *Disorders of War*, 137, 201; House Jour., Jan. 23, 1789.
81. House Jour., Mar. 4, 1789; Cooper and McCord, *Statutes of South Carolina*, V, 82.
82. Cooper and McCord, eds., *Statutes of South Carolina*, I, 184–193; David Duncan Wallace, *The South Carolina Constitution of 1895* (Columbia, S.C., 1927), 12–14; *City Gaz., and Daily Adv.*, May 26, June 1, 1790; *St. Gaz. of South-Carolina*, June 3, 1790.

Backcountry representatives won some significant concessions at the State Constitutional Convention of 1790. With Columbia established as the new state capital, backcountry legislators were less likely to be absent from legislative sessions. Distance would now work to the disadvantage of the coastal contingent. Although the inland districts, with four-fifths of the white population in 1790, still controlled less than half of the lower house, representatives from Charleston and the surrounding parishes (Charleston District) declined from 46 percent of the lower house in 1789 to about 38 percent in 1790. At the same time, Beaufort and Georgetown grew in influence, from 14 percent in 1789 to 18 percent in 1790. As Jerome J. Nadelhaft points out, Georgetown and Beaufort, together with the backcountry, had the power to control the state government.[83]

The problem, from the point of view of the majority of backcountry representatives, was that Georgetown and Beaufort were far from reliable backcountry allies, particularly on matters involving reapportionment itself. Although inland and coastal representatives joined together on a number of issues during the 1780s and 1790s, backcountry efforts to achieve further reform in the system of apportionment met with solid opposition in the legislature for nearly two decades following the State Constitutional Convention of 1790. Not until 1808 did inland leaders win sufficient support from the coastal parishes to effect another, more substantial change in the system of representation.

In retrospect, the South Carolina Constitution of 1790 represented a step toward the political unification of South Carolina's planter class, but contemporaries saw it as a qualified triumph for the coastal planters and merchants who had long dominated the state government. William L. Smith was disturbed that Columbia was to be the new capital and enraged "at the almost incredible treachery" of the lowcountry delegates who voted against their region. At the same time, he believed that the new Constitution was "much better than the former one," and he was able to compliment Edward Rutledge and other delegates "whose labors obtained such advantages for the low country." Along with Smith, Gadsden had hoped that the legislature would be even further reduced in size and wished that the governor's veto had been restored, but he was less concerned about "the fixing of the Seat of Government," which he considered "rather a matter of Conveniency." As

---

83. Nadelhaft, *Disorders of War*, 202–211. For earlier interpretations, see William A. Schaper, *Sectionalism and Representation in South Carolina* (New York, 1968 [orig. publ. Washington, D.C., 1901]), 380; John Harold Wolfe, *Jeffersonian Democracy in South Carolina* (Chapel Hill, N.C., 1940), 47; Wallace, *S.C. Constitution*, 12–14.

of May 30, 1790, Gadsden was "far from thinking" the new Constitution "a Bad one."[84]

viii

The State Constitutional Convention of 1790 capped a decade in which the coast-dominated legislature succeeded in quelling opposition to civil authority and limiting challenges to the Charleston-area elite by making limited concessions to opposition groups. With the backcountry smoldering in the aftermath of a near–civil war, the government managed to contain violence by establishing inland courts, passing a vagrancy law, and adopting confiscation and amercement schemes. The legislature quelled an artisan opposition movement by reorganizing the city government. In 1785, with debtors closing courts throughout the state, the legislature passed a series of limited debtor measures that answered to the needs of wealthy planters. It also established a county court system that benefited the small-scale debtors and creditors who dominated the backcountry. Angered by the limited response to postwar grievances, backcountry settlers pressed for reapportionment, but, again, the legislature succeeded in containing the opposition without relinquishing the authority of the coastal planters and merchants who continued to wield power beyond their numbers under the second South Carolina Constitution.

The success of South Carolina's new government derived not only or even primarily from the savvy of the state's political leaders. Throughout the decade, interregional alliances were promoting limited compromise. Lowcountry representatives, particularly from the distant coastal parishes, joined the backcountry on a number of key debtor votes, and—much to the dismay of William L. Smith—coastal defectors enabled backcountry leaders to win a state convention and an inland capital. At the same time, a small contingent of inland leaders from the middlecountry and the western piedmont were consistently voting in opposition to their own region. By 1790, members of this group were already becoming the mediators between the backcountry and the coastal leadership.

The clearest testimony to the limits of constitutional reform is that backcountry leaders renewed the struggle for reapportionment within four years of the first Columbia convention. Smith and Gadsden may have underestimated the advantages accorded to backcountry representatives by the Con-

84. William L. Smith to Edward Rutledge, June 28, July 4, Aug. 8, 1790, Smith Papers; Gadsden to Thomas Morris, May 30, 1790, in Walsh, ed., *Writings of Gadsden*, 251.

stitution of 1790, but they were correct in observing that the convention had retained coastal control of the state government. During the 1790s, in clear sectional votes, the legislature defeated each move toward reform. The important question to ask is, not simply how backcountry representatives continued their advance to the constitutional reform of 1808, but why that reform did not come sooner than it did.

CHAPTER 5

Backcountry Republicans

Political leaders of the South Carolina backcountry shared with other Americans of the post-Revolutionary generation a network of assumptions about government, power, liberty, and property. They believed that property was essential to individual liberty and that a just government would necessarily protect the independence of its citizens by safeguarding their possessions from arbitrary seizure. Fearful of governmental corruption, they thought that popular representation, grounded in an independent and hence virtuous citizenry, was the best defense against despotism. They looked with suspicion upon inherited political privilege and sought to stifle signs of incipient "aristocracy" in their own midst. At the same time, they feared unrestrained majority rule because the resulting "anarchy" would prove ripe ground for demagogues who, in turn, could threaten the very independence that they designed their government to protect.[1]

1. In a classic article, Robert M. Weir analyzed the way in which South Carolina's pre-Revolutionary political elite used "the country ideology" and approximated an elite republican ideal. See Weir, " 'The Harmony We Were Famous For': An Interpretation of Pre-Revolutionary South Carolina Politics," *WMQ*, 3d Ser., XXVI (1969), 473–501. Other invaluable explorations of 18th-century republicanism are J.G.A. Pocock's seminal article, "Machiavelli, Harrington, and English Political Ideologies in the Eighteenth Century," *WMQ*, 3d Ser., XXII (1965), 549–583; Gordon S. Wood, *The Creation of the American Republic, 1776–1787* (Chapel Hill, N.C., 1969); Edmund S. Morgan, *American Slavery, American Freedom: The Ordeal of Colonial Virginia* (New York, 1975); David Brion Davis, *The Problem of Slavery in the Age of Revolution, 1770–1823* (Ithaca, N.Y., 1975), esp. 164–212, 255–342; Drew R. McCoy, *The Elusive Republic: Political Economy in Jeffersonian America* (Chapel Hill, N.C., 1980). For a useful discussion of the earlier historiography of American republicanism, see Robert E. Shalhope, "Toward a Republican Synthesis: The Emergence of an Understanding of Republicanism in American Historiography," *WMQ*, 3d Ser., XXIX (1972), 49–80. I have also relied heavily on Donald L. Robinson, *Slavery in the Structure of American Politics, 1765–1820* (New York, 1971), esp. 54–97. Republicanism, in its various 18th-century guises, described and reinforced a world in which the household, or "family," remained the primary context of production and in which male heads of households entered the politi-

Republican political ideas, as interpreted by South Carolina's leaders, reflected and reinforced a confident commitment to slavery. The notion of independence that formed the bulwark of their political vision presumed that the social order consisted in relations of inequality. South Carolina leaders assumed, in other words, that men who entered the political arena as citizens would be presiding over households composed of dependents. Throughout the later years of the eighteenth century, no state representative questioned the assumption that independence was a prerequisite to citizenship; no one openly proposed an extension of political rights to dependent household members, black or white. South Carolinians debated the extent of political equality only with respect to independent white men.

Nonetheless, the network of republican symbols and assumptions that linked coastal and inland representatives in their fundamental commitment to slavery also allowed considerable room for contention. In the twenty-five years following the Revolution, it became clear that South Carolinians, along with other Americans, differed in their image of what form the new state and national governments should take. Inland settlers, together with artisans in the port city of Charleston, pressed for democratic reforms intended to make the state government more representative of its independent citizenry. Backcountry leaders, sensitive to the inclinations of their predominantly yeoman constituency and eager for access to the center of state power, subscribed to a particular formulation of republican thought that enraged many of their coastal counterparts.

i

The political outlook that distinguished inland leaders from most of their coastal counterparts derived in part from their distinctive position as slaveholders in a predominantly yeoman region. Whereas the majority of lowcountry South Carolinians continued to live amid an overwhelming black majority, the backcountry remained, at the turn of the century, a predominantly white yeoman area. By 1800, slaves in the lowcountry (excluding the city of Charleston) composed about 84 percent of that region's total popu-

---

cal arena as citizens. It was no coincidence that republicanism remained the dominant language of politics in antebellum South Carolina. See, especially, Drew Gilpin Faust, *James Henry Hammond and the Old South: A Design for Mastery* (Baton Rouge, La., 1982); Lacy K. Ford, Jr., "Social Origins of a New South Carolina: The Upcountry in the Nineteenth Century" (Ph.D. diss., University of South Carolina, 1983), esp. 517–582. See also Ford, *Origins of Southern Radicalism: The South Carolina Upcountry, 1800– 1860* (Oxford, 1988), which appeared as this work was going into production.

lation. In the upcountry, slaves composed 17 percent of the total population.[2]

Regional differences lay not only in the number of slaves relative to whites but in the proportion and nature of slaveowning households (see table 8). In 1800, slaveholders composed more than two-thirds of all households in the parishes surrounding and south of the city of Charleston. More than a third of all households in the same region included at least twenty slaves, and more than two-thirds included more than five slaves. Although the proportion of upcountry slaveholders had grown during the course of the preceding decade—from 23 percent in 1790 to 28 percent in 1800—the region was still a predominantly nonslaveholding area. Less than 1 percent of all upcountry households included at least twenty slaves, and two-thirds of all slaveholders held fewer than five slaves.[3] In short, the upcountry remained a region in which the vast majority of households continued to operate without help from slaves. The majority of slaveholders continued to work in the fields, and substantial planters were extremely scarce by comparison with the coastal parishes.

The lower backcountry, or middlecountry, remained, in 1800, a transitional area. Slaves in that region composed about a third of the whole population, and slaveholders composed about a third of all households. But these composite figures somewhat obscure the fact that the spread of cotton culture into the lower part of the old circuit court district of Camden—including Camden itself, the new state capital, and the area formerly designated as the High Hills of Santee—was transforming much of that region into a slave-plantation area. By 1800, slaves in the lower part of Camden District composed two-fifths of the population, and more than two-fifths of the area's households included slaves.[4]

These figures should not be used to suggest that the backcountry and lowcountry were entirely distinct or to minimize the yeoman influence on the coast. With a proportionately smaller slave population than the parishes to the south, the coastal region north of Charleston (Georgetown District) shared many characteristics with the middlecountry, particularly lower Camden.[5] Georgetown's slave population composed about 53 percent of the whole, and slaveholders composed about 52 percent of all households.[6]

2. Federal Population Census, South Carolina, 1800, NA microfilm.
3. *Ibid.*
4. *Ibid.*
5. This region was designated as Georgetown District until the Court Act of 1800 divided it into two districts, Marion and Georgetown.
6. Federal Population Census, South Carolina, 1800.

Table 8. Distribution of Slaveowning Households, 1790, 1800

Region	Proportion of Slaveowning Households, by No. of Slaves					No. of Households
	0	1–4	5–19	20+	Total	
1790						
Lowcountry						
Southern coastal parishes (Beaufort District)	40%	17%	18%	25%	100%	966
Central coastal parishes[a]	28	16	25	31	100	1,924
St. Philip and St. Michael parishes	35	31	31	2	99	1,869
Northern coastal parishes (Georgetown District)	54	17	19	10	100	1,876
Middlecountry						
Orangeburg	71	16	10	3	100	2,387
Cheraws	72	15	10	3	100	1,344
Lower Camden	75	11	11	3	100	2,079
Upcountry	77	16	7	1	101	13,591
1800						
Lowcountry						
Central and southern coastal parishes[a]	30	20	14	36	100	3,774
Northern coastal parishes	52	17	20	11	100	1,969
Middlecountry						
Orangeburg	69	19	10	2	100	2,738
Cheraws	70	16	12	2	100	2,202
Lower Camden and Lancaster	58	19	17	6	100	2,755
Upcountry	72	18	9	1	100	19,094

Sources: U.S., Bureau of the Census, *Heads of Families at the First Census of the United States Taken in the Year 1790: South Carolina* (Washington, D.C., 1908); Federal Population Census, South Carolina, 1800, NA microfilm.

[a] Excluding St. Philip and St. Michael parishes.

Although convergences between the northern coastal region and the middlecountry influenced the political behavior of representatives from both areas, much of the backcountry remained, throughout the early years of the nineteenth century, a yeoman area in which small-scale farming and household manufactures predominated. Even in the lower part of old Camden District—the backcountry region where slavery had made deepest inroads—substantial planters were scarce by comparison with the coastal parishes. Only 6 percent of Camden-area households included at least twenty slaves, as compared to 11 percent of all households in Georgetown District.[7]

An observer who traveled through South Carolina during the mid-1790s noted the farm economy that prevailed in the backcountry and distinguished that region from the coastal parishes.

> In the middle, and especially in the upper country, the people are obliged to manufacture their own cotton and woollen cloths, and most of their husbandry tools; but in the lower country the inhabitants, for these articles, depend almost entirely on their merchants. Late accounts . . . inform us, that the inhabitants manufacture, entirely in the family way, as much as they have occasion for.

Thomas Sumter was singing the praises of his own region when, in 1800, he made a public toast to "the yeomanry, mechanics and manufactures of the United States, whose intelligence and patriotism support our constitution as their labors do our lives."[8]

In one important respect, the backcountry's political leadership differed from the majority of those whom they represented: of the more than 350 backcountrymen who served in the state legislature from 1786 to 1808, only 11 (6 from the middlecountry and 5 from the upcountry) were non-slaveholders. The South Carolina constitutions of 1776, 1778, and 1790 established stiff property requirements for officeholders that virtually ensured the state government would be dominated by slaveholding representatives. Appointed by the legislature, county judges were drawn almost exclusively from the ranks of slaveholders. Not until 1808 did South Carolina voters elect their own sheriffs, and, even then, successful candidates had to post bonds of sufficient size to ensure that only wealthy men or their friends would ever run for the office.[9]

Nonetheless, deep identifications bound the backcountry's slavehold-

7. *Ibid.*
8. William Winterbotham, *An Historical, Geographical, Commercial, and Philosophical View of the American United States, and of the European Settlements* . . . (London, 1795), III, 255; *City Gazette, and the Daily Advertiser* (Charleston), July 21, 1800.
9. Thomas Cooper and David J. McCord, eds., *The Statutes at Large of South Caro-*

ing leadership and nonslaveholding majority and distanced both from the coastal elite. With few exceptions, the wealthiest and most prominent backcountry political figures had arisen from humble origins, at least by the standards of coastal leaders. Even such leading men as Wade Hampton, Thomas Sumter, and John Chesnut had received little, if any, formal education. Although prominent backcountry families held slaves before their arrival in South Carolina, most, like the Calhouns, had been small-scale planters.

Prosperous by comparison with their own constituency, inland leaders were, for the most part, considerably less opulent than their coastal counterparts, and that distinction contributed to the divergence between coastal and backcountry political outlooks. Andrew Pickens, for example, was one of the most widely respected inland leaders and, with thirty-three slaves in 1790, the most substantial planter in Pendleton County. When he was elected to the United States House of Representatives in 1793, Pickens was living in a two-story house that, according to the Charlestonian William L. Smith, contained "decent" if "not elegant" furnishings. One of Pickens's counterparts on the coast was Ralph Izard, who, as the most substantial slaveholder of his parish, held more than five hundred slaves at his various residences. His home plantation at Goose Creek was a showplace, with artfully designed gardens, walkways, and fruit groves. Ralph Izard was not typical even of his region, but, as a group, coastal representatives were wealthier than their backcountry counterparts. The lowcountrymen who served in the state legislature from 1786 to 1808 eventually accumulated, on average, more than one hundred slaves. Their middlecountry counterparts accumulated an average of fifty, and the upcountrymen accumulated only twenty-three (see table 9).[10]

Coastal representatives also had more formal education than their backcountry counterparts. Most wealthy South Carolinians received their education at or close to home, but at least forty-seven (nearly 10 percent) of the lowcountry group had received legal, medical, or a general university education abroad, and at least twenty-three attended American colleges.

---

lina (Columbia, S.C., 1836–1841), I, 131–132, 138–141, 184–186, V, 257–259, 669–670, VI, 122, 142.

10. U.S., Bureau of the Census, *Heads of Families at the First Census of the United States Taken in the Year 1790: South Carolina* (Washington, D.C., 1908) (hereafter cited as *Heads of Families, 1790*); George C. Rogers, Jr., *Evolution of a Federalist: William Loughton Smith of Charleston (1758–1812)* (Columbia, S.C., 1962), 127, 244; Walter B. Edgar *et al.*, eds., *Biographical Directory of the South Carolina House of Representatives* (Columbia, S.C., 1974–1984), II, III, IV; Federal Population Census, South Carolina, 1800, 1810, NA microfilm.

Table 9. Slaveowning by Representatives in the
South Carolina House, 1786–1808

Region	No. of Representatives	Average No. of Slaves Held near to Term	Average Maximum No. of Slaves Owned
Lowcountry	473	86	103
Middlecountry	179	36	50
Upcountry	177	17	23

Sources: Walter B. Edgar *et al.*, eds., *Biographical Directory of the South Carolina House of Representatives* (Columbia, S.C., 1974–1984); U.S., Bureau of the Census, *Heads of Families at the First Census of the United States Taken in the Year 1790: South Carolina* (Washington, D.C., 1908); Federal Population Census, South Carolina, 1800, 1810, NA microfilm.

Eighty-four (nearly 18 percent) were lawyers or physicians. Lawyers and physicians were also well represented among the backcountry contingent. Fifteen (8 percent) of the upcountrymen and twenty (11 percent) of the middlecountry group were trained in those professions. Only seven upcountry and seven middlecountry representatives, however, can be identified as having attended colleges or universities, and of these only one (the son of Joseph Kershaw) received his education abroad.[11]

Not surprisingly, state representatives reflected the religious and ethnic affiliations that characterized their respective regions. More than two-thirds of the 150 lowcountry representatives whose religious affiliation can be identified were Episcopalian, and three-fifths of those whose birthplace can be identified were native lowcountrymen. Backcountry representatives came from markedly different backgrounds. Those from the upcountry were predominantly Presbyterian, but middlecountry representatives were more evenly divided between High Church and various dissenting groups. The birthplace of backcountry representatives is more difficult to deter-

---

By the first decade of the 19th century, backcountry representatives were still far behind their coastal counterparts in the acquisition of slaves. Of those representatives who served in the House of Representatives at some time from 1786 through 1800 (7th–13th sessions of the lower house), the lowcountry group eventually accumulated an average of 105 slaves; middlecountrymen accumulated an average of 48 slaves; and upcountrymen accumulated an average of 22 slaves. Of those representatives who served in the legislature at some time between 1800 and 1808, the lowcountry group accumulated an average of 107 slaves; middlecountrymen accumulated an average of 61 slaves; and upcountrymen accumulated an average of 25 slaves. Edgar *et al.*, eds., *Biographical Directory of the House*, II, III, IV: *Heads of Families, 1790*; Federal Population Census, South Carolina, 1800, 1810.

11. Edgar *et al.*, eds., *Biographical Directory of the House*, II, III, IV.

Backcountry Republicans

Table 10. Birthplace of Representatives in
the South Carolina House, 1786–1800

| | Representatives, by Region | | | | | |
| | Lowcountry | | Middlecountry | | Upcountry | |
Birthplace	No.[a]	Share	No.[b]	Share	No.[c]	Share
Backcountry	1	1%	8	14%	7	9%
Lowcountry	75	60	9	16	0	0
Colonies or states north of South Carolina	19	15	30	53	58	71
England	12	10	3	5	4	5
Ireland	6	5	3	5	11	13
Other	11	9	4	7	2	2

Sources: Walter B. Edgar *et al.*, eds., *Biographical Directory of the South Carolina House of Representatives* (Columbia, S.C., 1974–1984); U.S., Bureau of the Census, *Heads of Families at the First Census of the United States Taken in the Year 1790: South Carolina* (Washington, D.C., 1908); Federal Population Census, South Carolina, 1800, 1810, NA microfilm.
[a]349 unidentified representatives are excluded from calculations.
[b]121 unidentified representatives are excluded from calculations.
[c]177 unidentified representatives are excluded from calculations.

mine, but more than half of those whose birthplace can be identified were migrants from states to the north of South Carolina (see table 10).[12]

Despite the obvious gap between the prosperous inland leadership and the nonslaveholding backcountry majority, the two groups could still feel a greater identification with each other than with the established coastal families that dominated the state government. Robert Anderson inadvertently linked the experience of inland voters and representatives when, at the State Constitutional Convention of 1790, he observed that "those who held lands below were opulent, many of their ancestors in the class of original settlers of the soil, long in possession of various advantages," whereas backcountry settlers "were new comers, who had not time to accumulate much wealth." Edward Hooker, a New Englander who traveled through the backcountry during 1805 and 1806, noted the same distinction. Describing the representatives who assembled at Columbia, he observed that "some have showy and costly dresses; but not a small number are plain, rustic sort of folks dressed in their own manufactures. Some

12. *Ibid.*

speak like foreigners, as they probably are: Some have the polished language of the Charlestonians: and Some the Coarser and more blunt language of the mountaineers."[13]

The political style and rhetoric that characterized inland representatives grew out of their complex relationship with yeomen constituents. Edward Hooker, a Federalist, observed the process with some dismay. Upon his arrival at the Pendleton plantation of John Taylor, a militia major, state representative, and owner of about thirty slaves, Hooker found "a worthless, drinking, brawling fellow at the house whom Taylor evidently wished to have gone, but did not like to order away." Hooker suspected that Taylor was fearful of losing his reputation as "a *lover of the people.*" The man shook hands with Taylor "three or four times as if about to go—came back again—called him Jack Taylor and took the liberties of a familiar friend."[14] Prominent backcountrymen knew that such demonstrative respect for the yeomanry was the price of local influence.

Inland representatives adopted a style of studied simplicity. Wade Hampton, who would own, by 1810, more than six hundred slaves and thousands of backcountry acres, was, according to Hooker, "a great enemy to finery and treats it with marked contempt." The colonel dressed "in good clothes" but had "nothing showy about him." Wade Hampton's brother was also "a very plain man," and Hooker observed that "everything connected with his domestic arrangements seems to be on a plain and economical scale." The younger Hampton showed Hooker a suit of clothes that had been "made in his own family." Samuel Mays, a militia colonel and state representative with several upcountry plantations and more than seventy slaves, also modeled his life on a vision of republican simplicity. Hooker, who visited Mays's Saluda River plantation, noted that the colonel, "though wealthy, for the upper country . . . lives in a one Story house, that has only plain window shutters, without glass windows." Mays told Hooker that he "often labors himself, as do other farmers in his neighborhood," and his respect for productive labor extended to other members of the household. Hooker was particularly impressed by Mays's daughters, who, "while sitting by the fireside in the evening, were at the same time engaged in knitting." In another room, someone was at work on a spinning wheel.[15]

13. *City Gaz., and Daily Adv.*, May 21, 1790; Edward Hooker, Journal, Nov. 23, 1805, I, 136, CHS. Edited selections from the journal have been published: see J. Franklin Jameson, ed., "Diary of Edward Hooker, 1805–1808," American Historical Association, *Annual Report, 1896*, (Washington, D.C., 1897), I, 842–929. References are to the manuscript.

14. Edgar *et al.*, eds., *Biographical Directory of the House*, IV, 553; Hooker, Journal, Sept. 29, 1805, I, 74.

15. Hooker, Journal, Nov. 5, 1805, Jan., Feb. 17, 1806, I, 94–95, II, 33, 50–51.

There is no reason to think that Samuel Mays and the Hampton brothers were insincere in their show of moderation, but they undoubtedly knew that those who bore the marks of ostentation were subject to ridicule by the voters. In the midst of a congressional election, Hooker overheard two piedmont farmers joking about the three candidates. Lemuel Alston, the wealthiest, was, according to the farmers, "in favor of the Stamp Act and too rich a man."[16]

The son of a middlecountry planter recalled comparable class resentment in the neighborhood where he grew up. High Hills had long been one of the wealthiest plantation areas of the middlecountry, and, by the turn of the century, it was attracting wealthy coastal families for summer and permanent residence. Apparently the people of Salem and the Black River area were "averse from the people of the Hills, as being too aristocratic."[17] The political style that prevailed among backcountry representatives was, in part, a response to precisely that sort of sentiment among the yeoman majority.

Backcountry spokesmen emphasized ties between representatives and constituents in their own region by portraying the backcountry as a bastion of republican simplicity and the coast as a scene of opulent decadence. They made physical health a metaphor for republican virtue by contrasting their own salubrious climate to hazardous conditions in the lowcountry. Describing the Pacolet Springs of the upper piedmont, a published letter from Ninety Six observed in 1786 that nature had "been abundantly kind to this part of our globe; and did men but once learn to pursue happiness rather than riches, and to enjoy life, than to spend it in dissipation and luxury, this would be the place that would gratify the pursuit, or answer the end proposed." Seven years later, an upcountry grand jury invited coastal residents to "come and taste the sweet waters flowing from the pure and rapid springs of our Blue Mountains," to "behold the ruddy faces of our children," and to "make the *experiment* of health!"[18]

A keynote of backcountry republicanism was its emphasis on the "aristocracy of talent" and glorification of simple virtues believed to derive from productive labor rather than from wealth, station, or education. In 1784, Thomas Sumter had expressed the prevailing outlook by observing that the

16. *Ibid.*, Sept. 22, 1806, II, 134.

17. William M. Wightman, *Life of William Capers, D.D., One of the Bishops of the Methodist Episcopal Church, South; Including an Autobiography* (Nashville, Tenn., 1859), 50.

18. *South-Carolina Evening Gazette*, Jan. 23, 1786; *State Gazette of South-Carolina* (Charleston), June 28, 1793. See also *South-Carolina Gazette* (Charleston), July 23, 1772.

people of his district, despite their "defects in point of *literary* merit," were "replete with *native* good sense, mother wit, unshaken fortitude, and anti-torified and anti-aristocratical principles." Nearly twenty years later, he repeated his call for ability, rather than station, as a criterion for leadership. "I have," wrote Sumter, "beheld *there* [abroad] war and desolation wielding a general and premature destruction—while *here* I have beheld my fellow citizens, happy in the enjoyment of equal rights, everyone rising in proportion to his talents." In 1793, grand jurors from the upcountry district of Washington urged the judge to "dispense with formalities," noting that "men should be only distinguished by their virtues." Addressing his constituents in 1804, Robert Anderson observed that he was "for all mankind the poor equal with the rich, enjoying equal rights in every respect both civil and religious."[19]

Differences between coastal and inland republicanism on this point were more a matter of degree than of kind. Not all coastal representatives would have disagreed with the celebration of talent over the advantages of birth, but leading coastal conservatives were straightforward in expressing their suspicion of the backcountry position. Ralph Izard disdained the prevailing inland outlook when, in 1785, he complained to Thomas Jefferson: "Our governments tend too much to Democracy. A handicraftsman thinks an apprenticeship necessary to make him acquainted with his business. But our back countrymen are of opinion that a politician may be born such (sic) as well as a poet." Francis Kinloch, a coastal planter and merchant with more than two hundred slaves, expressed the extreme position that Sumter and others were up against. Kinloch was an open advocate of monarchy who sought for his children "all the Rights to rank, and distinction, which is to be claimed from Ancestry."[20]

Such inland leaders as Sumter and Anderson were not, of course, attacking wealth and hierarchy per se. Their democratic-republican vision focused on equal political rights among citizens, and their calls for an "aristocracy of talent" actually sanctioned the position of wealthy backcountrymen who had, presumably, attained independence through ability and good character

19. *Gazette of the State of South-Carolina* (Charleston), Apr. 29, 1784; campaign broadside, May 1, 1802, Thomas Sumter Papers, II, LC; *St. Gaz. of South Carolina*, June 28, 1793; speech by Robert Anderson, Aug. 16, 1804, Robert Anderson Papers, SCL.

20. Ralph Izard to Thomas Jefferson, June 10, 1785, "The Letters of Ralph Izard," *SCHM*, II (1901), 197; Francis Kinloch to Thomas Boone, May 26, 1788, in Felix Gilbert, ed., "Letters of Francis Kinloch to Thomas Boone," *Journal of Southern History*, VIII (1942), 104. According to the federal census of 1790, Kinloch had 212 slaves in Prince George, Winyah, Parish and 12 slaves in Charleston. His guardian was the former royal governor, Thomas Boone, and he received legal training at the Inns of Court. *Heads of Families, 1790*; Edgar *et al.*, eds., *Biographical Directory of the House*, III, 402–405.

rather than through the advantages of birth. Property qualifications for voting and officeholding remained unchallenged until the first decade of the nineteenth century, and inland representatives assumed that men of wealth would best be able to carry out the responsibilities of office.

It would, in fact, be misleading to describe political practices in the post-Revolutionary backcountry as *democratic* in any modern sense of that word: not only were slaves, women, and propertyless men excluded from political participation, but local leaders extended their personal influence over the election process itself. The appointment, by the legislature, of three or more local managers for each election site enabled representatives to ensure that elections in their respective districts would be supervised by people whom they knew and trusted. It was no coincidence that managers were generally drawn from the ranks of planters and prosperous slaveholding yeomen. As a mark of trust, the very appointment as manager of an election reinforced ties of obligation between the particular representatives and appointees. In part because backcountry districts were so large, the legislature often designated private houses, in addition to county courts, as official polling places.[21] Presumably, location contributed to the choice of election sites, but here, too, representatives were able to exercise some control over the election process.

As one contested election suggests, managers held considerable power despite the apparent prevalence of ballot box voting. In January 1791, Henry Felder, an Orangeburg planter with twenty-one slaves, complained of misbehavior on the part of the election manager Samuel Rowe. Rowe was a neighboring planter with seventeen slaves. According to Felder, Rowe had taken it upon himself to appoint William Steel, another planter, as a replacement for the second official manager, a man who was too ill to preside at the election. Then, Rowe and Steel had "opened the Tickets, and read the Names of the persons wrote on the Tickets, before they put them into the Balloting Box." Felder insisted that a man sitting beside the managers had simply removed those ballots that Rowe and Steel "did not like and offered other tickets in lieu thereof." The House Committee on Privileges and Elections decided that Rowe had done nothing more than to help illiterate

21. Election managers and election sites were generally listed in the legislative journals. See, for example, South Carolina House of Representatives Journal, Nov. 3, 1788, Dec. 20, 1791, in Theodora J. Thompson *et al.*, eds., *Journals of the House of Representatives*, The State Records of South Carolina (Columbia, S.C., 1977–), *1787–1788*, 625–626, *1791*, 437–441; South Carolina House of Representatives Journal, Dec. 19, 1807, SCDAH (hereafter cited as House Jour.); *Heads of Families, 1790*; Federal Population Census, South Carolina, 1800.

voters put their ballots in appropriate boxes. It declared the election results legitimate.[22]

Whether or not Felder's complaint was justified, the incident reveals a great deal about election practices in the backcountry. In the first place, the House committee, despite its observation that "the opening of Votes tends to defeat the benefits of Voting by ballot," failed to prohibit the practice. It simply "recommended that the opening of Votes on any account, be, at any future election discouraged by the Managers and Voters at such elections." Apparently the representatives allowed for the possibility that managers, under certain circumstances, might find it necessary to bend the rules. Second, the incident points to the special vulnerability of illiterate voters and the capacity of managers to manipulate their votes. Given the small size of voter turnouts, several altered ballots could make a great difference.[23]

In retrospect what seems most striking about the dispute was Felder's failure to point out that Samuel Rowe was himself a candidate in the contested election. The House committee also failed to notice the apparent conflict of interest when it proclaimed Rowe "duely elected to Represent the District of Orange." Just how common it was for managers to preside over their own elections remains a question, but we can be sure that Rowe was not alone. In 1807, Reuben Arthur, a planter with thirty slaves, managed a Kershaw election that ended with him as one of the victorious candidates for a seat in state legislature. There is no evidence that anyone saw the procedure as improper.[24] The point is that managers, whether or not they served simultaneously as candidates, were part of a system in which representatives and other leading men extended their influence to the polls. At the very least, the elections of Rowe and Arthur suggest that backcountry-men expected or tolerated the presence of candidates at election sites, and it

22. House Jour., Jan. 15, 19, 1791, in Thompson *et al.*, eds., *Journals of the House, 1791*, 15, 81.

23. *Ibid.*, 81. Given the scarcity of early backcountry election returns and tax records, it is not possible to be precise in determining voter turnout. Nonetheless, scattered returns are suggestive. The winning candidates in the election protested by Henry Felder won 78 and 75 votes, respectively. In 1790, winning candidates to the state House of Representatives from Spartanburg received 219 and 152 votes respectively. The federal census of 1790 listed about 1,200 adult males in Spartanburg, of whom not all could have been eligible to vote. Returns for Spartanburg County and Orange Parish, Election Returns, 1790, nos. 20, 37, SCDAH; *Heads of Families, 1790*.

24. House Jour., Jan. 19, 1791, in Thompson *et al.*, eds., *Journals of the House, 1791*, 81; House Jour., Dec. 19, 1807; Edgar *et al.*, eds., *Biographical Directory of the House*, III, 619–620, IV, 42; *Heads of Families, 1790*; Federal Population Census, South Carolina, 1810.

was precisely that sort of influence that South Carolinians, from all regions of the state, apparently took for granted.

The pervasive custom of "treating" also testifies to the personal influence that characterized relations between representatives and constituents in the backcountry and, it seems, throughout the eighteenth- and early nineteenth-century South. Apparently, candidates for election would personally treat the voters to liquor on or before election day. During the congressional campaign of 1806, Edward Hooker noted with disgust that the incumbent and victor, Elias Earle, "presided over the Whiskey jugs himself. Standing behind it like a shop boy behind his counter and dealing out to any who would honor him so much to come up and partake of his liberality." The New Englander was alarmed by the "ludicrous" scene and especially by Earle, who *"loved the people more than any of them."* Two years later, a speaker at Pendleton's Hopewell Academy solemnly observed that "of all the despicable modes of obtaining votes, that of doing it by the distribution of liquor and promoting intoxication is the worst." Nonetheless, another Pendleton resident believed in 1810 that the practice was on the rise. "How often," he queried, "do we see men selling their liberty of choice for the lowest of all prices, a drink of grog?"[25]

The style of electioneering that so disgusted Edward Hooker simultaneously presented candidates as "lovers of the people" and accentuated social distinctions within the backcountry. By treating the voters to whiskey, candidates were reinforcing a system of social relations in which leading men won local influence by performing a variety of favors and necessary services for surrounding settlers. These shows of "liberality" displayed the personal power of candidates as much as they demonstrated the candidates' requisite deference to the voters. Elias Earle's ostentatious generosity on election day emphasized not only his image as a "lover of the people" but his position as one of the wealthiest and most powerful men in Pendleton.[26]

Public displays of political influence could become a point of pride for local leaders. In 1800 the Laurens District Grand Jury was distressed that there was "nothing more common, than for a militia officer to have a place appointed for his men to meet him, or some other influential character that he may appoint, in order to prepare their votes for such person or persons as he may think proper." Apparently some officers were sufficiently confident to march their men "to the very election." A few even marched with

25. Hooker, Journal, Sept. 27, 1806, I, 143–144; *Miller's Weekly Messenger* (Pendleton), Aug. 16, 1808, Sept. 29, 1810.
26. The custom of "treating" is explored in Charles S. Sydnor, *Gentlemen Freeholders: Political Practices in Washington's Virginia* (Chapel Hill, N.C., 1952); Rhys Isaac, *The Transformation of Virginia, 1740–1790* (Chapel Hill, N.C., 1982), 107–113.

their men "into the house to give their votes; as if it was an honor for them to appear at the head of the men, whose votes they had endeavored to influence."[27]

Whether or not such marches were "common," the militia did play an important role in shaping the relationship between local leaders and their yeomen constituents. Militia companies met not only at official musters but at public occasions, most notably on the Fourth of July. These events gave officers an opportunity to voice their respect for the yeomanry and to demonstrate what one backcountry correspondent described as "that cordial and brotherly esteem so characteristic of true republicans." A Fourth of July celebration held in Pendleton in 1800 was characteristic of such occasions. According to the correspondent, "Capt. Sloan's and Capt. Bar's companies of volunteer horse, with Captain Strong's company of riflemen, assembled early, to do honour to the day, and went through a variety of evolutions, under the eye of Bayles Earle, esq. their colonel." After Major John Taylor "delivered, in his animated way, an oration suited to the occasion . . . the military companies, with a body of citizens, partook of a civic feast." Concluding the many patriotic toasts was one to "the militia throughout the union—That bulwark of its country's safety."[28]

While militiamen celebrated their "brotherhood" as citizens, the very organization of militia companies embodied the unequal social relationships that republican political ideas alternatively camouflaged and justified. In effect, militia musters and other patriotic occasions reflected the tension that lay at the heart of backcountry republicanism. The planters, who generally held top-ranking positions and made the speeches on the Fourth of July, used the occasions to demonstrate their deference to the yeomanry, but in so doing they expected, and generally received, acceptance as men deserving of local influence and political position.[29] Any conflict between the militiamen's sense of fraternity and the planters' dependence on rank ap-

27. *City Gaz., and Daily Adv.*, Dec. 23, 1800.

28. *Ibid.*, Oct. 30, 1799, Aug. 7, 1800. Bayles Earle, the brother of Elias, held 24 slaves in 1800 and more than 4,000 backcountry acres. He was a state representative in 1785–1786 and served as a justice on the Spartanburg County Court from 1784 to 1791. John Taylor accumulated 33 slaves and served as a state representative from Pendleton from 1802 until 1805. See Edgar *et al.*, eds., *Biographical Directory of the House*, III, 208–209, IV, 553. For additional descriptions of backcountry Fourth of July festivities, see *City Gaz., and Daily Adv.*, July 21, 1798, July 19, 27, 1799, July 21, 1800, July 16, 1804, July 19, 1808.

29. For a discussion of the political role of militia companies in 18th-century Virginia, see Isaac, *Transformation of Virginia*, 112. I have made particular use of Edmund S. Morgan's analysis of the social and political uses of the militia. See Morgan, *Inventing the People: The Rise of Popular Sovereignty in England and America* (New York, 1988), 153–173.

pears to have paled before a common identity as independent citizens and a shared resentment against more powerful men on the coast.

In short, the distinctive political outlook that characterized inland representatives through the first decade of the nineteenth century cannot be understood independently of complex social relations that gave it meaning. Certainly, backcountry leaders had to show their respect for republican simplicity and for the majority of inland voters who lived, of necessity, in a simpler style than the people who represented them. As parvenus, excluded from the center of state power, they also shared with the yeomanry a sense of grievance against the coastal elite, a determination to expand their own representation in the state government, and an inclination to make the state and national governments more, rather than less, responsible to the citizenry. But despite their ostentatious deference to the yeomanry and repeated challenges to the coastal elite, backcountry political leaders shared the republican assumptions that defined the limits of political discourse throughout the state, and they protected the unequal social relationships that shaped their political practices.

ii

Sectional differences in political outlook were clearly apparent at the State Convention of 1787 that ratified the United States Constitution. Although the delegates who met in Charleston were, by all appearances, unanimous in their desire for congressional regulation of trade, they differed greatly in their conceptions of the national government. Fearful of federal encroachments on individual liberty and concerned that the new government would be insufficiently representative of the citizenry, most inland delegates opposed the proposed constitution. Coastal delegates, who almost unanimously favored ratification, were victorious only because representation at the convention was apportioned on the same basis as the state legislature.[30]

By 1785, South Carolina's various political factions were united in an effort to give the Confederation Congress greater power in the regulation of commerce. Angered by the loss of markets and the advantages allowed to British trade, planters, merchants, and artisans hoped that a strong congress, with powers to institute navigation laws, would help to ease the

30. The ratification process in South Carolina has been explored in Rogers, *Evolution of a Federalist*, 135–158; Jerome J. Nadelhaft, *The Disorders of War: The Revolution in South Carolina* (Orono, Maine, 1981), 173–190; Marvin R. Zahniser, *Charles Cotesworth Pinckney, Founding Father* (Chapel Hill, N.C., 1967), 87–101; Jackson Turner Main, *The Antifederalists: Critics of the Constitution, 1781–1788* (Chapel Hill, N.C., 1961); Forrest McDonald, *We the People: The Economic Origins of the Constitution* (Chicago, 1958).

state's economic crisis. Complaining that "trade with Great Britain on the present footing is ruinous and disgraceful as they have the carrying trade in their own hands, without our having any adequate counter advantage," petitioners from Camden argued that it was "highly necessary to vest congress with full powers to adopt a general system of commercial regulations for this as well as other states in the Union." Also in 1785, a "memorial of sundry persons," initiated by artisans and merchants in Charleston, urged that Congress "for a limitted time, may be vested with full power to regulate Trade" with nations that had no commercial treaties with the United States. Even the state's resident British merchants favored the proposal for congressional trade regulation, because they recognized that, under a stronger federal Congress, states would be unable to pass debtor laws such as the Sheriffs' Sale Act. In March 1787, the legislature, with near unanimity, passed an act proposing that the Articles of Confederation be altered so as to give Congress the power to regulate trade (excepting trade in slaves) for fifteen years.[31]

Fearful of social unrest within their own state, many prominent lowcountrymen hoped that a strengthened federal government would not only regulate trade but serve as a check on popular involvement in federal as well as state politics. Many had traveled north during the summer of 1786, and they were acutely aware of social disturbances beyond their own borders. Having just returned from a session of the Confederation Congress, the Charlestonian David Ramsay observed that most of the new state governments were "elective despotisms" that had "but feeble barriers against tyranny." He believed many legislators were "committing blunders from ignorance" and feared that the nation had "neither honesty nor knowledge enough for republican governments." Besieged by a mounting attack on their own leadership, members of the Charleston-area elite could easily sympathize with such northerners as John Jay, who feared that "too much" had been "expected from the Virtue and good Sense of the People."[32]

Chosen by the state legislature, South Carolina's delegation to the Consti-

31. Petition from Camden, Petitions to the General Assembly, 1785, no. 104, SCDAH (hereafter cited as Petitions); House Jour., Sept. 26, 1785, Mar. 8, 1787, in Thompson *et al.*, eds., *Journals of the House, 1785–1786*, 320, *1787–1788*, 193–194; Rogers, *Evolution of a Federalist*, 148–149; Cooper and McCord, *Statutes of South Carolina*, IV, 720. See also South Carolina Senate Journal, Sept. 29, 1785, SCDAH (hereafter cited as Senate Jour.). The "memorial of sundry persons" is identified and discussed in Nadelhaft, *Disorders of War*, 174.

32. Rogers, *Evolution of a Federalist*, 141–145; David Ramsay to Benjamin Rush, Aug. 6, 1786, in Robert L. Brunhouse, ed., *David Ramsay, 1749–1815: Selections from His Writings*, American Philosophical Society, *Transactions*, N.S., LV, pt. 4 (1965), 105; John Jay quoted in Wood, *Creation of the American Republic*, 425.

tutional Convention at Philadelphia consisted entirely of lowcountrymen. With the exception of Pierce Butler, the group was drawn from the heart of the Charleston-area elite. General Charles Cotesworth Pinckney, his younger cousin Charles Pinckney, and the former governor John Rutledge were staunch opponents of the Charleston opposition movement and of inland demands for political parity. On the defensive within their own state, they were more fearful of democracy than were their Virginia counterparts. At Philadelphia, the South Carolinians struggled simultaneously to create a strong central government in which popular involvement would be clearly delimited and to protect slavery and the slave states from federal interference.[33]

With support from the other South Carolinians, General Pinckney worked to prevent men of middling means from winning seats in the legislature and to distance the national legislature from the people at large. He spoke out against senatorial stipends, observing that as the upper house "was meant to represent the wealth of the Country, it ought to be composed of persons of wealth." The South Carolinians voted with the minority against James Madison's proposal to allow fixed salaries for representatives, and they were adamantly opposed to popular election of senators and representatives. Charles Pinckney noted that "the people were less fit Judges [in such a case]," and, along with the others, he believed that the president should be chosen by the national legislature rather than by the voting public.[34]

The South Carolinians worked to keep the central government from becoming so powerful as to threaten state (specifically, slave state) interests, but to allow it sufficient power to overcome popular rebellions. Thus General Pinckney believed that the term of senators should be shortened from six to four years so as to prevent their losing "sight of the States they represent," and Butler insisted that members of the upper house must be "controlled by the states, or they will be too independent." After failing in their attempt to prevent senators from receiving salaries, the South Carolinians argued that the stipends should be provided by the state rather than the national government. At the same time, the delegation supported the formation of a national army. The United States, according to the younger Pinckney, had "been making an experiment without it, and we see the

33. South Carolina's involvement in the Constitutional Convention is explored in Robinson, *Slavery in the Structure of American Politics*, 207–247; Ulrich B. Phillips, "The South Carolina Federalists," I, *American Historical Review*, XIV (1908–1909), 542; Zahniser, *Charles Cotesworth Pinckney*, 87–101; Nadelhaft, *Disorders of War*, 178–179; Ernest M. Lander, Jr., "The South Carolinians at the Philadelphia Convention, 1787," SCHM, LVII (1956), 134–135.

34. Max Farrand, ed., *The Records of the Federal Convention of 1787*, rev. ed. (New Haven, Conn., 1911–1937), I, 69, 91, 211, 215–216, 426.

consequence in their rapid approaches toward anarchy." South Carolina's delegates also favored a strong president. Charles Pinckney gently mocked those who feared a monarchy by observing that the Confederation Congress, if its executive powers extended to peace and war, would become "a Monarchy, of the worst kind, towit an elective one."[35]

John Rutledge and General Pinckney were explicit in drawing connections between their views on national government and their recent experiences at home. Arguing against the majority plan to make the lower house the sole originator of money bills, Rutledge observed that the "experiment in S. Carolina" had produced the "very bad" result of "continually dividing and heating the two houses." Pinckney also drew on his South Carolina experience when he suggested that national representatives be elected by the state legislatures. "An election of either branch by the people" was, he claimed, "totally impracticable," because the people in many states, particularly his own, were "scattered." He reminded the assembled delegates that the majority in South Carolina had been "notoriously for paper money." The legislature had refused the request only because it was not directly representative of the state population.[36]

Given their own political inclinations and the well-known disposition of the state's Philadelphia delegation, inland settlers were highly suspicious of the proposed constitution. When it came to a vote, delegates to the State Ratification Convention supported ratification by 149 to 73, with most of the negative votes coming from the backcountry contingent. The lowcountry supported the proposed constitution by a vote of 121 to 16, and the backcountry opposed by a vote of 57 to 28. Among the 16 coastal delegates who voted with the backcountry, 5 represented St. Bartholomew Parish, which, with its own extensive frontier area, resembled inland districts. Three others were from the distant coastal parish of Prince Frederick. Of the 28 inland delegates who favored ratification, 17 represented middle-country districts. A number of these inland Federalists were not enthusiastic in their support. Two days before the vote on ratification, Thomas Sumter, a firm Antifederalist, had proposed the convention be postponed for five months. Although the motion lost by a majority of 46, the backcountry supported Sumter by a vote of 72 to 15. In other words, a number of inland delegates who cast their votes for ratification would have preferred time for further reflection and consultation.[37]

South Carolina's state leadership debated the proposed constitution first

35. *Ibid.*, I, 64–65, 409, 434, II, 332; Zahniser, *Charles Cotesworth Pinckney*, 93–96.
36. Farrand, ed., *Records of the Federal Convention*, I, 137, II, 279–280.
37. Jonathan Elliot, ed., *The Debates in the Several State Conventions on the Adoption of the Federal Constitution . . .*, 2d ed. (Philadelphia, 1941 [orig. publ. Philadelphia,

in the legislature and later at the State Ratification Convention, but back-country Antifederalists, overwhelmed or intimidated by their coastal counterparts, said little in either forum. They allowed Rawlins Lowndes, the only Antifederalist member of the Charleston contingent, to speak for the opposition. Lowndes focused his critique on what he saw as an ominous threat to slave state interests. He argued that, under the proposed constitution, the northern states could be expected to have a stronger voice than the southern states in both the executive and legislative branches of the federal government. Given the proposed extension of federal powers, southern states would be vulnerable on several fronts. "The Northern States," suggested Lowndes, "would so predominate as to divest us of any pretensions to the title of a republic." In drawing attention to the proposed ban on the slave trade, Lowndes articulated his key concern: "Why confine us to twenty years, or rather why limit us at all? . . . They [the northern states] don't like our slaves, because they have none themselves, and therefore want to exclude us from this great advantage."[38]

James Lincoln, owner of thirty-three slaves in Abbeville County, was the only backcountry representative to speak at length during South Carolina's constitutional debates, and the emphasis of his comments differed from Lowndes's. Whereas the Charlestonian objected primarily to a perceived imbalance of power between the northern and southern states, Lincoln was particularly concerned about protecting the liberties of citizens under the new government and ensuring governmental responsibility to the electorate. Lincoln began his critique by recognizing the need for reform of the Articles of Confederation. He had "long since perceived that not only the federal but the state Constitution required much the hand of correction and revision." What troubled him was that officials in the new government would not be sufficiently subject to popular control. Drawing on the recent experience of backcountry settlers, Lincoln feared that a government located so far from the voters would not be responsive to their needs. "What," queried Lincoln, "have you been contending for these ten years past? Liberty! What is liberty? The power of governing yourselves. If you adopt this Constitution, have you this power? No: you give it into the hands of a set of men who live one thousand miles distant from you."[39]

Backcountry spokesmen expressed special concern about the power of

---

1836]), IV, 338–340; Nadelhaft, *Disorders of War*, 180–182; Main, *Antifederalists*, 218–219.

38. Elliot, ed., *Debates on the Federal Constitution*, IV, 265–266, 271–274, 287–291, 297–298, 308–312, quotations on 272.

39. *Heads of Families, 1790*; Elliot, ed., *Debates on the Federal Constitution*, IV, 312–315.

the presidency. Lincoln and others were disturbed that the proposed constitution established infrequent presidential elections and no limitation on the number of terms in office. "This man," admonished Lincoln, "you say, shall not be elected for more than four years; and yet this mighty, this omnipotent governor-general may be elected for years and years." Aedanus Burke, representing the District between the Broad and Saluda Rivers, moved that the delegates resolve "that the eligibility of the President after the expiration of four years is dangerous to the Liberties of the people" and that the office was likely "in a short time to terminate in what the good people of this State highly disapprove of [,] An hereditary Monarchy." Most of the supporters of Burke's motion came from the backcountry, but, with Charleston and the surrounding parishes voting in almost solid opposition, the proposed resolution lost by a vote of 139 to 68.[40]

South Carolina Antifederalists were also disturbed that the proposed constitution lacked a bill of rights. Lincoln suspected that the framers had purposely neglected to ensure liberty of the press, and Patrick Dollard of Prince Frederick pointed out that his constituents opposed the proposed constitution because it gave over to the national congress their "birthright, comprised in Magna Charta." To Dollard it seemed that the constitution was "particularly calculated for the meridian of despotic aristocracy."[41]

With the Pinckney cousins as their principal spokesmen, Federalists argued that the central government would in fact be responsive to the people and protective of slave state interests, but that it would prevent the social discord that endangered all republics. Referring specifically to recent disturbances in Rhode Island and Massachusetts, Charles Pinckney observed that the new government would "give an opportunity to the more temperate and prudent part of the society to correct the licentiousness and injustice of the rest." Calling himself "Caroliniansis," a Federalist writer carried Pinckney's point a step farther. "Should a popular insurrection happen" in one of the thirteen states, "the others," observed the author, would "be able to quell it."[42] Both supporters and opponents of the proposed constitution believed that the government should be responsible to the people, but while inland Antifederalists were most concerned about the danger of aristocracy, coastal Federalists, based on their own recent experience, were much more fearful of democracy.

Responding to Lincoln's call for a bill of rights, Charles Cotesworth Pinckney identified another, even more fundamental point of dispute be-

40. Elliot, ed., *Debates on the Federal Constitution*, IV, 314. See also the Antifederalist arguments by "Cato" in *St. Gaz. of South-Carolina*, Dec. 10, 1787.
41. Elliot, ed., *Debates on the Federal Constitution*, IV, 337–338.
42. *Ibid.*, 327, 329; *Columbian Herald* (Charleston), Jan. 3, 1788.

tween prominent Federalists and their inland opponents. Pinckney reminded backcountry leaders that their egalitarian outlook could, if sanctioned by the national government, threaten the slave system. One reason, recalled Pinckney, that "weighed particularly, with the members from this state, against the insertion of a bill of rights" was that "such bills generally begin with declaring that all men are by nature born free." A Federalist calling himself "Back Wood's Man" identified the nub of the argument when he attributed the strength of Antifederalism to "the mistaken notions of liberty entertained by some men, and those too, whose example may have powerful effects on the bulk of the people."[43]

Finally, Federalist spokesmen appealed to recent memories by pointing out that the proposed constitution would make it impossible for state governments to pass debtor measures. Charles Pinckney was appealing to merchants and artisans when he exulted that the constitution would "rescue your national character from that contempt which must ever follow the most flagrant violations of public faith and private honesty! No more shall paper money, no more shall tender-laws, drive their commerce from our shores, and darken the American name in every country where it is known." In a more guarded allusion, Pinckney observed that republics were too often threatened by "the imbecility of the laws." He insisted that the proposed constitution would guard against that danger.[44]

The simple identification of Antifederalists as debtors and Federalists as merchant creditors hardly bears repeating. Although Pinckney and others were correct in suggesting that the center of Antifederalism was also the locus of support for debtor legislation, they neglected to mention that many coastal delegates who supported early debtor measures also supported ratification. Backcountry delegates, representing the region that was pressing hardest for paper currency and stay laws, may well have been concerned about the constitutional prohibition of such measures, but it is significant that Antifederalist spokesmen voiced no objections to national trade regulation or currency control. They were far more concerned with governmental responsibility and individual liberties.[45]

Although the dispute over debtor legislation cannot sufficiently account for divisions between Federalists and Antifederalists, it can help to explain why Charleston artisans, including members of Alexander Gillon's group, were willing to join with British merchants and wealthy rice planters in supporting the proposed constitution. Apparently their eagerness for com-

43. Elliot, ed., *Debates on the Federal Constitution*, IV, 316; *Col. Herald*, May 8, 1788.
44. Elliot, ed., *Debates on the Federal Constitution*, IV, 329, 336.
45. Nadelhaft, *Disorders of War*, 190.

mercial expansion and resentment of debtor legislation enabled them to overlook Federalist political arguments that they may well have found objectionable. Writing under the name of "Civis," Henry Perroneau, formerly a leader of the Marine Anti-Britannic Society, expressed what must have been the feeling of many merchants and artisans. He urged his readers to be on their "guard against the misrepresentation of men who are involved in debt." Such people, he suggested, might oppose the constitution because it prohibited states from issuing paper currency and from passing "any *expost facto* law, or law impairing the obligation of contracts." These provisions, according to "Civis," would "doubtless bear hard on debtors who wish to defraud their creditors, but it will be of real service to the honest part of the community." Having suffered great hardship during the postwar economic crisis, Charleston artisans were willing to unite with their former enemies in the interest of commercial expansion and currency control.[46]

Their divergent reactions to the news of South Carolina's adoption of the Constitution indicate how far apart radical artisans and backcountry settlers had grown since the years immediately following the Revolution, when they had shared in a fierce opposition to returning loyalists. In Charleston, where, according to Aedanus Burke, there were "not fifty inhabitants" who opposed the proposed constitution, an enormous procession marched in celebration of ratification. Every sort of artisan from ships' carpenters to musical instrument makers carried "decorated emblems of their crafts." The butchers provided an ox, "to which the People sat chearfully down, without distinction." Joined by "gentlemen planters" and clergymen of all denominations, "a joyful spirit of *Republicanism* seemed to pervade" the procession. Meanwhile, the more numerous Antifederalist contingent reacted angrily to the news. "In the interiour country," observed Burke, "all is disgust, sorrow, and vindictive reproaches against the system, and those who voted for it." In some areas, "people had a coffin painted black, which, borne in funeral procession, was solemnly buried, as an emblem of the dissolution and interment of publick liberty."[47]

iii

Criticism of the United States Constitution all but vanished after ratification, but the system of beliefs that had informed backcountry Antifederal-

46. *Col. Herald*, Feb. 4, 1788. "Civis" is identified in *Gazette of the State of South-Carolina* (Charleston), Aug. 9, 1788. For an excellent discussion of artisan perspectives on the United States Constitution, see Eric Foner, *Tom Paine and Revolutionary America* (New York, 1976), 204–209.

47. *Col. Herald*, May 29, 1788; Aedanus Burke to John Lamb, June 23, 1788, John Lamb Papers, NYHS, also quoted in Rogers, *Evolution of a Federalist*, 156–157.

ism persisted and contributed to distinctly sectional voting patterns on
many issues involving state and local government.[48] Suspicious of the
Charleston-area elite, fearful of potential infringements on individual liberties, and committed to the principle of governmental responsibility to the
electorate, inland representatives supported measures that limited the power of the state government while increasing direct popular participation in
the choice of officeholders. Even on issues that did not affect the sectional
balance of power, backcountry representatives favored efforts to make state
and local officeholders more directly responsible to their constituency.

Backcountry representatives did not always vote as a bloc, but, to a large
extent, differences among them corresponded to differences between the
middlecountry and upcountry. It is not surprising that representatives from
the former area were somewhat more likely to vote with the coast than were
the upcountrymen. By the same token, the underrepresented coastal parishes to the north of Charleston were somewhat more inclined than other
coastal areas to vote with the backcountry.

A series of House votes spanning the period from 1787 to 1810 illustrates these tendencies. It was, for example, backcountry representatives
who, in 1794, pressed for the election of militia officers by the rank and file.
Upcountry representatives favored the provision by a vote of twenty-three
to four, but representatives from Georgetown and the middlecountry districts were divided. Charleston and the surrounding parishes opposed the
proposal by a vote of thirty-one to seven. They were joined by eight of nine
representatives from Beaufort. Defeated by only one vote, inland proponents of the measure were more successful in 1803, when, by a vote of fifty
to forty-seven, the House passed a similar bill.[49]

Throughout the 1790s and the early 1800s, backcountry representatives
continued to demonstrate their suspicion of appointed officials and their
commitment to broadened popular participation in government. In 1799,
inland leaders led an unsuccessful effort to vest equity jurisdiction in the

48. Jackson Turner Main analyzed state assembly votes before 1790 in all thirteen
states. He explained sectional voting patterns in South Carolina by pointing to a division
between backcountry "localists" and lowcountry "cosmopolitans." My discussion has
benefited greatly from Main's study, but I have tried to avoid his terminology because it
tends to obscure distinctions within the backcountry and the extent of backcountry
involvement in the statewide market. See Main, *Political Parties before the Constitution*
(Chapel Hill, N.C., 1973), 268–295. Using Main's categories, Patrick S. Brady analyzed
roll calls in the South Carolina legislature from 1790 to 1833 and concluded that the
most fundamental division centered around attitudes toward state government. See Patrick Stone Brady, "Political and Civil Life in South Carolina, 1787–1833" (Ph.D. diss.,
University of California, Santa Barbara, 1971), esp. 10–48.

49. House Jour., May 5, 1794, Dec. 6, 1803.

state's common law judges. They disliked the court of equity because it operated without juries and assumed functions previously performed by the royal council. Backcountry representatives supported the proposal by a vote of thirty-nine to eleven. Again, the upcountry contingent was almost united, whereas representatives from the middlecountry and Georgetown District divided their votes. Charleston and Beaufort opposed the proposal by a vote of thirty-nine to three. In 1806, petitioners from Edgefield and Laurens districts requested popular election of sheriffs, and, two years later, inland representatives successfully pushed the proposal through the legislature. Finally, it was from backcountry grand jurors that the legislature, in 1809, heard the first call for manhood suffrage.[50]

As backcountry representatives supported measures that tended to increase popular representation in government, they also demonstrated a marked concern about corruption among state officials. Spurred by their suspicion of the Charleston-area elite, inland leaders were more fearful and intolerant of official misconduct than were their coastal counterparts. Although many prominent South Carolinians were involved in speculative schemes, inland leaders were less inclined to be lenient when public officials misbehaved. Most striking was their reaction to the case of Alexander Moultrie, a state attorney general who, in 1793, was convicted by the Senate for attempting to profit by channeling public funds into the South Carolina Yazoo Land Company. Only nine representatives, eight of whom were from the Charelston area, had dissented from the House decision to impeach, but representatives divided over an earlier attempt to ease Moultrie's punishment. Before the impeachment vote, representatives considered a proposal that would have enabled Moultrie to avoid further penalties by mortgaging his estate to the Commissioners of the Treasury until the extent of his debt could be determined. Representatives from Charleston District and Beaufort favored the proposal by a vote of twenty-six to eleven. Five of six Georgetown representatives joined their backcountry colleagues who opposed leniency by a vote of thirty-seven to five. Only one piedmont representative joined Moultrie's coastal sympathizers.[51]

Backcountry representatives also tended to oppose any increase either in the number of state officials or in the size of their respective salaries. In 1787, Patrick Calhoun argued against an increase in the governor's salary

50. Brady, "Political and Civil Life," 44; William A. Schaper, *Sectionalism and Representation in South Carolina* (New York, 1968 [orig. publ. Washington, D.C., 1901]), 425–426; Cooper and McCord, eds., *Statutes of South Carolina,* V, 569; House Jour., Dec. 1, 1799, Nov. 29, 1806.

51. Brady, "Political and Civil Life," 43; Senate Jour., Dec. 19, 1792; House Jour., Dec. 18, 1792; *St. Gaz. of South-Carolina,* Dec. 21, 1793.

by observing, "Such murmurings prevailed amongst the backcountry people on account of the civil list, that if it was not reduced, considerably reduced, the taxes would not be paid." From 1787 to 1810, backcountry representatives opposed the Charleston-area contingent on all matters involving salaries for judges, governors, house ministers, treasurers, and even constables. Again, piedmont representatives were more consistent in their opposition than were their middlecountry counterparts, and Charleston-area representatives came closer to unanimity than those from Georgetown and Beaufort. Serving as a state representative from Charleston in 1791, Jacob Read had no doubt about the backcountry's impact on judges' salaries. "The Yahoos," Read informed his friend Judge Grimké, "have had no mercy on the Lawyers. They have really cut us out of feather!" One year later, petitioners from Abbeville and Pendleton opposed the federal excise tax by observing, "Nothing tends with more speed and certainty to the ruin of a Country, than swelling Numbers of Officers with high Salaries—the pregnant parent of baneful Pride, Luxury and Immorality."[52]

For obvious reasons, backcountry representatives were more supportive of state expenditures when the allowances involved were their own, but their position was not entirely inconsistent. So long as Charleston remained the state capital, inland representatives saw coastal efforts to limit legislative allowances as an effort to discourage backcountry attendance at the legislature. In 1787, when Thomas Bee of Charleston proposed that the per diem payment (distinct from the additional travel allowance) be reduced, Patrick Calhoun countered by observing that he would "willingly agree when the legislature met at Columbia to give up any allowance for expenses." Arthur Simkins also believed that the reduction would "destroy the freedom of representation, for if gentlemen of the backcountry could not receive sufficient money to pay their expenses, very few of them will serve." He, too, "hoped that when the place of meeting was held at the new town then every member might support himself." Lowcountry representatives were divided over Bee's proposal, but, with the backcountry almost unanimous in opposition, the motion went down in defeat.[53]

Once Columbia was established as the new capital, inland representatives

52. *Charleston Morning Post, and the Daily Advertiser*, Feb. 14, 1787; House Jour., Feb. 2, 5, Mar. 21, 1787, Feb. 20, 26, 1789, Feb. 4, 10, 1791, in Thompson *et al.*, eds., *Journals of the House, 1787–1788*, 42–44, 52–56, 244–245, 1789–1790, 166–167, 194–195, 1791, 209–211, 230–231; House Jour., May 10, Dec. 3, 1794, Nov. 28, Dec. 8, 1801, Dec. 7, 9, 1803, Dec. 19, 1805, Dec. 17, 1806; SCDAH; Jacob Read to John F. Grimké, Feb. 12, 1791, Grimké Family Papers, SCHS; Main, *Political Parties before the Constitution*, 277–279; petition from Abbeville and Pendleton, Petitions, 1792, no. 41.
53. *Chas. Morn. Post, and Daily Adv.*, Feb. 14, 1787; House Jour., Feb. 14, 1787, in Thompson *et al.*, eds., *Journals of the House, 1787–1788*, 89–90.

were less concerned about establishing a substantial per diem. In 1795, when the House voted on a proposal to increase daily allowances from 7s. to $2, twenty of thirty-nine inland representatives opposed the measure. Charleston and the coastal parishes divided their votes, with the result that per diem payments were not increased. More than half the upcountry representatives voted against the increase, even though they lived farther from Columbia than many of their inland and coastal counterparts.[54] In other words, the region that was least inclined to support high civil salaries also tended to oppose higher allowances for legislators. Many backcountry representatives were consistent in their belief that public officials should be motivated solely by sense of civic duty, and many shared the prevalent coastal assumption that legislators should be sufficiently independent to afford the inevitable expenses associated with public office.

Inland representatives gave further evidence of their staunch republicanism when, in 1802, they were almost alone in opposing a resolution to use the House chamber as a ballroom. All thirty-four Charleston-area representatives favored the resolution, but more than three-fourths of the eighteen upcountry representatives opposed it. Beaufort and Georgetown split eleven to six in support of the ball, and they were joined by fourteen of nineteen middlecountry representatives. Adopting a position that must have annoyed the urbane Charlestonians, opponents of the resolution expressed their belief that frugality and simplicity were necessary correlates of good government.[55]

Finally, backcountry leaders were more protective of local independence and more suspicious of centralized state power than were their coastal counterparts. In 1798, they succeeded in defeating a bill for the establishment of a state bank. Sixteen of the upcountry's twenty-three representatives opposed the bank bill. They were joined by fourteen of the remaining sixteen inland representatives and seventeen of fifty-two representatives from the coast. During the same legislative session, a small majority of backcountry representatives demonstrated their commitment to local autonomy by supporting a motion that would have forced individual districts to pay for their own courthouses instead of relying on state coffers. Despite its cost to inland settlers, nine of twenty-three upcountry representatives supported the proposal, along with thirteen of nineteen representatives from the middlecountry. At the same time, coastal representatives opposed the district-payment plan by a vote of twenty-six to eighteen. It seems that many lowcountrymen preferred sharing the cost of the new courthouses to

54. House Jour., Dec. 18, 1795.
55. House Jour., Dec. 7, 1802; see also Dec. 12, 1801.

allowing the backcountry greater local independence. The result was that the state, rather than the districts, paid for the new buildings.[56]

Although inland leaders were markedly suspicious of measures that enhanced the power of the state government, it would be a mistake to portray them as isolated "localists," lacking any interest in the statewide market. Their persistent struggle to maintain an open slave trade and their continual efforts to improve inland navigation provide ample testimony to wider ambitions. It is significant that in 1789, while the backcountry was still suffering the effects of the postwar economic crisis, inland representatives supported Alexander Gillon's proposal to establish a state fund for inland navigation. Whereas coastal representatives opposed the plan by a vote of sixty-two to three, inland representatives supported Gillon by a vote of twenty-nine to nineteen. Influenced by their yeoman constituency and by enduring struggles to achieve political influence within South Carolina, backcountry leaders were more fearful of governmental corruption, and more democratic in orientation, than most of their coastal counterparts. But they were also ambitious men whose purpose was to enter, not reject, the state's political and economic elite.[57]

iv

Divisions in the South Carolina contingent to the First United States Congress reflected ideological divisions between inland and coastal representatives and anticipated future party alignments in the state. With Daniel Huger, representing Georgetown and Cheraws, absent because of illness, William L. Smith of Charleston was often isolated from other members of his delegation. Thomas Tudor Tucker of Ninety Six, Aedanus Burke of Orangeburg, and Thomas Sumter, representing Camden, were leading advocates of the Bill of Rights. All felt that the ten amendments proposed by the House of Representatives committee were insufficient, and Tucker proposed an additional amendment requiring representatives to obey the wishes of their constituents. By contrast, Smith voted with the majority in urging that the House amendments be accepted quickly and without change. Smith differed from the other South Carolinians in supporting the establishment

56. *Ibid.*, Dec. 10, 20, 1798; Brady, "Political and Civil Life," 46.
57. House Jour., Feb. 2, 1789; Patrick S. Brady, "The Slave Trade and Sectionalism in South Carolina, 1787–1808," *Jour. So. Hist.*, XXXVIII (1972), 601–620. Coastal representatives were not opposed to inland navigation per se, but they were unwilling to interfere with private navigation companies. Inland representatives apparently felt that the private companies were moving too slowly. See also Chapter 8.

of a federal court system, a national bank, and a standing army. He also differed from his fellows by voting for the federal excise tax.[58]

Backcountry representatives on the state and national levels were suspicious of centralized political power, protective of local and individual political liberties, and resentful of taxes imposed for the support of a complex state or federal structure. Following a Fourth of July celebration in 1799, an upcountry correspondent gave clear expression to the republican spirit that predominated in his region. "We are," he observed, "the most determined enemies of kingly government, or of hereditary succession, and will be the resolute opposers of adding even the shadow of a power to the President, denied by the constitution." The correspondent noted, "Not a few among this enlightened body of citizens keep a keen and watchful eye upon public men and public measures."[59]

The problem, from the point of view of coastal conservatives, was that inland republicanism might, if unchecked, develop into a deeper attack on planter power. Artisan and debtor protests of the 1780s heightened those fears, and, during the 1790s, as the French Revolution became associated with emancipation in Saint Domingue, coastal leaders became more convinced of the need to limit republicanism at home. Acutely conscious of the backcountry's nonslaveholding majority, they insisted that the inland spread of slavery would be the only secure antidote to the democratic-republican threat.

There was, however, considerable room for ideological and political compromise. The difference between inland and coastal republicanism was by no means absolute. Slavery was never a point of contention among South Carolina political leaders, nor did backcountry representatives ever press for full political equality even among independent white men. In any case, on any given point of dispute, there was some convergence between coastal and backcountry representatives, particularly those from the middlecountry and the lowcountry parishes distant from Charleston. Drawn together by common concern for the protection of planters throughout the southern states, certain leading men from both regions managed to forge a political alliance among planters that spanned South Carolina sections.

58. 1st Cong., 3d Sess., *Debates and Proceedings in the Congress of the United States, 1789–1824* [Annals of Congress] (Washington, D.C., 1834–1856), 1884, 1960; William L. Smith to Edward Rutledge, July 25, 1790, William L. Smith Papers, 11-476, SCHS; Rogers, *Evolution of a Federalist*, 167–180, 193–207, 217–219.

59. *City Gaz., and Daily Adv.*, July 27, 1799.

CHAPTER 6

The Politics of Land

When the duc de La Rochefoucault Liancourt traveled through the United States during the 1790s, he referred to the country as "the land of speculation." In this South Carolina was not exceptional. Planters and merchants throughout the state sought quick profits and new sources of credit by joining the boom in land speculation that swept the nation during the post-Revolutionary decades. By 1794, Samuel Green, a Richland County merchant, was admonishing his brother for discouraging his ambitions as a speculator: "I want to know what you were about last year when I wrote you about the speculation on land in this country. You treated the business quite indifferently. Col. Wade Hampton will make clear upward of 500 Sterling in this business and many others have made themselves very handsome fortunes." Later that year, Green attempted to purchase "soldiers tickets for land," but was unable to find any. "I fear," he wrote to his brother, "they have been principally bought up we have so many men who are transacting from here to the northward."[1]

Although the land-grab that swept South Carolina between 1784 and 1795 failed to yield the anticipated economic rewards, it did have an important political and social impact. In the midst of divisive political disputes between inland and coastal representatives, the speculative boom of the 1780s and 1790s extended bonds between leaders in both sections and contributed to the formation of an interregional political opposition to the Charleston-area elite. At the same time, the widespread corruption and land engrossment associated with speculation created social tensions within the backcountry.

1. François Alexandre Frédéric, duc de la Rouchefoucault Liancourt, *Travels through the United States of North America, the Country of the Iroquois, and Upper Canada, in the Years 1795, 1796, and 1797*, trans. Henry Neuman, 2d ed. (London, 1800), I, 261; Samuel Green to Timothy Green, Sept. 27, Nov. 29, 1794, Samuel Green Papers, SCL.

i

The voracious appetite for land that overwhelmed South Carolinians during the last two decades of the eighteenth century was not an entirely new phenomenon. Interest in land acquisition was inevitable in a world in which partible inheritance prevailed as the most common mode of property transmission—a world in which fathers continued to demonstrate an interest in providing their sons and occasionally their daughters with a farm or plantation. Free headright grants had drawn migrants to the backcountry before the Revolution and enabled settlers with large households to acquire hundreds and, in some cases, thousands of acres. Nonetheless, South Carolina's royal land policy together with a tax system that assessed all land at a flat rate had limited the extent of land engrossment in the backcountry. Although wealthy individuals such as Joseph Kershaw and John Chesnut managed to accumulate vast tracts before the Revolution, they were exceptional. Most backcountrymen acquired tracts of fewer than three hundred acres.

In 1784 the South Carolina legislature passed a land act that opened the land office after a closure of nearly ten years and lifted restraints on large-scale engrossment and speculation. Writers of the act attempted to discourage speculation by limiting the size of grants to 640 acres and requiring that purchasers begin cultivating their property within two years of receiving the grant or one year of resale. The House of Representatives gave some hope to speculators, however, when it rejected proposals to establish a fixed price of $60 for each hundred acres and settled on a price of £10. During the same year, the legislature passed a land tax that, for the first time in South Carolina's history, based assessments on land value. Proponents of the measure probably designed it not only to appease owners of inland acreage but to ease the way for speculation. In March 1785, the legislature reduced the price of granted property to $10 for each hundred acres, and, in September of that year, Patrick Calhoun proposed that the land act be further altered, having been found "extremely inconvenient." He and others successfully pressed for a new act that opened the way for speculation by eliminating the limit on acreage and repealing the cultivation requirement.[2]

Patrick Calhoun was not personally involved in speculation, but, as a backcountryman, his sponsorship of the liberalized land act is significant.

2. South Carolina House of Representatives Journal, Mar. 13, 1784, in Theodora J. Thompson *et al.*, eds., *Journals of the House of Representatives*, The State Records of South Carolina (Columbia, S.C., 1977), 1783–1784, 266; Thomas Cooper and David J. McCord, eds., *The Statutes at Large of South Carolina* (Columbia, S.C., 1836–1841), IV, 590–592, 707–710; *Charleston Evening Gazette*, Sept. 27, 1785.

Of the 253 identifiable South Carolinians who acquired grants in tracts of 2,000 or more acres from 1785 through 1794, 163, or 64 percent, were from the backcountry. They accumulated more than 4,500,000 acres in speculative tracts; their lowcountry counterparts received comparable grants totaling about 1,070,000 acres. If grants to unidentifiable grantees are included, more than 8,000,000 South Carolina acres were granted in speculative tracts during this period. The bulk of this land (about 89 percent) was located in the backcountry, where the sparsely settled pine barrens of Orangeburg District became the scene of the most frenetic speculative activity. There, more than 2,700,000 acres were granted in tracts of at least 2,000 acres, and many thousands more were granted in smaller quantities.[3]

Some of the more than ninety people who acquired speculative grants in 1786 probably hoped not simply to profit from the sale of valuable property but to pay creditors with worthless land. It cannot be a coincidence that the legislature adopted the revised land act during the same session in which it passed the Sheriffs' Sale, or Pine Barren, Act. Opponents of debtor legislation saw the connection. Thomas Bee believed "it had become common for people to purchase grants of pine barren which they offered to their creditors." John Wickley, who later led a riot at the Winton County Court, must have expected his post-Revolutionary grants of more than thirty thousand acres in Orangeburg, Camden, Ninety Six, and Cheraws would enable him to pay his debts. Had the legislature renewed the Sheriffs' Sale Act in 1786, he and other speculators might well have succeeded.[4]

Other speculators hoped to profit by the sale of their recently acquired

3. In all, 326 people received individual grants of 2,000 or more acres from 1785 through 1794, including those who received simultaneous or consecutive grants that totaled at least 2,000 acres. Not all recipients were necessarily interested in speculation, but the size of the tracts suggests that most were. In any case, the South Carolina Senate, in December 1793, identified grants exceeding 2,000 acres as "excessive" and speculative. South Carolina Senate Journal, Dec. 7, 1793, SCDAH (hereafter cited as Senate Jour.); *Columbian Herald* (Charleston), Feb. 3, 1794. In addition, 409 people received individual grants of between 1,000 and 2,000 acres during the same period. The likelihood is that some members of this group, whose holdings totaled considerably more than 2,000 acres, were also interested in speculation. Index to State Grants, SCDAH; U.S., Bureau of the Census, *Heads of Families at the First Census of the United States Taken in the Year 1790: South Carolina* (Washington, D.C., 1908) (hereafter cited as *Heads of Families, 1790*); Tax Returns, 1787–1793, Orangeburg District, District Eastward of Wateree, Ninety Six District (two returns), 1787, box 3, nos. 8, 9, 10, 11, SCDAH; Tax Returns, 1800, Winton County, Comptroller General Tax Record Books, box 107, folder 2, SCDAH.

4. *Charleston Morning Post, and Daily Advertiser*, Feb. 22, 1787; Index to State Grants. See also Chapter 4.

acreage. As early as 1784, Wade Hampton, the most audacious land speculator in South Carolina, had his eye on lands as far west as what would become the state of Alabama. That year, he became a member of the Muscle Shoals Land Company, organized by William Blount. The members planned to acquire and resell property at the Muscle Shoals region of the Tennessee River. Since Georgia and South Carolina both made claims to the territory, Blount, who later became governor of Tennessee, wanted titles from both states. He was present in Charleston during the opening legislative session in 1784 and probably established his connection with Hampton at that time. The following year, Hampton, along with several partners, acquired grants for 107,760 and 131,160 on the Tennessee River. (The lands were in territory that would eventually become Alabama, but in 1785, the region was still claimed by South Carolina.) Fearing that these western acquisitions would provoke the Indians, inland and coastal representatives joined together and disallowed all grants to territory west of the Cherokee boundary line. In 1786, South Carolina ceded its claim to the far western territory.[5]

After their state abandoned its western claims, a group of South Carolinians looked with new interest to Georgia, which, until 1797, made claims to the entire territory of what would become Mississippi and Alabama. In 1789, William Clay Snipes of St. Bartholomew joined the state attorney general, Alexander Moultrie, and Isaac Huger, a representative from St. Thomas and St. Dennis, in organizing the South Carolina Yazoo Land Company. Their purpose was to acquire and resell Georgia grants to territory along the Mississippi and Tennessee rivers. Together with comparable companies based in Tennessee and Virginia, they actually received grants to about sixteen million acres, but extensive Indian settlements made it difficult for any of the Yazoo land groups to attract purchasers. Moultrie, in an unsuccessful attempt to prevent the South Carolina company from defaulting on its payments, siphoned off £60,000 in state funds for the Yazoo venture. In 1792, he was impeached by the South Carolina House of Representatives and, one year later, convicted by the Senate.[6]

5. Index to State Grants; Ronald Edward Bridwell, "The South's Wealthiest Planter: Wade Hampton I of South Carolina, 1754–1835" (Ph.D. diss., University of South Carolina, 1980), 285–300.
6. Senate Jour., Dec. 19, 1792; Bridwell, "South's Wealthiest Planter," 302–304; C. Peter Magrath, *Yazoo: Law and Politics in the New Republic: The Case of Fletcher v. Peck* (Providence, R.I., 1966), 1–5; A. M. Sakolski, *The Great American Land Bubble: The Amazing Story of Land-Grabbing, Speculations, and Booms from Colonial Times to the Present* (New York, 1932), 125–139; Walter B. Edgar *et al.*, eds., *Biographical Directory of the South Carolina House of Representatives* (Columbia, S.C., 1974–1984), III, 515–517.

In 1795, several years after the first Yazoo ventures fizzled, four new companies appeared on the scene. None was based in South Carolina, but several prominent speculators from the state were deeply involved. Most notable were Robert Goodloe Harper, who was then serving as a United States congressman from Ninety Six District, and Wade Hampton. These companies, backed by a number of politically prominent national figures, succeeded in purchasing grants from the Georgia legislature, but, one year later, the same body, under fire from its own constituency, rescinded. Ultimately the matter was settled by the United States Supreme Court, which ruled in favor of the Yazoo companies, and by a United States Senate decision, four years later, to provide compensation. The principal beneficiaries were New England merchants, who were the largest investors in the second Yazoo scheme. Such small-scale speculators as Samuel Green, who, by February 1796, wished he "had never heard of the Yazoo Lands," probably did not see a profit.[7]

Most South Carolina speculators concentrated on lands within their state's borders. The largest grants went to a group of men who were already becoming the backcountry's leading planters and political figures. Well aware of a mounting backcountry movement to bring the state capital inland, a number of backcountry speculators accumulated extensive holdings at likely sites. Following in the footsteps of Joseph Kershaw and John Chesnut, whose pre-Revolutionary grants accounted for most of Camden Township, they hoped to profit by selling or renting lots at centers of local trade. The Winn family of Fairfield County owned the entire village of Winnsboro. The town of Sumter grew up on a 14,288-acre tract granted to Thomas Sumter in 1788. Sumter also owned most of the lands that eventually became Stateburg, but he lost his bid to make it the location of the new capital. That victory went to Colonel Thomas Taylor, his brother James Taylor, and Wade Hampton, who held extensive grants to the lands at Congarees that eventually became Columbia. Like Hampton and Sumter, the Taylors had emigrated from Virginia to South Carolina before the Revolution. Settling near Congarees, they became leading planters and political figures of their region.[8]

7. Bridwell, "South's Wealthiest Planter," 361–378; Magrath, Yazoo, 5–19, 70–100; Samuel Green to Timothy Green, Feb. 9, 1796, Samuel Green Papers.
8. Anne King Gregorie, Thomas Sumter (Columbia, S.C., 1931), 212–213; Buford S. Chappell, The Winns of Fairfield County (Columbia, S.C., 1975); Kate Furman, "General Sumter and His Neighbors," Southern History Association, Publications, VI (1902), 495; Cooper and McCord, eds., Statutes of South Carolina, IV, 751–752; Index to State Grants; Index to Colonial Land Grants, SCDAH.

It did not take long before speculators, capable of influencing local surveyors, began acquiring property that was already settled. In 1787, the House received a petition from settlers living between the Broad and Saluda rivers who complained that Jonas Beard, a former representative from Saxe Gotha, had obtained a fraudulent grant for fifty-one thousand acres. They claimed that the survey, which consisted of nothing more than a line drawn between rough sketches of the two rivers, encompassed lands that were well settled and previously granted. Beard had drawn his own plat and, instead of notifying the surrounding settlers as required by law, told them that he was "laying out a road and wanted for *that purpose to inform himself of the County Line.*" He then went directly to Charleston and registered the grant "so Suddenly that none of the parties concerned had time and information of the proceedings to put a caveat before it was too late." The House upheld the petitioners. Beard had been so blatant in his fraud that the legislature, of which he had been a member, pronounced his behavior an act of "profligate rapaciousness" and passed a special ordinance voiding his grant.[9]

Beard typified the ambitious backcountry planters and merchants who were becoming involved in speculation. An ardent whig during the Revolution, he was one of the militia officers who had worked to aid the Reverend William Tennent and William Henry Drayton during their tour of the backcountry. Beard owned a plantation at Congarees, but he was also a local storekeeper, surveyor, and justice of the peace. He served in the South Carolina House of Representatives through 1786, and his misdeeds as a speculator did not prevent him from attending the State Constitutional Convention of 1790 as a delegate from Saxe Gotha.[10]

In an effort to circumvent more such protests, the legislature, in 1787, passed an act "to Restrain particular persons therein described, from obtaining grants of Land." The act nullified all grants "for lands situate, lying, and being within lines, buttings, and boundings of former plats and grants." It also prohibited the surveyor general, deputy surveyors, and secretary of state from taking elapsed grants (grants for which the designated grantee had not paid within the allotted time) for themselves. In a further effort to prevent rampant speculation, the act prohibited the purchase of grants on credit. During the same session, the House and Senate passed an ordinance that attempted to protect prior grantees from speculators by prohibiting the

9. House Jour., Feb. 27, 1787, Feb. 8, 1788, in Thompson *et al.*, eds., *Journals of the House, 1787–1788*, 148, 411–412; Edgar *et al.*, eds., *Biographical Directory of the House*, III, 59–60; Cooper and McCord, eds., *Statutes of South Carolina*, V, 74.

10. Edgar *et al.*, eds., *Biographical Directory of the House*, III, 59–60.

signing of any grant in excess of one thousand acres while the legislature was in recess and for forty days thereafter.[11]

Despite these efforts, violations and protests continued. In 1788, seventy residents of Lancaster and Chesterfield counties, not one of whom held more than one slave in 1790, complained that the large surveys were "a means which has and does Distress many poor honest Families not able as yet to secure their lands, but intending to do it when able, now have lost there improvements." They suspected that they were "in a likely way to suffer the owners Extortioning them in there price of there land and there not being able to purchase." Those receiving the "excessive" grants could, according to the petitioners, have only been interested in speculation, for they had "there possessions in Lancaster County and will come over into Chesterfield County and lay the surveys of thousands of acres of land there." This appeared to the petitioners "to be of no other view but to make gain and distress the poor." In addition, they feared loss of the open areas used for pasturage and believed that the final result of the speculative boom might be to drive people off the land, thereby producing "a thin settled Country."[12]

The legislature took no further action on the land question until 1789, when it received another protest against an excessive grant. This time the petitioners, many of whom had signed the earlier petition from Lancaster and Chesterfield counties, designated themselves as "Inhabitants of the Great and Little Lynches Creeks" and directed their attention to John Marshall, a former Regulator who had attempted to obtain a grant for thirty-five thousand acres in Chesterfield. Like Beard, Marshall was a justice of the peace and a colonel in the whig militia. He also kept at least thirty-six slaves at his plantation in Lancaster. According to the settlers, Marshall's survey enclosed "many Entire Surveys which is mostly inhabited by poor Families." They accused Marshall of obtaining a fraudulent plat and insisted that "there could not be an accurate platt made only from Running them Lines."[13]

11. House Jour., Mar. 27, 28, 1787, in Thompson *et al.*, eds., *Journals of the House, 1787–1788*, 285–286, 304; Cooper and McCord, eds., *Statutes of South Carolina*, V, 38–41.

12. *Heads of Families, 1790*; petition from Lancaster and Chesterfield counties, Petitions to the General Assembly, 1788, no. 87, SCDAH (hereafter cited as Petitions); House Jour., Feb. 4, 1788, in Thompson *et al.*, eds., *Journals of the House, 1787–1788*, 389–390.

13. Petition from the Inhabitants of Great and Little Lynches Creek, Petitions, 1789, no. 105; House Jour., Jan. 7, 1789, in Thompson *et al.*, eds., *Journals of the House, 1789–1790*, 43–44; Richard M. Brown, "Prosopography of the Regulators," MS, 104–106.

Not all of the petitioners were members of "poor families." David Perkins, one of the signers, owned twenty slaves in 1790, and Richard Bettis, another signer, owned seven slaves. Bettis was himself involved in speculation. In 1793, he received a survey for thirty-five thousand acres in Chesterfield. Although his plat was not identical to Marshall's, Bettis's concern in 1789 may well have arisen from his interest as a competing speculator rather than from genuine fear of dispossession. Nonetheless, the majority of the petitioners were small planters and nonslaveholders. Nineteen of the fifty-two signers were unable to write their names, and only four, including Bettis and Perkins, owned slaves.[14]

Despite its apparent recognition of the potential social problem, the legislature was unable or unwilling to adopt strong measures. Although the House upheld the claims of the Lynches Creek petitioners by disallowing the grant to John Marshall, it did not address the deeper problem. Given the extent of participation in the postwar land-grab and the number of speculators who held public office, the ambivalence of the legislature is not surprising. Marshall himself went on to serve as a delegate to the State Constitutional Convention of 1790 from the District Eastward of Wateree.[15]

ii

The second phase of land speculation in South Carolina began in 1791 with another change in the state's land law. After deciding that "all the valuable lands" had already been granted, the legislature decided to grant remaining and predominantly pine barren lands to anyone, so long as the grantee paid official processing fees to the commissioner of locations, secretary of state, and deputy surveyor. According to one student of speculation in South Carolina, the act enabled people to acquire grants of any size for £2 per grant and a halfpenny per acre. The new law, which took effect in April 1792, signaled an explosive speculative boom. During 1792 and 1793 alone, more than three million acres were granted in tracts of two thousand or more acres.[16]

14. Petition from the Inhabitants of Great and Little Lynches Creek, Petitions, 1789, no. 105; *Heads of Families, 1790*; Index to State Plats, SCDAH; *Col. Herald*, Feb. 3, 1794.

15. House Jour., Jan. 27, 30, 1789, in Thompson *et al.*, *Journals of the House, 1789–1790*, 76–77, 94; Francis M. Hutson, ed., *Journal of the Constitutional Convention of South Carolina: May 10, 1790–June 3, 1790* (Columbia, S.C., 1946), 3–6, 33.

16. Cooper and McCord, eds., *Statutes of South Carolina*, V, 168–169; Bridwell, "South's Wealthiest Planter," 305–311; Index to State Grants.

The linchpin of the second South Carolina land-grab was Robert Morris, superintendent of finance under the Articles of Confederation and United States senator from Pennsylvania from 1789 to 1795. Morris became involved in his various land schemes through his association with a young man named John Nicholson, who began his career as a clerk in Morris's finance office. Between 1782 and 1784, Nicholson served as comptroller general of Pennsylvania. The position gave him extensive influence in the dispensation of vacant land in the state, and he did not hesitate to use the office to his personal advantage. He accumulated more than 4,000,000 acres in Pennsylvania and, together with Morris, bought up enormous tracts throughout the southern states. Other Philadelphia speculators were involved in the purchase of South Carolina lands, but none equaled Morris and Nicholson, who, in South Carolina alone, acquired 1,261,256 acres.[17]

What Morris and Nicholson did was simply to purchase huge tracts from intermediaries who had managed to accumulate land by speculating in soldiers' indents and purchasing grants from the land office. By the summer of 1793, Samuel Green informed his brother, "There has been great speculation in land in this state and Georgia . . . and even at present all the pine barrens in the country have been taken up as it is said to sell to George [Robert] Morris of Philadelphia." The next year, one of Nicholson's associates informed him that "Every Land Jobber in the South . . . think you will purchase anything called land."[18]

The fraud and the potential for social unrest were, by 1793, so great that even Governor William Moultrie declined signing "several Grants containing surveys for very large quantities of land," some of which were, in his words, "laid in parts of the state that are thickly inhabited where I do not conceive that such large bodies of vacant land can lie." One has only to look at the many careless plats drawn by deputy surveyors for land in sparsely settled parts of Orangeburg District to see that the drawings could have borne little relation to the actual terrain. The South Carolina Senate responded by passing a resolution prohibiting the governor from signing any grant for land in excess of five hundred acres. It also directed the secretary

---

17. Robert D. Arbuckle, *Pennsylvania Speculator and Patriot: The Entrepreneurial John Nicholson, 1757–1800* (University Park, Pa., 1975), 165–201; Ellis Paxson Oberholtzer, *Robert Morris: Patriot and Financier* (New York, 1968 [orig. publ. New York, 1903]), 312–313; Bridwell, "South's Wealthiest Planter," 320–323. Among the other Philadelphia speculators who were purchasing South Carolina state grants were Abraham Morhouse and Ezekiel King. Deeds of Feb. 3, Apr. 14, 1795, County Deeds, WPA Trans., Anderson County, no. 27 (MS, 174–176, 418–419), SCDAH.

18. Samuel Green to Timothy Green, Aug. 31, 1793, Samuel Green Papers; Oberholtzer, *Robert Morris*, 312–357; John Stockdale to John Nicholson, Dec. 26, 1794, quoted in Arbuckle, *Pennsylvania Speculator and Patriot*, 172 (see also 165–357).

of state to publish the names of everyone who had received grants of two thousand or more acres that were awaiting the governor's signature. The legislators presumably intended this measure to alert the people whose plantations or prior grants were threatened. Included on the list of "excessive" surveys were sixty-one separate grants to thirty people for a total of about two million acres.[19]

Participation in the land schemes of the 1790s was perfectly consistent with the earlier behavior of rising backcountry planters who were eager to extend their holdings in land and slaves. Of the thirty men identified by the secretary of state as recipients of questionable, speculative surveys, at least nineteen were from the backcountry. Among them were such prominent backcountrymen as Thomas Sumter, his son Thomas Sumter, Jr., and John Hampton, brother of Wade. Laurence Rambo, another suspected speculator, was the son and brother of prosperous planters who, as Regulators, had participated in the whipping of John Harvey in 1769. The secretary of state listed Rambo as having received a suspect warrant for 55,543 acres in the Orangeburg pine barrens. At the time, he was living in Edgefield County and owned four slaves. Although South Carolina had already ceded her western claims, Christopher Lewis, owner of four slaves in Claremont County, received a suspect warrant for 27,920 acres located on the south side of the Tennessee River. The lands were originally surveyed for Richard Hampton and Thomas Sumter.[20]

A number of the suspect grantees were deputy surveyors. Richard Bettis of Cheraws, owner of seven slaves in 1790, surveyed his own warrant for 35,000 acres in his home district, and David Squier surveyed 95,750 acres for himself in Cheraws. William Minor of Orangeburg drew surveys for himself totaling more than 140,000 acres. John Bynum surveyed two tracts in Orangeburg for himself and his uncle, John Hampton. The surveys totaled 60,914 acres. Finally, Alexander Boling Stark surveyed 39,308 acres in Orangeburg for his brother, Robert Stark.[21]

In a final effort to counter this pervasive "spirit of speculation and land-jobbing," the legislature, at the end of 1794, passed a comprehensive land act. The act accused speculators of trying to "impose upon, deceive and cheat unwary foreigners, by sales of such pretended vacant lands." The

---

19. Senate Jour., Nov. 30, 1793; South Carolina House of Representatives Journal, Nov. 30, 1793, SCDAH (hereafter cited as House Jour.); *Col. Herald*, Feb. 3, 1794. For an example of a careless "excessive" grant, see plat of July 9, 1793, State Plats, XXIX, 173–175, SCDAH.

20. *Col. Herald*, Feb. 3, 1794; Brown, "Prosopography of the Regulators," 133–137; *Heads of Families, 1790*; Index to State Plats.

21. *Col. Herald*, Feb. 3, 1794; *Heads of Families, 1790*; Index to State Plats.

result, according to the authors, would be to "oblige the inhabitants who are settled within the boundaries and limits of the aforesaid plats to produce their titles, or, if they had lost them in the war or by other accidents, to seize their lands as vacant." In order to "prevent the alarms of the people," the act closed the land office for four years and limited future grantees to five hundred acres. It made holders of excessive surveys liable to legal prosecution by any proprietors whose lands were subsumed in the large surveys and called for prosecution of surveyors who drew fraudulent plats.[22]

The limited efforts of South Carolina's legislature were not sufficient to halt the issuance of speculative grants. In 1794, before Governor Moultrie left office, thirty-nine individuals, including such large-scale speculators as Thomas Sumter and Minor Winn, received grants for 2,000 or more acres. Most of the grantees simply divided the acreage into 1,000-acre segments. Thus, Hugh Middleton, an Edgefield planter and former state representative, along with two inland associates, received joint title to nearly 195,000 acres in Pendleton. The property was divided into 195 separate tracts. In similar fashion, the Charlestonian Robert Brodie received title to 219,173 acres in Camden. Thomas Sumter, whose grant to 19,000 acres in Camden had already been listed by the legislature as "excessive" and illegal, did not even bother to divide the property into smaller, consecutive surveys.[23]

Nor did legislative attention prevent the signing of the largest speculative grants. Governor Moultrie, who himself held more than two thousand acres in Ninety Six, signed all of the surveys that the legislature had specifically earmarked as "excessive." In December 1794, with a new governor in office, a Senate committee determined that "all large Grants which the legislature fully intended should not be signed and delivered out, have, since the last meeting of the Legislature received the signature of the late Governor." Though the committee recommended that "all those Grants ought to undergo a judicial determination in the Circuit Courts," there is no indication that such legal measures were ever taken. Camden's circuit solicitor did follow the legislature's instructions by ordering the ten recipients of excessive Camden-area grants to appear in the district court during the November session, but the group, which included Thomas Sumter and his son, never appeared. They had already disposed of their lands.[24]

Morris and Nicholson, who acquired most of the publicized "excessive" grants along with hundreds of thousands acres in additional South Carolina

22. Cooper and McCord, eds., *Statutes of South Carolina*, V, 233–235; Senate Jour., Dec. 7, 1793.

23. Index to State Grants.

24. Senate Jour., Dec. 19, 1794; Camden Court of Common Pleas, Journal, Apr. 1794, II, 64, SCDAH; Bridwell, "South's Wealthiest Planter," 313–314.

grants, relied upon a number of politically prominent local contacts. Wade Hampton and his partners, Dr. John Hall and Gideon Denison, both of Georgia, were the primary agents for the Philadelphians. By the end of 1794, they had purchased 1,261,256 acres in South Carolina, consisting primarily, though not exclusively, of the "excessive" grants illegally signed by Moultrie. They sold most of the property to the Philadelphia speculators. Working along with Hampton as an intermediary was William Tate, owner of ironworks in the upper piedmont. In 1793, Thomas Sumter also received a power of attorney from Morris and Nicholson, presumably for the purpose of purchasing backcountry lands. He may well have intended to transfer some of his own substantial holdings. At least one tract of nearly 41,000 acres surveyed for Sumter in Ninety Six District was sold through another intermediary to Morris and Nicholson.[25]

The scheme that signaled the downfall of Morris and Nicholson was initially intended to bolster their faltering enterprises. Following a rush of purchases in 1793 and 1794, the partners formally consolidated their property into a corporation they called the North American Land Company. They planned to issue shares on the basis of their six-million-acre holdings in Pennsylvania, Virginia, North Carolina, South Carolina, and Georgia. Though they sent agents throughout the United States and Europe, Morris and Nicholson were unable to raise the much-needed credit or to sell a substantial number of shares. Pressed by creditors and tax collectors, they were, by 1796, already in dire straits. In 1797, they went bankrupt, and soon thereafter both men entered the debtors' apartment of Philadelphia's Walnut Street Prison.[26]

Having paid their associates with personal notes, the partners managed to bring down with them many of the local speculators from whom they had purchased land. Harper suffered serious financial setbacks, and speculation probably contributed to Thomas Sumter's continuing financial woes. Wade Hampton, who emerged unscathed from his speculative ventures, was probably unique.[27] Recalling his own role in the land-grab of the early

25. Bridwell, "South's Wealthiest Planter," 314–318, 332–343; Indenture from Robert Morris, Esq. and John Nicholson, Esq. to John Greenleaf, Esq., Private Papers, Sumter Family, Mortgages, box 1, SCDAH; Thomas Sumter to John Nicholson, Jan. 29, 1793, Thomas Sumter Papers, SCL, deeds of Nov. 28, Dec. 1–2, 1794, County Deeds, WPA Abs., Anderson County, no. 26, B, 27, C–D (MS, 53–54, 317–322). Thomas Ruston, the Philadelphia physician who purchased Sumter's land, was an associate of Morris and Nicholson. See Arbuckle, *Pennsylvania Speculator and Patriot*, 189.

26. Arbuckle, *Pennsylvania Speculator and Patriot*, 167–201; *Robert Morris*, 312–313.

27. "List of Creditors Who Have Proved Their Debts in the Case of Robert Morris," newspaper clipping, n.d., Simon Gratz Collection, Old Congress, case 1, box 9, HSP;

1790s, Robert Goodloe Harper ruefully described the time when "Morris and Nicholson, then in such credit that their notes passed as cash, were engaged in those extensive purchases of Southern lands which led finally to the ruin of themselves and so many other persons." By 1796, even Samuel Green was longing "to be rid of speculation." It was, he now believed, "a very troublesome companion. It will scarce let me sleep. I think it much worse than love."[28]

iii

Although speculation failed to fulfill the economic aspirations of land-hungry South Carolinians, it did foster complex bonds between leading political figures of the backcountry and the lowcountry, even in the midst of the political conflicts that divided the state during the 1780s and 1790s. The explosion of speculation that began after the Revolution contributed to the formation of a political alliance that was opposed to British merchants in Charleston and increasingly sympathetic to inland demands for political parity. A number of lowcountrymen who became extensively involved in speculation were already distanced from the Charleston-area elite, and, for such men, the acquisition of backcountry lands both reflected and furthered political identifications with that region.

Whether they turned to speculation in order to recoup losses suffered at the hands of British merchants or because their hostility toward the Charleston-area elite drew them to the backcountry, leading members of the Charleston opposition became involved in the land-grab. Most notable was Alexander Gillon, who, by the time of the Revolution, already owned nearly six thousand acres near the Congaree River in addition to fifteen town lots in Charleston. In 1783 and 1784, he received grants that totaled nearly fifteen hundred acres in Ninety Six. Beset by financial woes, Gillon sold his elegant home in St. Andrew Parish and, in 1793, one year before his

---

Robert Goodloe Harper, "Autobiographical Sketch," Robert Goodloe Harper Papers, MHS; Bridwell, "South's Wealthiest Planter," 319–378. At the time of his death, Sumter had mortgaged all his slaves. He was saved from relentless creditors by the citizens of Sumter and Kershaw districts who, in 1827, successfully petitioned the state legislature for aid in order to "extricate Genl. Sumter from Embarrassments . . . and restore tranquility to the declining years of this old soldier." The petition was probably organized by Sumter's son. Gregorie, *Thomas Sumter*, 270–274; Memorial of Sundry Inhabitants to the House of Representatives, [1827], Lyman C. Draper Manuscripts, Ser. VV, Thomas Sumter Papers, I, no. 178, SHSW.

28. Harper, "Autobiographical Sketch"; Samuel Green to Timothy Green, Feb. 21, 1796, Samuel Green Papers.

death, moved to his plantation on the Congaree River. His new residence was not far from the home of Wade Hampton, and Gillon's inland holdings led him to support Hampton and Taylor in pressing for Columbia as the site of the new state capital. According to one account, he and Thomas Sumter nearly came to blows as they disputed the point. Gillon's hatred of British merchants, financial troubles on the coast, and landed interest in the backcountry made him a natural ally of inland leaders. In 1788, he ran unsuccessfully against William L. Smith, a Charlestonian who was closely tied to the British merchant community, in a bid for a seat in the First United States Congress. By that time he was already serving as a representative from the middlecountry district of Saxe Gotha.[29]

Other outspoken opponents of the British merchant community also had landed interests in the backcountry. In 1786 and 1787, Dr. John Budd received Orangeburg grants for 2,000 and 1,874 acres, respectively. He already had nearly 3,000 acres in Georgetown, Camden, and Ninety Six. In 1786, O'Brien Smith, a representative from St. Bartholomew and a close friend to Aedanus Burke, received joint ownership of an Orangeburg grant for 11,001 acres. A native of Ireland, Smith had moved to South Carolina during the early 1780s after inheriting lands in Ninety Six. He chose to live in St. Bartholomew, but shared certain backcountry concerns. Firmly opposed to Charleston's resident British merchants, Smith supported backcountry efforts to move public records to an inland location. Although he did not go so far as to favor the call for state constitutional reform, he did join the inland delegates who opposed ratification of the United States Constitution. Both Smith and Alexander Moultrie later joined Charleston artisans and backcountry settlers as enthusiastic supporters of French expansionist schemes in Florida and Louisiana.[30]

Thomas Tudor Tucker never became actively involved in the Charleston opposition movement, but he was a leading advocate of state constitutional reform and, along with Gillon, moved with ease into the backcountry political environment. Born in Bermuda, Tucker arrived in Charleston before the Revolution and found it difficult to establish his medical practice there. He turned instead to St. George, Dorchester, and served intermittently as a state representative from that parish until 1787. Tucker was no friend to the

29. Index to State Grants; Edgar *et al.*, eds., *Biographical Directory of the House*, III, 268–272; Joseph Johnson, *Traditions and Reminiscences, Chiefly of the American Revolution in the South* (Charleston, S.C., 1851), 137–138.

30. Index to State Grants; Edgar *et al.*, eds., *Biographical Directory of the House*, III, 103–104, 667–669; Johnson, *Traditions and Reminiscences*, 436–437; House Jour., Feb. 25, 1789; List of Members of the Republican Society Established in Charleston, S.C., Apr. 14, 1794, Republican Society of South Carolina Papers, BPL. See also Chapter 7.

powerful Goose Creek contingent. In 1786, Ralph Izard worked successfully to prevent Tucker's reelection. After the defeat the two men met in a
duel, at which Tucker received a serious wound in the leg. He won some
satisfaction by defeating Izard's cousin in a special election the same year,
but Tucker's attention was already moving inland. Also in 1786, Tucker
took advantage of the state's liberalized land law to acquire a grant to 3,517
acres in Camden. He purchased smaller tracts in Ninety Six and, by 1799,
had nearly 8,000 acres divided among Charleston and the two inland districts. Tucker was also a planter with thirty-one slaves. He represented
Ninety Six District in the First and Second United States Congresses and
subsequently became a member of the state's Republican coalition.[31]

Speculative interests also played a key role in drawing Robert Goodloe
Harper into the backcountry political orbit. A native of Fredericksburg,
Virginia, Harper attended Princeton and moved to Charleston in 1785 in
order to study law. In 1787, having decided that his prospects in Charleston
looked dim, he moved to Abbeville in Ninety Six District. Two years later,
for reasons that are not clear, Harper returned to Charleston, where his
most consuming interest was land speculation. By 1791, he was a lawyer for
the South Carolina Yazoo Land Company and a substantial shareholder.
During a trip to Columbia in the summer of 1794, he met Wade Hampton,
an old acquaintance, who convinced him of the profits to be won by acting
as an agent for Morris and Nicholson. In an arrangement with Hampton,
Harper proceeded to purchase several hundred thousand acres from local
grantees for resale to the Philadelphians. Harper's speculative activities in
the backcountry may well have influenced his decision to establish a residence at Ninety Six. In 1794, the same year in which he offered himself as a
backcountry congressional candidate, he purchased a plantation on credit,
expecting the proceeds from his land sales to Morris and Nicholson to
cover the cost. Harper lived to regret his speculative ventures. If his autobiography is to be believed, he never received the promised sum from Wade
Hampton.[32]

Harper's involvement in speculation extended and reflected what must
have been deeper sources of identification with backcountry leaders. Although his opposition to debtor legislation and growing Federalist sympathies on national issues tied him to the Charleston-area elite, his staunch

31. George C. Rogers, Jr., *Evolution of a Federalist; William Loughton Smith of
Charleston (1758–1812)* (Columbia, S.C., 1962), 128; Edgar et al., eds., *Biographical
Directory of the House,* III, 725–726; Index to State Grants.

32. Joseph W. Cox, *Champion of Southern Federalism: Robert Goodloe Harper of
South Carolina* (Port Washington, N.Y., 1972), 11, 14–24; Harper, "Autobiographical
Sketch"; Bridwell, "South's Wealthiest Planter," 326–332.

support for constitutional reform identified him firmly with his inland constituency. In 1794, at the height of his involvement in the speculative bubble, he became the spokesman for the backcountry Representative Reform Association, a group whose purpose was to achieve political parity for inland counties. Not coincidentally, Wade Hampton was a member of the association's General Committee.

During the 1790s, Harper became a lawyer for Pierce Butler, who, more than anyone else, illustrates the complex relationship between speculation and interregional political connections. Butler was a wealthy planter of Beaufort District with more than four hundred slaves by 1810. His personal background and landed interest in the backcountry drew him into a deepening political identification with inland leaders. The son of a minor Irish aristocrat, Butler arrived in Charleston in 1767, while serving in the British army. There he arranged an elopement with the wealthy heiress Elizabeth ("Betsy") Izard, but members of the Izard family sabotaged the plan. Despite the threat of a lawsuit by the Izards, Butler remained in Charleston and acquired a fortune by marrying into the wealthy Middleton family. With the outbreak of the Revolution, he became a strong supporter of the whig cause. As a newcomer to South Carolina, eager to make his fortune, Butler shared certain fundamental traits with the inland leadership. He also shared backcountry concerns about the British merchant community in Charleston. Involved in an extended litigation during the 1780s and 1790s with the British merchant Hercules Bize, Butler had personal experience of the problem. From 1784 into 1785, he traveled to Holland with the hope of securing an alternative source of credit. In 1788, he led an unsuccessful effort in the House to pass a new valuation bill.[33]

Butler's involvement in land speculation strengthened his ties to the backcountry. Between 1772 and 1788, he obtained grants to nearly eleven thousand acres in addition to the Beaufort property acquired through marriage. Among his extensive holdings were more than eight thousand acres in the backcountry. In the midst of the Revolution, Butler became involved in a speculative enterprise with the merchants Joseph Atkinson and Daniel Bourdeaux, and, by 1786, he was a partner with Wade Hampton and John

---

33. Pierce Butler to Robert Goodloe Harper, Feb. 18, 1792, Mar. 6, 1794, Pierce Butler Letterbook, 1790–1794, II, 170–172, 338, Pierce Butler Papers, SCL; George D. Terry, ed., "Pierce Butler's Letters to the Leaders of the South Carolina Backcountry, August 27, 1791 to March 6, 1794," introd., ix, SCL; Edgar *et al.*, eds., *Biographical Directory of the House*, III, 108–113; *Dictionary of American Biography*, s.v. "Butler, Pierce"; *City Gazette, and the Daily Advertiser* (Charleston), Feb. 9, 1788. John Lewis Gervais attempted to follow Butler's example by seeking credit from the Dutch. See Gervais and John Owen to Leonard De Neufville, Apr. 13, 1786, John Lewis Gervais Papers, SCL.

Rutledge in another speculative scheme. Butler was probably involved in
the first South Carolina Yazoo Land Company as well. His most valuable
inland holding was a one-hundred-thousand-acre tract in Ninety Six that he
acquired in 1792. Originally granted to the British merchant Joseph Salvadore before the Revolution, the property had been of interest to Butler for
some years. Butler was finally able to obtain partial ownership by standing
as security for one of his former partners; however, with pressure from
creditors, his title to the property remained insecure. Butler attempted to
sell part of the tract to Morris and Nicholson, and he probably had other
business connections to the Philadelphians. It was concerning these lands in
Ninety Six that he secured legal assistance from Harper.[34]

Recognizing the necessity of establishing inland contacts to facilitate his
speculative endeavors, Butler set about gaining influence among backcountry leaders. Along with other speculators, he was concerned about the danger of Indian war and the location of western boundary lines. Butler was
particularly solicitous of Andrew Pickens, who was involved in negotiations
with the western Indians. "I would," wrote Butler to Pickens in 1792, "express myself more fully could I be certain that this letter would fall into no
hand but your own, but there is so much curiosity afloat that it would not
be expedient to be very explicit." The following year he asked Pickens to
write "as often as you can make it convenient" and indicated that he would
do what he could to make Pickens's son, Andrew Pickens, Jr., a congressman. Butler went so far as to arrange the appointment of his friend James
Seagrove as superintendent of Indian affairs. "It is expected," Butler informed Seagrove, "that you will be much among the Indians and gain an
ascendancy over them. Give constant information and I expect a copy of
what you write that I may be as well informed as the others." "I have," he
added, "a prospect of settling my private affairs to my satisfaction, if I
succeed you shall also."[35]

Butler also depended upon prominent backcountrymen for advice and
help in the sale of his extensive inland holdings. In 1794, he assured a
prospective purchaser of a tract from his Salvadore lands that John Hunter,

34. Index to Colonial Land Grants; Index to State Grants; Edward Rutledge to Samuel
Saxon, Sheriff of Ninety Six, Aug. 5, 1791, Testimony by Robert Goodloe Harper, Jan.
24, 1792, Payment of Debt by Richard and Wade Hampton, in partnership with Pierce
Butler, John Rutledge, *et al.*, July 6, 1792, Miscellaneous Records, bk. A(3), 373, 471–
472, SCDAH (hereafter cited as Misc. Records); Edgar *et al.*, eds., *Biographical Directory of the House*, III, 109–110; Pierce Butler to John Nicholson, Mar. 19, 20, 1793,
Gratz Collection, First Congress, case 1, box 28.
35. Pierce Butler to Andrew Pickens, Nov. 22, 1792, Feb. 2, 1793, Butler to James
Seagrove, Sept. 28, 1791, Butler Letterbook, II, 239, I, 137–138, Butler Papers, SCL.

a former surveyor who was soon to become a congressman from Ninety Six, had examined the property. Hunter had provided assurances the lands would be salable to the tenants and neighboring settlers for a substantial sum. Andrew Pickens also knew Butler's property "as well as any man can know it" and advised his friend on its value. Undoubtedly, such services reinforced Butler's opinion that there were "not two more respectable men in the district [of Ninety Six] than General Pickens and Mr. Hunter." Several years later, Butler sent Thomas Sumter a power of attorney and requested that the general do his best to sell some lands on the Wateree River.[36]

As Butler's landed interests drew him toward the inland leadership, a personal dispute deepened his alienation from the Charleston-area elite. In 1792, a wealthy widow, Elizabeth Izard Blake, died, leaving a substantial property to Butler's children. A cousin of the deceased Mrs. Butler, Elizabeth Blake had been careful to insist that Pierce Butler be kept from the property, which was to be managed by her executors, Edward Rutledge and the Pinckney brothers, Charles Cotesworth and Thomas. According to Cotesworth Pinckney's account, Butler was deeply angered when the executors honored the widow's request.[37]

Butler's antagonism toward British merchants and resentment of powerful coastal acquaintances converged with his landed interest in the backcountry and his personal identification with certain backcountry leaders to make him a leading proponent of inland demands for political parity and an inland capital. As a United States congressman in 1790, Butler could not attend the State Convention that framed the new South Carolina Constitution, but he was careful to inform a friend of his sentiments. Butler urged that Charleston not be allowed "the preposterous Representation she now has which gives Her an unjust Ascendancy in all the measures of Government." In Charleston he observed "a strong bias to aristocracy in a great part of the citizens." Unlike many of his colleagues from Beaufort District, Butler was not satisfied with the new Constitution. When, in 1794, he heard that backcountry leaders had organized the Representative Reform Association, he wrote to Harper, "with Great satisfaction . . . on the dawning of light and perception in the minds of our fellow citizens of the partial and unjust state of representation under our new as well as old State Consti-

36. Pierce Butler to W. T. Franklin, Aug. 21, 1793, Jan. 22, 1794, Butler Letterbook, II, 308, 312, Butler Papers, SCL; Pierce Butler to Thomas Sumter, Feb. 9, 1796, Pierce Butler Letterbook, 1787–1822, HSP.
37. Rogers, *Evolution of a Federalist*, 184.

tution."[38] Butler's backcountry identification on statewide matters would also influence his positions on national affairs. Although he joined his low-country fellows as a leading Federalist at the State Convention that ratified the United States Constitution, he shortly came out as an opponent of the first administration and a leader of the backcountry Republican coalition.

It would be a mistake to conclude that lowcountry speculators in back-country land were uniformly sympathetic to backcountry critiques of the state government or that speculation in land somehow became an index of political attitudes among the state leadership. The list of South Carolinians who received speculative grants after the Revolution includes several clear opponents of inland and artisan challenges to the Charleston-area political elite. Gabriel Manigault of Charleston and St. James, Goose Creek, re-ceived a grant in 1786 for 2,163 acres in Camden. He had already inherited nearly 25,000 acres, most of which were located in the lowcountry. Mani-gault's inland holdings in no way weakened his attachment to the social and political faction that was most closely aligned to the British merchants in Charleston.[39]

John Rutledge, former governor of South Carolina, was more deeply involved in speculation than Manigault, and although his political views remained somewhat more ambiguous, he, too, was an opponent of inland and artisan opposition movements. In addition to the substantial backcoun-try acreage acquired before the Revolution, Rutledge acquired more than twenty thousand backcountry acres in state grants. In 1786, he joined Pierce Butler and others in a speculative enterprise, and, at the time of his death in 1800, he maintained a residence at Camden. Along with the Pinckneys, Rutledge was firmly opposed to the British merchant community in Charleston, and he refused to align himself with the conservative Izard-Manigault wing of the coastal elite. But he never became a political ally of Gillon, Sumter, Butler, or the leadership in Ninety Six.[40]

38. Pierce Butler to John McPherson, Feb. 13, 1790, Nov. 6, 1792, Pierce Butler to Robert Goodloe Harper, Mar. 6, 1794, Butler Letterbook, I, 9, II, 226, 338, Butler Papers, SCL.

39. Index to State Grants; Edgar *et al.*, eds., *Biographical Directory of the House*, III, 470–472; Rogers, *Evolution of a Federalist*, 80–92, 124–129. Manigault was firmly opposed to the establishment of an inland capital and to backcountry pressure for consti-tutional reform. See House Jour., Jan. 23, Feb. 28, Mar. 4, 1789, in Thompson *et al.*, eds., *Journals of the House, 1789–1790*, 61, 199, 221.

40. Index to Colonial Land Grants; Index to State Grants; Taxable Property, Oct. 1, 1791, John Rutledge Papers, SCL; Payment of a Debt by Richard and Wade Hampton, in partnership with Pierce Butler, John Rutledge, *et al.*, July 6, 1792, Misc. Records, bk. A(3), 471–472; will of John Rutledge, Feb. 20, 1803, County Wills, Kershaw County, WPA Trans., I, bk. C, 65–66, SCDAH; Lisle A. Rose, *Prologue to Democracy: The*

Manigault and Rutledge were not unique, but the fact remains that the majority of post-Revolutionary speculators were from the backcountry and that most politically prominent lowcountry speculators had political ties to the inland leadership. Involvement in speculation did not force coastal leaders to develop political identifications with the backcountry, but the great land-grab did attract the sort of ambitious or economically troubled men who were already likely to have experienced some degree of alienation from the Charleston-area elite. Speculation strengthened the bonds between such men and the inland leadership.

iv

An intriguing question remains: What finally became of settlers living on lands included in the "excessive" grants, and how did the land engrossment associated with speculation affect class relations within the backcountry? One thing is certain: Those settlers who actually signed the three petitions directed against specific speculative grants were only a small minority of the people affected. Although in those cases the legislature upheld the claims of the petitioners, it was ineffective in limiting speculation on a wider scale. Even after the collapse of the land bubble, individual backcountrymen were left with enormous tracts that inevitably encompassed lands inhabited by squatters, renters, or prior grantees.

Two backcountry tax lists from the southern part of Orangeburg District suggest that speculation contributed to the formation of larger and somewhat more concentrated holdings in land among taxpayers in that area. In 1787, during the first phase of the speculative boom, the top 10 percent of Orangeburg landholders held 44 percent of the taxable acreage and an average of 1,110 acres. Thirteen years later, the top 10 percent of the region's landholders owned 50 percent of the taxable land and an average of 2,722 acres. The largest single holding on the 1787 list was 2,327 acres. By 1800, the largest landholders were speculators with vast holdings ranging to nearly 24,000 acres. Most of these speculative tracts were located entirely in the pine barrens, but the largest single holding was valued at a sufficiently high rate to suggest that the owner either lacked the requisite local influence with the assessor or that his property included acreage suitable for farming.[41]

Federalists in the South, 1789–1800 (Lexington, Ky., 1968), 106–107; Rogers, *Evolution of a Federalist,* 115, 191–192.

41. Tax Returns, 1787–1793, Orangeburg District, 1787, box 3, no. 8; Tax Returns,

The very absence of more widespread protest is surprising. That the situation never did provoke "the alarms of the people" suggests that many large-scale owners worked out acceptable arrangements with prior settlers in order to avoid conflict. In the case of the predominantly pine barren lands transferred to Morris and Nicholson and other Philadelphia speculators, the "excessive" grants probably made no difference whatsoever. The North American Land Company failed because the partners were unable to sell their extensive holdings. That the jailed Philadelphians held essentially worthless and ill-defined grants to much of South Carolina's least valuable acreage was probably irrelevant to settlers and squatters who were actually living on the property.

In cases where South Carolinians retained their "excessive" grants, the situation was more complex. Some large-scale owners simply dispossessed settlers or squatters. William Moultrie's agent in the backcountry appears to have taken the practice for granted. As he informed Moultrie in 1792, "I have been and seen your land about the Piney Bluff both upwards and Downwards, But as the Surveyor has not surveyed it, I cannot find its Bounds and so I am not able to Warn any one off." Andrew Pickens provided similar services for Cotesworth Pinckney, who, by 1804, owned substantial acreage in Pendleton. Pickens informed Pinckney that there were "many intruders" on the land. In addition, wrote Pickens, "there are two small tracts which are Settled under Grants of an old date which I presume will hold the land, the others I believe will not contend." Prior grantees, though threatened, had legal recourse, but many others, whose stories have been lost, faced eviction. With the spread of cotton into the backcountry, large-scale landowners had added reason to turn squatters off the more fertile acreage.[42]

Where lands were valuable, owners might try to transform squatters into renters. This, at least, was the arrangement that Butler tried to establish on the one-hundred-thousand-acre Salvadore tract, but his limited success points to the dilemma confronted by large-scale owners. In January 1794, anticipating sizable profits from renting, Butler urged his attorney to "fix

1800, Winton County, Comptroller General Tax Record Books, box 107, folder 2. The 1787 list appears to include a small area within the region that was designated as Winton County in 1785. The earlier record lists only 148 taxables, while the Winton list includes 802. Backcountry tax records provide only limited help in probing the impact of speculation on class relations in the backcountry. The problem lies not only in the small number and often fragmentary nature of the surviving 18th-century backcountry tax lists but also in the failure of those records to include squatters who did not own taxable property.

42. Joseph Martin to William Moultrie, July 24, 1792, William Moultrie Papers, SCL; Andrew Pickens to Cotesworth Pinckney, Jan. 2, 1804, Andrew Pickens Papers, SCL.

on some of the heads or principal settlers that refuse to pay rent, and bring Ejectments against them without loss of time." Those, he added, "who are orderly and acknowledge themselves my tenants may have a lease for one year." The problem, as Butler soon discovered, was that many of the settlers were unwilling and unable to pay. According to Butler's upcountry agent, William Tennent, those who lived on the more than ninety settlements encompassed by the Salvadore tract were "generally very poor, many of whom do not cultivate more than three or four acres of land and some less." Some of the settlers, recognizing that they had no legal title to their farms, may have followed Butler's directive and departed, but the majority apparently refused. In July 1797, Tennent, "after much difficulty," succeeded in collecting slightly more than £59 in rent, but after deducting £50 for his own services, he left a rather paltry sum for Butler. In 1805, Butler was still struggling to collect rents on his Salvadore lands. His new agent, Eldred Simkins, believed that "the great bulk of citizens now on the land . . . would pay rent and perhaps a great number would consent to buy." But Simkins advised Butler to "commence *a few suits* . . . to try the principle," in order to put pressure on recalcitrant settlers.[43]

If Butler's experience was characteristic of problems confronted by large-scale owners, it is not difficult to understand why Joseph Kershaw was eager to sell land to prior settlers rather than attempting to rent. Finding himself seriously in debt after the Revolution, Kershaw attempted to take advantage of the state's liberalized land law by acquiring more than seven thousand additional acres in Camden. In 1787, he was forced to sell a plantation along with various tracts of land in his home district and in Ninety Six. In advertising the sale, he recognized that people had already "set down upon the Lands" and promised to give those settlers preference.[44]

Settlers on a speculative tract in Orangeburg who struggled successfully to protect their lands testify to the limits within which large-scale owners were forced to operate. According to Robert Goodloe Harper, Jacob Rumph, a leading planter and political figure of Orangeburg District, purchased his grant to 181,000 acres in Orangeburg "without any expectation of making anything by them, but merely with a view of preventing some poor people, who had settled on them, from being molested." With some

43. Pierce Butler to William Tennent, Jan. 28, 1794, Butler Letterbook, II, 317, SCL; William Tennent to Pierce Butler, Oct. 20, 1794, July 13, 1797, Eldred Simkins to Pierce Butler, Aug. 18, 1805, Butler Family Papers, Major Pierce Butler, box 3, HSP. Settlers are identified by name in William Tennent to Pierce Butler, June 14, 1794, Butler Family Papers, Major Pierce Butler, box 3.
44. *State Gazette of South-Carolina* (Charleston), Nov. 26, 1787.

persuasion, Rumph agreed to sell the property, but only on the condition that Harper "take steps to secure" the settlers. Wade Hampton eventually sold 150,000 acres of Rumph's tract to Morris and Nicholson. "The rest," according to Harper, "was deducted for the claims of the settlers." It seems doubtful that Rumph, in purchasing the lands, could have been entirely uninterested in the possibility of profiting by them, and subsequent events suggest that settlers played a larger role in their own protection than Harper's account would allow. When Harper engaged a man to resurvey the acreage before reselling it to Morris and Nicholson, the settlers were still suspicious and careful to protect their individual holdings. Some years later, the surveyor recalled:

> The inhabitants residing within the Limits of the said Patent or Grant were much dissatisfied and had expressed a determination not to permit their line to be closed or run through or upon nor to permit the resurvey to be made—and as I conceived it both a difficult and laborious under-taking even with the aid and assistance of the inhabitants there being a very great quantity of older granted land within the said patent, and mostly in small Tracts.

The surveyor was so intimidated by the opposition that he refused to finish the job. He recommended that someone else, better acquainted with the settlers, take over.[45]

On much of the land included in the speculative surveys of the 1780s and 1790s, tenantry or resale to squatters would have been inconceivable. Even Butler had difficulty attracting tenants to the less desirable areas of his tract in Ninety Six, and it seems unlikely that owners of less fertile land in more sparsely settled regions could have been any more successful.[46] In other words, large-scale owners of infertile acreage had little reason to involve themselves in the inevitable difficulties that accompanied efforts to enforce tenantry agreements or ejectments. Thomas Sumter's situation provides an illuminating case in point. His nineteen-thousand-acre grant in Camden District encompassed the lands of at least three planters in addition to a tract that Sumter's own plat labeled simply as "persons unknown." Another

45. Harper, "Autobiographical Sketch"; indenture between R. G. Harper, John Hall, and Jacob Rumph, Sept. 10, 1794, Robert Goodloe Harper Papers, SCL; deposition taken from John Bynam (Bynum) April 18, 1804, General Court, Western Shore Maryland, MHS. I am grateful to Ronald Bridwell for informing me of this deposition and for providing me with a transcript of it.

46. Referring to Andrew Pickens's report on the Salvadore tract, Butler wrote, "The Land no. 3 in the platt is the very best Land in So Carolina. . . . He [Pickens] says he knows it was let for 3s an acre for such parts as were cultivated by the Tennents, but that tennents could not be got to take one half of it." Butler to Franklin, Aug. 21, 1793, Butler Letterbook, II, 308, Butler Papers, SCL.

grant for eleven thousand acres in the same district enclosed at least four prior surveys held by four prosperous planters.[47] Given the size and location of these holdings, it seems almost certain that there were others living on the property either with or without prior grants.

Apparently Sumter was lenient toward those who lived within the bounds of his enormous grants. According to tradition, he allowed "Indians and half breeds . . . and a number of tenants" to remain on his property without paying rent. During the first decade of the nineteenth century, Sumter sold many small tracts that totaled more than ten thousand acres. Undoubtedly such transactions put squatters at great risk, but, for purposes here, it is more important to note that Sumter did not bother to evict prior settlers on property to which he held title.[48] Along with others whose vast landholdings exceeded anything they could have used for cultivation, Sumter retained both legal and economic power over squatters. Even when he acknowledged the prior title of individual planters, Sumter enjoyed considerable authority simply through his ownership of the surrounding acreage. So long as he did not exercise his authority too strenuously—and there was no particular incentive for him to do so—he could avoid divisive struggles and enhance his own prestige.

The will of Robert Anderson, written in 1810, illustrates the type of relationship that apparently developed between some large-scale landowners and settlers living on the property. Although he was not directly involved in speculation, Anderson did own a substantial amount of acreage in Pendleton County. At his death, he bequeathed 2,514 acres. Included was a tract of about 500 acres that he had agreed to sell to two farmers. Anderson wrote that one of the farmers, a man named Mr. Cunningham, had "lived on the land for several years" without ever having "paid one cent for it." Nor, observed Anderson, had "any writings been drawn for the evidence of any bargain." But rather than forcing payment or calling for Cunningham's eviction, Anderson insisted that the land not be sold and that "the old man shall live upon it during his life if he chooses to do so."[49]

The case of Anderson's second resident farmer, Luke Hubbert, is even more striking. Many years before, Anderson, according to his own account, had agreed to sell Hubbert a portion of land near the tract farmed by

47. Plats of Nov. 15, 1786, Oct. 1, 1793, bk. A(2), 50, 167. State Plats.
48. Gregorie, *Thomas Sumter*, 264. Contested evictions would have appeared in the records of the Camden District Court. Camden Court of Common Pleas, Journal, 1786–1799. During the first decade of the 19th century, Sumter sold several small tracts to people who were already living on the land. See County Deeds, WPA Trans., Sumter County, nos. 841–845.
49. Will of Robert Anderson, Jan. 9, 1813 (written Jan. 25, 1810), County Wills, WPA Trans., Anderson County, I, bk. A, 145–155, SCDAH.

Cunningham. Anderson believed that Hubbert had "lived nearly one year upon it, and left of his own accord." Such departures had occurred several times, but Hubbert had always returned and promised to pay for the property. According to Anderson, Hubbert never remained longer "than was necessary to build a cabin." He had never paid anything for the acreage and was absent when the will was written. Nonetheless, Anderson provided that the lands be retained for Hubbert's return.[50]

v

Of the many small-scale farmers living in the backcountry, only a small fraction could have been involved in the type of arrangement established by Jacob Rumph, Thomas Sumter, and Robert Anderson. With the spread of cotton into the backcountry, evictions from fertile acreage undoubtedly increased. As we shall see, between 1800 and 1810, the state and region experienced not only a net loss of population but a growing problem of vagrancy. It may well be that speculators of the preceding decades, eager to maximize use of their best acreage, contributed to the problem by doing what they could to force squatters off the land.

Nonetheless, Butler's experience and the story of settlers on Jacob Rumph's Orangeburg tract suggest that ejectment was not an easy or automatic process. The very absence of more widespread protest suggests that many large-scale owners, particularly those with infertile lands, resigned themselves to the presence of prior settlers and, like Sumter and Anderson, began to cast themselves in the role of protector. In such a way, they transformed a potential assault on their prerogative into an arrangement that reinforced their power and prestige.

In short, land speculation had a complex impact in the backcountry and throughout the state as a whole. Although the land engrossment associated with speculation threatened to provoke an inland crisis, it also served to strengthen the local standing of politically prominent, large-scale landowners. At the same time, involvement in the speculative schemes of the postwar decades fostered contacts and alliances between political leaders of the lowcountry and the backcountry. Most notable was Pierce Butler, who became a pivotal figure not only in the movement for constitutional reform but in the development of an interregional Republican alliance. Speculation was not tied to either national party, but, within South Carolina, hostility to British merchants, alienation from the coastal elite, and a voracious appetite for land contributed to the development of an interregional challenge to lowcountry Federalism.

50. *Ibid.*

CHAPTER 7

The French Revolution in South Carolina

Despite the steady development of interregional political allegiances among leading men, the mid-1790s was a period of heated sectional conflict in South Carolina. New and unsuccessful backcountry efforts to win constitutional reform coincided with a dispute over national foreign policy that pitted coastal Federalists against inland Republicans. Together with Charleston artisans and a small group of coastal speculators, backcountrymen were the most enthusiastic proponents not only of the French Revolution but of French expansionist schemes into Canada and the Southwest. At the same time, many leading lights of the coastal elite saw the French Revolution as a warning signal against reapportionment in the state government.

Although members of the backcountry's political elite had long demonstrated their attachment to slavery, their democratic-republican rhetoric, in the wake of the French Revolution, provoked considerable concern among the coastal elite. The problem, from the point of view of coastal leaders, was twofold. First was the possibility that democratic-republican political ideas might be taken in dangerously radical directions not only by nonslaveholders but by slaves. The revolution of slaves and free blacks in Saint Domingue and the influx of hundreds of refugees from the island seemed to confirm these fears. Second, backcountry representatives appeared, as a group, incapable of maintaining a firm grip on their own region, too closely identified with their yeoman constituency, and insufficiently sensitive to the most radical implications of the pro-French sentiment that prevailed in their own region. These concerns provided the context within which coastal leaders heard and rejected renewed backcountry calls for state constitutional reform. Distrust of the backcountry was the glue that held South Carolina Federalism together even after national Federalist policies had all but lost their appeal in the southern states.

In the midst of the deepening conflict over constitutional reform in the state, Pierce Butler set about organizing an interregional political coalition that was dedicated to defeat of the Federalist contingent on the coast. In effect, coastal Federalists boxed themselves into a political corner. Their ties to Charleston's merchant community, their baldly elitist vision of the social order, and their identification with a national administration that alienated planters and yeomen on several key issues made it difficult to muster support in their own state, particularly among leading men of the backcountry. Butler's group stepped into the breach. Identified with Jefferson's Republican contingent, its members sought to contain the most democratic implications of backcountry republicanism in order to build a political coalition that could safeguard the interests of planters throughout the southern states.

i

More than any other issue debated in the Third Congress of the United States, the war between England and France, and the internal conflict it sparked, became the focal point of deepening tensions within South Carolina. In April 1793, President George Washington had delighted leading commercial interests by issuing a Proclamation of Neutrality, but, as the British began seizing ships that appeared to be trading with the French West Indies, many in Congress advocated a more aggressive anti-British policy. Sympathetic to their former Revolutionary ally and hostile to their former enemy, many were enraged by the administration's refusal to support the revolutionary government of France. Predictably, William L. Smith, the Federalist congressman from Charleston, opposed a congressional plan to suspend the importation of British goods, but South Carolina's backcountry congressmen voted with the Republican majority.[1]

Despite Smith's pro-British stance, support for France ran high in the port city not only among artisans but among merchants who looked to France (or the French West Indies), rather than to England, as a trade partner. During the summer of 1793, residents of the city organized the Republican Society of South Carolina, which was dedicated to the support of France and the suppression of lurking "aristocracy" at home. At least forty-four of the seventy-seven identifiable members were city craftsmen or mechanics, and at least twelve were native merchants. For such men, participation in the Republican Society of South Carolina was an extension of long-standing

1. 3d Cong., 1st Sess., *Debates and Proceedings in the Congress of the United States, 1789–1824* [Annals of Congress] (Washington, D.C., 1834–1856), IV, 604–606 (hereafter cited as *Annals*).

grievances against British merchants and coastal planters. The society's first printed Declaration observed:

> In as much as an aristocratic ambition has already manifested itself in the conduct, even of some Americans, and has lately been more strongly marked, by its whispers of dissatisfaction to the cause of France, and of mankind: WE do hereby declare, pledging ourselves to each other and to the world, that we, and each of us, will contribute to the utmost of our ability, towards the support of equal liberty and national justice, as well in respect to the French republic, as of the United States, against tyranny and iniquitous rule, in whatever form they may be presented, by any character or body of men appearing in these United States.

A statement issued in August of that year was even more explicit in identifying liberty at home with the cause of the revolution in France. According to the author: "The interest and preservation of France is that of America. If she is oppressed, if she is reduced to slavery, the fate of our land is decided." The following spring, three hundred Charlestonians signed a memorial to Congress protesting British seizures of American ships and insisting that "the present degrading neutrality" was "more injurious to the interests . . . of the republic, than the actual state of war."[2]

By spring 1793, support for France was also mounting in the backcountry, and contemporaries were quick to identify that region as the locus of pro-French sentiment. William L. Smith noticed that the Republican *National Gazette* was the most conspicuous newspaper in the inland counties, and in July, a merchant in Columbia included Thomas Paine's *Rights of Man* on his list of salable books. During his visit to South Carolina, the French consul Michel Angel Bernard de Mangourit observed that the "friends" of France were "all the good farmers and not the pompous planters . . . nearly all of the officers and men who poured out their blood to become free."[3]

Inland settlers, who founded branch organizations of the Republican So-

2. Eugene Perry Link, *Democratic-Republican Societies, 1790–1800* (New York, 1942), 71–72; Republican Society of South Carolina, Declaration, July 13, 1793, in Philip S. Foner, ed., *The Democratic-Republican Societies, 1790–1800: A Documentary Sourcebook of Constitutions, Declarations, Addresses, Resolutions, and Toasts* (Westport, Conn., 1976), 379, 382; *South-Carolina State-Gazette* (Charleston), suppl., Apr. 10, 1794.

3. William L. Smith to Alexander Hamilton, Apr. 24, 1793, in Harold C. Syrett *et al.*, eds., *The Papers of Alexander Hamilton*, XIV (New York, 1969), 338–341; Samuel Green to Timothy Green, July 20, 1793, Samuel Green Papers, SCL; Citizen Mangourit to Minister of Foreign Affairs, 10 Xbre 1793, in Richard K. Murdoch, ed. and trans., "Correspondence of the French Consuls in Charleston, South Carolina, 1793–1797," *SCHM*, LXXIV (1973), 73.

ciety in the piedmont districts of Pinckney, Greenville, and Pendleton, identified the cause of France with their own domestic struggles.[4] Inspired by the arrival of Edmond C. Genêt in April 1793, grand jurors in Washington District addressed Judge Thomas Waties "in the language of republicanism . . . following the glorious example of France" and reiterated inland demands for paper money, public schools, publication of legislative acts, improved postal service, and constitutional reform. Members of the Pinckneyville Democratic Society resolved that "population is the only true principle of representation among a free people." Challenging coastal claims that apportionment should be based on regional tax returns, they observed, "Wealth causes its own influence and ought not to be directly represented." In a thinly veiled challenge to the Charleston-area elite, the Madison Society of Greenville resolved that "all the officers of a free government ought to be divided as equally as possible among the citizens." The four hundred members of Pendleton's Franklin Society protested "the collecting of taxes, or other duties to be paid in money" and insisted that seizures of property and sheriffs' sales were "highly injurious and destructive to the laborious and honest farmer and his family." They also claimed, as the "inherent right of every free man," the right to vote for his militia officers. Camden residents did not have their own Republican society, but in 1794 they celebrated Bastille Day with a large dinner and ball. At a tavern owned by the old Regulator Joshua Dinkins, they concluded their holiday toasts with salutes to "the fair Sans Culottes of America" and "perpetual Union between France and America."[5]

In fact, defenders of the French Revolution saw the conflict between France and England as a magnified image of struggles occurring within their own state and nation. "The world," according to an editorial in the *State Gazette of South-Carolina,* "is at this moment engaged in the important contest—whether the people shall rule or be slaves, the success or ruin of the French republic decides the question." Meanwhile, insisted the writer,

> the aristocracy of all countries are employing every engine that fear, or art, or revenge can devise, to secure and increase their power. . . . They

4. For a list of Republican Societies in South Carolina and throughout the United States, see Link, *Democratic-Republican Societies,* 13–15. That the Republican Society of St. Bartholomew Parish, organized in 1795, was the only such group in any of the coastal parishes besides Charleston is a further indication that coastal support for the French Revolution was centered among city artisans.

5. *State Gazette of South-Carolina* (Charleston), June 28, 1793; Foner, ed., *Democratic-Republican Societies,* 395, 391, 397; *City Gazette, and the Daily Advertiser* (Charleston), Aug. 14, 1794.

throw off the mask, and declare in the Senate, that "The people (whom they call rabble) has no part in the constitution; that an aristocracy forms the essence of it; that wealth makes power and right."

Another defender of France attacked his state's coastal elite by suggesting that an opponent was "bouyed up with that *self importance* which *vanity inspires,* and which *weak minds* derive from the possession of more wealth than their neighbors, regardless of the measures or fortuitous circumstances, by which it was acquired, or the good fortune by which it has been preserved."[6]

Writers on behalf of the French republic went out of their way to defend the Jacobin phase of the Revolution. A Charlestonian defined "Jacobin" as "a man who is a friend to the people, a patron of liberty and equality, of the democratic government, and a hater of tyrants and tyranny." Countering an article by "A Moderate Man," a member of a French Republican Society must have enraged coastal conservatives by suggesting that "aristocrats under the name of *moderate men . . .* caused all the internal divisions in France" and that it was "now necessary to gillotine them as the only way to stop the civil wars." The writer preferred being "a fanatic for the welfare of the people" to being "a support of aristocracy under the colour of a *moderate man.*" Invoking recent charges against South Carolina loyalists, another writer likened critics of Maximilien Robespierre to signers of congratulatory addresses to General Charles Cornwallis.[7]

Interest in speculation strengthened support for the French republic and cemented ties between Charleston and inland Republicans. Alexander Moultrie, recently convicted for embezzling public funds, joined O'Brien Smith, William Tate, and other speculators as leading members of Charleston's Republican Society of South Carolina. They looked to France for aid in ousting Spanish forces and hostile Indians from the western territories. Even Governor William Moultrie, whose son belonged to the Charleston group, may well have been drawn to support for the French cause by his involvement in the land-grab. In August 1794, he wrote a private letter to the French Council of Safety sending "health and brother love" and identifying "Citizen William Tate . . . as one worthy of trust and confidence."

6. *St. Gaz. of South-Carolina,* Nov. 8, Aug. 24, 1793; see also Jan. 10, Feb. 5, Apr. 30, May 2, 14, 1794. Numerous general studies have explored the impact of the French Revolution in the United States. I have relied most heavily on Lance Banning, *The Jeffersonian Persuasion: Evolution of a Party Ideology* (Ithaca, N.Y., 1978), 208–245; John C. Miller, *The Federalist Era, 1789–1801* (New York, 1960), 99–182.

7. *St. Gaz. of South-Carolina,* July 24, Sept. 3, Dec. 17, 1793.

Along with backcountry settlers, such land-hungry men as the Moultries were eager to open the western territories to settlement and the Mississippi River to American commerce.[8]

Joined by western traders who hoped to capture the lucrative Indian fur trade from Spanish and British firms, speculators encouraged French efforts to mobilize a "Republican Army" whose mission would be to attack Spanish forces in Florida and Louisiana. With the help of Stephen Drayton, they planned to send an armed ship from Charleston for a sea attack on St. Augustine. At the same time, they began recruiting soldiers in the western part of the state for an attack by land. By October 1793, the French consul reported that recruitment was "taking place with an ardor so great that instead of 1500 men, we have almost 4000."[9]

Apart from Stephen Drayton, the president of Charleston's Republican Society of South Carolina, all of the identifiable participants were backcountrymen. When a House committee investigated the French recruitment scheme, it identified Jacob R. Brown and John Hamilton, in addition to the Tate brothers, as leading members of a group who had "received and accepted Military Commissions from M. Genet." Brown and Hamilton owned fifteen and three slaves in Newberry and Pendleton counties, respectively. William Urby, also mentioned by the House committee, was a Newberry planter with six slaves. LeRoy Hammond's nephew Samuel was aiding Mangourit as well, but he apparently had sufficient political influence to escape mention by the legislature. In December 1793, the House voted to prosecute Drayton, Hamilton, the Tate brothers, and another participant named Richard Speke for attempting to raise recruits for the French government and "commit acts of hostility against nations at peace with the United States of America."[10]

8. List of Members of the Republican Society Established in Charleston, Apr. 14, 1794, Republican Society of South Carolina Papers, BPL; Link, *Democratic-Republican Societies*, 65–66, 77–78, 133–135; William Moultrie to the French Council of Safety, Aug. 9, 1794, William Moultrie Papers, SCL.

9. Link, *Democratic-Republican Societies*, 65–69; 135–136; *St. Gaz. of South-Carolina*, Apr. 17, 1793; Mangourit to Minister of Foreign Affairs, 10 Xbre of 1793, in Murdoch, ed. and trans., "Correspondence of the French Consuls," *SCHM*, LXXIV (1973), 76.

10. South Carolina Senate Journal, Dec. 7, 1793, SCDAH (hereafter cited as Senate Jour.); U.S., Bureau of the Census, *Heads of Families at the First Census of the United States Taken in the Year 1790: South Carolina* (Washington, D.C., 1908) (hereafter cited as *Heads of Families, 1790*); Members of the Republican Society, Apr. 14, 1794, Samuel Hammond to Mangourit, Mar. 3, 1794, Republican Society Papers; Link, *Democratic-Republican Societies*, 77; John A. Chapman, *History of Edgefield County from the Earliest Settlements to 1897* (Newberry, S.C., 1897), 133. Stephen Drayton subsequently sued the House committee, which consisted of Robert Anderson, Henry William Desaussure, John Rutledge, Jr., Timothy Ford, John Drayton, James Green Hunt, and the back-

In a letter to Genêt, Alexander Moultrie gave clear expression to the interests and outlook that prompted land-hungry South Carolinians to become enthusiastic proponents of French expansionist schemes. Referring to "the Yazoo territory on the Mississippi," Moultrie observed that area was

> the great nursery of the growing strength and future athletic power of America—here will be her riches, here her population and here her weight in the great scale of political Influence.—An intimate connection here formed by the Republic of France with America in politics and commercial interests will be the best cement of French and American Friendship and virtue.

But Moultrie did not rest his case with this celebration of the commercial benefits to be won by French incursions into the Mississippi territory. He also pointed to backcountry settlements as the seedbeds of true republicanism and suggested that westward expansion would weaken aristocratic influences on the coast. "If we look," he continued, "into the state and History of the lower Country of America on her sea borders, we find the soil degenerating fast, the Country depopulating and mostly a foreign interest and mercantile aristocracy of the most poisonous kind prevailing there." Moultrie hoped that backcountry farmers would dominate the political life not only of the state but of the nation. He glorified commercial expansion precisely because he thought that the opening of the Mississippi and the development of trade relations between the United States and France would contribute to the extension of western settlement and thereby increase the political power of the most virtuous segment of the population. The farmer, wrote Moultrie,

> thinks for himself; no implicit faith governs his mind, he asks no boon from greatness or his fellow man [save] the kind Courtesies of social equality: Independent in circumstances he is so in thought and knows no rulers but the social compact of legislation made by himself. Health, competence and Liberty therefore will give to this country that population which has begun and now increases with such rapidity.

Moultrie believed that the mouth of the Mississippi would give rise to "the great Emporium of the new age."[11]

---

countryman William Butler. *S.-C. St.-Gaz.*, May 14, 1794; South Carolina House of Representatives Journal, Dec. 18, 1793, SCDAH (hereafter cited as House Jour.).

11. Alexander Moultrie to Citizen Genêt, Jan. 9, 1794, Edmond C. Genêt Papers, LC. This discussion has profited from Drew R. McCoy's account of the relationship between Republican attitudes toward westward expansion and political economy. See McCoy, *The Elusive Republic: Political Economy in Jeffersonian America* (Chapel Hill, N.C., 1980), esp. 76–104.

ii

If support for France ran high in the backcountry and the port city, many prominent coastal Carolinians were quickly alienated by the pro-French contingent. These loosely organized coastal Federalists shared a deep suspicion of the backcountry and a firm commitment to the maintenance of coastal control of the state government. Conscious of challenges within their own state and beyond its borders, they were opposed to democratic innovations, disturbed by Thomas Jefferson's egalitarian rhetoric, and frightened by the enthusiastic response accorded to the Jacobin phase of the French Revolution. They saw backcountry republicanism not only as a challenge to their personal political power but as a threat to slavery itself. Thus Federalism in South Carolina can best be understood not simply as a defense of the British commercial interest but as a defensive response to the more democratic political ideology that predominated in the backcountry and among artisans of the port city.

Despite their shared suspicion of the backcountry, the Charleston-area Federalist elite was by no means entirely unified. As the historian George C. Rogers has shown in his study of state politics during the 1790s, four family factions competed for federal patronage and exerted powerful but often divergent influences over state politics, maintaining different degrees of identification with the British merchant community. Although William L. Smith was skeptical of the French Revolution from the outset, other Federalist leaders more gradually distanced themselves from the nation's former ally. The Pinckneys and Rutledges, actively hostile to the British mercantile community, initially hailed the Revolution in France, and, when the French minister arrived in South Carolina, both Charles Cotesworth Pinckney and Ralph Izard gave him a warm welcome. Even among coastal leaders, Smith was in the minority by refusing to participate in the festivities surrounding the minister's visit. Writing to Alexander Hamilton in April 1793, Smith could not resist noting that a public dinner planned for Genêt in Camden was "a foolish thing entre nous."[12]

12. George C. Rogers, Jr., *Evolution of a Federalist: William Loughton Smith of Charleston (1758–1812)* (Columbia, S.C., 1962), 180–192, 247; Marvin R. Zahniser, *Charles Cotesworth Pinckney: Founding Father* (Chapel Hill, N.C., 1967), 102–106, 117–118; Smith to Hamilton, Apr. 24, 1793, in Syrett *et al.*, eds., *Papers of Hamilton,* XIV, 341. For another excellent account of Federalism in South Carolina, see Lisle A. Rose, *Prologue to Democracy: The Federalists in the South, 1789–1800* (Lexington, Ky., 1968). In an excellent study, George D. Terry found that South Carolinians did not become actively concerned about the French Revolution until summer of 1793, when hundreds of refugees began flocking to Charleston. See Terry, "A Study of the Impact of

Although representatives throughout the state were duly alarmed when the slaves of Saint Domingue emancipated themselves in 1791, not until the fall of 1793, after France had recognized the revolution in Saint Domingue by issuing an emancipation decree, did coastal conservatives identify the French Revolution as a dangerous threat to slavery. France's general emancipation decree of February 1794 heightened these fears by proclaiming the liberation of slaves throughout the French colonies. With refugee planters and slaves flocking to the state, South Carolina's legislature demonstrated its sympathy by granting £2,000 for relief of "the unfortunate French who were Victims of Convulsions in St. Domingo." In April 1794, members of Charleston's wealthy Huguenot church expelled their minister, John Paul Coste, for including French patriotic hymns in a service, and, in June, the Charleston merchant Nathaniel Russell informed Ralph Izard of a meeting at which he hoped that "some effective measure will be adopted to prevent any evil consequences from that diabolical decree of the national convention which emancipates all the slaves in the french colonies, a circumstance the most alarming that could happen to this country."[13]

Terrified by events in Saint Domingue, coastal leaders became frightened by the conspicuous presence of Genêt and Mangourit. Well aware of the democratic-republican political ideology that prevailed among backcountry settlers and Charleston artisans, South Carolina Federalists were fearful that the French Revolution might spread to the slaves. As events in their own state turned many coastal leaders against the revolution abroad, events in France and Saint Domingue gave an increasingly ominous cast to their image of inland republicans. Mangourit complained of rumors that linked him to suspected slave conspiracies, and refugees from Saint Domingue fueled suspicions with angry letters to Charleston newspapers. A writer for the *Columbian Herald* declared in December 1793 that Genêt was threatening to create disturbances in South Carolina comparable to the Massachusetts Shays's Rebellion, and, during the winter of 1794, the newspaper published several scathing critiques of the French Revolution. In February of that year, William L. Smith drew connections between international, national, and local events. He informed Edward Rutledge that "the proceedings of Drayton, Moultrie, and Genêt are all of a peace with that spirit

---

the French Revolution and the Insurrections in Saint-Domingue upon South Carolina, 1790–1805" (master's thesis, University of South Carolina, 1975).

13. House Jour., Dec. 18, 1793; Senate Jour., Dec. 21, 1793; John Paul Coste to Mangourit, Apr. 14, 1793 (typescript translation), Republican Society of South Carolina Papers; Nathaniel Russell to Ralph Izard, June 6, 1794, quoted in Ulrich B. Phillips, "The South Carolina Federalists," II, *American Historical Review*, XIV (1908–1909), 735.

of anarchy which has been infusing itself into our affairs gradually for a few years past and which increases with a rapidity correspondent with the increasing of the anarchy in France." Ralph Izard was fearful of joining the French war, not simply because such participation would disrupt British trade but because it "would occasion a prodigious number of the lower order of Frenchmen to come to this Country, who would fraternize with our Democratical clubs, and introduce the same horrid tragedies among our Negroes, which have been so fatally exhibited in the French Islands."[14]

iii

Such fears were not confined exclusively to members of the coastal elite. Within the backcountry there were politically prominent men who sought to limit democratizing tendencies within their own region. Recognized as "moderate" men by the state's most outspoken Federalists, these inland political leaders eventually helped to make the republican outlook that predominated in the backcountry more palatable to wealthy coastal planters. Although such men as Robert Anderson, Andrew Pickens, John Hunter, and John Ewing Colhoun represented piedmont counties in the state legislature, they demonstrated a willingness to vote with the coastal majority in opposition to their own region. During the 1790s, they formed the bulwark of a statewide Republican coalition spearheaded by Pierce Butler.

Drawn to the backcountry by his personal identifications, hostility to British merchants, and speculative connections, Butler was, by 1792, already seeking to strengthen his ties to politically influential inland leaders and to organize a national Republican faction within South Carolina. Although he had been a supporter of the administration during his first term as a United States Senator from Beaufort-Orangeburg District, he was, by the time of his election to the Third Congress in 1793, a firm ally of the opposition. His antagonism to the national administration may well have been exacerbated by his failure to win a coveted diplomatic post, but there is no reason not to believe his own explanation for his growing disaffection from Federalist measures. Writing in 1792 to John McPherson, a repre-

14. Mangourit to Minister of Foreign Affairs, 10 Xbre 1793, in Murdoch, ed. and trans., "Correspondence of the French Consuls," *SCHM*, LXXIV (1973), 15; *Columbian Herald* (Charleston), Dec. 27, 1793; William L. Smith to Edward Rutledge, Feb. 15, 1794, William Loughton Smith Papers, SCHS; Ralph Izard to Mathias Hutchinson, Nov. 20, 1794, Ralph Izard Papers, SCL. For articles critical of the French Revolution, see *Col. Herald*, Jan. 10, 17, 20, 1794. For examples of letters by French refugees that attacked French officials, see *St. Gaz. of South-Carolina*, Dec. 7, 12, 21, 1793. The French emancipation decrees and American responses are explored in David Brion Davis, *The Problem of Slavery in the Age of Revolution, 1770–1823* (New York, 1975), esp. 113–163.

sentative and fellow planter from Prince William Parish, Butler recalled, "When the present constitution was established, and the gentlemen who were made choice of to carry it into operation assembled . . . a majority of us brought with our power of acting too lively a sense of the imperfections and weakness of the government established under the confederation of 1775." It was, he continued, "one of the aptness's or imbecilities of the human mind to run from one extreme to the other." Butler hoped that "freemen throughout the United States" would check this tendency toward aristocracy before "it gets the strength to curb them." By January 1793, Butler was sufficiently disenchanted with the national Federalists to inform Robert Anderson that "the Republican party in both houses . . . aim at nothing more than parrying a continuation of measures that have not only been partial in their benefit but highly injurious to the Agricultural Interest." Referring to recent events in France, he observed that Americans were "benefitting in some degree by their success" because the Revolution abroad would serve as a "small check on the aristocratic part of our government."[15]

In fact, the shift in Butler's political attitudes was not so sudden or complete as some have suggested. His overriding concern at the Constitutional Convention had been to protect southern slaveholders from possible encroachments by a strengthened federal government. That same concern contributed to his early disaffection from Federalist policies. By August 1789 he believed that "locality and partiality" in the national Congress was threatening the "Southern interest." Writing to Edward Rutledge the following year, he gave assurances that he would support the plans for funding and assumption of state debts by the federal government because South Carolina, with its large unpaid war debt, would benefit by assistance. Nonetheless, Butler was concerned about the extension of federal powers implied by the acts and wondered whether "posterity in Carolina" would thank him for his actions. In a letter to Robert Goodloe Harper, Butler was more explicit. Referring to a lengthy debate over the apportionment of representatives for each state, he noted that the issue was "a fair southern and Northern question," and he expressed particular displeasure that "some Southern men quit the Southern ground."[16]

15. Pierce Butler to John McPherson, Nov. 6, 1792, Pierce Butler to Robert Anderson, Jan. 5, 1793, Pierce Butler Letterbook, 1790–1794, II, 225, 249, Pierce Butler Papers, SCL. Butler's apparent change of sentiment has been attributed to personal disappointments. See *Dictionary of American Biography*, s.v. "Butler, Pierce"; Lewright Browning Sikes, "The Public Life of Pierce Butler" (Ph.D. diss., University of Tennessee, 1973); Rogers, *Evolution of a Federalist*, 184; Malcolm Bell, Jr., *Major Butler's Legacy: Five Generations of a Slaveholding Family* (Athens, Ga., 1987), 91–92.

16. Pierce Butler to James Iredell, Aug. 11, 1789, quoted in Phillips, "South Carolina Federalists," II, *AHR*, XIV (1908–1909), 731; Pierce Butler to Edward Rutledge, May

Butler's suspicion of merchants in general, and his antipathy toward British merchants in particular, also informed his national political opinions. Like many eighteenth-century Americans, Butler assumed that property in land was inherently more virtuous than less tangible wealth derived from mercantile pursuits. He did not object to commerce so long as it served the needs of farmers and planters. The problem, he believed, was that merchants, with help from the national government, threatened to reduce farmers and planters to dependency. Butler was deeply involved in speculation, and his repeated insistence that the Federalist administration was "tending to prostrate the Landed Interest at the feet of Speculators and the monied interest" makes sense only when considered in the light of these concerns. By attacking "speculators," Butler was referring to creditors, whom he perceived as a personal and political threat. Writing to Andrew Pickens in 1793, Butler might almost have been referring to Charleston's resident British merchants when he described his distress at seeing "upstart speculators not known in America during the war, wallowing in the wealth of nabobs, enjoying the earnings of the war worn soldier or fair industrious farmer or planter." Opposing the Federalist plan for a national army, Butler remarked with apparent approval that some saw "the Yeomanry as the natural defense of the Country." He was displeased by the style of government under the Federalist administration and could not resist noting that Philadelphia had been "very gay this winter a continued scene of dissipation."[17]

Butler's mounting suspicion of Hamilton's economic program arose from his fear that it represented a threat to farmers and planters. Butler insisted that the national bank would be of "no benefit to the landed interest for no Farmer or Planter within even twenty miles of the seat of the Bank could or can get a note of his or her own discounted without laying himself under an obligation to a merchant Resident in the town." "Principles teach us," suggested Butler, "that commerce should be the consequence not the means of agriculture." He believed that Hamilton's ties to commercial interests were threatening to bring on a resurgence of "aristocracy." The secretary of the Treasury was "narrowing as much as possible the powers and influence of the Government within a few hands" and "drawing to himself by such contrivances the support of the monied and commerical Interest and that

---

15, 1790, Pierce Butler to Robert Goodloe Harper, Feb. 18, 1792, Butler Letterbook, I, 41, II, 171–172, Butler Papers, SCL.

17. Butler to Anderson, Jan. 5, 1793, Pierce Butler to Andrew Pickens, Feb. 2, 1793, Butler to Harper, Feb. 18, 1792, Butler Letterbook, II, 171–172, 249, 257–258, Butler Papers, SCL. See also Pierce Butler to John Hunter, Feb. 6, 1793, II, 260–261.

Aristocratick influence and support that his very measures tend to promote and increase."[18]

Butler shared with his Federalist counterparts an aversion to social unrest among the yeomanry, but he suggested an alternative antidote. Writing in September 1794, he was sufficiently disturbed by the uprising of farmers in western Pennsylvania to reconsider his opposition to a national army, but he blamed the situation on the partiality and "malpractices" of the Federalist administration. Somewhat ambiguously, Butler observed that South Carolinians might "avert the Evil [of unrest] by a timely and Judicious Arrangement—by Fraternizing and uniting as One Family—by agreeing to some fixed lines or principles." For Butler, constitutional reform within the state and commitment to Republican policies nationally were the best insurance against social disorder.[19]

Given the direction of his political outlook, it is not surprising that Butler turned to backcountry leaders for support and that Cotesworth Pinckney, in 1794, referred to him as an "upper country" senator. Among Butler's personal and political correspondents were John Hunter, Robert Anderson, Robert Goodloe Harper, Andrew Pickens, Wade Hampton, Thomas Sumter, and John Ewing Colhoun, a nephew of Patrick Calhoun. In repeated letters, Butler urged a united effort to elect men of "republican characters" to national office.[20] Writing to Anderson in September 1792, Butler observed, "Dr. Tucker discharged the Trust committed to him by his fellow citizens of Ninety-Six with an attentive regard to their rights." But Butler was concerned about rumored lowcountry plans to propose congressional elections by a general ticket rather than by districts because "nineteen times in twenty the District of Charleston will . . . name the Six members[.] There will scarce ever be so general an understanding in the Back Country as to fix a Ticket." Two months later, he wrote approvingly of Commodore Gillon as "a republican in principle" and urged McPherson to support his candidacy for the United States Congress.[21]

Members of Butler's inland circle did not represent the most radical ten-

18. Pierce Butler to James Jackson, Jan. 24, 1791, Butler to Anderson, Jan. 5, 1793, *ibid.*, I, 103–104, II, 250. See also McCoy, *Elusive Republic*.

19. Pierce Butler to Thomas Sumter, Sept. 11, 1794, Thomas Sumter Papers, II, LC. For a discussion of Butler's advocacy of state constitutional reform, see Chapter 6.

20. Charles Cotesworth Pinckney to Ralph Izard, Dec. 20, 1794 (copy), Charles Cotesworth Pinckney Papers, DUL. Many of Butler's letters to backcountry leaders are collected in Butler Letterbook, Butler Papers, SCL.

21. Pierce Butler to Robert Anderson, Sept. 18, 1792, Butler to McPherson, Nov. 6, 1792, Butler Letterbook, II, 206, 226, SCL; Butler to Sumter, Sept. 11, 1794, Sumter Papers, II, LC.

dencies of inland republicanism. They had, in other words, proven their willingness to support coastal leaders on key issues. John Hunter of Laurens County was one of only twenty-eight backcountry delegates (the great majority of whom were from the middle districts of Cheraws and Orangeburg) who favored ratification of the United States Constitution. In 1793, Robert Anderson chaired the legislative committee responsible for investigating charges that the French were recruiting in the backcountry. The following year, he and John Ewing Colhoun (also representing Pendleton) were among five piedmont representatives who voted against a plan to allow privates and battalion officers to elect field officers. In a public defense of his position, Anderson expressed his own reservations about the progress of events in France. He observed that the French nation had "just revolved from a very despotic monarchical government," but that "the experience of past ages sufficiently shews that in all revolutions the revolving party generally embraces the opposite extreme."[22]

Colhoun was more closely identified with the coastal elite than were Butler's other backcountry correspondents. Colhoun moved from Long Canes to Charleston during the 1770s in order to study law and was admitted to the bar in 1783 following his Revolutionary service in the South Carolina militia. Through marriage, Colhoun acquired a sizable plantation in St. John, Berkeley. He also held thousands of acres throughout the backcountry and spent summers at his Pendleton residence. Before he entered the United States Senate in 1801, he served, sequentially, as a state representative from Ninety Six, St. Stephen, and Pendleton. As an upcountry representative, he frequently voted in opposition to his region. In 1799, he joined Andrew Pickens and three other piedmont representatives in opposing a motion to vest equity power in the state's common law judges. Soon after Colhoun's election by the state legislature as a United States senator, Henry William Desaussure referred to him as "a man of real worth" who possessed "a strong understanding together with some prejudices." His opinions were, according to Desaussure, "tenacious" but "moderate."[23]

Sumter, whose actions in state and national politics placed him more firmly in the Republican camp, was not so closely tied to Butler as were other inland leaders. Despite Butler's efforts to draw the general into the

22. Jonathan Elliot, ed., *The Debates in the Several State Conventions on the Adoption of the Federal Constitution . . .* , 2d ed. (Philadelphia, 1941 [orig. publ. Philadelphia, 1836]), IV, 340; House Jour., Dec. 18, 1793, May 3, 5, 1794; *City Gaz., and Daily Adv.*, Apr. 8, 1794.

23. Walter B. Edgar *et al.*, eds., *Biographical Directory of the South Carolina House of Representatives* (Columbia, S.C., 1974–1984), III, 146–148; House Jour., Dec. 11, 1799; Henry William Desaussure to John Rutledge, Jr., Jan. 13, 1802, John Rutledge, Jr., Papers, SHC.

backcountry political network, he questioned Sumter's "steady republicanism" and apparently favored Hunter's selection as the backcountry choice for a Senate seat.[24] Butler was organizing a statewide political coalition that he could trust to protect the interests of planters on the national level while restraining the most radical implications of republicanism at home. Sumter, who was far more consistent in supporting debtor legislation during the 1780s and the pro-French contingent during the 1790s, was never fully accepted into Butler's circle.

By 1794, Butler believed that national politics were reaching a crisis "owing to some characters grasping at more than the constitution admits or holds out," and he began early in an attempt to unify backcountry leaders behind the opposition. "I need not tell you," he wrote to Anderson, "how important it is to get a Republican Senator." Fearful of competition between leading men of Camden and Ninety Six, Butler urged that "district jealousies and district distinctions ought to be lay'd aside, and that [a] republican character who is likely to unite most votes shou'd be taken up." He begged Anderson to "*consult—advise—agree* and support the election of the man likely to unite most Republican votes" and asked him to "exert" his "weight and well merited influence" toward that end. Writing to Wade Hampton two days later, Butler again insisted that unanimity "among the friends to Republicanism is essentially necessary," and that "very great reliance is had on your activity and judgement in uniting Parties and Men."[25]

Although Hunter was clearly a moderate by the standards of coastal Federalists, even the Rutledge-Pinckney faction was sufficiently threatened by backcountry republicanism to reunify with the pro-British group. Initially, it supported David Ramsay for the Senate seat rather than the arch-Federalist Jacob Read, but when opponents raised questions about the depth of Ramsay's commitment to slavery, the candidate lost favor. According to Cotesworth Pinckney, Ramsay's supporters eventually threw their support behind Read "notwithstanding . . . his antigallican prejudices" because they wanted to prevent Hunter's victory. The moderate Federalists suffered a similar setback in the congressional election for Charleston District. Despite their hostility toward William L. Smith and his British connections, the Rutledge-Pinckney faction refused to support Thomas Tudor Tucker, formerly a congressman from Ninety Six who had the support of the city's pro-French faction. Instead it brought forward its own candidate

24. Pierce Butler to Iredell, Apr. 3, 1794, Butler Letterbook, II, 333, Butler Papers, SCL.

25. Pierce Butler to Robert Goodloe Harper, Mar. 6, 1794, Pierce Butler to Robert Anderson, Feb. 1, 1794, Pierce Butler to Wade Hampton, Feb. 3, 1794, Butler Letterbook, II, 322–323, 329, Butler Papers, SCL.

for Charleston's congressional seat, the young John Rutledge, Jr. As a result, Smith won a narrow victory.[26]

The elections of 1794 illustrate not only the power of the British merchants in state politics and the extent of the rift within the coastal elite but also the underlying unity of coastal Federalists in opposition to backcountry challenges. Whereas Butler saw the creation of an interstate Republican coalition as the best protection of "southern," or planter, interests, Federalist leaders such as Smith and Izard believed that backcountry Republicans might place slavery itself in jeopardy. Writing from Philadelphia in the autumn of 1792, Senator Ralph Izard had cut to the heart of Federalist concerns: "The time is at no very great distance when the property in negroes will be rendered of no value." Izard may have been thinking of recent Quaker efforts to prohibit the slave trade when he continued by observing, "The enthusiasm of a considerable part of this Country, as well as of Europe on this subject, can not fail of producing a convulsion which will be severely felt by the Southern States." For that reason, he thought it especially important that the southern states "send men of good characters, of abilities, and of property to the general government, that their interests may be protected." He was distressed that many of his fellow southerners appeared "to be of a different opinion."[27] For Izard and other members of the coastal elite, the struggle to limit the extent of backcountry influence among the state's congressional delegation was part of a broader effort to protect the interests of slaveholders throughout the South. He and Butler shared the same fundamental goal, but, as an insider in the state's increasingly defensive coastal elite and as a man with close ties to the state's resident British merchants, Izard identified backcountry Republicans as the most dangerous threat to the southern system. By the first decade of the nineteenth century, most South Carolinians disagreed.

iv

The spreading news of the Jay Treaty placed coastal Federalists in an awkward situation by straining ties between South Carolina planters and the national administration. Passage of the treaty seemed to confirm Republican accusations that Federalists were unwilling to resist dangerous subservience to the British and that southern interests were insufficiently protected by Federalist policies. At the same time, the furious antitreaty protests that

26. Cotesworth Pinckney to Izard, Dec. 20, 1794; Rogers, *Evolution of a Federalist*, 266–269.

27. Ralph Izard to Edward Rutledge, Sept. 28, 1792, Dreer Collection, Members of the Old Congress, III, Ser. 7:1, HSP.

erupted in Charleston and the backcountry confirmed the staunchest Federalists in their belief that Republicans within the state posed a dangerous threat to social order.

South Carolinians from all sections were quick to condemn John Jay's efforts. They joined planters throughout the South in their outrage at the British refusal to compensate American slaveowners for slaves taken or freed by British troops during the Revolution. That Jay failed to press the point heightened planter suspicions of northern Federalists, whose antislavery pronouncements were difficult to ignore. Many were also alarmed by restrictions placed on commerce with the West Indies and by other limits placed on the southern carrying trade. Already angered by the power of British traders within their own state and offended that the administration had chosen John Jay as negotiator even though Thomas Pinckney had been serving as a minister in London, the Rutledges initially gave their support to a furious outcry against the administration and against Jacob Read, who, as senator from South Carolina, had cast the decisive supporting vote. In July 1795, after news had spread of ratification, William Read, brother of the senator, walked along Charleston Bay in order to hear what "gentlemen" had to say about recent Senate actions. He found to his dismay that "nobody defend'd the Treaty and nobody spared Mr. Jay from censure, so far were the People from defending him." Opposition was so widespread that the state legislature quickly passed a resolution declaring the treaty "Highly Injurious" to the interests of the United States.[28]

A stormy popular protest in Charleston persuaded Senator Read to remain out of state until the winter. According to his brother, a mob, led by Stephen Drayton, assembled first at the Exchange and then at the senator's house, where they "burnt the Treaty and groan'd thrice." They returned later in greater numbers and "chopt the door and beat at it with sticks." Some men threatened to set the house on fire. General Pinckney and a Mr. Dawson urged restraint, but one of the leaders was heard to say: "Tonight we play the farce. Tomorrow you shall have the Play." A rumor circulated in town that Read had received a gift of expensive plate from British merchants, and some in the crowd promised to return the next day to get it. Apparently these threats were not carried out, but, in the evening after Bastille Day, another crowd assembled and "lay'd hold of several Persons who were accused of saying something in favor of the Treaty and british nation. . . . They pumpt one Berry almost to death and chased others." The

28. Rogers, *Evolution of a Federalist*, 275–281; Rose, *Prologue to Democracy*, 108–116; Zahniser, *Charles Cotesworth Pinckney*, 121–130; Miller, *Federalist Era*, 164–182; William Read to Jacob Read, July 21, 1795, Read Family Papers, SCHS; House Jour., Dec. 11, 1795.

crowd attacked the house of one man and "pursued him thro the Town with vengeance." "Would to God," William Read wrote his brother, "you had remained quietly at home in a private station if this is the reward for public services when a Man acts to the best of his opinion."[29]

Protests in the backcountry were at least as widespread as disturbances in Charleston. In Edgefield, a meeting attended by a number of the county's leading slaveowners and militia officers burned effigies of "John Jay, the envoy and Jacob Read, the aristocratical senator." They inflicted "every indignity . . . which the treacherous behavior of those detestable characters have justly excited." Samuel Green believed that people in that area would "likewise burn the President himself if he should place his signature to the treaty." In Pendleton, a general meeting appointed a committee consisting of Robert Anderson, Andrew Pickens, the Reverend Thomas Reese, and John Ewing Colhoun to consider the treaty. The members issued a series of resolutions pointing to the danger of association with the "monarchical and unregenerated" nation of Britain. After the resolutions were read to Pendleton's assembled militiamen, "a Liberty Tree was erected, with the cap of Liberty and the colours of the United States, and an inscription on its base expressive of the general detestation of the Treaty." A citizens' group in Laurens wrote a public letter commending Senator Pierce Butler for voting against ratification, and public meetings in Washington and Camden districts issued antitreaty resolutions.[30]

Announcing his determination to establish a newspaper in Pendleton County, the printer of the Charleston-based *South-Carolina State-Gazette* pointed to the Republican bond between inland settlers and city artisans. He observed that the central government, for several years past, had been tending "in a most alarming degree, to undermine the liberties of our country—to strip the planter, the mechanic, the manufacturer, and the useful labourer, of all influence, and of all importance—to consign them to contempt, or at best to the sad privilege of murmuring without redress!" He called for more frequent elections and suggested that more public officials be chosen by the electorate rather than the legislature.[31]

The intensity of protest in Charleston and the backcountry again placed certain coastal Federalists in an uncomfortable position. Ralph Izard, who harbored doubts about the treaty, refused to express his thoughts in public because he did not want to encourage the artisan and backcountry opposition. He waited anxiously for the storm to pass. Cotesworth Pinckney also

29. William Read to Jacob Read, July 21, 1795, Read Family Papers.

30. *City Gaz., and Daily Adv.*, Oct. 20, 26, 27, 28, 1795; Samuel Green to Timothy Green, Aug. 2, 1795, Samuel Green Papers.

31. *S.-C. St.-Gaz.*, Nov. 26, 1795.

remained aloof. According to William Read, Edward Rutledge "was afraid to give a loose to his tongue in speaking his sentiments fully, lest it should raise the People into a ferment." Writing to Jacob Read in November 1795, Izard suggested that "the minds of the people in this state begin to be calmed" and was hopeful that "everything may be avoided which will be likely to rekindle the flame which has already given us too much trouble." In December, William Read informed his brother that many of the "anti-Treaty men," having found themselves "leagued with men of deeper designs," were "sick and ashamed of their Conduct.... Old ER [Edward Rutledge] has then adopted the moderate side of the question it would seem in opposition to some more violent."[32]

v

In the spring of 1794, in the midst of rising tensions over national and international affairs, backcountry leaders renewed their call for political parity. They based their demands on the democratic-republican political assumptions that predominated in their region, and, in so doing, they terrified coastal leaders, who looked with growing alarm to events in France and Saint Domingue. The ensuing debate put backcountry republicanism to the test and forced the leaders of the constitutional reform movement to modify their rhetoric so as to accommodate the particular interest of planters throughout the state.

In April, following an unsuccessful effort to increase representation for Richland County, prominent political figures from all regions of the backcountry met in Columbia to organize the Representative Reform Association. Determined to effect a change in the system of apportionment, the association used recent returns from the federal census to point out that the backcountry, with nearly four-fifths of South Carolina's white population, was granted fewer than half of the state representatives. The founding group consisted of leading inland planters. Such men as Wade Hampton, John Kershaw (son of Joseph Kershaw), Ephraim Ramsay (an Abbeville planter with twenty-six slaves in 1800) and William Falconer (a Chester-

---

32. Zahniser, *Charles Cotesworth Pinckney*, 123–126; Rogers, *Evolution of a Federalist*, 277–284; Rose, *Prologue to Democracy*, 117; William Read to Jacob Read, July 27, 1795, Read Family Papers; Ralph Izard to Jacob Read, Nov. 17, 1795, Emmet Collection, NYPL; William Read to Jacob Read, Dec. 16, 1795, Jacob Read Papers, SCL. In October 1795, William Read informed his brother that Ralph Izard had "expressed much displeasure at his being accused of disapproving of the treaty. . . . He added that what he did say was very different, had been grossly perverted he said 'that he would not have agreed to the 12th article if he could have avoided it.'" William Read to Jacob Read, Oct. 27, 1795, Miscellaneous Manuscripts, NYPL (hereafter cited as Misc. MSS).

field planter with twenty-four slaves in 1800) signed the association's open-ing statement. Special committees were established in six backcountry dis-tricts. Their purpose was to disseminate information and correspond with members of the General Committee, who planned to meet in Columbia while the legislature was in session. Robert Goodloe Harper, serving as a representative from Ninety Six, wrote a long accompanying address. Sign-ing his name "Appius," he formulated a critique of the state government and in so doing articulated the fundamental political assumptions that pre-vailed among inland leaders. Setting out for Columbia in November 1794, Cotesworth Pinckney expected to "have a very disagreeable session owing to the appian politics."[33]

Harper's address might almost have been designed to antagonize coastal planters, who looked with growing suspicion upon the pro-French stance of their backcountry counterparts. There is no evidence of a direct link be-tween the Republican and Democratic societies and the Representative Re-form Association other than John Kershaw, Jr., who we can be sure, be-longed to both organizations. Nonetheless, the two groups presented com-parable arguments for constitutional change and apparently presented comparable threats to political leaders on the coast. Harper began by ob-serving that, when men entered into society, they had equal rights and that representation was necessitated simply by the impracticality of pure democ-racy. It followed that government could not safeguard the equal rights with which each individual was born unless each member of the community held the same proportion of power through his representative that he would have held "had the government been administered by all the people in person." "The very definition of aristocracy," continued Harper, "is a com-munity, where a small part of the people have the power of making laws to bind the rest."[34]

In contradicting coastal claims that property deserved to be represented along with population, Harper issued his most radical challenge. He began by observing that "society is prior to property" and that property, "being a mere creature of government and laws, can have no influence in their origi-nal formation." In language almost identical to that of the Pinckneyville

33. *City Gaz., and Daily Adv.*, July 29, 1794; [Robert Goodloe Harper], *An Address to the People of South-Carolina, by the General Committee of the Representative Reform Association at Columbia* (Charleston, S.C., 1794); Federal Population Census, South Carolina, 1800, NA microfilm; Cotesworth Pinckney to Ralph Izard, Nov. 5, 1794, Manigault Family Papers, SCHS. See also William A. Schaper, *Sectionalism and Repre-sentation in South Carolina* (New York, 1968 [orig. publ. Washington, D.C., 1901]), 171–183.

34. Members of the Republican Society, Apr. 14, 1794, Republican Society Papers; [Harper], *Address to the People*, 4–5.

Democratic Society, Harper insisted that wealth would "always acquire influence enough in every government to protect itself." He elaborated:

> The possessors of it commonly have a better education, more extensive means of acquiring knowledge, and improving their talents, more leisure for attending to public affairs, better opportunities of making friends, establishing connections and forming parties. A rich citizen, without having more votes, or choosing more representatives than his poor neighbours, will very speedily obtain ten times as much influence in the government. . . . You cannot prevent this wealth from uniting itself with talents, and obtaining influence. But you ought to counteract this disposition as much as possible. Strip wealth of as many advantages as you can, still it will have enough, and more than enough.

Challenging coastal claims that greater contributions in taxes entitled them to additional representation, Harper observed that wealthy men received greater benefits from government and should not also have greater power.[35]

Harper was not, of course, suggesting that property be equalized or property rights disregarded. Along with other leading backcountrymen, he argued only for an equality of political rights, noting that "in an assembly of the people at Athens, the lowest mechanic, or labourer, had a vote." Coastal representatives might have taken comfort in his observation that the great majority of citizens in every community were "intermediate classes. . . . possessed of more or less property," who would, while passing laws to protect their own possessions, "equally protect those of the richest members."[36]

Nonetheless, as Harper proceeded to identify differences in interest and outlook between coastal and inland areas, he gave lowcountry representatives ample reason to fend off demands for proportional representation. The "upper and lower countries," he suggested,

> have opposite habits and views in almost every particular. One is accustomed to expence, the other to frugality. One will be inclined to numerous offices, large salaries, and an expensive government. The other, from the moderate fortunes of the inhabitants, and their simple way of life, will prefer low taxes, small salaries, and a very frugal, civil establishment. One imports almost every article of consumption, and pays for it in produce: The other is far removed from navigation, has very little to export, and must therefore supply its own wants. . . . One wishes for slaves; the other will be better without them.

When two groups in a single community had "such opposite inclinations

35. [Harper], *Address to the People,* 14–15, 16–17.
36. *Ibid.,* 15, 17–18.

and customs," it was, according to Harper, "fit that the most numerous should govern."[37] Coastal leaders drew precisely the opposite conclusion.

No argument could have persuaded opponents of constitutional reform to grant the requested change in apportionment, but Harper weakened his case by failing to emphasize the extent of slaveownership among the backcountry leadership. His ambiguous statement that the upper country would "be better without" slaves is particularly curious given the composition of the Representative Reform Association. Writing in the midst of growing agitation over events in Saint Domingue, Harper may have been expressing a widespread desire to limit the influx of new slaves into the state. Perhaps, as one of his critics suggested, Harper was influenced by Jefferson's critique of slavery and believed that the "morals of the people" would be better without the institution.[38] Whatever its intent, the statement did not accurately describe the backcountry's complex relationship to slavery and gave no reassurance to coastal leaders who feared that a slaveholding inland leadership would be unable to keep reigns on the nonslaveholding and staunchly Republican majority.

The most outspoken defenders of the existing South Carolina Constitution were the Charleston lawyers and arch-Federalists Timothy Ford and Henry William Desaussure. Despite certain differences of emphasis, both wove the same central theme through their lengthy letters to the *City Gazette, and the Daily Advertiser*. They believed that Harper's abstract arguments for political equality would, if applied to South Carolina society, endanger the property interest of coastal planters and provoke serious social disruptions. Ever sensitive to the potential danger from their own black population, lowcountry spokesmen believed that the very rhetoric of equality upon which inland leaders premised their demands for equal representation threatened slavery itself.[39]

Ford, the more theoretical of the two writers, began by insisting that

37. *Ibid.*, 30–31.
38. *City Gaz., and Daily Adv.*, Oct. 13, 1794.

39. Americanus [Timothy Ford], *The Constitutionalist; or, An Enquiry How Far It Is Expedient and Proper to Alter the Constitution of South Carolina* (Charleston, S.C., 1794), 15–16; Phocion [Henry William Desaussure], *Letters on the Questions of the Justice and Expediency of Going into Alterations of the Representation of the Legislature of South-Carolina* (Charleston, S.C., 1795), 15–16. These letters were published in the *City Gaz., and Daily Adv.* in October and November 1794. See Joseph W. Barnwell, ed., "Diary of Timothy Ford, 1785–1786," *SCHM*, XIII (1912), 132–133. This discussion has benefited from Jack P. Greene's analysis of the Ford and Desaussure letters. See Greene, " 'Slavery or Independence': Some Reflections on the Relationship among Liberty, Black Bondage, and Equality in Revolutionary South Carolina," *SCHM*, LXXX (1979), 193–214, esp. 204–212.

Harper's postulated state of nature was mere fantasy. People, he insisted, were from the outset social beings who began to accumulate property and form associations before the establishment of civil society. He suggested that the rights to life and property were essentially identical, since no one, stripped of all possessions, would survive. Whereas Harper had argued that government preceded property, Ford believed that property preceded government and that men entered into civil society not simply in order to protect their lives and liberties but to safeguard their vested interests and acquired possessions. The universal natural rights to life and liberty should, according to Ford, be guaranteed by all constitutions, but "the real situation of each people ought to govern their own institutes, and make them peculiar to themselves." In other words, a constitution that was perfectly just within the context of one society might bring destruction to another.[40]

In a statement that anticipated the arguments of later proslavery theorists, Ford distinguished between civil equality and "equality of condition." Whereas all men were born with equal rights to possess what they acquired, equal rights to legal protection, and equal personal liberties, they were manifestly unequal in ability. That nature, according to Ford,

> created all men free and equal *in their rights*; and that in this respect she has not one favorite in all her progeny, I most religiously believe. But in the endowment of natural gifts and faculties, nature has instituted almost every gradation. . . . Her views in the *human condition* are evidently to inequality. Why hath she made one man strong and another weak; one nimble and alert, another heavy and inactive; one industrious and another slothful? why hath she dropped scarcely a solitary spark of her celestial fire into one mind, and beamed into another the richest and most copious effulgence? why are some men bold and others timid; some sagacious and others dull; some successful and others unfortunate?

"Inequality of condition," concluded Ford, was one of "nature's laws."[41]

The problem, according to Ford, was that excessive claims to equal rights could easily become a call for equality of condition. In South Carolina, where wealth was not evenly distributed, a system of absolute majority rule would threaten the acquired property interests of coastal planters. Ford used the sectional distinctions drawn by Harper to argue against the reformers. He suggested that the most fundamental division in society was between "those who pursue and must pursue their occupations by *slaves*, and those who pursue, or may pursue, their occupations of themselves." Whereas backcountry farmers might part with their slaves without giving up their source of livelihood, coastal planters, living in the midst of danger-

40. Americanus [Ford], *Constitutionalist*, 10, 3–11.
41. *Ibid.*, 33.

ous swamplands, would be ruined by the loss of their slaves. It followed that inland settlers could not be trusted to safeguard the essential property rights of the coastal elite. Challenging Harper's claim that property would always acquire influence without additional representation, Ford observed that it was "not probable that a poor man at Enoree or Tyger, being told that the low country was very rich, would feel himself much influenced to *protect* those riches."[42]

Ford must have incensed backcountry readers when he illustrated his point by suggesting that inland farmers were as threatening to lowcountry interests as frontier hunters were to planters. He asked his readers to imagine that one hundred men were left in the forest "with a bow and hatchet each." In the course of a year, "20 of these clear ten acres of land each, build a house and set down to agriculture: twenty more catch and tame ten head of cattle each, and subsist upon the milk and the young of the flocks." The remaining sixty, Ford described as wandering hunters who "depend upon the precarious chance of their bow, perhaps upon pilfering, for daily subsistence." Obviously, the majority would not be entitled to equal political rights. "Strange state," exclaimed Ford, "where the rights of the citizen diminish in proportion as his industry and acquisitions increase." Speculating on the type of laws likely to meet approval by the hunting majority, Ford suggested that none would be passed "against pilfering and plundering, robbery or rapacity: no laws to check idleness and vagrancy; no laws to protect property, and no other laws in short, but such as would authorize the lounging crew to prey upon the industrious." In terms that were sure to have an impact on backcountry readers, Ford was groping for a social theory that would guarantee slaveholders' rights in a society of nonslaveholders. He was reminding inland representatives of their own struggle to safeguard their property and of the persistent threat from people who had less and lived differently.[43]

Desaussure, like Ford, was careful not to dispute the principles of equal rights defined by Harper; rather, he suggested that particular conditions in South Carolina "must forever prevent their application in the extent laid down." "Appius," observed Desaussure, had erected his whole argument on a set of abstract axioms,

> one of which is, that "equality is the natural condition of man," the application of which to the state of South-Carolina would ruin the country, by giving liberty to the slaves, and desolating the land with fire and

42. *Ibid.*, 15–16, 37–38.
43. *Ibid.*, 34–35.

sword in the struggles between master and slave: a fate which has attended the French West India Islands from the too hasty adoption of these axioms in all their extent.[44]

Ralph Izard also drew ominous implications from Harper's argument. Writing to Cotesworth Pinckney of recent disturbances in western Pennsylvania, Izard observed, "Mr. Genêt and his offspring the Democratical Societies, have certainly by their Lucubrations promoted this scandalous business." He feared that "the author of Appius" had "laid the foundation of greater trouble in So Carolina" and believed that their claims, if adopted, would "inevitably destroy all security of Property and Government."[45]

Critics of constitutional reform recognized that Harper's claims could threaten the position of southern states within the national government. After all, southern delegates to the Constitutional Convention had sought to protect slave state interests by establishing the three-fifths rule—a system of apportionment based on white population and slave property. "With what propriety," queried Desaussure, "shall South-Carolina . . . have claimed and obtained a rule of representation in the general government . . . and yet refuse to admit the same rule in her own internal arrangements?" Another critic made precisely the same point. He observed, "If the doctrine of Appius was to be admitted in a representative reform in this state, the eastern and northern states would then erect a battery on a foundation built by Carolinians."[46]

Acutely aware of events in France, Desaussure was also fearful that reform might lead to revolution at home. He warned would-be reformers against "lightly seeking a change," for "though they may be easy to commence it may be difficult to terminate internal dissensions." Desaussure recalled the fate of the French people who "in their noble, but dreadful struggles for liberty, have paid a price in blood and in treasure, beyond all calculation." Timothy Ford expressed similar concerns when he urged backcountry leaders to "beware, lest in arraying liberty with the omnipotence of a deity, or the captiousness of an arbitrary monarch, they convert her into a tyrant."[47]

Unlike Harper, whose abstract argument had created the fiction of a

44. Phocion [Desaussure], *Letters on the Questions,* 8, 29–30.

45. Ralph Izard to Cotesworth Pinckney, Nov. 21, 1794, Ralph Izard to Mathias Hutchinson, ———, 1794, Izard Papers.

46. Phocion [Desaussure], *Letters on the Questions,* 14; *City Gaz., and Daily Adv.,* Oct. 13, 1794.

47. Phocion [Desaussure], *Letters on the Questions,* 27; Americanus [Ford], *Constitutionalist,* 31.

uniform backcountry consisting of semisubsistence farmers, both Ford and Desaussure appealed to the property interests of inland planters. Ford suggested that Harper had misrepresented the middle districts of Orangeburg, Camden, and Cheraws, where planters made extensive use of slave labor in the production of staple crops. He wondered whether the people of the middle districts would "be willing to have their commercial advantages sacrificed for the advantage of back country manufactures." Desaussure was even more direct when he pointed out that Harper's egalitarian principles would be "nearly as destructive to the upper country, since independently of the loss of its market, its title to its own slaves would be destroyed."[48]

vi

The Representative Reform Association sparked a massive petition campaign and forced a vote in the legislature. When the House, against the wishes of inland representatives, decided to form itself into a committee of the whole, it essentially adopted the arguments propounded by Ford and Desaussure. The committee report declared that the system of apportionment established by the existing South Carolina Constitution "was founded in a spirit of compromise and in an Equipoise of interests between the different parts of the state." By a strictly sectional vote of fifty-eight to fifty-three, the House accepted the report and defeated the move for reform. Only five lowcountrymen, all from Georgetown District, joined the inland representatives who supported reform, and only two backcountrymen, from St. Matthew and Camden, joined the coastal opposition.[49]

Several days after their defeat in the legislature, backcountry representatives and senators met at Columbia to discuss and revise their campaign for reform. Abandoning their earlier call for proportional representation, they argued that South Carolina was actually characterized by three regions, each of which should have an equal voice in the government. Slaves in the coastal districts of Charleston, Beaufort, and Georgetown composed 72 percent of the population; in the "middle country" districts of Orangeburg, Camden, and Cheraws, 30 percent, and in the "upper country" districts of Ninety Six, Pinckney, and Washington, 15 percent. The assembled representatives insisted that the middle region would always protect the interests of

48. Americanus [Ford], *Constitutionalist*, 48; Phocion [Desaussure], *Letters on the Questions*, 8.
49. House Jour., Dec. 12, 1794.

the lowcountry and would serve as "a connecting link in the chain."[50] The authors of the address were identifying a pattern of South Carolina politics. Throughout the 1780s and 1790s, piedmont representatives had voted more consistently in opposition to Charleston than had their middlecountry counterparts.

Authors of the new address also abandoned the abstract language of equal rights. They attempted to assuage coastal fears by pointing to the backcountry's actual interest in slaves. "We too," they insisted, "have slaves, though not so many as you. There is not one member of the legislature from the middle and western districts who is not a slave owner. . . . As for the middle division, its wealth consists in slaves." The address pointed out that backcountry representatives would be defeating their own interests by proposing emancipation or imposing burdensome taxes on slaves.[51] Again, they were arguing from experience, since inland representatives had consistently demonstrated their commitment to slavery and opposition to taxation in any form.

Coastal leaders remained unconvinced. The stakes were too high. Whereas the South Carolina Constitution of 1790 had extended the influence of backcountry representatives without giving them a majority voice in the legislature, the proposed reform would have given the balance of power to the staunchly republican middlecountry. Concerned about social unrest at home and abroad, coastal representatives deemed it "inexpedient" to grant the request of a new group of inland petitions. In 1796, by a vote of fifty to fifty-seven, the House opposed the more conservative move for reform. Again the vote was strictly sectional. Only three lowcountrymen voted with the minority, while five backcountrymen—all from the middle districts— voted with the coast. Writing to Jacob Read, the clerk of the House observed that the session had been "very tranquil—the Appian business passed over without the least murmur."[52]

The very manner by which inland representatives maintained local credibility—their outspoken adherence to a more democratic-republican vision and their continuing support for the French Revolution—gave coastal leaders reason for apprehension. Although backcountry representatives gave

50. "An Address by Senators and Representatives from the Middle and Western Districts Met in Columbia, December 17, 1794," *Col. Herald*, Oct. 29, 1795. See also Schaper, *Sectionalism and Representation*, 183–190.

51. "An Address by Senators and Representatives, December 17, 1794," *Col. Herald*, Oct. 29, 1795.

52. Schaper, *Sectionalism and Representation*, 188; John Sandford Dart to Jacob Read, Dec. 21, 1796, Misc. MSS.

consistent evidence of their firm commitment to slavery, they had, in the
eyes of coastal leaders, failed to demonstrate sufficient inclination or capacity to maintain a firm grip on their own region. Concerned about events
in France and Saint Domingue, not to mention western Massachusetts and
Pennsylvania, coastal leaders remained uneasy about potential challenges
from the backcountry. The Charlestonian John Brown Cutting gave clear
expression to these fears when he referred to "that fierce column of rural
representation which when influenced by any popular passion rushes to
whatsoever may be the object of the hour with an irresistible impetuos-
ity."[53] Not until backcountry leaders could be trusted to control their region and safeguard the state's interest in slaves would coastal leaders willingly grant another reform in the system of apportionment.

vii

Coastal Federalists did what they could to extend their influence among
politically prominent backcountrymen. They managed to identify a group
of men whom they found acceptable, but they did not succeed in winning
substantial support for Federalism in the backcountry. A brief period of
ascendancy during the later 1790s only highlights the limits of the Federalists' appeal and their weakness throughout the state.
    William L. Smith sought to win backcountry support for the national
Federalists in the spring of 1793 when he set out for the inland districts to
meet with newly elected congressmen and other influential men. After
spending a day with Andrew Pickens, he was hopeful that the general
would "do well" in the House of Representatives. At Union Court House,
he met a "smart young" lawyer whom he found to be in "very good dispo-
sitions." The man was probably Abraham Nott, a Yale-educated native of
New England who, in 1799, became the second Federalist congressman
from the western piedmont. Moving on to Winnsboro in Fairfield County,
Smith visited with General Richard Winn, a wealthy planter and speculator
who was also the newly elected congressman from Camden. He had "great
hopes" that Winn would "go right." Smith missed seeing Lemuel Benton,
recently elected to the United States Congress from Cheraws. He also
missed John Hunter, but, upon his return to Charleston, Smith did see
Alexander Gillon, who had just been elected to Congress by the voters of

---

53. John Brown Cutting to John Rutledge, Jr., Feb. 21, 1789, John Rutledge, Jr.,
Papers, SHC.

the Beaufort-Orangeburg District. Gillon said only that he knew about the parties in Congress and would "judge for himself."[54]

By the time Smith made his foray into the backcountry, John Chesnut, the wealthy planter and merchant of Camden, was already linked to the coastal Federalists. In 1790, Cotesworth Pinckney had described him as "a Gentleman of great worth and influence in our interior country." Four years later Pinckney arranged for Mrs. Ralph Izard to visit his friend's plantation in Camden, and, in 1795, he sent Chesnut a portrait of himself as a token of friendship. These social connections were not unrelated to politics. Chesnut was the only representative from the District Eastward of Wateree to support the repeal of the Confiscation Act, and, as a member of the State Ratification Convention, he was the only delegate from the same district to vote in favor of ratification.[55]

Although Chesnut won a position in the South Carolina Senate, neither he nor his Federalist friends ever gained a strong political foothold in the backcountry. With the exception of Robert Goodloe Harper, who by 1795 had become a leading Federalist spokesman after his election by Ninety Six District to the Fourth Congress, the majority of backcountry representatives to the United States Congress identified themselves with the Republicans. Alexander Gillon and Wade Hampton, who represented the Beaufort-Orangeburg District in the Third and Fourth Congresses, respectively, were also members of Butler's circle and identified with the Republicans. Thomas Sumter, a staunch opponent of the Federalist administration, remained the dominant political figure in Camden District throughout the 1790s. He lost his bid for election to the Third Congress to Richard Winn, but he ran successfully for office in 1797 and continued to serve as a congressman and later as a senator through 1810.[56]

Richard Winn, a leading planter, merchant, and land speculator of Fairfield in Camden District, was more acceptable to coastal Federalists than was his predecessor, but it would be a mistake to see him as their ally.

54. Smith to Hamilton, Apr. 24, 1793, in Syrett *et al.*, eds., *Papers of Hamilton*, XIV, 338–341; Rogers, *Evolution of a Federalist*, 242–246.

55. Cotesworth Pinckney to Brig. General Steward, July 10, 1790, Charles Cotesworth Pinckney Papers, SCL; Cotesworth Pinckney to Izard, Nov. 5, 1795, Manigault Family Papers; Cotesworth Pinckney to John Chesnut, Aug. 31, 1796, George Washington to John Chesnut, June 26, 1791, John Laurence Manning Papers, DUL; South Carolina House of Representatives Journal, Feb. 21, 1787, in Theodora J. Thompson *et al.*, eds., *Journals of the House of Representatives*, The State Records of South Carolina (Columbia, S.C., 1977–), *1787–1788*, 125; Elliot, ed., *Debates on the Federal Constitution*, IV, 333.

56. Edgar *et al.*, eds. *Biographical Directory of the House*, III, 270–271, 309–310, 696, IV, 262–263.

Whereas Sumter had opposed William L. Smith in forty of fifty-nine votes, Winn opposed his Federalist colleague in only fourteen of thirty votes at which both were present. However, he joined the Republicans on crucial issues such as support for nonintercourse with Great Britain and the amendment proposed by William Branch Giles of Virginia that called upon Congress to prohibit French émigrés from using aristocratic titles in America.[57]

As members of the Third Congress from the western piedmont, Andrew Pickens and John Hunter followed roughly the same path as Richard Winn. They split their votes about evenly between Federalist and Republican camps and opposed William L. Smith about as often as they supported him. Unlike Thomas Sumter, they did not belong to the solid core of the Republican group, but they did consistently support that faction on issues involving the struggle between Britain and France, and they apparently shared Republican fears of creeping aristocracy at home. Both Pickens and Hunter joined Winn and opposed Smith in favoring commercial discrimination against Great Britain and supporting the Giles Amendment.[58]

Only Robert Goodloe Harper became a firm ally of the Federalist faction in Congress, but it seems he won favor with his constituents in spite, rather than because, of that affiliation. His election to Congress probably reflected widespread support for his activities on behalf of the movement for state constitutional reform. Although Harper proved to be a staunch ally of the administration during his three and one-half terms as a congressman from Ninety Six, he had difficulty reconciling his constituents to his national political opinions. Unlike William L. Smith, who defended the Jay Treaty by pointing to the commercial advantages of the British connection, Harper felt the need to stress his attachment to the French nation and to the principle of equal political rights. In defending the treaty, he reminded the inland electorate of his labors to alter the state government in those areas where he "thought it hostile to the rights of a great majority of the people." Harper also insisted that John Jay had no special attachment to British interests. Had the minister been "an avowed enemy to France," there would, according to Harper, "surely have been a sufficient reason for rejecting him." In 1796, Harper decided not to resign his congressional seat, in part because

57. In 1794, Richard Winn joined the Republicans in supporting commercial sanctions against Great Britain. 3d Cong., 1st Sess., *Annals*, IV, 595–606, 735–736, 2d Sess., *Annals*, IV, 1056–1057; J. F. Grimké to H. D. Ward, Oct. 19, 1798, J. F. Grimké Papers, SCL; Edgar *et al.*, eds., *Biographical Directory of the House*, III, 779–781.

58. 3d Cong., 1st Sess., *Annals*, IV, 154, 166, 254–255, 454–455, 459, 476–477, 497–498, 563, 596, 600–606, 656–657, 666–672, 682–687, 694–696, 699, 707–709, 711–713, 715–716, 723–726, 730, 738–741, 744–745, 757, 760, 765–769, 781–782,

he believed that his place "would most probably be filled by a person of contrary opinions." A group "of officers and leading men" from Newberry indicated that Harper was probably correct. They commended the congressman on his decision to support the treaty even though "near nine tenths" of his constituents "were pointedly opposed" to its ratification. Pierce Butler also believed that Harper had violated the trust of his constituents by writing in support of the treaty. He referred to Harper as a man who held political opinions that were "the very opposite to those of the western country of Carolina."[59] It would seem, in other words, that voters of Ninety Six chose Harper to represent them *despite* his Federalist sympathies.

In 1797 and 1798, deepening tensions between the United States and France helped to unify the coastal Federalists and enabled them to muster a flurry of support in the inland districts. Angered by the Jay Treaty, French officials had responded by refusing to receive the newly appointed ambassador, Cotesworth Pinckney. The provocative act met with widespread condemnation in Pinckney's native state and brought the Rutledges back into the Federalist fold. Early in 1798, President John Adams dispatched three commissioners to negotiate an end to French depredations on American shipping, but, when the public learned of efforts to bribe the American officials, support for the French government was sorely weakened throughout the United States. Fearful of an invasion by French forces, national and state governments began mustering for war. Under those circumstances, the Rutledge-Pinckney wing of the coastal elite was willing to join forces with William L. Smith and the arch-Federalists. According to Edward Rutledge, his nephew John Rutledge, Jr., who was then serving as a congressman from the Beaufort-Orangeburg District, had hoped that France would be a de-

---

2d Sess., *Annals*, IV, 943–945, 965–966, 977–978, 1000, 1057–1058, 1161, 1222, 1269, 1280.

59. Robert Goodloe Harper, *An Address from Robert Goodloe Harper, of South-Carolina, to His Constituents, Containing His Reasons for Approving the Treaty of Amity, Commerce, and Navigation, with Great-Britain* (Philadelphia, 1795), esp. 14, 35; [William L. Smith], *A Candid Examination of the Objections to the Treaty of Amity, Commerce, and Navigation, between the United States and Great Britain, As Stated in the Report of the Committee, Appointed by the Citizens of the United States, in Charleston, South-Carolina* (Charleston, S.C., 1795); *City Gaz., and Daily Adv.*, May 12, 1796; Robert Goodloe Harper, "Autobiographical Sketch," Robert Goodloe Harper Papers, MHS; Butler to John Hunter, Nov. 10, 1795, Pierce Butler Letterbook, 1787–1822, HSP. Joseph Cox has argued that the extent of Harper's change of sentiment has been exaggerated and that his election reflected more widespread support for Federalist policies in Ninety Six. Cox's study did not make use of Pierce Butler's correspondence, which suggests that Butler, at least, deemed Harper to be within the Republican fold before his election. See Joseph W. Cox, *Champion of Southern Federalism: Robert Goodloe Harper of South Carolina* (Port Washington, N.Y., 1972), 40–171.

pendable ally, but "when he saw her over-running innocent Countries; maintaining her armies in plunder; seducing the people from their government . . . insulting our beloved Pinckney, seizing our vessels without a cause . . . and threatening to divide our citizens from the Government . . . he took fire" and joined the administration.[60]

Mounting terror of slave insurrection contributed to the nervous mood of planters throughout the state and increased their fears of French invasion. Throughout the 1790s, South Carolinians sought to insulate their own slaves from slaves who had been influenced by northern or French antislavery thought. They also grew increasingly concerned about the size of their own black majority. The state legislature repeatedly renewed an act of 1792 that prohibited the importation of slaves from Africa and the northern United States. In 1797, Charlestonians received news of a planned slave insurrection that they believed "originated among the French negroes and was to be executed by them alone" with the help of some whites. That year, memorialists from Charleston asked that all free blacks of French origin, who had arrived after 1790, be forced to leave the state. By 1798, the mood was one of crisis. Governor Charles Pinckney warned of "the danger of suffering either free person of colour or slaves to be introduced from these Islands [the West Indies]." He urged immediate passage of a law establishing severe penalties for any captain or owner of a ship that imported any "slave or person of colour from any island in which an insurrection has taken place."[61]

John Rutledge, Jr., was particularly concerned about the impact of the anticipated French invasion in the backcountry. In 1798, he informed his father-in-law that he and others in Philadelphia had "strong reasons for believing that a project is now carrying on by the French to take Canada and the floridas and to revolutionize a great portion of our western country." Rutledge was sufficiently alarmed to advocate an active campaign to oust French supporters from office. Revealing his persistent suspicion of the backcountry leadership, he observed that "a crisis" had arrived that rendered "it the duty of every good citizen to exert himself, by all possible means, to purge our councils of the Jacobins who infest them."[62]

60. Rose, *Prologue to Democracy*, 143–144, 167–204; Miller, *Federalist Era*, 210–227; Senate Jour., Nov. 30, 1798; House Jour., Nov. 28, Dec. 14, 17, 20, 1798; Edward Rutledge to Capt. Dunbar, Fall 1798, John Rutledge, Jr., Papers, SHC.

61. House Jour., Nov. 28, 1798; Thomas Cooper and David J. McCord, eds., *The Statutes at Large of South Carolina* (Columbia, S.C., 1836–1841), VII, 430–436, 444–449; J. Alison to Jacob Read, Dec. 5, 1797, Jacob Read Papers, DUL; Memorial from Charleston, Petitions to the General Assembly, 1797, no. 87, SCDAH.

62. John Rutledge, Jr., to Rev. Smith, Apr. 1, 1798, John Rutledge, Jr., Papers, SHC; John Rutledge, Jr., to John F. Grimké, July 30, 1798, Grimké Family Papers, SCHS.

In fact, backcountry settlers also had cause to fear an invasion by France. They were concerned not only that a French invasion might provoke a new frontier war with the western Indians but that their own slaves, many of whom were newly arrived from Africa, might be moved to rebellion. Despite their persistent efforts to keep the slave trade open, upcountry representatives had been sufficiently concerned about Saint Domingue to join in the unanimous House vote of 1792 to impose a temporary ban on all slave imports. In 1798, news of a rumored slave conspiracy on John Ewing Colhoun's Pendleton plantation exacerbated and possibly reflected inland concerns about slave rebellion.[63]

By the summer of 1797, the leading men of Pendleton were showing some signs of discomfort in their references to France. At a Fourth of July celebration presided over by Robert Anderson, a toast was made to General Lafayette, but not to the Republic of France. One speaker, in a veiled reference to relations between the United States and France, hoped that "the tone of the American People" would "manifest to all nations" not only a "sincere and unchanging solicitude for peace" but a "fixed resolution, if it cannot be obtained by negotiation, to repel hostility." The correspondent who reported on the festivities tried to clarify the sentiments of his fellows for readers of the *City Gazette*. Recognizing that the Fourth of July toasts might appear to indicate declining sympathy for France, he insisted, "Our sentiments of gratitude, of affection for that truly magnanimous nation, are as much alive as ever." But he also observed that residents of Pendleton could not "help feeling tenderly" for the nation's "wounded honor through the French Directory." One year later, the Pendleton Fourth of July toasts were more pointed. "May France," declared one speaker "regardful of her real interests, return to her true, her sincere friends, 'ere too late. Let her reflect cooly, how greatly she has wounded our feelings and our interests, by the unexampled treatment of our envoys, and unwarranted depredations on our commerce."[64]

A roll call in the South Carolina House of Representatives on a defense bill sponsored by leading Federalists is perhaps the best indication of the party's strength during the crisis of 1798. By a vote of fifty-five to forty, the House agreed to purchase five thousand guns for resale to the militia. The supporters included forty-three lowcountrymen, five representatives from the middlecountry, and seven upcountrymen. Opponents included fifteen middlecountry representatives, fifteen from the upcountry, and only seven from the lowcountry. Although Charleston and the coastal parishes contin-

63. House Jour., Dec. 8, 1792; Rose, *Prologue to Democracy*, 193–196; Trial of Slaves Accused of Attempted Murder of Their Master, 1798, John Ewing Colhoun Papers, SCL.
64. *City Gaz., and Daily Adv.*, Aug. 8, 1797, July 21, 1798.

ued to be the center of Federalist strength, the vote reveals some inroads into the backcountry.[65]

Whatever gains coastal Federalists enjoyed during the later 1790s were short lived. With the reduction of international tensions, upcountry settlers reaffirmed their enthusiastic support for France. In 1800, a speaker at Pendleton's traditional Fourth of July festivities hoped that success would "attend our embassy to the Republic of France, in a happy and speedy termination of all differences," and the correspondent to the *City Gazette* observed, "The prospect of an amicable accommodation of our differences with France, added not a little to the pleasure of the day." The following May, a speaker at a Pendleton militia muster included a simple toast to "the Republic of France."[66]

By 1800, leading backcountry political figures were solidly in the Republican fold. Both Anderson and Pickens were serving as Jefferson electors. The following year, Anderson revealed his own distance from the Federalist faction by writing to congratulate John Ewing Colhoun "upon what we have done ourselves, in making General Sumter your colleague from the State to the Senate." Anderson thought it particularly fortunate that Sumter and his opponent John Rutledge, Jr., "stood precisely upon the same ground, inasmuch as they were both upon the spot, and were both cloathed with equal honors by this State, so that the triumph of Sumter (correctly speaking) may be called a triumph of Principle in Carolina." With the reduction of international tensions, Nott was unable to win a second congressional election, and, by 1801, a correspondent observed that if Harper had been a candidate that year, "he would have been rejected by a vast majority" of voters in Ninety Six. Several years later, when Edward Hooker made his trip through the backcountry, he noted that "to this day, in all the electioneering campaigns throughout the old District of Ninety Six . . . there is no weapon, with which a candidate can be more successfully annoyed by his opponent, than the public exhibition of him as 'one of Harper's men.' "[67]

The Federalists proved incapable of sustaining inland support. Their leaders were too rigidly elitist, and their national party was too closely associated with northern commercial interests. It was the Republicans who were best able to accommodate to the various groups within South Carolina

65. House Jour., Dec. 17, 1798; Rose, *Prologue to Democracy*, 185–186.
66. *City Gaz., and Daily Adv.*, Aug. 7, 1800, May 30, 1801.
67. *South-Carolina State Gazette and Timothy's Daily Advertiser* (Charleston), Dec. 2, 1800; Robert Anderson to John Ewing Colhoun, Dec. 3, 1801, SCL; *City Gaz., and Daily Adv.*, May 27, 1801. Edward Hooker, Journal, May 23, 1803, I, 83, CHS.

and to slaveholders' interests throughout the South. When Federalists on the coast felt secure that backcountry Republicanism would not bring with it the threat of social revolution, their party was effectively defunct.

Emerging politically dominant within the backcountry during the 1790s was Pierce Butler's Republican coalition. Andrew Pickens, Robert Anderson, John Ewing Colhoun, Wade Hampton, and Thomas Sumter were culturally and ideologically identified with their region, but, with the exception of Sumter, they also succeeded in winning respect from arch-Federalists on the coast. Among the leading planters of their region, Butler's group was able to form a bridge between conservatives in the Charleston area and staunch Republicans in the backcountry. Their ascendancy worked to contain the most democratic version of backcountry republicanism, thereby contributing to the political unification of South Carolina.

CHAPTER 8.

The Political Unification of South Carolina

The inland spread of cotton culture affected the course of South Carolina and, for that matter, United States history, not by creating a class of inland planters, but by increasing their numbers and enhancing their regional power. During the half-century that preceded South Carolina's constitutional reform of 1808, inland leaders accumulated land and slaves as they established economic, political, and personal ties to members of the coastal elite. Cotton expansion facilitated the growing ties between sections, but it did not initiate the process. From the Regulator period onward, slave acquisition had been a dominant concern of inland leaders. Cotton enabled backcountry planters to make more extensive purchases, but it did not transform their aspirations.

Throughout the later eighteenth century, the primary source of sectional tension had been the small slaveholders and nonslaveholders who composed the inland majority. Opponents of inland demands for political parity suspected that inland leaders might capitulate too readily to the reckless whims of their yeoman constituency. They feared, in other words, that the democratic-republican vision that prevailed in the backcountry might develop, among yeomen, into a more dangerous assault on South Carolina planters. Even the most adamant Federalists maintained personal respect for individual political figures from the backcountry, but their personal ties could not overcome more serious fears. Cotton resolved—or nearly resolved—that problem.

In fact, cotton expansion capped a series of interregional efforts to unify South Carolina's sections. In response to persistent inland demands for constitutional reform, lowcountry leaders, including a number of prominent Federalists, sought to render the backcountry leadership and constituency less threatening to the coastal elite. In so doing, they joined prominent inland political leaders in a revival of two Regulator goals: the establishment of educational institutions and the development of staple agriculture throughout the backcountry. These early efforts to bind backcountry settlers to the coast provide further testimony to the common concerns that, despite sectional tensions, linked political leaders from both regions.

i

From the Regulator period onward, inland and coastal leaders pressed for the development of backcountry schools as a basis for social order and state unity. In 1777 and 1778, the legislature incorporated several societies whose purpose was to establish schools for poor children in the backcountry. The largest and most successful of these was the Mount Zion Society, which set up a school in Winnsboro, Fairfield County. The officers and nearly four hundred members represented the broad spectrum of state leadership. On the society's membership roster, Charles Cotesworth Pinckney joined such prominent Republicans as Alexander Gillon, Aedanus Burke, and William Tate and such leading backcountrymen as Andrew Pickens and Richard Winn. The Mount Zion Society also included several former Regulators.[1] In 1784 the leading men of Ninety Six set up a public school on land donated by John Ewing Colhoun, and the next year the legislature incorporated colleges in Abbeville County and Charleston. Trustees for the school at Ninety Six included not only the most prominent men of that region but the Federalist Thomas Pinckney and various other lowcountrymen.[2] In 1786, Thomas Sumter, together with the Charleston Baptist leader Richard Furman, advertised the opening of an inland school at the High Hills of Santee, and, throughout the 1780s and 1790s, the legislature incorporated societies in Claremont, Clarendon, and Kershaw counties for the purpose of educating poor and orphaned children. Finally, in 1811, the state established its first system of public schools.[3]

1. Thomas Cooper and David J. McCord, eds., *The Statutes at Large of South Carolina* (Columbia, S.C., 1836–1841), VIII, 114–119; *Gazette of the State of South-Carolina* (Charleston), May 26, 1777; *South-Carolina Weekly Gazette* (Charleston), Mar. 8, 1783; *South Carolina Gazette, and Public Advertiser* (Charleston), July 16, 1785; Ellen Heyward Jervey, comp., "Items from a South Carolina Almanac," *SCHM*, XXXII (1831), 75; William A. Schaper, *Sectionalism and Representation in South Carolina* (New York, 1968 [orig. publ. Washington, D.C., 1901]), 166–167; Eugene Perry Link, *Democratic-Republican Societies, 1790–1800* (New York, 1942), 171.

2. Indenture between the Reverend John Harris, Andrew Pickens, Robert Anderson, Patrick Calhoun, William Moore, and John Bowie, Nov. 25, 1784, John Ewing Colhoun Papers, SCL; South Carolina Senate Journal, Mar. 14, 1785, SCDAH (hereafter cited as Senate Jour.).

3. *Charleston Morning Post, and the Daily Advertiser*, May 8, 1786; Cooper and McCord, eds., *Statutes of South Carolina*, IV, 674, V, 198, 639.

In part, this post-Revolutionary interest in the development of backcountry schools and colleges represented a continuation of Regulator efforts to reduce crime by instilling habits of industry in the poor or predominantly hunting population. The free-school movement reflected a common belief that the landless or poor population constituted a fundamental threat to inland, and hence statewide, stability. Aedanus Burke echoed Regulator concerns when he insisted that the "spreading of knowledge and learning thro' the Land would have this good effect, the Youth in our Back Country would become valuable useful men, instead of being, as they are at present, brought up deer-hunters and horse thieves, for want of Education." Robert Anderson expressed a similar sentiment when, in 1790, he "asked if it would be proper to cast them [inland planters] off because they were poor? Certainly not—rather let us encourage their industry. Why were we so pestered with horsethieves—entirely owing to men degenerating into habits of idleness preferring dangerous pursuits to those of honest industry." Six years later, a correspondent from Pendleton observed that the establishment of county schools would be "the only means of promoting general industry, and consequently of rooting out our too general vicious habits . . . and that it would be the best security for maintaining our liberties." Comparable concerns undoubtedly prompted grand jurors of Washington District to request the establishment of "two grammar schools in Pendleton and Greenville counties, to be supported out of the public taxes, *free to all*."[4]

A detailed educational plan described by the Abbeville merchant John De La Howe reveals a good deal about the motives that underlay the free-school movement in general. At his death in 1797, De La Howe left funds for the establishment of a school at his home in Abbeville County. Originally planned in 1787, the school was to house, clothe, and feed twenty-four boys and girls, with priority given to orphans. In addition to teaching the students reading, writing, and arithmetic and the boys, in particular, geography, geometry, and "practical surveying," masters were to give instruction "in such chemical principles as the success of their different operations depends upon, as melting, brewing, distilling, baking, fixing different colors, making vinaigre, soap, cheese, butter, etc. etc." Students were to "manufacture such of their cloathing themselves as can be made out of the produce of the farm." A correspondent from Pendleton County summed up

4. Aedanus Burke to Arthur Middleton, July 1782, in Joseph W. Barnwell, ed., "Correspondence of Hon. Arthur Middleton, Signer of the Declaration of Independence," *SCHM*, XXVI (1925), 204; *City Gazette, and the Daily Advertiser* (Charleston), June 1, 1790, Aug. 26, 1796; *State Gazette of South-Carolina* (Charleston), June 28, 1793. See also South Carolina House of Representatives Journal, Nov. 29, 1798, SCDAH (hereafter cited as House Jour.); Presentment from ———, General Assembly, Grand Jury Presentments, Kershaw District, 1804, SCDAH.

the free-school philosophy when, in 1796, he observed that the establishment of county schools would be the "only means of promoting general industry, and habits" and a "certain method of *preventing* crimes."[5]

Proponents of free schools also believed that the spread of education would help make citizens more dependable. This notion was hardly unique to South Carolinians, but it had particular resonance in a state where coastal leaders had expressed such persistent fears about the inland majority. Coastal founders of the Mount Zion Society declared it their object to "promote knowledge as the firmest cement of a State." In 1795, a year in which backcountry representatives renewed their call for legislative reapportionment, Governor Arnoldus Vanderhorst urged the establishment of schools throughout the state, "so that knowledge and information may be generally diffused, and morals and virtue, the necessary effect, adorn and characterize the citizens of South Carolina." Education was, he believed, "one of the most important objects of Governments where the private lives and Morals of individual Citizens and their Freedom of Conversation and Agency have most effect and influence on public conduct." Two years later, Governor Charles Pinckney delivered a message to the legislature in which he observed, "No real stability can be expected unless the minds of the citizens are enlightened and sufficiently impressed with the importance of the principles from whence these blessings proceed." Pinckney insisted that the morals of the citizenry could not "degenerate whilst Education and early discipline hold them fixed and permanent."[6]

In pressing for the development of inland schools, lowcountry leaders were also hoping to strengthen ties between coastal and inland elites. Prompted by coastal Federalists but supported by representatives from all sections, the legislature, in 1801, incorporated South Carolina College. Governor John Drayton saw the proposed college as a means by which "the friendships of our young men would . . . be promoted, and strengthened throughout the State, and our political union be much advanced thereby." Two years later, Governor James Burchill Richardson declared that "the youths of our State educated in the early habits of intimacy, will form attachments that will grow with them . . . and when the charge of Government devolves on the rising generation, those attachments will produce the most happy effects, and will tend to the complete annihilation of all divisions in our State." He believed that the friendships formed at the new

5. Will of John De La Howe, Sept. 7, 1796, County Wills, WPA Trans., Abbeville County, I, 167–173, SCDAH; *City Gaz., and Daily Adv.*, Aug. 26, 1796.
6. Preamble to Act of Incorporation of the Mount Zion Society, quoted in Schaper, *Sectionalism and Representation*, 166; Senate Jour., Nov. 18, 1795; House Jour., Nov. 27, 1797. See also Cooper and McCord, eds., *Statutes of South Carolina*, VIII, 114–115.

college would "insure a just regard for the whole State, divested of confined partialities for particular parts." Henry William Desaussure was also delighted that the legislature had "founded and endowed a College at Columbia where the youth of all parts of the state may be educated, and a greater union of opinion produced in our state." Several years later he wrote to Ezekiel Pickens, the son of Andrew Pickens, that "the diffusion of education gives the hope that we shall have able and worthy men for every department of government."[7]

The very terms in which coastal leaders advocated the establishment of inland schools represented a triumph for the backcountry elite, whose demands for political parity had been premised on the assumption that ability and moral character, rather than the benefits of wealth and birth, should be the foundation of state leadership. Governor Charles Pinckney, having already defected to the Republican fold, justified his enthusiastic call for free schools by observing, "Poverty or loss of parents ought not to be the means of withholding from this Country and burying in Obscurity those who might have promised its most distinguished Ornaments." In 1803, Governor Drayton also insisted that the state, by establishing inland schools, would be "enabled to acquire for the public service the most distinguished abilities, in whatsoever station they may be placed, and which otherwise would have been lost in oblivion." Drayton proposed that each district free school send one promising student to South Carolina College, where, if necessary, he would be maintained at public expense. Both Pinckney and Drayton echoed the Mount Zion Society founders, who had urged others to "reflect on the many fine geniuses in the remote part of the State who are entirely buried in oblivion through lack of education."[8]

Apart from the highly successful college at Columbia, the free-school movement ended in failure. The widespread pattern of settlement and the tendency of yeomen to keep their children home for farm work inhibited the development of public schools throughout the southern states. Mount Zion College in Winnsboro and the proposed college in Abbeville failed before they got off the ground. By 1800, the farm school at John De La Howe's

7. Cooper and McCord, eds., *Statutes of South Carolina*, V, 403; Senate Jour., Nov. 27, 1801, Nov. 25, 1803; Henry William Desaussure to John Rutledge, Jr., Jan. 13, 1802, John Rutledge, Jr., Papers, SHC; Henry William Desaussure to Ezekiel Pickens, Oct. 27, 1805, Henry William Desaussure Papers, SCL. See also Daniel Walker Hollis, *The University of South Carolina*, I, *South Carolina College* (Columbia, S.C., 1951), 3–21.

8. House Jour., Nov. 27, 1797; Senate Jour., Nov. 25, 1803, Nov. 23, 1802; Preamble to Act of Incorporation of the Mount Zion Society, quoted in Schaper, *Sectionalism and Representation*, 166.

Abbeville plantation was foundering.[9] Nonetheless, the free-school movement was significant. As an interregional effort to stabilize the backcountry and strengthen the inland leadership, it testified to a shared vision of state unity.

It was, in the end, through private academies that this vision was at least partially fulfilled. Established primarily by Presbyterian ministers and incorporated by the state, academies drew support from planters in both lowcountry and backcountry. These institutions assumed primary responsibility for educating the sons of South Carolina's elite and preparing them for college. They also admitted a small number of poor boys on scholarship. By 1850, there would be more than two hundred academies operating in South Carolina alone. In the early years of the nineteenth century, private academies were, in the same way as South Carolina College, providing a meeting ground for future planters and political leaders within South Carolina and throughout the southern states as a whole. Of these, none was more important to the backcountry's planter class than Moses Waddel's academy in Abbeville, which opened in 1804. A native of North Carolina, Waddel was a Presbyterian minister who enjoyed close ties to the leading men of the western piedmont. His first marriage was to the daughter of Patrick Calhoun, and his young brother-in-law, John C. Calhoun, was among his first students. The roster of graduates from Waddel's school includes a number of men who became prominent political leaders in the antebellum years.[10]

Of course, backcountry leaders had personal reasons for involving themselves in the education movement. Many inland planters probably shared Andrew Pickens's edge of defensiveness about his own lack of schooling. As an elderly man, Pickens wrote that he had been "raised on the frontiers of new settlements [and] had not an opportunity of receiving even a good English education." Pickens was careful to note that his two eldest sons had

9. Petitions from the Mount Sion Society and Francois Rene LeRoy Decerquel, Petitions to the General Assembly, 1798, no. 27, 1800, no. 1, SCDAH (hereafter cited as Petitions); Patrick S. Brady, "Political and Civil Life in South Carolina, 1787–1833" (Ph.D. diss., University of California, Santa Barbara, 1971), 157–166; Schaper, *Sectionalism and Representation*, 167–170.

10. Edgar W. Knight, *The Academy Movement in the South* [Chapel Hill, N.C., 1919 (?)], reprinted from *High School Journal*, II, nos. 7–8 (n.d.), III, no. 1 (n.d.), 6, 13–24; Edgar W. Knight, *Education in the United States*, 3d rev. ed. (Boston, 1951), 372–380; John N. Waddel, *Memorials of Academic Life: Being an Historical Sketch of the Waddel Family* (Richmond, Va., 1891), 44–60, 67–69; William B. Sprague, *Annals of the American Pulpit; or, Commemorative Notices of Distinguished American Clergymen of Various Denominations, from the Early Settlement of the Country to the Close of the Year Eighteen Hundred and Fifty Five*, IV, (New York, 1859), 63–71.

received "a classical education and studied the law." Robert Anderson was among the many inland planters whose wills made special provision for the "liberal education" of sons or grandsons. Both Pickens and Anderson, together with Elias Earle, served as trustees for Hopewell Academy in Pendleton, which was founded as a preparatory school for admission to South Carolina College at Columbia.[11] The involvement of such men, and many others, in the South Carolina education movement suggests that the post-Revolutionary demand for inland schools and colleges was more than an effort by lowcountry leaders to educate ignorant frontiersmen; it also reflected the determination of a rising inland leadership to educate itself.

ii

Coincident with the education movement was a renewed interregional effort to encourage the development of staple agriculture throughout the state by improving transportation between Charleston and the backcountry. The call for inland navigation arose in response to economic crisis, but it also reflected the political concerns of lowcountry leaders who were seeking ways of drawing the inland majority into an identification with the coast. In 1784, when Governor William Moultrie called a special legislative session to cope with the postwar debtor crisis, he urged the House of Representatives "to bestow a very particular attention to all our Roads, Causeys, Bridges, Ferries, Cuts and Inland Navigation . . . to the great ease and Comfort of the Inhabitants, and very much to the good of the State." He was particularly interested in "that Valuable but Bulkey Article of Tobacco," which, he predicted, would "in a few years be one of our great staples." From 1784 through 1809, the legislature responded to such calls by passing twenty-seven acts for clearing rivers and building canals. These, in addition to acts establishing tobacco inspections, ferries, and road improvements, reflected a widespread interest in the unification of South Carolina sections through the development of commercial agriculture in the backcountry.[12]

Funds for the major improvements in interregional transportation came, not from the state, but from private investors, whose interest in navigation schemes both reflected and reinforced growing ties between South Caroli-

11. Andrew Pickens to Henry Lee, Aug. 28, 1811, Andrew Pickens Papers, SCL; will of Robert Anderson, Jan. 25, 1810, County Wills, WPA Trans., I, Anderson County, bk. A, 145–155; *Miller's Weekly Messenger* (Pendleton), Sept. 24, 1807.

12. South Carolina House of Representatives Journal, Feb. 2, 1784, Feb. 17, 1785, in Theodora J. Thompson *et al.*, eds., *Journals of the House of Representatives*, The State Records of South Carolina (Columbia, S.C., 1977–), *1783–1784*, 402, *1785–1786*, 98; Cooper and McCord, eds., *Statutes of South Carolina*, IV, V.

na's sections. In 1786, the legislature incorporated the first of four navigation companies. Its purpose was to build a canal between the Santee and
Cooper rivers to facilitate the flow of goods from the backcountry directly
into Charleston. The idea had been articulated before the Revolution, but
not until after the war did the plan get under way. The officers of the Santee
Cooper Canal Company included a broad spectrum of South Carolina political figures. Ralph Izard, John Rutledge (the former governor), Thomas
Sumter, Aedanus Burke, Wade Hampton, John Chesnut, and William Moultrie were among those who, despite political differences, joined together to
establish the company.[13]

Other navigation companies represented similar interregional efforts. Established in 1787, the Catawba Company sought to construct a canal between the Catawba River in Camden and the North Carolina line. Along
with Thomas Sumter and leading men from the Camden area, a number of
prominent Federalists were heavily involved in the project. The most notable among these were William L. Smith and Henry William Desaussure.
Another company, involved in cutting a canal between the Edisto and Ash-
ley rivers to improve "the communication between the north-western parts
of this State, and the city of Charleston," drew on a similarly broad base of
support, as did the company for cutting a canal between the Broad and
Pacolet rivers. Business connections forged in these navigation companies
inevitably contributed to the development of a statewide leadership even in
the midst of sectional conflict. In January 1792—a time of deepening political tension within South Carolina and the nation at large—Thomas Sumter
was still able to dine with William L. Smith at the home of Ralph Izard. Not
surprisingly, conversation centered on the Santee and Catawba canals.[14]

Participants in these early navigation schemes had complex motives. Undoubtedly men such as Wade Hampton and Thomas Sumter considered
the profitable impact of improved transportation on their own substantial
holdings. Even the Federalists John Rutledge and Thomas Pinckney, who
owned land in the backcountry, must have considered the advantages to be
gained from improved transportation. Ralph Izard had dreams of establishing a village called "Izardtown" on his plantation near the Santee end of the
canal. It seems likely that participants also hoped to profit by speculat-

13. House Jour., Mar. 22, 1786, in Thompson *et al.*, eds., *Journals of the House,
1785–1786*, 595; George C. Rogers, Jr., *Evolution of a Federalist: William Loughton
Smith of Charleston (1758–1812)* (Columbia, S.C., 1962), 130–133; *St. Gaz. of South-
Carolina*, Apr. 19, May 21, 1787; Cooper and McCord, eds., *Statutes of South Carolina*,
VII, 541–543.
14. Cooper and McCord, eds., *Statutes of South Carolina*, VII, 545–547, 549–551,
558–560; Rogers, *Evolution of a Federalist*, 133–134; William L. Smith to Edward
Rutledge, Jan. 16, 1792, William Loughton Smith Papers, SCHS.

ing in lands granted to the companies by the initial incorporating acts. Finally, Charleston merchants, distressed at losing backcountry trade to Augusta and Savannah, also supported the navigation plans. It is not coincidental that such prominent merchants as Nathaniel Russell and Aaron Loocock were among the original petitioners for the Santee Cooper Canal Company.[15]

At the same time, lowcountry leaders had political reasons for supporting inland navigation. Ralph Izard was probably not alone in seeing the development of canals as a solution to the sectional conflict. Reflecting in 1795 on the probability that the recent "attack upon the constitution of the state would be renewed," Izard had "no doubt that in a few years a considerable change will take place in the representation." If, he insisted, "Appius's plan were adopted immediately, the lower country would be considerably injured, and the whole state disgraced. Taxes would be partially laid, and the Offices of Government would not be filled by the most respectable characters." Izard hoped and believed that the "evil" would, "in a great measure be removed by the inland navigation, when carried farther than is at present contemplated." When, he continued, "men of property and education are distributed through all parts, an exact apportionment in the representation whatever may be the standard, will be of much less importance than it is at present."[16]

iii

As with the movement for inland navigation, the search for a new staple crop was a response to economic crisis. Suffering from a series of post-Revolutionary crop failures and the loss of the British bounty, indigo planters were eager to find a substitute. Encouraged by the growth of British demand for cotton, South Carolinians also began seeking ways to expand production of the fiber. In 1787, a correspondent lamented, "The culture of cotton is so much neglected in this state" and observed that the northern states, Great Britain, and other European nations might be expected to "purchase it with avidity." One year later, a writer noted that backcountrymen were "very anxious to get the machines for ginning, carding and spin-

15. Index to State Grants, SCDAH. For a discussion of Ralph Izard's plan for "Izardtown," see Henry Savage, Jr., *River of the Carolinas: The Santee* (Chapel Hill, N.C., 1968), 244. See also Carl L. Epting, "Inland Navigation in South Carolina and Traffic on the Columbia Canal," South Carolina Historical Association, *Proceedings*, 1936, 19; Cooper and McCord, eds., *Statutes of South Carolina*, VII, 541–543, 545–547, 549–551.

16. Ralph Izard to Charles Cotesworth Pinckney, Jan. 18, 1795, Ralph Izard Papers, SCL.

ning cotton," and he urged lowcountry planters to improve the healthfulness of their region by draining swamplands and growing cotton instead of rice.[17]

Throughout the late 1780s, South Carolinians searched for improvements in the small hand gins used for separating the lint from the cotton seed. In 1788, John Hart petitioned the legislature for patent rights on a proposed gin. It is unclear whether he received the patent, but, the following year, someone else advertised roller gins designed upon "a new plan," which, "for utility and cheapness . . . exceeds anything of that kind that has yet appeared." In 1790, William L. Smith worked to obtain a gin invented in the Bahamas, and, in 1793, Pierce Butler also hoped to increase his yield in cotton by acquiring new gins. That year he asked a friend in Nassau whether a "Famous Ginn maker could be prevailed on to come to America." Butler had already made inquiries about a young inventor who was residing in Georgia. He believed that the young man's machine was superior to the thirty-six small gins that he had recently purchased in Philadelphia.[18]

The young Georgia inventor was Eli Whitney, and it was his saw-toothed gin that won widest acceptance in South Carolina and throughout the southern states. Once the Whitney gin came into general use, South Carolina cotton exports soared. Using the early hand gins, a worker might have expected to clean about five pounds of cotton each week; Whitney's earliest roller gin could clean about fifty pounds each day. Between 1790 and 1800, the state's cotton exports rose from 9,840 pounds to more than 6,425,000 per year. During the same period, exports of indigo declined dramatically. In 1800, Governor John Drayton proclaimed it a "matter of National Joy to find that so valuable a staple as cotton is now added to the produce of this State." Observing that indigo and tobacco had "become in less demand," Drayton exulted, "The planting of cotton increases annually both in the lower and upper country."[19]

17. *City Gaz., and Daily Adv.,* Dec. 6, 1787, May 29, 1788; see also June 24, 1788.
18. Petition from John Hart, Petitions, 1788, no. 22; *City Gaz., and Daily Adv.,* Feb. 17, 1789; William L. Smith to Edward Rutledge, Apr. 29, 1790, Smith Papers; Pierce Butler to Nathanial Hall, Sept. 16, 1793, Pierce Butler Letterbook, 1790–1794, II, 272, Pierce Butler Papers, SCL. Smith was referring to Joseph Eve, a Bahamian inventor who immigrated to Georgia in an effort to get patent rights on his roller gin. See Ulrich Bonnell Phillips, *American Negro Slavery: A Survey of the Supply, Employment, and Control of Negro Labor as Determined by the Plantation Regime* (Baton Rouge, La., 1966 [orig. publ. New York, 1918]), 158.
19. Phillips, *American Negro Slavery,* 156–158; Lewis Cecil Gray, *History of Agriculture in the Southern United States to 1860* (Gloucester, Mass., 1958 [orig. publ. New York, 1941]), II, 680; Savage, *River of the Carolinas,* 255–258; John Drayton, *A View of South Carolina, As Respects Her Natural and Civil Concerns,* (Charleston, S.C., 1802), 135–168; Marjorie Stratford Mendenhall, "A History of Agriculture in South Carolina,

Piedmont settlers were slower to turn to cotton than were growers in the middlecountry and coastal districts. In fact, most of the cotton produced in South Carolina before 1800 was probably grown on middlecountry and lowcountry plantations. Tobacco exports rose steadily during the 1780s and remained more or less stable during the subsequent decade—a clear indication that piedmont planters had not yet turned to cotton. In 1794, as he opposed backcountry efforts to win constitutional reform, Timothy Ford was able to distinguish between the middlecountry districts, which were likely to be transformed by the introduction of cotton, and the upcountry districts, which still seemed to be unaffected by the crop. Two years later, Robert Goodloe Harper confirmed that observation when he complained that people in his region continued to "persevere obstinately in the cultivation of tobacco." As late as 1802, John Drayton observed that tobacco remained the primary money crop in the piedmont, although cotton production had begun to increase.[20]

Nonetheless, by the first decade of the nineteenth century, cotton was making inroads throughout the backcountry. The trend was apparent to Edward Hooker during his tour of 1805. Before leaving Charleston, Hooker noted that backcountrymen were coming down "pretty numerously with their corn and cotton." Those crops, he believed, were "their chief articles for the market." Tobacco, he had heard, was "very little raised by them." On the route to Columbia, Hooker passed through Granby, Orangeburg District. The town had once been the site of a large tobacco inspection, but Hooker found, "since the culture of cotton has superseded that of tobacco, its trade has dropped, and the tobacco warehouses are shut up, and going to decay." When he finally reached the piedmont, Hooker admitted to having had "no conception till now of the immense benefit produced to the Southern States by the invention of the ingenious Mr. Whitney of New Haven." The gins were then "in universal use." By the first decade of the nineteenth century, some tobacco warehouses were being converted to cotton.[21]

Cotton boosters in South Carolina believed that the new staple would bring prosperity to the inland poor. In 1796, petitioners from Camden

1790 to 1860: An Economic and Social Study" (Ph.D. diss., University of North Carolina, Chapel Hill, 1940), 42; House Jour., Nov. 25, 1800.

20. Mendenhall, *History of Agriculture*, 39–44; Americanus [Timothy Ford], *The Constitutionalist; or, An Enquiry How Far It Is Expedient and Proper to Alter the Constitution of South Carolina* (Charleston, S.C., 1794), 46; Robert Goodloe Harper to a Gentleman in Philadelphia, Sept. 16, 1795, in *Observations on the North American Land Company, Lately Instituted in Philadelphia* ... (London, 1796), 143; Drayton, *View of South Carolina*, 135–168.

21. Edward Hooker, Journal, Nov. 15, 4, 1805, I, 78, 119, CHS.

District requested passage of a cotton inspection law in order to raise the price of South Carolina's crop on the foreign market. They insisted that cotton, "by finding employment for Numbers of our poor fellow citizens would be the means of procuring to themselves and families many of the necessities and Comforts of life, of which they would be otherwise destitute." Writing in 1808, David Ramsay was convinced that cotton made the greatest impact on the nonslaveholding population. He noted that cotton production did not require the sort of initial capital outlay demanded by rice or indigo and suggested that the crop enabled "the poor" to become "of value, for they generally were or at least might be elevated to this middle grade of society." Ramsay believed that cotton "had a large share in moralizing the poor white people of the country" by giving them incentive to work.[22]

In fact, there is no reason to believe that the inland spread of cotton culture transformed those backcountry "vagrants" or marginal people so much complained of during the Regulator era. In the absence of an early agricultural census, it is virtually impossible to say whether the years of the cotton boom saw an increase in their numbers, but continuing complaints against them testify to their presence during the early antebellum era. Ramsay himself noted that "squatters" who lived by hunting and pilfering "have been at all times nuisances." Also in 1808, Henry William Desaussure expressed his opposition to manhood suffrage by observing, "The principle would be mischievous in all large towns, and in some of the districts where there is a floating population not attached to the soil." He suspected that the "levelling effects would be more felt in the upper than in the lower country." Some years later, a grand jury of Kershaw—a former Regulator area in which a wealthy plantation area was surrounded by infertile sandhills—protested on behalf of those planters who were "wantonly and cruelly beaten, and often maimed by disorderly vindictive and intemperate persons who frequently possess no sufficient property from which compensation could be obtained."[23]

Whatever its impact on the "floating population," cotton expansion exerted diverse pressures on the backcountry yeomanry and sparked a flood of out-migration. Most migrants were probably seeking larger tracts in the Southwest in order to take better advantage of rising cotton prices and to

22. Petition from Sundry Inhabitants of Camden District, Petitions, 1796, no. 96; David Ramsay, *History of South Carolina from Its First Settlement in 1670, to the Year 1808* (Newberry, S.C., 1858 [orig. publ. Charleston, S.C., 1809]), II, 248–249.

23. Ramsay, *History of South Carolina*, II, 231; Henry William Desaussure to Ezekiel Pickens, Sept. 12, 1808, Desaussure Papers; Kershaw grand jurors, quoted in Brady, "Political and Civil Life in South Carolina," 135 (see also 119–139).

Political Unification

Table 11. White Population and Households, 1790–1810

Area	People, *Households*				
	No.			Increase	
	1790	1800	1810	1790–1800	1800–1810
Lowcountry					
Coastal districts excluding city of Charleston	20,555	24,233	25,096	18%	3%
	4,851	*5,743*	*5,779*	*18%*	*1%*
City of Charleston	8,089	9,630	11,568	19	20
	1,933	*1,240*	*—*	*−36*	
Middlecountry					
Orangeburg	12,412	15,350	19,321	24	26
	2,387	*2,738*	*3,489*	*15*	*27*
Cheraws	7,418	13,138	13,279	77	1
	1,344	*2,202*	*2,239*	*64*	*2*
Lower Camden[a]	11,571	18,722	19,838	62	6
	1,596	*2,755*[b]	*2,961*	*73*	*7*
Upcountry[c]	80,133	114,590	126,097	43	10
	12,547	*18,004*	*19,190*	*43*	*7*

Sources: U.S., Bureau of the Census, *Heads of Families at the First Census of the United States Taken in the Year 1790: South Carolina* (Washington, D.C., 1908); *Return of the Whole Number of Persons within the Several Districts of the United States* (Washington, D.C., 1802); Federal Population Census, South Carolina, 1800, 1810, NA microfilm.
[a]Household figures for Richland are excluded because they are missing from the 1800 census; household figures for Lancaster are included because, before the formation of Kershaw County in 1791, it extended into the middlecountry.
[b]Because part of the 1800 census for Sumter District is missing, this figure is low.
[c]Because much of the 1800 census for Chester District is illegible, it is excluded from the upcountry figures.

provide more fully for their offspring. At the same time, as landowners turned their acreage to the cultivation of cotton, they "warned off" squatters onto unproductive marginal land or out of the state completely. Charles Cotesworth Pinckney was not alone when, during the first decade of the nineteenth century, he decided to cultivate his backcountry tract. Those living on lands without grants had no choice but to leave. Finally, moral opposition to slavery impelled some backcountrymen to head for the Midwest. Though their numbers remain unknown, Newberry Quakers and antislavery Presbyterians in the western piedmont left South Carolina during the early years of the nineteenth century.[24]

In all backcountry areas except Orangeburg, the most sparsely settled region of the state, the rate of increase of the white population dropped dramatically between 1800 and 1810 (see table 11). A similar decline occurred in the rate of increase of backcountry households. During the first decade of the nineteenth century, several upcountry districts lost white population. In the upcountry as a whole, the rate of increase among whites declined from 43 percent between 1790 and 1800 to 10 percent during the following decade. At the same time, the rate of increase of upcountry households declined from 43 percent to 7 percent. Individual districts saw even more dramatic changes. Between 1790 and 1800, before cotton became the dominant market crop in the region, the white population in Fairfield increased by 32 percent. During the subsequent decade, the number of Fairfield whites declined by 4 percent. Newberry's white population increased by only 1 percent between 1800 and 1810, having grown by nearly 19 percent the preceding decade.[25] In other words, there is little question that untold numbers of upcountry settlers were departing the area just as cotton was taking root.

Among those who remained, the shift to cotton production opened new opportunities for the acquisition of slaves. The years of the cotton boom saw a notable increase in the number of slaveholding households. The most marked transformation occurred in the middlecountry, particularly the lower part of old Camden District (see table 12). There the number of slaveholders rose from 26 percent of all households in 1790 to 47 percent of all households in 1810. The proportion of slaveholders in the middlecountry district of Cheraws changed relatively little between 1790 and 1810, but the spread of cotton did bring marked transformation to the old district of Orangeburg. There the proportion of slaveholders grew from 29 percent to about 43 percent of all households.

The rise in the number and proportion of middlecountry slaveholders reflected a dramatic increase in the number of slaves (see table 13). Between 1790 and 1810, the slave population throughout the entire backcountry grew from 29,094 to 85,654—an increase of 194 percent. During the same

24. Andrew Pickens to Charles Cotesworth Pinckney, Jan. 2, 1804, Andrew Pickens Papers, SCL. Patrick S. Brady found evidence that yeoman families and poor whites were leaving South Carolina during the early years of cotton expansion. See Brady, "Political and Civil Life in South Carolina," 119–139. See Chapter 9 for a discussion of Newberry Quakers and antislavery Presbyterians.

25. Federal Population Census, South Carolina, 1800, 1810, NA microfilm; *Return of the Whole Number of Persons within the Several Districts of the United States* (Washington, D.C., 1802).

Table 12. Slaveowning Households in the Backcountry, 1790, 1810

Area	Proportion of Households Owning Slaves				
	No. of Slaves				Total
	0	1–4	5–19	20+	
Middlecountry					
Orangeburg[a]					
1790 (N = 2,387)	71%	17%	10%	3%	101%
1810 (N = 3,489)	58	22	16	4	100
Cheraws[b]					
1790 (N = 1,344)	72	15	10	3	100
1810 (N = 2,239)	70	15	12	4	101
Lower Camden[c]					
1790 (N = 2,079)	74	11	11	4	100
1810 (N = 3,755)	53	20	19	8	100
Upcountry					
1790 (N = 13,591)	77	15	7	1	100
1810 (N = 20,589)	64	21	13	2	100

Sources: U.S., Bureau of the Census, *Heads of Families at the First Census of the United States Taken in the Year 1790: South Carolina* (Washington, D.C., 1908); Federal Population Census, South Carolina, 1810, NA microfilm.
[a]By 1810, the area that had been Orangeburg District included Barnwell, Lexington, and Orangeburg districts.
[b]By 1810, the area that had been Cheraws District included Chesterfield, Marlboro, and Darlington districts.
[c]In 1790, Lower Camden included Claremont, Clarendon, Lancaster, and Richland districts; in 1810 it included Kershaw, Lancaster, Richland, and Sumter (figures for Sumter are incomplete).

period, the slave population of lower Camden District grew by 323 percent, from 5,519 to 23,369. In 1790, 32 percent of the region's population was enslaved; by 1810 the proportion had risen to 53 percent. With the lower part of old Camden District solidly in the Black Belt, the middlecountry was beginning to look more like the coastal parishes, where, in 1810, 72 percent of the population was slave and 60 percent of all households (excluding the city of Charleston) held slaves. One visitor to South Carolina sensed these distinctions as early as 1802 when he defined the "lowcountry" as the entire area from the coast to "a hundred and fifty miles inland." By this definition

Table 13. Slave Population, 1790–1810

| | Slaves | | | | |
| | No. | | | Increase | |
Area	1790	1800	1810	1790–1800	1800–1810
Lowcountry					
Coastal districts excluding city of Charleston	70,316	87,351	96,586	24%	11%
City of Charleston	7,684	9,819	11,671	28	19
Middlecountry					
Orangeburg	5,931	7,046	12,628	19	79
Cheraws	3,229	4,877	6,079	51	25
Lower Camden	5,519	13,202	23,369	139	77
Upcountry	14,415	23,856	43,578	65	83

Sources: U.S., Bureau of the Census, *Heads of Families at the First Census of the United States Taken in the Year 1790: South Carolina* (Washington, D.C., 1908); *Return of the Whole Number of Persons within the Several Districts of the United States* (Washington, D.C., 1802); Federal Population Census, South Carolina, 1810, NA microfilm.

the traveler was including the village of Camden—once a center of Regulator activity—as part of the lowcountry.[26]

The upcountry remained, in 1810, a predominantly yeoman area, but there, too, slavery was making significant inroads. Between 1790 and 1810, the slave population rose from 18 to 26 percent of the whole, and the proportion of slaveowning households increased from 23 to 36 percent. By the first decade of the nineteenth century, the slave population in the upcountry was growing at a more rapid rate than in any other region of the state. Between 1800 and 1810, when cotton took hold, the number of slaves in the upcountry grew by 83 percent, as compared to only 11 percent in the lowcountry districts (excluding Charleston) (table 13). In 1790, only

26. U.S., Bureau of the Census, *Heads of Families at the First Census of the United States Taken in the Year 1790: South Carolina* (Washington, D.C., 1908) (hereafter cited as *Heads of Families, 1790*); Federal Population Census, South Carolina, 1810, NA microfilm (figures for St. Philip and St. Michael parishes missing); F. A. Michaux, *Travels to the Westward of the Allegany Mountains . . .* (London, 1805), 285. See also Brady, "Political and Civil Life in South Carolina," 19–137.

Table 14. Distribution of Slaves, 1790–1810

Area	1790 (N = 107,094)	1800 (N = 146,151)	1810 (N = 193,911)
Lowcountry	73%	67%	56%
Middlecountry			
Cheraws	3	3	3
Orangeburg	6	5	7
Lower Camden	5	9	12
Upcountry	13	16	22
Total	100	100	100

Sources: U.S., Bureau of the Census, *Heads of Families at the First Census of the United States Taken in the Year 1790: South Carolina* (Washington, D.C., 1908); *Return of the Whole Number of Persons within the Several Districts of the United States* (Washington, D.C., 1802); Federal Population Census, South Carolina, 1800, 1810, NA microfilm.

13 percent of all South Carolina slaves resided in the upcountry (see table 14). By 1810, the proportion had risen to 22 percent. During the same period, the proportion of South Carolina slaves in the lowcountry dropped from 73 to 56 percent.[27]

The backcountry's growing demand for slaves provoked a last flurry of sectional tensions over the slave trade. Lowcountry representatives continued to express the fear that new imports would promote social instability, but they were probably more concerned about maintaining high prices for their own surplus slaves while guaranteeing that coastal planters would be the primary suppliers for the backcountry. In any case, inland representatives continued to press for an open trade, whereas lowcountry planters favored maintaining a ban on importation. In 1803, when thirty-six of forty-nine inland representatives supported a motion to permit slave imports from other states within the United States, not a single lowcountry member joined the inland minority. The ban on the interstate trade remained in effect through 1804, and, that year, lowcountry representatives urged passage of a bill that would have extended the prohibition. Again, backcountry members tried to amend the proposed legislation so as to allow entry of slaves from other states. Of the thirty representatives who favored the amendment, twenty-nine came from the backcountry. The proposed continuation of the ban finally met with defeat in the Senate, where, again, most of the negative votes came from inland senators. In 1805,

27. *Heads of Families, 1790*; Federal Population Census, South Carolina, 1810.

backcountry senators succeeded in defeating another proposed ban on slave imports. At that time, an opponent of the measure declared that the act would be unfair to upcountry planters, for, as they were "just becoming rich enough to buy slaves, they are prevented by the laws, while the lower country are already supplied."[28]

Even while the ban on importation remained in effect, backcountry planters managed to circumvent the legislation. Wade Hampton was rumored to have smuggled in slaves from North Carolina. In 1803, Governor James Burchill Richardson complained, "The law prohibiting the importation of negroes into this State . . . has been without success." He raised the possibility that "the Interest of the Citizens is so interwoven with that species of property that it prevents their aiding the law."[29]

This new wave of slave importation swelled the ranks of substantial backcountry planters (see table 15). Again, the most significant shift was in Camden, where planters with twenty or more slaves increased from 14 to 17 percent of all slaveholding households. (By 1810 planters in the low-country districts, excluding the city of Charleston, composed 38 percent of all slaveholders.) In the upcountry districts, the proportion of substantial planters increased only slightly, from 3 to 5 percent of all slaveholding households. Holders of fewer than five slaves remained predominant, but, even there, the proportion of wealthier planters was growing slightly in relation to small-scale slaveholders. That is, farmers who held between one and five slaves formed a smaller proportion of the slaveholding population in 1810 than they had in 1790. The spread of slavery through the backcountry was reflected in the region's tax assessments. Between 1768 and 1800, backcountry contributions to South Carolina taxes rose from 12 to 27 percent of the whole. By 1809, inland settlers held 34 percent of the state's taxable property.[30]

In 1810, the backcountry's planter class was not, for the most part, composed of recent migrants. The majority of backcountry planters with twenty or more slaves had been living in the region for at least twenty years. The

28. House Jour., Dec. 13, 1803, Dec. 14, 1804; Senate Jour., Dec. 8, 1804, Dec. 14, 1805; Hooker, Journal, Dec. 2, 1805, I, 148. See also Patrick S. Brady, "The Slave Trade and Sectionalism in South Carolina, 1787–1808," *Journal of Southern History*, XXXVIII (1972), 601–620.

29. Hooker, Journal, Nov. 5, 1805, I, 93–94; Senate Jour., Nov. 25, 1803.

30. *Heads of Families, 1790*; Federal Population Census, South Carolina, 1800, 1810; Public Treasurer, General Tax Receipts and Payments, 1761–1769, Account of the General Tax Collected for the Charges of the Government, 1768 (for the year 1767), SCDAH; Aggregate of the Taxes for 1799, Acts and Resolutions, 1800, in Records of the States of the U.S. (S.C.) Sessions Laws, 1791–1806, LC microfilm; General Assembly, Annual Report of the Comptroller General, 1809, inclosure 12, SCDAH.

Table 15. Distribution of Slaves among
Backcountry Slaveowners, 1790, 1810

| Area | Proportion of All Slaveholding Households | | | |
| | No. of Slaves Owned | | | |
	1–4	5–19	20+	Total
Middlecountry				
Orangeburg[a]				
1790 (N = 699)	57%	33%	11%	101%
1810 (N = 1,487)	53	38	10	101
Cheraws[b]				
1790 (N = 381)	54	35	11	100
1810 (N = 672)	49	39	12	100
Lower Camden[c]				
1790 (N = 528)	43	43	14	100
1810 (N = 1,747)	42	41	17	100
Upcountry				
1790 (N = 3,131)	69	28	3	100
1810 (N = 7,331)	60	35	5	100

Sources: U.S., Bureau of the Census, *Heads of Families at the First Census of the United States Taken in the Year 1790: South Carolina* (Washington, D.C., 1908); Federal Population Census, South Carolina, 1810, NA microfilm.

[a] By 1810, the area that had been Orangeburg District included Barnwell, Lexington, and Orangeburg districts.

[b] By 1810, the area that had been Cheraws District included Chesterfield, Marlboro, and Darlington districts.

[c] In 1790, Lower Camden included Claremont, Clarendon, Lancaster, and Richland districts; in 1810 it included Kershaw, Lancaster, Richland, and Sumter (figures for Sumter are incomplete).

middlecountry district of Sumter, formerly lower Camden, had more low-country migrants than any of the other six census districts studied, but even there only 30 of the 180 planters can be identified as having migrated from the lowcountry between 1790 and 1810. About 110, or 61 percent, of Sumter's planters were probably living in the backcountry at the time of the first federal census. In areas farther north and west, native backcountrymen were even more predominant among the planters. In Kershaw—the district that included the old village of Camden—49 of 62 substantial slaveholders were native backcountrymen, and most of those can be traced to families that had arrived in South Carolina before the Revolution. Only 2 Kershaw planters can be clearly identified as new arrivals from the lowcountry. Fairfield presents an even more striking picture. There, 24 of 41 planters with twenty or more slaves in 1810 were either living in the Fairfield area in 1790 or were born into Fairfield County families. In Abbeville—an area that included the old settlement at Long Canes—22 of 35 planters were probably living in the backcountry in 1790; only 3 can be reasonably identified as lowcountrymen. Finally, in the upper piedmont districts of Laurens and Union, 31 of 49 substantial slaveholders were long-standing residents of the backcountry. Only 3 can be reasonably identified as migrants from the coastal area.[31]

Wade Hampton was only the most spectacular example of upward mobility. With 87 slaves in 1790, he had hardly been destitute, but, by 1810, the number had risen to 635. In 1811, Hampton purchased a sugar plantation in Louisiana, and, at his death some twenty years later, he was rumored to have owned 3,000 slaves. Austin Peay of Fairfield owned no slaves in 1790, but he held at least 70 in 1810. His great prosperity appears not to have resulted from inheritance, for no member of the Peay family held more than 5 slaves in 1790. Elias Earle of Pendleton held 11 slaves in 1790, and his brother Samuel owned 5. By 1810, the numbers had risen to 30 and 49, respectively. Finally, Thomas Sumter, who paid taxes on 39 slaves in 1783, held 57 in 1810.[32]

In short, cotton expansion not only enabled backcountry yeomen to increase their holdings in slaves; it also enlarged and enriched the region's planter class. The lower part of old Camden District saw the most dramatic changes, but upcountry yeomen and planters were drawing thousands of slaves into their own region as well. The process was reassuring to the coastal elite, who, for the first time, were able to see the backcountry—at least portions of it—in their own image.

iv

The inland spread of cotton culture weakened the position of coastal opponents of reapportionment. It is no coincidence that the South Carolina Federalists, whose lowcountry leadership had formed the bulwark of oppo-

31. *Heads of Families, 1790*; Federal Population Census, South Carolina, 1800, 1810; Ge Lee Corley Hendrix and Morn McKoy Lindsay, comps., *The Jury Lists of South Carolina, 1778–1779* (Greenville, S.C., 1975); Thomas J. Kirkland and Robert M. Kennedy, *Historic Camden*, pt. I, *Colonial and Revolutionary* (Columbia, S.C., 1905); Walter B. Edgar *et al.*, eds., *Biographical Directory of the South Carolina House of Representatives* (Columbia, S.C., 1974–1984), III, IV.

32. *Heads of Families, 1790*; Federal Population Census, South Carolina, 1800, 1810; Edgar *et al.*, eds., *Biographical Directory of the House*, III, 308–310; Tax Returns, 1783–1784, District Eastward of Wateree, 1783, box 1, no. 6, SCDAH.

sition to backcountry demands for political parity, declined in influence during the early years of the cotton boom. After 1798, the party steadily lost ground until the election of 1804, when the Republicans emerged triumphant, even on the coast. By 1803, Henry William Desaussure was already so filled with "dread" at the "ultimate effects of a degrading, calumnating democracy," that he contemplated moving north.[33]

The demise of the Federalist contingent resulted in part from differences with the national Federalist leadership. South Carolina coastal planters resented Federalist tariff policies, and they felt snubbed by the Federalist-dominated Senate that had refused to confirm the appointment of John Rutledge to the Supreme Court. Jefferson's Louisiana Purchase was extremely popular throughout the South, and it probably won lowcountry Federalists to the Republican camp. Thomas Sumter, Jr., believed that opposition was confined to "a few mad-dog federalists," but he found that "many of the moderates of that party . . . approve of the acquisition." Most important, the antislavery leanings of leading northern Federalists had already alienated many southerners. The decision to run Charles Cotesworth Pinckney together with John Adams in the presidential election of 1800 represented an effort to hold together a party already rent with sectional tensions.[34]

There were, however, other, more compelling reasons for the Federalists' loss of influence. The diminishing political strength of South Carolina's arch-conservatives was a clear indication that lowcountry planters felt less threatened by the staunchly Republican backcountry. Throughout the 1790s, Federalists within the state had appealed to voters who feared that inland settlers posed a serious challenge to slavery on the coast. The revolution in Saint Domingue and growing tensions between the United States and France had made lowcountry leaders particularly sensitive to the danger of internal social upheaval. As relations between the United States and France improved and as cotton expanded the backcountry's slave population and planter class, inland settlers appeared less threatening. Federalists in South Carolina lost their primary leverage.

This is not to suggest that the early years of the nineteenth century witnessed an end to sectional tensions. Indeed, the presidential election of

33. James H. Broussard, *The Southern Federalists, 1800–1816* (Baton Rouge, La., 1978), 235–246; John Harold Wolfe, *Jeffersonian Democracy in South Carolina* (Chapel Hill, N.C., 1940), 121–123, 155–160, 197–202; Rogers, *Evolution of a Federalist*, 342–355, 362–364; Henry Desaussure to John Rutledge, Jr., July 12, 1803, John Rutledge, Jr., Papers, SHC.

34. Broussard, *Southern Federalists*, 58–60, 87, 236–242; Rogers, *Evolution of a Federalist*, 348; Thomas Sumter, Jr., to James Monroe, Dec. 11, 1803, James Monroe Collection, NYPL.

1800 sparked a renewed battle between coastal conservatives and back-country Republicans. Leading Federalists organized themselves in an effort to sweep the state, and Charles Pinckney began organizing Republican forces throughout South Carolina. Writing to John Rutledge, Jr., in September 1800, Thomas Pinckney observed that the line between the parties was "becoming every day more distinct." He feared that South Carolinians would soon "arrive at the acme of political rancour and malevolence which the Pennsylvanians seem to have first reached."[35]

Supporters of Thomas Jefferson emphasized themes that had long marked the political rhetoric of inland leaders. At a public dinner held in Stateburg on Bastille Day to honor Thomas Sumter, a speaker toasted Thomas Jefferson, "whose character still rises in the estimation of his country, though attacked by shafts of calumny." Sumter himself evoked a central tenet of backcountry republicanism by emphasizing links between artisans and farmers. He toasted "the yeomanry, mechanics, and manufactures of the United States, whose intelligence and patriotism support our Constitution, as their labors do our lives." Several months later, an Orangeburg Republican attacked the snobbery of coastal Federalists, declaring that people in his region were "too well acquainted with the merits of Mr. Jefferson" to be swayed by Federalist pamphlets. "Though we are," the writer concluded, "called '*Yahoos*' we can distinguish between an honest man and *a knave*."[36]

South Carolina Republicans went out of their way to challenge the openly elitist outlook of Federalists on the coast and to emphasize Jefferson's commitment to individual liberties. A public letter from "A Back-Countryman" declared that, despite "inflammatory newspaper scribblers," the people of America knew that Thomas Jefferson was "the uniform, undeviating friend of the rights and liberties of his fellow citizens." Another Republican writer mocked his opponents by detailing a mock recipe for the creation of a Federalist.

> Begin by asserting a pre-eminence in *abilities, virtue,* and *patriotism . . .* and the *exclusive* right of governing. Attribute the worst *motives* to every man who does not adopt *your* political creed. Advocate standing armies, sedition acts, *efficient* governments, not stopping at monarchies. Call the liberty of the press, licentiousness; ridicule the sovereignty of the people. . . . Use on all occasions, the words *Jacobinic, democratic,* etc.; apply them indiscriminately to any thing that does not accord with your

35. Rogers, *Evolution of a Federalist,* 348–350; Thomas Pinckney to John Rutledge, Jr., Sept. 23, 1800, John Rutledge, Jr., Papers, SHC.
36. *City Gaz., and Daily Adv.,* July 21, Oct. 2, 1800.

own opinions; abominate every thing that is French and extol every thing
that is *English.*

Finally, an Abbeville resident who called himself "Impartialis" challenged
the Federalist Sedition Act and declared that Thomas Jefferson held "a
higher place than any other man in the public estimation."[37]

Coastal Federalists mustered all their forces in opposition to what they
saw as a dangerous threat from within their own state and the nation at
large. They pressed older, respected men to run for the legislature so that
they would be able to sway South Carolina for Adams and Pinckney, and,
with help from Robert Goodloe Harper, they sought inland allies as well.
Wade Hampton noted that Federalists in Charleston had made "extraordinary exertions . . . in favour of General Pinckney and have turned their
views to every part of the state."[38]

Federalists from Charleston succeeded in electing most of their candidates to the state legislature, but, overall, they suffered a serious blow. With
Harper's defeat in Ninety Six and the election of Sumter in Camden, they
failed completely to solidify support in the backcountry. Moreover, Jeffer-
son-Burr electors won decisively in the legislature, with the result that South
Carolina swung the national election for the Republicans. Federalists in
Congress further weakened their party by supporting Aaron Burr over Jefferson when the two were temporarily deadlocked in the contest for the
presidency. It was with good reason that Desaussure wrote in 1801 of the
"fearful apprehensions" experienced by lowcountry Federalists.[39]

Leaders of the old guard were horrified by the Republican victory. Henry
William Desaussure, a prominent coordinator of Federalist efforts in South
Carolina, declared that the object of the opposition was "to pull down
every man who has been respected in the community before the present
party was erected, and who is not within their pale." John Rutledge, Jr., was
concerned that Jefferson would "introduce into our Constitution *subver-
sion* and *revolution.*" He feared that a Constitution so altered would be
unable "to shelter liberty and property . . . when the rains fall and licentiousness howls in tempests about it."[40]

37. *Ibid.,* July 21, Aug. 23, Sept. 12, 1800. "Impartialis" is identified as an Abbeville
resident in the issue for Sept. 20, 1800.
38. Rogers, *Evolution of a Federalist,* 348; *South-Carolina State Gazette, and Timothy's Daily Advertiser* (Charleston), Dec. 15, 1800.
39. Rogers, *Evolution of a Federalist,* 350–351; Wolfe, *Jeffersonian Democracy in
South Carolina,* 155–161; Henry William Desaussure to John Rutledge, Jr., Dec. 19,
1801, John Rutledge, Jr., Papers, SHC.
40. Henry William Desaussure to John Rutledge, Jr., Aug. 25, 1801, John Rutledge,
Jr., to H. D. Ward, Jan. 3, 1801, John Rutledge, Jr., Papers, SHC.

There was nothing new in the charges leveled by both sides in the election of 1800; what was new was the isolation of the coastal Federalists. While Rutledge Junior worried about democratic tempests, celebration swept much of the state. Republicans met not only throughout the backcountry—in Camden celebrants met at Dinkins tavern, the former Regulator stronghold—they also congregated on the coast. In Charleston, "upwards of two hundred republican citizens dined together" to celebrate Jefferson's victory. At the head of the table was suspended a portrait of the new president, and large letters around his head spelled the words "Man of the People." After drinking to the militia of the United States, guests sang the "Marseillaise."[41]

Festivities were not confined to the city, where artisans exerted a Republican influence. The Ashepoo Social Club also gave a "Civic Feast" to celebrate the election, and a meeting of "respectable inhabitants" of Christ Church and Saint Thomas parishes held a "Republican Festival" honoring Jefferson's victory. Guests at the Christ Church dinner gave striking evidence of growing state unity by drinking toasts to Thomas Sumter and Robert Anderson. They also drank to "the French Republic" and its "exertions in defense of the rights of man." Toward the conclusion of the festivities, guests toasted the parish of Christ Church, "the only election district in the lower division of this state which voted with Republican unanimity"; they also toasted "the Republican Minority of St. Thomas' Parish."[42]

During the next few years, Federalist influence declined further. By 1801, Republicans in the state legislature were already working to pass a new election districting system that would diminish Federalist chances for success in the coming congressional elections. Desaussure was particularly alarmed that backcountry representatives were winning support from their coastal counterparts. He complained to Rutledge Junior "that men calling themselves friends to the low country, should venture to recommend this suicide."[43]

In 1802, when the Republican-dominated state legislature succeeded in passing a gerrymandering act, the fate of the Federalists was sealed. South Carolina's new system for electing representatives to the United States Congress linked the backcountry election districts of Richland and Orangeburg to the lowcountry district of Colleton. Even more damaging to the Federalists was the decision to join Barnwell and Beaufort to the strongly Republican and heavily populated district of Edgefield. The result was that John Rutledge, Jr., formerly a congressman from Barnwell and Beaufort, was

41. *City Gaz., and Daily Adv.*, Jan. 6, Mar. 14, 20, 1801.
42. *Ibid.*, Mar. 19, May 6, 1801.
43. Desaussure to John Rutledge, Jr., Aug. 25, 1801, John Rutledge, Jr., Papers, SHC.

effectively removed from the Congress. His friends decided not even to put him up for election in the newly defined district. According to Desaussure, the legislature had designed the new system "expressly to destroy the Federal voice," and Cotesworth Pinckney believed that the "openly avowed principle" of the plan was "to stifle the voice of federalism." As early as December 1802, a Republican legislator from Claremont informed Thomas Sumter that, regardless of the districting plan ultimately adopted, Federalism would be "taken care of."[44]

With the founding in 1803 of the *Charleston Courier*, the state's only avowedly Federalist newspaper, the party experienced a new surge of energy, but Republicanism was triumphant. Federalists did not get very far by complaining of their opponents as a "tribe of democrats" who stayed in power by "flattering the views of the multitude." In 1804, even Charleston failed to elect a Federalist congressman to the United States House of Representatives, and only a few members of the dwindling faction remained in the state legislature. That year, when Republican members of the state legislature met at a dinner in Columbia, they were able to drink a toast to "the republican parishes of the low country." Three years later the South Carolina House of Representatives agreed, by a vote of sixty-seven to twenty-two, to commend Thomas Jefferson and request that he present himself again as a presidential candidate. All save two of the dissenting representatives came from the lowcountry, and, of these, nine were Charlestonians.[45]

v

As Federalists declined in influence, backcountry leaders experienced growing success in their calls for state constitutional reform. In 1801, a majority of state representatives voted to support a resolution declaring that it was "expedient to go into an alteration of the representation as settled by the Constitution." Backcountry representatives succeeded because they were able to win crucial votes from the coast. Of the fifty-six supporters, eleven came from the lowcountry and forty-five from the backcountry. The fifty-one opponents included only four backcountrymen, and all were from the middlecountry districts of Clarendon, Orange, and St. Matthew. Henry Wil-

44. Cooper and McCord, eds., *Statutes of South Carolina*, V, 430–431; Henry William Desaussure to John Rutledge, Jr., Jan. 1803, John Rutledge, Jr., Papers, SHC; Cotesworth Pinckney to John Rutledge, Jr., Jan. 17, 1803, John Rutledge, Jr., Papers, DUL; A. [probably Anthony] Butler to Thomas Sumter, Dec. 9, 1802, Thomas Sumter Papers, II, LC. See also Rogers, *Evolution of a Federalist*, 354–355.

45. *Charleston Courier*, Apr. 1, 1803; *City Gaz., and Daily Adv.*, May 16, 1804; House Jour., Dec. 10, 1807.

liam Desaussure was, predictably, alarmed by the result. He informed John Rutledge, Jr., "The representation in the state legislature was assailed; and *for the first time*, a majority obtained by the assailants."[46]

The backcountry victory of 1801 was significant, but it did not result in reapportionment. Supporters of reform did not attain the two-thirds majority required for a constitutional amendment, and, according to Desaussure, piedmont representatives became alienated from the movement because the proposed bill diminished coastal representation and increased representation for the middlecountry without altering apportionment for their own region. Desaussure predicted that the lowcountry would be "saved" by backcountry "jealousies, not their justice." He hoped that his region would "be enabled to resist the appian scheme a considerable time long from the divisions of the middle and upper country."[47]

These divisions were of short duration. The following year petitioners from the piedmont districts renewed the struggle for equal representation. Appealing to long-standing republican assumptions, residents of Abbeville conceived themselves "intitled, by the principals of a Free Constitution to an equal participation of political Rights, with their fellow Citizens throughout the State." They reminded the legislature that the last federal census and a variety of other governmental documents "loudly proclaim this unpleasant truth that the freemen of the upper and middle Districts are not one twentieth part represented in the State Legislature, in proportion to their fellow citizens below." The Abbeville petition requested a constitutional convention or a legislative act to reform the system of representation. The House voted in favor of a resolution to grant the request of the piedmont petitioners, but a lowcountry maneuver succeeded in postponing the issue for another year, when, again, supporters of reform failed to achieve the two-thirds majority required for altering the South Carolina Constitution.[48]

During the next two years, a solid backcountry contingent, joined by a small group of lowcountry defectors, succeeded in maintaining a narrow House majority in favor of reform but failed to secure the necessary two-thirds margin. In 1803, after approval by the Senate, fifty-two state representatives supported a bill designed to alter the system of state representation. Only forty-four opposed the measure. Ten lowcountrymen joined the

46. House Jour., Dec. 12, 1801; Desaussure to John Rutledge, Jr., Dec. 19, 1801, John Rutledge, Jr., Papers, SHC.

47. Desaussure to John Rutledge, Jr., Dec. 19, 1801, Jan. 13, 1802, John Rutledge, Jr., Papers, SHC.

48. Petitions from Abbeville, Petitions, 1802, nos. 52, 53 (oversize); Senate Jour., Dec. 3, 1802; House Jour., Nov. 26, Dec. 7, 1802.

majority, but only four backcountrymen, all from the middlecountry, voted against reform. The following year, more or less the same thing happened. Supporters of reform won a narrow majority in the House. This time only one backcountryman, again from the middlecountry district of Clarendon, voted against his region, whereas nine coastal representatives supported reform. As in the past, representatives from the coastal districts north of Charleston (formerly Georgetown District) split their votes.[49]

It was probably not surprising to contemporaries that the last leading spokesman for constitutional reform came, not from the backcountry, but from the Georgetown area—a region that had displayed consistent sympathy for the backcountry. Joseph Alston, one of the wealthiest men of the Georgetown area, was also, linked to the state's leading speculators. Married in 1801 to Theodosia Burr, daughter of the vice-president, Alston subsequently loaned money to his father-in-law and became involved in Burr's plan to establish a western empire. Thomas Sumter and Wade Hampton, whose penchant for speculation may have drawn them to the periphery of the conspiracy, were also close friends with Aaron Burr and probably developed contacts to Alston as well. In any case, Alston had by 1804 become the state's most outspoken advocate of constitutional reform.[50]

In 1804, while serving as a representative from Christ Church, Alston delivered a lengthy speech outlining his case for reform. He began by alluding to familiar republican themes. Calling the current system of apportionment "arbitrary," he reminded coastal representatives that backcountrymen were "as virtuous, as intelligent, as patriotic as the inhabitant of the seacoast." Although they paid annual taxes on their property, they were "excluded from the most valuable right which results from a free government!"[51]

Recognizing that the backcountry had grown deeply committed to slavery, Alston sought to convince lowcountry representatives that they had nothing to fear from reapportionment. He admitted that "the circumstances of the times" formerly justified the system established by the Constitution of 1790. The point was that circumstances had changed. The inland expansion of cotton cultivation had "enabled and inclined the proprietors

49. House Jour., Dec. 15, 1803, Dec. 13, 1804; Senate Jour., Dec. 12, 1803. Dissenting lowcountrymen were from Christ Church; St. Andrew; St. James, Goose Creek; St. James, Santee; St. John, Berkeley; Williamsburg; and Marion.

50. Edgar *et al.*, eds., *Biographical Directory of the House*, IV, 32–35; George C. Rogers, Jr., *The History of Georgetown County, South Carolina* (Columbia, S.C., 1970), 188–192, 195–197; Thomas Perkins Abernethy, *The Burr Conspiracy* (New York, 1954), 45–46.

51. *Chas. Morn. Post, and Daily Adv.*, May 9, 1804.

of land to large purchases of slaves." As a result, the interests of South Carolina sections were virtually identical. Alston suggested that backcountry settlers had "advanced beyond all calculation, in wealth and number, in information, in every thing which can render a people respectable." He pointed out that "the same law . . . which oppresses the one, could not fail to bear hard upon the other." Alston mocked the "inconsiderable minority" who saw fit "to alarm themselves, unnecessarily by predicting dangers and evils which exist only in their imaginations, as the probable result of the majority's being invested with their rights."[52]

Alston's preference was for a system of apportionment based on white population alone, but he supported the compromise plan for a system based on some combination of population and wealth. Appealing to the more numerous skeptics, he suggested that defeat of the moderate plan would probably prompt backcountry representatives to press harder for the more democratic solution. "Would it not" queried Alston, "be wiser . . . at once to admit these claims, which will probably set the question forever at rest, than to risk being compelled, at some future day, to admit claims of a far more extensive nature?"[53]

The House was not sufficiently persuaded by these arguments to act on the reform proposal in 1804 or in 1806, when the matter came up again, but in December 1807 Alston made another plea for reform. As in his speech of 1804, he insisted that backcountry South Carolinians were firmly committed to slavery. "The cultivation of the soil," he observed, "is not only the common pursuit of every part of the state, but is everywhere carried on by the same description of persons." Although he admitted that "the number of slaves is greater in the Lower Country," Alston pointed out that there were "more persons in the Upper Country interested in that species of property." Few South Carolinians, he concluded "will be seriously suspected of want of interest on that head."[54]

Alston sought to persuade coastal representatives that they, too, would benefit by an alteration in apportionment. He reminded representatives from the northern coastal parishes that their region was also underrepresented. All Saints and Prince George, Winyah, were wealthier and better populated than smaller parishes to the south; yet they had fewer representa-

52. *Ibid.*, May 10, 1804.
53. *Ibid.*, May 9, 10, 1804.
54. Joseph Alston, *Speech of Joseph Alston, Member from Christ Church, in the House of Representatives for Winyaw in a Committee of the Whole to Which Was Referred the Bill for Amending the Third and Seventh Sections of the First Article of the Constitution of This State* (Georgetown, S.C., 1808), 12–13.

tives in the House. Alston also observed that the sense of grievance resulting from inequitable apportionment was the primary source of dissension
within the state. He believed that state unity would be achieved only when
that long-standing dispute had been resolved.[55]

The legislature did not act on Alston's suggestion that a convention be
called to implement the proposed reform, but, during a special session in
1808, the House finally passed a constitutional amendment establishing a
system of apportionment based on population and taxable property. There
were only two dissenting votes. By 1808, as Alston recognized, not even the
most conservative coastal planters could see reapportionment as a threat.
Henry Izard, serving as a senator from St. James, Goose Creek, was able to
inform his friend Gabriel Manigault that the legislature was "wonderfully
unanimous at Columbia on our Constitutional business." The same year, as
if to emphasize the transformation in South Carolina politics and society,
the Camden mills closed for lack of wheat. Cotton had replaced grain as the
key market crop in the middlecountry.[56]

The reform of 1808 amounted to an official recognition of the expanding
Black Belt. It provided a formula for combining white population and taxable wealth as a basis for apportionment and required that reapportionment occur every ten years. The reform allowed more representatives to
backcountry districts as they became absorbed by the slave-plantation system. Although the backcountry won a clear majority in both houses, the
amendment ensured that Black Belt representatives would control the legislature. The reapportionment plan of 1808 signaled an interregional agreement among political leaders throughout the state to give legislative control
to those representatives who would be least subject to influence by nonslaveholding voters and most sensitive to the potential threat of a slave
majority.

vi

It was the sons and grandsons of the Revolutionary generation who finally
sealed the process of state unification. Schooled, for the most part, at South
Carolina College together with their lowcountry counterparts, they were
more intimately tied to the coastal elite than their fathers had ever been.
Whereas the first generation of inland leaders had generally married women
of similar background, sons and daughters of the wealthiest and most

55. *Ibid.*, 6, 17–18.
56. Cooper and McCord, eds., *Statutes of South Carolina*, I, 193–196; Schaper, *Sectionalism and Representation*, 433–434; Henry Izard to Gabriel Manigault, July 6,
1808, DUL; Mendenhall, "History of Agriculture in South Carolina," 123.

prominent inland families began marrying into coastal families.[57] As cotton increased the value of upcountry land, sons of prominent coastal families began moving inland for summer or permanent residence. By the second decade of the nineteenth century, South Carolina names were less regionally specific, and, by the late 1830s, members of the Pinckney and Desaussure families were serving as state representatives from upcountry districts.[58]

Meanwhile, sons of prominent backcountry political figures outstripped their fathers in statewide and national political position. In 1802, James Burchill Richardson, son of the middlecountry planter and Regulator sympathizer Richard Richardson, became the first backcountryman—indeed the first non-Charlestonian—to serve as state governor. Twelve years later, Andrew Pickens, Jr., a graduate of Rhode Island College, became the state's first governor of piedmont origin. In 1808, John C. Calhoun, a graduate of Yale, assumed his first elective office as state representative from Abbeville. He emerged some years later as the leading political spokesman for planters throughout the southern states. That the younger Pickens and Calhoun received legal training in Desaussure's law office is further testimony to the unification of South Carolina's political leadership.[59]

Cotton had not been responsible for the advance of leading inland families to planter status and political prominence, nor had cotton alone prompted the formation of interregional political alliances. Bound together

57. At the start of the 19th century, interregional marriages were confined to the most prominent backcountry families. Most notable was the marriage of Wade Hampton's son to the daughter of Christopher Fitzsimmons, a wealthy Charleston merchant. John C. Calhoun married his lowcountry cousin, thereby sealing ties between the piedmont and coastal branches of his family. Ezekiel Pickens, son of Andrew Pickens, married John C. Calhoun's lowcountry sister-in-law. Emily Bellinger Reynolds and Joan Reynolds Faunt, *Biographical Directory of the Senate of the State of South Carolina, 1776–1964* (Columbia, S.C., 1964), 231, 289; Rogers, *Evolution of a Federalist*, 371; Robert L. Meriwether et al., eds., *The Papers of John C. Calhoun* (Columbia, S.C., 1959–1986), I, xxiv.

58. Lawrence Fay Brewster, *Summer Migrations and Resorts of South Carolina Lowcountry Planters* . . . (Durham, N.C., 1947), 3–73; William W. Freehling, *Prelude to Civil War: The Nullification Controversy in South Carolina, 1816–1836* (New York, 1966), 20–21; Edgar et al., eds., *Biographical Directory of the House*, I, 339. Tax records of 1809 suggest that coastal residents were acquiring extensive inland holdings. That year, residents of Charleston District (excluding the city) paid 20% of their taxes on property held out of the district. Residents of the lowcountry districts of Beaufort, Colleton, Georgetown, and Williamsburg paid 18, 13, 11, and 6% of their taxes, respectively, on property held elsewhere. Most piedmont districts paid only 1 or 2% of their taxes on property held in other areas, but residents of Richland and Kershaw paid 9% of their taxes on property held out of the district, and residents of Darlington held 13% of the taxable property in other areas of the state. See General Assembly, Annual Report of the Comptroller General, 1809.

59. Edgar et al., eds., *Biographical Directory of the House*, I, 273, IV, 92–96, 441–442, 475–476.

by their joint involvement in the slave system, inland and coastal leaders had fundamental interests in common even before the Revolution. The incorporation of backcountry areas into the Black Belt strengthened and extended these ties, but it did not create an inland leadership. The expansion of cotton culture helped to unify the state only because backcountry planters were already committed to slavery and eager for a new staple crop.

What cotton expansion did was to reassure coastal leaders that the backcountry could be a trusted ally in the struggle to protect slavery from any possible interference. With more inland settlers acquiring slaves and with more inland areas potentially vulnerable to black majorities, coastal representatives could finally rest assured that backcountry republicanism would not become a spearhead of antislavery. The formula for reapportionment reflected and resolved fundamental coastal concerns by ensuring that Black Belt districts would control the state legislature.

CHAPTER 9

Evangelical Revival and the
Definition of Christian Stewardship

i

Writing in 1788, in the midst of South Carolina's debtor crisis, the Presbyterian minister Thomas Reese reflected on the problem of social disorder and concluded that religion was necessary "to supply the imperfection of civil laws." Echoing republican fears of the propertyless poor and the luxury-loving rich, he observed, "Extreme poverty and want stimulate men to theft, robbery and many other dishonest practices," while "overgrown estates" were "often a curse and incumbrance to their owners, and a source of many evils in society, by introducing luxury, sensuality and effeminacy." Reese undoubtedly pleased many of his backcountry readers by suggesting that those "who are placed between the extremes of want and abundance, are generally the best members of society, most happy themselves, and contribute most to the happiness of others." Christianity would create virtuous citizens by "moderating our love of riches," on the one hand, and by promoting "diligence as the means of acquiring a comfortable subsistence," on the other.[1]

Reese linked his assault on the luxury-loving rich to a hierarchical social vision. Although he assumed that the spread of Christianity would narrow the difference between the extremes of wealth and poverty, he also believed that society as a whole, and the citizenry in particular, would always be characterized by some degree of difference in social rank. Christianity would promote social order by reconciling the lowly to their God-given station and by sensitizing the wealthy to their social obligations. "The real

1. Thomas Reese, *An Essay on the Influence of Religion, in Civil Society* (Charleston, S.C., 1788), 15, 65–66.

Christian," insisted Reese, "though he may possess an affluent fortune, to which you may add, if you please, a noble and refined taste, is careful to keep both in due subordination to the honor of God and the good of men." If poor, he would be "satisfied with the station, tho' humble, in which heaven hath fixed him" and would neither envy "the rich and the great" nor be "anxious for change." Reese was confident that "with such a temper as this," the devout Christian would be "an honest, quiet, and peaceable member of society."[2] Slavery was not the subject of this essay, but it hardly needs to be pointed out that Reese's vision of Christianity, based on the acceptance of social inequality, posed no problem for planters. This hierarchical religious outlook was not unique to South Carolina or even to the slave states, but it did provide the foundation for what later became a distinctive, proslavery Christianity.

For purposes here, Reese's essay is significant because Reese was personally and ideologically identified with leading planters of the backcountry. In 1788, he was still living in the middlecountry, but, by 1793, he was running an academy in the upcountry county of Pendleton while ministering to a church where both Robert Anderson and Andrew Pickens served as elders. (Anderson eventually married Reese's widow.) Like the political leaders with whom he associated, Reese linked a markedly inegalitarian social outlook to an attack on the opulent style of South Carolina's gentry. He died in 1796, about five years before the revival of religion that transformed his region and state, but his essay articulated themes that became central to the message of southern evangelicals generally.[3]

Reese's characterization of the Christian message captured the tension that lay at the heart of backcountry evangelicalism—and politics—at the turn of the century. By celebrating men of middling means and contrasting them to those with "overgrown estates," he was, in effect, minimizing distinctions between backcountry planters and yeomen. That construction of social order served the purposes of backcountry planters who had, for decades, emphasized their identifications with the far more numerous yeomanry, but it also signaled an arena of tension. Although backcountry planters felt constrained to demonstrate their deference to the yeomanry, they also struggled to establish their class prerogative. As Robert Anderson,

2. *Ibid.*, 25, 67.

3. William B. Sprague, D.D., *Annals of the American Pulpit; or, Commemorative Notices of Distinguished American Clergymen of Various Denominations, from the Early Settlement of the Country to the Close of the Year Eighteen Hundred and Fifty-Five* (New York, 1859–1869), III, 331–332; Walter B. Edgar *et al.*, eds., *Biographical Directory of the South Carolina House of Representatives* (Columbia, S.C., 1974–1984), III, 40–41, 552.

Andrew Pickens, and a number of prominent backcountrymen recognized, the yeomanry's claims to political equality could, if carried too far, threaten the prerogative of planters generally and thereby render slavery insecure. Reese, as a ministerial spokesman for his backcountry planter friends, dealt with that dilemma by insisting that the true Christian would willingly obey civil authority and accept the inequality among men as an expression of God's will. Nonetheless, for all the effort of ministers such as Reese, the early history of evangelicalism in the backcountry suggests that God's vision of the polity remained a matter of contention.

There were, however, important areas of growing, though tenuous, unity between yeoman and planter Christian visions. If backcountrymen differed in their sense of the right relationship among independent men, they shared a belief that the household or family was the fundamental unit of social order and that relationships within households were, of necessity, characterized by some degree of dependence and inequality. As slave ownership expanded through the backcountry population, yeomen demonstrated their willingness to identify slavery as a legitimate extension of the familial relationships that defined production through the household economy as a whole.[4]

To recognize that backcountry yeomen incorporated slavery into their notion of family order is not to say that the southern yeomanry was automatically or necessarily proslavery in orientation. During the latter half of the eighteenth century, evangelicalism became a vehicle for the expression of antiplanter sentiment among yeomen, and, in certain contexts, it devel-

---

4. The following explorations of religion in the Old South raise important questions about the widely held assumption that southern evangelicalism was inherently or necessarily egalitarian in its implications. They point to the widespread influence of ministers who saw slavery as the natural extension of a God-ordained hierarchy and suggest that the organic social vision at the heart of proslavery Christianity be seen in the context of the social relations that defined production in yeoman as well as planter households. See Eugene D. Genovese and Elizabeth Fox-Genovese, "The Religious Ideals of Southern Slave Society," *Georgia Historical Quarterly*, LXX (1986), 1–16; Eugene D. Genovese, " 'Slavery Ordained of God': The Southern Slaveholders' View of Biblical History and Modern Politics," 24th Annual Robert Fortenbaugh Memorial Lecture, Gettysburg College, 1985; Jack P. Maddex, Jr., " 'The Southern Apostasy' Revisited: The Significance of Proslavery Christianity," *Marxist Perspectives*, II, no. 3 (Fall 1979), 132–141; Maddex, "Proslavery Millennialism: Social Eschatology in Antebellum Southern Calvinism," *American Quarterly*, XXXI (1979), 46–62. Stephanie McCurry's pathbreaking work focuses attention on relationships within yeoman households of the South Carolina lowcountry and argues persuasively that the inequality of those relationships enabled yeomen to share in the planters' proslavery Christian vision. See McCurry, "Defense of Their World: Class, Gender, and the Yeomanry of the South Carolina Lowcountry, 1820–1861" (Ph.D. diss., State University of New York, Binghamton, 1988).

oped into a critique of slavery itself.[5] In other words, the evangelicals' challenge to gentry culture could and occasionally did turn into a more fundamental critique of the social relationships upon which planter power rested. In South Carolina, the spread of slavery into the upcountry and the vigilance of proslavery ministers nipped such tendencies in the bud, and the long history of accommodations by planters kept tensions under control. Rather than challenging slavery, the evangelical churches that expanded with cotton and slaves through the backcountry mediated the uneasy relationship between planters and yeomen and did what they could to locate slaves in a broader network of unequal familial bonds.

ii

South Carolina's evangelical revival occurred within the context of a society in which planters gave no sign of harboring any antislavery inclinations. The Revolutionary era saw a spate of private manumissions among planters in the Upper South, but no comparable impulse ever beset the planters of any region in South Carolina. Whereas Virginia's free black population increased by more than 7,000 between 1790 and 1800, free blacks in South

5. David Brion Davis has pointed out that southern antislavery, during the Revolutionary era, was short lived and confined, for the most part, to yeoman areas of the Upper South. He argues that any "indigenous questioning of slavery" was assimilated by planters and their ministers into a vision of Christian trusteeship. See Davis, *The Problem of Slavery in the Age of Revolution, 1770–1823* (Ithaca, N.Y., 1975), esp. 164–212. By interpreting the evangelical revival in pre-Revolutionary Virginia as a challenge to gentry culture, Rhys Isaac's work makes a compelling case for its anti-elitist and antislavery potential. Isaac does not explore the hierarchical assumptions that Virginia Baptists may have shared with their opponents; nor does he consider the assimilation by planters of evangelical thought. See Isaac, *The Transformation of Virginia, 1740–1790* (Chapel Hill, N.C., 1982), esp. 161–205. Other important studies of southern evangelicalism in the 18th and 19th centuries have drawn attention to its early anti-elitist or antislavery potentialities. Focusing primarily on Virginia, they tend to interpret proslavery Christianity as a retreat from or reaction to an essentially or initially egalitarian message. The case of South Carolina, which gave rise to an early, proslavery version of evangelicalism, raises questions about that perspective, but recognition of the diverse potentialities of the revival remains vital to an understanding of the early development of Christianity in the Old South. See Donald G. Mathews, *Religion in the Old South* (Chicago, 1977); Anne C. Loveland, *Southern Evangelicals and the Social Order, 1800–1860* (Baton Rouge, La., 1980), 186–218; James Oakes, *The Ruling Race: A History of American Slaveholders* (New York, 1982), 96–122; Richard R. Beeman, *The Evolution of the Southern Backcountry: A Case Study of Lunenburg County, Virginia, 1746–1832* (Philadelphia, 1984), 97–119, 186–200. For an important account of links between antiplanter and antislavery sentiment in pre-Revolutionary North Carolina, see Mark Haddon Jones, "Herman Husband: Millenarian, Carolina Regulator, and Whiskey Rebel" (Ph.D. diss., Northern Illinois University, 1983), esp. 47–77.

Carolina increased by fewer than 1,400. Coastal planters, eager to replenish their wartime losses of slaves, freed fewer slaves than planters in the back-country. Perhaps their more direct contact with refugees from Saint Domingue further convinced coastal planters to refrain from enlarging their own free black population. Between 1790 and 1800, the number of free blacks on the coast rose from 1,216 to 1,630. Excluding the district of Orangeburg, where the number declined absolutely, the free black population in the backcountry rose from 415 in 1790 to 1,349 in 1800. By 1800, about 3 percent of the inland black population was free. Still, the South Carolina backcountry as a whole contained absolutely and proportionately fewer freed slaves than the more established slave society of Virginia, where, by 1800, 5.5 percent of the total black population was free. Free blacks on the South Carolina coast composed less than 2 percent of the total black population in that region.[6]

Even the relatively small increase in the number of South Carolina free blacks should not be attributed to antislavery sentiment. Quakers in Cheraws may have been responsible for the more extensive manumissions in that area, and a group of antislavery Presbyterian ministers in Ninety Six freed their slaves during the 1790s. But, throughout most of South Carolina, manumissions appear to have been unrelated to feelings of guilt or apprehension about slavery. The South Carolina Act Respecting Slaves, Free Negroes, Mulattoes, and Mestizoes, passed in 1800, placed restrictions on private manumission and made no reference to antislavery sentiment. The act observed simply that it had "been a practice for many years past in this State for persons to emancipate or set free their slaves, in cases where such slaves have been of bad or depraved character, or, from age or infirmity, incapable of gaining their livelihood by honest means." From 1800, each act of manumission required approval from five local freeholders who could testify that the slaves in question were of "good character" and capable of providing their own subsistence.[7]

Wills from two counties, in Camden and Ninety Six, respectively, suggest that planters who made provision for manumission were more concerned

6. Ira Berlin, *Slaves without Masters: The Free Negro in the Antebellum South* (New York, 1974), 46–47; U.S., Bureau of the Census, *Heads of Families at the First Census of the United States Taken in the Year 1790: South Carolina* (Washington, D.C., 1908); Federal Population Census, South Carolina, 1800, NA microfilm.
7. Stephen B. Weeks, *Southern Quakers and Slavery: A Study in Institutional History*, Johns Hopkins University Studies in Historical and Political Science, extra vol. XV (Baltimore, 1896), 266–267; Margaret B. DesChamps, "Antislavery Presbyterians in the Carolina Piedmont," South Carolina Historical Association, *Proceedings*, 1954, 6–13; Thomas Cooper and David J. McCord, eds., *The Statutes at Large of South Carolina* (Columbia, S.C., 1836–1841), VII, 440–443.

with bestowing favor on individual slaves than with challenging the system itself. Twenty-four wills, written between 1770 and 1815, provided for manumission, but not one included any indictment of slavery. The 1783 will of William Pearson of the Camden area is typical. Pearson declared his "trusty negro fellow Jim" a free man and gave him twenty acres free of rent for life. Pearson was less solicitous, however, of his remaining seven slaves. Although he hoped that his personal estate, including slaves, might be kept together, he empowered his executors to sell all of the "Negroes except the young ones," if they thought the sale necessary.[8]

Of the religious groups that challenged slavery during the 1780s, only Quakers maintained a consistently antislavery stance, and, in South Carolina, they either became assimilated or, by 1810, had left the state. The most prominent of South Carolina's Quaker settlements was the Irish community that had migrated to Camden before the Revolution. Within two decades several members of this early Quaker settlement were among the leading slaveowners of what would become Kershaw County. Before the turn of the century, their meeting had disappeared. Inner doubts that may have troubled individual members of Camden's Quaker community were either stifled or transformed. In the end, there was little to distinguish the wills of slaveowning Quakers from their Presbyterian and Episcopalian fellows. John Adamson, who wrote his will in 1814 when he held more than eighty-five slaves, freed a favored slave woman and provided that she be supported for life. He bequeathed his remaining slaves in family units and took care to prevent their sale from the family in the event of an heir's death. Adamson's Quaker heritage may have inclined him to be particularly solicitous of his slaves' well-being, but it did not lead him to question the system as a whole.[9]

Samuel Mathis, son of a British immigrant, reportedly the first white baby born in Camden, expressed the dilemma of a more sensitive slaveowning Quaker. "As to my slaves," wrote Mathis, "I know not what to

8. Will of William Pearson, n.d. [written 1783], County Wills, WPA Trans., Kershaw County, I, bk. A(1), 29–30, SCDAH. The following residents of Kershaw and Abbeville counties wrote their wills between 1770 and 1815 and included provisions for manumission. Kershaw: John James, William Wyly, Sarah Brown, John Chesnut, Elizabeth Nott, John Adamson; Abbeville: John De La Howe, Higgason Barksdale, John Morrow, Sr., Mathew Donaldson, Benjamin Gant, Elizabeth Porter, Henry Wideman, Sarah Bell, William Dunlap, Gennet Donaldson, Rebecca Hutton, James Calhoun, Willis Breazele, Aaron Alexander, Elizabeth Crawford, John Brownlee, Thomas Hamilton.

9. Weeks, *Southern Quakers and Slavery*, 266–267; Thomas J. Kirkland and Robert M. Kennedy, *Historic Camden*, pt. I, *Colonial and Revolutionary* (Columbia, S.C., 1905), 285; will of John Adamson, May 25, 1816 [written 1814], County Wills, WPA Trans., Kershaw County, II, bk. G, 4–12.

say." On the eve of his death in 1823, he left a favored slave to his daughter and urged that she treat him well "for the sake of his father who is a friend of mine." Mathis wished that two other favored slaves might be "set free if ever the law admits it." Mathis's devotion to individuals and apparent inkling of self-doubt about slavery did not, however, diminish his matter-of-fact attitude toward "the rest and residue" of the personal estate "including negroes." He asked simply that these be divided at the discretion of his executors.[10]

Only in the nonplantation areas of the Upper South did Quakers remain true to their antislavery stance. Having settled along the Bush River in what would become Newberry County, the Quakers of Ninety Six District were less prosperous than their counterparts in Camden. Throughout the eighteenth century, they managed to avoid direct involvement in the slave system. As piedmont planters began bringing more slaves into the region, members of the Bush River community sold their lands and, at the turn of the century, departed for the Midwest. Little is known about the Pee Dee Quaker community except that it was probably responsible for the large free black population in Cheraws District and had, by 1810, left the state.[11]

Antislavery advocates gained no influence whatsoever among the backcountry's political leadership. Despite the fears most ably expressed by Timothy Ford and Henry William Desaussure, there is no evidence that any backcountry political figure ever drew antislavery conclusions from the rhetoric of the Revolution. Indeed, piedmont representatives, who might have been expected to entertain some reservations on the slavery question, demonstrated their commitment by voting consistently against efforts to close the African and interstate slave trade. As a group, backcountry representatives were less sensitive to the danger of slave insurrection and less concerned about the impact of democratic-republican political rhetoric than were their counterparts on the coast, but they were no less committed to slavery.[12] South Carolina's political leadership was unanimous in its an-

10. Kirkland and Kennedy, *Historic Camden*, pt. I, 101; will of Samuel Mathis, Dec. 19, 1823, County Wills, WPA Trans., Kershaw County, II, bk. K, 4–8.

11. Weeks, *Southern Quakers and Slavery*, 266–267; Memoirs of the Quakers in the Bush River Region of South Carolina, Written in 1872, John O'Neall Papers, DUL.

12. See Chapter 5. The only political leaders publicly to question slavery in the wake of the Revolution were Charlestonians. John Laurens, son of the merchant Henry Laurens, died in 1782, before the coastal elite had an opportunity to ostracize him politically. David Ramsay, a native of Pennsylvania, was a doctor and historian who represented Charleston in the South Carolina House of Representatives and Senate during the 1780s and 1790s. Although he retreated from his moderate antislavery position, his early remarks cost him a position in the United States Senate. Edgar *et al.*, eds., *Biographical Directory of the House*, III, 418–424, 590–594; Jerome J. Nadelhaft, *The Disorders of*

gry response to Quaker antislavery advocates from the North, and Alexander Gillon brought the matter before the State Constitutional Convention of 1790. He observed, "As the Quakers were a persevering people, their conduct ought to be carefully looked after and every precaution made use of to prevent five millions in property being sacrificed to their prejudices."[13]

Heightened tensions about events at home and abroad led South Carolina's leaders to secure their labor system by limiting the growth of their own free black population and by imposing further restrictions on their slaves. The Act Respecting Slaves, Free Negroes, Mulattoes, and Mestizoes not only reduced the possibility of manumission; it also strengthened the patrol system and prohibited assemblies of slaves or free blacks who "met together for the purpose of mental instruction," whether or not whites were present.[14]

iii

Not until the first decade of the nineteenth century did backcountry South Carolinians experience a massive revival of religion, but evangelical sects were expanding through the inland reaches of the state during the 1780s and 1790s, and it was during this period that they began to formulate a proslavery version of Christianity. Of the various evangelical sects, Baptists were most successful in attracting converts among the backcountry yeomanry, and, for that reason, they provide a particularly useful window into this process of definition.[15] Baptists had established a strong foothold among planters of the coast and middlecountry before the Revolution, and

War: The Revolution in South Carolina (Orono, Maine, 1981), 87–88; George C. Rogers, Jr., *Evolution of a Federalist: William Loughton Smith of Charleston (1758–1812)* (Columbia, S.C., 1962), 268; Arthur H. Shaffer, "Between Two Worlds: David Ramsay and the Politics of Slavery," *Journal of Southern History*, L (1984), 175–196.

13. 1st Cong., 2d Sess., *Debates and Proceedings in the Congress of the United States, 1789–1824* [Annals of Congress] (Washington, D.C., 1834–1856), II, 1197–1205; *State Gazette of South-Carolina* (Charleston), June 3, 1790; *City Gazette, and the Daily Advertiser* (Charleston), June 2, 1790. William L. Smith described the reaction of the South Carolina congressional delegation in two letters to Edward Rutledge, Feb. 13, 28, 1790, William L. Smith Papers, SCHS.

14. Cooper and McCord, eds., *Statutes of South Carolina*, VII, 440–443.

15. Presbyterians, who retained strict educational requirements for their ministry and whose ministers generally refused to settle in a neighborhood unless their prospective churches promised them a yearly salary, found it difficult to compete with denominations that made use of lay exhorters. See Margaret Burr DesChamps, "The Presbyterian Church in the South Atlantic States, 1801–1861" (Ph.D. diss., Emory University, 1952), 11–24. For a discussion of the significance of the Baptists in defining a proslavery version of Christianity, see Davis, *Problem of Slavery*, esp. 208–212.

they sought to limit more egalitarian interpretations of their own faith. Indeed, the post-Revolutionary struggle between the Charleston Association and the New Light churches of the backcountry reveals a great deal about the boundaries of evangelical religion in South Carolina's expanding slave society.

By the third quarter of the eighteenth century, planters were already well represented among lowcountry and middlecountry Baptist churches, whereas upcountry churches consisted primarily of yeomen. Of 661 likely Baptists who can be located on the 1790 census, 433, or 66 percent, were nonslaveholders, and, of these, nearly 90 percent lived in the piedmont. Of the 228 identifiable slaveholding Baptists, only 21 owned more than twenty slaves, and, of these, only 3 lived in the piedmont. However, more than half of the slaveholding Baptists with fewer than twenty slaves lived beyond the fall line. Of the 100 known preachers and licentiates who were active between 1780 and 1800, at least 40 were slaveowners.[16] In sum, the majority of substantial slaveowning Baptists were situated in the lowcountry or middlecountry and belonged to churches that maintained early ties to the Charleston Association, but most small-scale slaveholders and nonslaveholding Baptists belonged to piedmont churches that were, at least initially, inclined to adopt New Light practices. Middlecountry churches, most notably the Baptist church at Welsh Neck, counted among their members some of the most substantial plantation men and women from that region, but piedmont church members were chiefly nonslaveholders. The unification of South Carolina Baptists involved the gradual incorporation of church groups in which nonslaveholders were the majority into an organization dominated by more substantial planters.

Tensions between New Light and Regular Baptists had been apparent during the Regulator struggles and emerged once again as lowcountry whigs worked to win support for the Revolutionary cause. By sending Oliver Hart on the tour with William Henry Drayton and William Tennent, the Council of Safety revealed its well-founded suspicion that inland Separates would be less than sympathetic to the Revolutionary cause. Members of the whig Committee of Secrecy, Intelligence and Observation in North Carolina had already ordered a Separate preacher named James Perry into custody. They believed that his "influence with the People, especially with those of his own profession, on account of his being a Preacher . . . rendered his political Doctrine more pernicious in its Consequences than otherwise it might

16. Leah Townsend, *South Carolina Baptists, 1670–1805* (Florence, S.C., 1935), 280–281.

have been." Thomas Norris, minister of a church in what would become Union County, exerted a similar influence by preaching nonresistance. When Oliver Hart attempted to address a group assembled by Norris, he had been "a little decomposed on account of Mr. Norris being unwilling that I should say anything about national affairs, and had not much freedom in preaching that I could have wished." Located in what would become Newberry County, Philip Mulkey's community had demonstrated great antagonism toward the lowcountry establishment, and all of Hart's efforts failed to win its support.[17]

After the establishment of South Carolina as an independent state, members of the Charleston Association sought to extend their influence among the new political leadership. Their immediate goal was passage of a state constitution that would place Baptists on a par with other religious groups. In 1777, still fearful that the New Light connection would impede their efforts, they sought to gain influence by expanding their inland membership while distancing themselves from the Separates. Oliver Hart gave clear expression to the concerns of leading Regulars when he wrote to the middle-country minister, Richard Furman, urging union between inland and low-country Regular churches.

> I hope we shall have your Voice and influence for the junction there proposed. We have now no prospect of association with the churches on the Frontier (the Separates). If you and the Congarees will come into the Plan it will be strengthening of us all. I am much of Opinion, it would be much to the Advantage of the Baptist Interest in this State; and the more so on account of our new Constitution, which will necessarily render us more conspicuous to the State, by which we expect all our Privileges, civil and religious.

Hart was especially eager for union because he feared that "some of the Baptists on the Frontiers will be deemed unfriendly to the Government." He asked that all who were "willing to stand up in support of our happy Constitution united together in one band," so as to "be more respectable in the eyes of the Government." Meanwhile, members of the Charleston Association reaffirmed their commitment to South Carolina's civil authority by declaring that the ministers were "happy in being able to say that there is

17. Walter Clark, ed., *The State Records of North Carolina* (Goldsboro, N.C., 1895–1905), XXII, 752: Glenwood Clayton and Loulie Latimer Owens, eds., "Oliver Hart's Diary of the Journey to the Backcountry," *Journal of the South Carolina Baptist Historical Society*, I (1975), 24, 30. For a discussion of New Light Baptists in 18th-century Virginia, see Isaac, *Transformation of Virginia*, 161–205; Beeman, *Evolution of the Southern Backcountry*, 97–119.

not one in this Association but heartily joins in the measures taken by America in general, and this State in particular to secure our liberties."[18]

Even after the Regulars achieved their object in the South Carolina Constitution of 1778, they continued to emphasize their support for the various forms of civil authority. At a meeting in November 1779, the Charleston Association could not "forebear adding, that it becomes us in general to manifest the unshaken Fidelity which we have to the government under which we live." Some years later, the association observed, "The laws of our country are the barrier by which our persons, reputations and property are secured from the cruel depredations of the robber, the slanderer and the assassin. And while we ourselves regard these laws as sacred, we should mark those who do not." Charleston Regular Baptists had reason to fear for the reputation of Baptists in the state at large. It was probably in reference to the New Lights that the South Carolina House of Representatives, in 1786, urged passage of a bill to "Oblige Clergymen and Preachers officiating in this State to take an Oath of Allegiance and Fidelity to the same." The Presbyterian Patrick Calhoun must also have been thinking of New Lights when he expressed doubts "on the too great latitude allowed in religion" by the United States Constitution.[19]

The unwillingness of upcountry New Lights to become active on behalf of the whig cause was not the only source of tension among South Carolina Baptists. According to one early historian of the Baptists, New Lights permitted the appointment of female elders and deacons much to the annoyance of the Regulars. Whatever the actual extent of this alleged New Light practice, the slaveholding Regulars gave special attention to the maintenance of gender hierarchy in Baptist churches. The Charleston Association, in 1783, was careful to point out that "female members may, when called upon, act as Witnesses in a Church; and when aggrieved are to make known their Case . . . and must have a proper Regard paid them: But they are excluded from all Share of Rule or Government in the Church." The

18. Oliver Hart to Richard Furman, Feb. 20, 1777, in Wood Furman, *A Biography of Richard Furman*, ed. Harvey Toliver Cook (Greenville, S.C., 1912), 57; Charleston Association, Minutes, Feb. 3–5, 1777, in *Minutes of the Charleston Association* (Charleston, S.C.), 1777, 3, SCL microfilm.

19. Charleston Association, Minutes, Nov. 9, 1779, Oct. 29, 1796, in *Minutes of the Charleston Association*, 1779, 3, 1796, 8; South Carolina House of Representatives Journal, Feb. 11, 1786, in Theodora J. Thompson et al., eds., *Journals of the House of Representatives*, The State Records of South Carolina (Columbia, S.C., 1977–), *1785–1786*, 394; Jonathan Elliot, ed., *The Debates in the Several State Conventions on the Adoption of the Federal Constitution . . .* , 2d ed. (Philadelphia, 1941 [orig. publ. Philadelphia, 1836]), IV, 312.

Regulars gave evidence of like concerns when they accused the New Lights'
primary spokesman, Philip Mulkey, of adultery and the "Practice of Crimes
and Enormities at which humanity shudders." Mulkey's actual behavior
remains unknown, but the charges against him bear further witness to the
heightened interest of slaveholding Baptists in the protection of patriarchal
authority and household order.[20]

Concerned about the establishment of civil authority and social inequality, Regulars were uneasy about the New Lights' rituals of humility
and offended by their adherence to uneducated ministers. In 1791, one year
after excommunicating Mulkey, the Charleston Association urged member
churches to allow no person into the ministry "but such as afford good
evidence that they are truly pious and of promising gifts." The association
suggested that "at least two, but rather three" of the most "generally es-
teemed" ministers assist in the process of ordination and that the young
preachers "use every rational and proper means for their improvement."[21]

Baptist injunctions concerning dress are also revealing of the Regulars'
concern for the maintenance of social hierarchy. Responding to a query
from the Baptist church at High Hills, the Charleston Association declared
in 1788 that, in dress, "both extravagance and neglect should be carefully
avoided" and that "due respect be paid to the age, circumstances and sta-
tions of persons, and to the customs of the place where we reside; also our
income should not be exceeded, as we are under moral obligations to improve our subsistence for necessary and useful purposes." Along with
Thomas Reese, these coastal and middlecountry Baptists rejected the lavish
display of the lowcountry elite, but they were, at the same time, going out of
their way to acknowledge social distinctions that they saw as intrinsic to
God's order. The association gave further evidence of the inegalitarian social outlook that bound its members when, in 1794, it sent a circular letter
that attempted to explain the inevitability of religious diversity. "Grace,"
according to the letter, did "not occasion an equality of intellect"; rather,
"the human powers are the same *after* conversion as *before*."[22]

The person who was almost single-handedly responsible for the formal
unification of South Carolina Baptists was the backcountry minister Rich-

20. See Chapter 1; Townsend, *S.C. Baptists*, 123–124; *Summary of Church-Discipline,
Shewing the Qualifications and Duties, of the Officers and Members, of a Gospel-
Church, by the Baptist Association in Charleston, South-Carolina* (Wilmington, 1783),
7; Floyd Mulkey, "Rev. Philip Mulkey, Pioneer Baptist Preacher in Upper South Carolina," Southern Historical Association, *Proceedings*, 1945, 12.

21. Charleston Association, Minutes, Nov. 5, 1791, in *Minutes of the Charleston
Association*, 1791, 2.

22. Charleston Association, Minutes, Oct. 27, 1788, Nov. 1, 1794, *ibid.*, 1788, 3,
1794, 7.

ard Furman. The son of a wealthy planter, merchant, surveyor, and school-master of what would become Sumter County, Furman personally bridged the gap between Separates and Regulars. As a child, he moved with his family from New York to Charleston and then, in 1770, to a large planta-tion near Stateburg. He experienced conversion by the New Light preacher Joseph Reese and, along with his mentor, departed from the position of nonresistance advocated by Philip Mulkey. Furman became an active sup-porter of the whig cause. His friendship with Oliver Hart began during the 1770s, and it was to Furman that Hart turned for aid in attracting inland churches into the Charleston Association. In 1787, Furman moved to Charleston, where, for his remaining thirty-eight years, he served as pastor of the city's First Baptist Church. Furman's early ties to the backcountry New Lights ideally suited him to assume a role as unifier of Regulars and Separates. Unlike the Charlestonian Oliver Hart, he was at ease among inland settlers. He also lacked the social snobbery common among coastal planters and merchants. According to tradition, Furman acquired influence within the backcountry by serving as a surveyor for indigent neighbors and practicing medicine among the backcountry poor.[23]

Nonetheless, Furman's class identification and social connections were with planters of the backcountry and coast. Although he was more sympa-thetic to the New Lights than were most of the Regulars, he resisted their antihierarchical inclinations. Furman was a strong advocate of an educated ministry, and, in 1791, he observed, "A great part of our ministers as well as members are very illiterate men; which is a great hindrance to the Baptists having that weight in the state that they would be entitled to, and has in many instances, in the interior part of the country, opened the door to enthusiasm and confusion among them." In subsequent years, Furman sought to extend Baptist influence by involving himself in various plans to educate poor boys for the ministry. It is significant that he joined with Thomas Sumter and other wealthy Claremont planters in establishing a grammar school in Stateburg.[24]

It is possible only to glimpse the process of compromise by which New Light Baptists won acceptance by the Regular organization and gradually lost their Separate identity. In 1775, the Charleston Association included only twelve member churches, of which four were from the backcountry. By

23. Furman, *Biography of Furman*, ed. Cook, 2–13; James A. Rogers, *Richard Fur-man: Life and Legacy* (Macon, Ga., 1985), 1–100.

24. Furman to Rev. Pierce, Feb. 12, 1791, quoted in Furman, *Biography of Furman*, ed. Cook, 42 (see also 15); *Charleston Morning Post, and Daily Advertiser*, May 8, 1781; Rogers, *Richard Furman*, 49–50, 117–133; First Baptist Church, Columbia, Minutes, Oct. 14, 1810, WPA Trans., SCL.

1789, the association consisted of twenty-two churches, including eleven from the backcountry. That year, New Light churches northwest of Columbia and in neighboring North Carolina formed the Bethel Association and opened friendly communications with Charleston. In 1791, a poor community on the Little Pee Dee River applied for membership, but the association had some doubts about "their state" and sent two representatives to visit the church. One year later, the Little Pee Dee church won acceptance. By that time, according to an early historian of the Baptists, the words "Separate" and "Regular" were falling into disuse. Individual church groups retained certain New Light rituals, and members of the upcountry Bethel Association never placed the same emphasis on the education of their ministry as did members of the Charleston group, but none continued to engage in the full range of Separate "peculiar practices."[25] That complaints against New Lights had virtually ceased by the 1790s is perhaps the best testimony to the extent of Baptist unification.

In the absence of any surviving South Carolina New Light church records, it is not possible to recover the extent or shape of the New Lights' challenge to social hierarchy, but the early tension among South Carolina Baptists reveals a great deal about the Regulars.[26] Eager for approval among the planters with whom they were identified, sensitive to the threat of social upheaval in the aftermath of the Revolution, and mindful of the anti-elitist inclinations of the yeomanry, Furman and the Charleston Association were struggling to demonstrate that their denomination would bolster, rather than challenge, the position of planters generally. The process of unification between Regulars and New Lights says less about the actual practices of the latter group than it does about efforts by prosperous slaveholding Baptists to define the acceptable boundaries of their own faith.

iv

The formal unification of the South Carolina Baptists preceded, by a decade, the evangelical revival that swept the state during the first four years of the nineteenth century. Concentrated in the upcountry, it swelled the

25. The process of unification is discussed in David Benedict, *A General History of the Rise and Progress of the Baptist Denomination in America and Other Parts of the World* (Freeport, N.Y., 1971 [orig. publ. New York, 1813]), II, 154–164; Townsend, *S.C. Baptists*, 111–182; Rogers, *Richard Furman*, 63–65. See also Charleston Association, Minutes, Feb. 6, 1775, Feb. 3, 1777, Nov. 9, 1779, Oct. 29, 1787, Dec. 12, 1789, Nov. 5, 1791, Nov. 3, 1798, in *Minutes of the Association*, 1775, 1, 1777, 1, 1779, 1, 1787, 3, 1789, 1, 1791, 4, 1798, 15.

26. The earliest surviving South Carolina New Light Baptist church records date from the 1780s but concentrate on the decades after 1790, when distinctions between New

ranks of Baptist as well as Presbyterian and Methodist denominations. During the peak year of 1802, thousands attended camp meetings at Lancaster, Waxhaws, and Spartanburg in addition to smaller gatherings throughout the state. The number of Methodist churchgoers in South Carolina doubled between 1802 and 1805, from 7,443 to 16,089. During the same period, thirty-five additional Baptist churches came into existence, most located in the upcountry. The leading student of the South Carolina Baptists estimated that black and white membership in churches of that denomination numbered about 10,000 by 1803—an 80 percent increase over the preceding three years. Robert Anderson gave ample testimony to the influence of religion in the upcountry when, in 1804, he publicly defended himself against allegations that he hoped "to establish the Presbyterian religion, in exclusion of the other religious societies." The story, insisted Anderson in a published speech, was "a monstrous and artful insinuation, fabricated to withdraw the confidence of that respectable body of people, the Baptists."[27]

Contemporaries were quick to see a potential for disruption in the religious movement, and it is significant that they tended to focus attention on sexual disorders. The fear, it seems, was that the emotions unleashed at camp meetings would disrupt household order by providing an opportunity for illicit sexual activity. Thus, in 1804, a Charleston newspaper carried a letter from an upcountry writer who insisted that a married woman in York District who "got exorcised to go and have some talk with a handsome young man who lived near," wound up being "exorcised again to sleep with the young man on a Pallet made down by the fireside" in her own home. She allegedly did so with the misguided approval of her husband, who saw the event as an operation of "the Holy Spirit." Richard Furman articulated comparable concerns when he returned from a camp meeting at Waxhaws. He questioned some "incidental evils" that arose at "love feasts" as "men of an enthusiastic disposition have a favorable opportunity at them of diffusing their spirit." Furman was concerned that "the too free intercourse between the sexes in such an encampment is unfavorable."[28] Such accusations point not only to the observers' preoccupation with the preservation of household order but to the probability that the emotionalism of the

---

Lights and Regulars were on the decline. See Padget's Creek Baptist Church Book, 1784–1874, SCL typescript and microfilm.

27. John B. Boles, *The Great Revival, 1787–1805: The Origins of the Southern Evangelical Mind* (Lexington, Ky., 1972), esp. 185; Townsend, *S.C. Baptists*, 301–305; speech by Robert Anderson, Aug. 16, 1804, Robert Anderson Papers, SCL.

28. *City Gaz., and Daily Adv.*, Oct. 17, 1804; Richard Furman to Dr. Rippon of London, Aug. 11, 1802, quoted in George Howe, *History of the Presbyterian Church in South Carolina* (Columbia, S.C., 1870–1883), II, 112–113.

revivals and the intimacy of camp meetings did, in fact, push at the boundaries of acceptable sexual behavior.

As evangelicalism spread through South Carolina, it threatened to have a more direct impact on the order of slaveholding households. James Gilleland, a young Pendleton District preacher, was one of a small group who began speaking out against slavery. Soon after his ordination in 1796, he received a directive from the Presbyterian Synod of South Carolina to keep his antislavery opinions to himself. In 1804, Gilleland, having found it impossible to obey the injunction, moved to Ohio, where he became an abolitionist. At what point William Williamson, a minister at Greenville, decided to emancipate his own slaves remains unclear, but he, too, had migrated to Ohio by 1805 along with some members of his congregation. The Reverend Robert G. Wilson of Greenville followed a similar course. That all three participated in the Spartanburg camp meeting of 1802 suggests the potentialities of the evangelical movement; that they all departed the state within three years testifies to its limits.[29]

Despite their recognition that the revival contained disruptive, egalitarian potentialities, Furman and other slaveholding ministers were confident that the primary effect of religious awakening would be to secure social order by promoting acceptance of a God-ordained hierarchy. Outlining his position in a Fourth of July sermon delivered in the midst of the revival of 1802, Furman described the religious revival as an extension of processes begun during the Revolution. He observed that the Revolution had been "effected by the special agency of God" and that it placed Americans, like the Israelites of the Old Testament, in a divine covenant. The expanded "influence of vital religion" was both a sign of God's approval and a means to the fulfillment of the divine purpose. "Let us not," declared Furman, "rest satisfied with the establishment of republicanism alone, virtue must be added to make us truly respectable and happy." Echoing the position outlined years before by Thomas Reese, Furman declared, "Without virtue there can be no real happiness, either to individuals or the body politic; and without religion, there can be no genuine, stable virtue." Furman was speaking before the Society of the Cincinnati, an organization of Continental officers that had been an object of attack by radical artisans after the Revolution. He doubtless pleased his audience by observing that virtuous citizens would "have due respect for the persons who are constitutionally, or legally, invested with authority."[30]

29. Howe, *History of the Presbyterian Church*, I, 634–635, II, 129, 135; DesChamps, "Antislavery Presbyterians in the Carolina Piedmont," South Carolina Historical Association, *Proceedings*, 1954, 6–11.
30. Richard Furman, *America's Deliverance and Duty: A Sermon Preached at the*

Furman revealed his deepest political assumptions by drawing analogies between society and the family. The sort of man who acknowledged familial obligations was, he insisted, most likely to fulfill public responsibilities, because the public was essentially an extension of the familial realm. "Will that man," asked Furman, "be kind, generous and faithful to his neighbour, who neglects and abuses his own parents and family? and can we suppose *he* will be faithful to his country, who is not faithful to his God?" In effect, Furman was arguing that religion would bind society much as it strengthened the bonds between parents and children. Two years later, in a statement that Furman probably authored, the Charleston Association made the point most clearly.

> In the exercise of authority, whether in public or domestic life, unite it with mercy and kindness; that if possible, you may rule by consent of the governed, and promote their happiness; but support your authority with purity, dignity and firmness; for rulers are the ministers of God and accountable to him. When authority is not so supported, how many vices are tolerated in society, both civil and religious; and how many children are ruined, both in soul and body, for want of seasonable reproof, needful restraint, and due subjection to their parents and governors.[31]

The message was clear: governmental authority was analogous to parental authority because the state was, or should be, a family writ large.

It was this faith in the inherently familial quality of the social order that enabled Furman and other slaveholding ministers to view with optimism the impact of the revival on slaves. The Reverend James M'Corkle, owner of six slaves, gave a revealing description of his own experience at a camp meeting held in Randolph, North Carolina, in 1802. M'Corkle, who later participated in a number of camp meetings in upcountry South Carolina, admitted to having "viewed with horror," and with "some degree of disgust," the scene of "men, women, children, white and black" who "fell and cried for mercy; while others appeared in every quarter, either praying for the fallen, or exhorting bye-standers to repent and believe." M'Corkle initially wondered whether "this scene of seeming confusion" could have "come from the Spirit of God," but he was comforted upon viewing the effects. Among the scenes he noted was that of a "black woman grasping

Baptist Church in Charleston, South-Carolina, on the Fourth Day of July, 1802, before the State Society of the Cincinnati, the American Revolution Society, and the Congregation Which Usually Attends Divine Service in the Said Church (Charleston, S.C., 1802), esp. 7, 13, 17–19.

31. *Ibid.*, 17; Charleston Association, Minutes, Nov. 3, 1804, in *Minutes of the Charleston Association, 1804*, 8.

her mistress' hand and crying 'O mistress you prayed for me when I wanted a heart to pray for myself. Now thank God he has given me a heart to pray for you and every body else.'" M'Corkle did not reflect on the shades of meaning that those words may have held for the slave. Filled with confidence in his own Christian vision, he saw in the incident confirmation of his belief that the conversion experience would enable slaves to accept, even appreciate, subordination. Thus M'Corkle concluded his observations by defending the revival against charges that it bred disorder.

> Where then is that disorder which involves guilt? It is in a multitude of improper, incoherent and wandering thoughts. Do such thoughts pass through the minds of the exercised, or of serious spectators? No.—An awful sense of the Majesty of God—a painful sense of sin—an earnest desire to be delivered from it, etc. etc. surely there is no disorder here.

M'Corkle believed that God, through the revival, was bringing personal and social order out of seeming chaos. The result, he suggested, would be to "reform mankind," not by breaking the bonds of social order, but by grounding unequal relationships in a love of God.[32]

The Methodist minister James Jenkins shared similar assumptions concerning the impact of conversion on slaves. Born in 1764, Jenkins was the son of a prosperous Baptist planter from the Pee Dee area. A staunch advocate of religious education for slaves, Jenkins gave a laudatory account of a camp meeting at which a slave assumed the role of a preacher among whites. At the meeting, which was held at the height of the revival in 1802, Jenkins was pleased to see "a negro man, belonging to brother Bell" begin "preaching near one of the tents." He recalled that "some of us soon joined him—his master among the rest—and the people having collected from every quarter, the work broke out and spread through all the company." Jenkins, who betrayed no hint of disaffection from his class, celebrated the incident, not because he favored a leveling of social distinctions, but because he took social hierarchy for granted. He appears to have assumed, in other words, that religion, properly understood, would strengthen, rather than undermine, the master-slave relationship. Indeed, those black as well as white congregants who failed to accept their station aroused Jenkins's irritation. He later recalled being disturbed about "some difficulties with an influential coloured man, who desired further promotion in the church." Noting that the man "became quite impatient and troublesome," Jenkins

---

32. Rev. James M'Corkle to ———, Jan. 8, 1802, in James Hall, *A Narrative of a Most Extraordinary Work of Religion in North Carolina, by the Rev. James Hall; Also a Collection of Interesting Letters from the Rev. James M'Corkle, to Which Is Added the Agreeable Intelligence of a Revival in South Carolina* (Philadelphia, 1802), 21, 23–34.

reflected that he had "generally found that these people cannot bear promotion: like too many white people, they become proud."[33]

Slaveholding Baptists were perfectly clear in suggesting that conversion would spark recognition of the obligations attending one's position in a God-ordained hierarchy. The member churches of the Charleston Association insisted that masters owed slaves protection, religious instruction, and a decent standard of physical treatment and that slaves owed masters submission and respect. As early as 1785, the prosperous Welsh Neck church promised:

> If we should be possessed of negro or other slaves, that we will act a truly Christian part by them, by giving them good advice, laying our commands on them to attend the worship of God in public on Lords day and in private in our Families when convenient, and we do also promise that we will not treat them with cruelty, nor prevent their obtaining religious knowledge.

Although the churchmen would "endeavor to prevent their rambling," they also promised to encourage literate slaves to instruct others. In 1800, the Charleston Association also assured its members that the "scriptural doctrine on the station and duties of servants, is clear and decided." According to the association, the doctrine required of slaves "faithfulness, submission, quietude and obedience." In return, it asserted the "obligations of masters to rule their servants with justice and moderation; to afford them a reasonable portion of the comforts as well as the necessaries of life; and to regard with seriousness their religious interests." There is no reason to believe that such injunctions reflected a retreat from any antislavery inclination. Rather, the member churches of the Charleston Association were giving voice to an organic vision of social order that celebrated slavery as a natural extension of familial relationships. The Presbyterian Patrick Calhoun inadvertently revealed this underlying assumption when, in 1795, he referred to "my family, both whites and blacks."[34]

William Capers, a prominent South Carolina Methodist minister, got to the heart of the evangelical position on social hierarchy and slave conversion. Born in 1790, Capers was the son of a middling Methodist planter.

33. [James Jenkins], *Experience, Labours, and Sufferings of Rev. James Jenkins of the South Carolina Conference* (n.p., 1842), 110, 117, 212.

34. Welsh Neck Baptist Church, Minutes, 1785, WPA Trans., 37, SCL; Charleston Association, Minutes, Nov. 1, 1800, in *Minutes of the Charleston Association*, 1800, 7. Patrick Calhoun to John Ewing Colhoun, Sept. 30, 1795, Patrick Calhoun Papers, SCL. The inland Mechanicsville church urged masters to instruct their slaves in religion "and supply them with food and raiment becoming their station." See Baptist Church, Mechanicsville, Minutes, 1803, in Cashaway Church, Minutes, WPA Trans., SCL.

While still a child, he moved with his family from Georgetown to the middlecountry. In his autobiography, Capers admitted to being socially ambitious as a young man, eager for acceptance among his father's more prosperous neighbors. In 1806, Capers was deeply moved at a camp meeting at High Hills, but it was another two years before he renounced his political ambitions and devoted himself to the ministry. In making this decision, Capers was, with admitted reluctance, renouncing certain aspects of gentry culture. He recalled that his first act as a Methodist had been to "rip off the frill" from his shirt after a friend reminded him that "Methodists did not wear superfluous ornaments." Capers also gave up dancing, which he linked to the fashionable balls of the planters who lived near his father's plantation.[35]

These acts of renunciation may well have expressed Capers's underlying hostility toward the wealthy families among whom he sought acceptance, and they undoubtedly gave him credibility among the "very poor people" to whom he frequently preached, but they did not signal a rejection of social hierarchy per se. Capers did not question his commitment to slavery, nor did he break off his friendly relations with planters. Indeed, he wrote with apparent pride of attending South Carolina College with a number of young men who later became prominent in southern political circles.[36] Capers was turning his back on certain representations of class, but, rather than challenging social hierarchy, he and others like him expected to place social distinctions on a more solid foundation.

Only by recognizing Capers's essentially unegalitarian social outlook can we begin to comprehend his glowing account of the great free black preacher Henry Evans. By 1810, when the two men met in Fayetteville, North Carolina, Evans, a shoemaker by trade, had won the respect of neighboring planters, but earlier he had been forced to elude "the hands of the mob." Only gradually had planters begun "to suspect their servants of attending his preaching not because they were made worse, but wonderfully better." It was, according to Capers, "not long before the mob was called off by a change in the current of opinion." In 1810, Evans was preaching to a church that included numerous planters and their wives as well as slaves. Apparently he knew how to quell the fears of slaveholding Christians. Evans proved his "inoffensiveness" to Capers and others by

> never speaking to a white man but with his hat under his arm; never allowing himself to be seated in their houses; and even confining himself to

35. William M. Wightman, *Life of William Capers, D.D., One of the Bishops of the Methodist Episcopal Church, South; Including an Autobiography* (Nashville, Tenn., 1859), 11–59, 75–76.

36. *Ibid.*, 59–60, 78.

the kind and manner of dress proper for negroes in general, except his plain black coat for the pulpit. "The whites are kind to me, and come to hear me preach," he would say, "but I belong to my own sort, and must not spoil them."[37]

The content of Evans's sermons and religious beliefs remains unknown, but his survival as a preacher depended upon his ability to appear unthreatening. In the process, Capers and his slaveholding friends in Fayetteville found support for their belief that right religion would reconcile slaves and free blacks to their subordinate place in the social order.

Richard Furman shared Capers's perspective. Not long after Furman's death, an acquaintance recalled the following encounter between the minister and an elderly slave woman. Furman had been

> present in a small company of brethren who had assembled to dine with a common friend, when the usual style by which they addressed each was that affectionate appellation of brother. Those present were very exact in using this mode of address. While their conversation was in progress, and they were freely brothering each other, there came in an aged colored woman well known for her piety and good character. The brethren present saluted her, one in this manner and another in that,—Thus: "Well old Woman," "How-de momma," "How-de Clarinda" and so on. When she came to Dr. Furman, he leaned forward, extended to her his hand and said, "How do you do, Sister Clarinda!" He might have designed his salutation to the old woman as a gentle reproof to these present who did not seem to feel the true equality in which all who know the religion of Christ stood as brethren.

Yet Furman, for all of his apparent respect for slave piety and equality in faith, demonstrated no ambivalence in his acceptance of slavery. In 1805, he complained of having run "into Debt in the purchase of Negroes, to increase my Planting Interest." Rather than challenging slavery, he consistently advocated religious instruction of slaves, and, on his own plantation, he sought to live up to a standard of Christian stewardship.[38]

An essay published in an 1807 edition of the upcountry *Miller's Weekly Messenger* articulated the Christian vision shared by the ministerial spokesmen for the region's planter class. "Are they," queried the author, "obscure in the world, of no account or consideration among men? Are they poor and obliged to act in the quality of servants to others?" If so, the thought

37. *Ibid.*, 124–128.

38. "As Younger Contemporaries Saw Him," from an editorial in *Southern Watchman*, 1838, in Furman, *Biography of Furman*, ed. Cook, 122; Richard Furman to ———, Apr. 21, 1805, Elizabeth Furman Talley Papers, II, 39, SHC typescript; Rogers, *Richard Furman*, 221–230.

that God "is pleased to place them in this low station ... enables the meanest employment: it shows them, that they cannot be obscure so long as they are counted worthy of the notice of God." The Gospel reconciles people "to the most gloomy events" by enabling them to see "that the whole frame of nature is under the dominion of their friend and benefactor."[39] Like Furman and other leading ministers, the author of "The Gospel Morality" was arguing that inequality was essential to God's order and that right religion would reconcile the lowly to their preordained place in the hierarchy.

v

In 1802, Furman and other Baptist ministers from all regions of the state embarked upon an effort to implement their vision through a change in the law. They petitioned the legislature for an alteration of the 1800 Act Respecting Slaves, Free Negroes, Mulattoes, and Mestizoes, which had virtually prohibited religious meetings among slaves. According to the petitioners the restrictions imposed by the act would "have a strong *indirect* tendency to produce the evil it was designed to prevent; by making that class of negroes who value religious privileges and are disposed to support good principles consider themselves oppressed." They recognized that the situation was "delicate" and urged that a distinction be made between "innocent" meetings and those gathered "under the pretense of religion which would in their operation, destroy the foundations of peace and social order."[40]

That the ministers succeeded is the best evidence of their political influence, particularly in the backcountry. When, in 1803, the issue came to a vote, the House supported the Baptist petitioners by fifty to forty-four. The new act altered the act of 1800 by legalizing religious meetings that included slaves. The only qualifications were that such meetings be held before nine in the evening and that the majority of participants be white. Twenty-one of twenty-nine piedmont representatives supported the ministers, along with nine of sixteen middlecountry representatives and twenty of forty-nine representatives from the coastal parishes. As usual, the northern coastal parishes voted with the inland majority, and most Charleston-area representatives opposed the petitioners.[41] The sectional meaning of the vote

39. *Miller's Weekly Messenger* (Pendleton), Sept. 3, 1807.

40. Petition from Richard Furman and others, Petitions to the General Assembly, 1802, no. 181, SCDAH (hereafter cited as Petitions).

41. Cooper and McCord, eds., *Statutes of South Carolina*, VII, 449; South Carolina House of Representatives Journal, Nov. 29, 1803, SCDAH (hereafter cited as House Jour.).

remains somewhat ambiguous. The early spread of evangelicalism through-out the upcountry undoubtedly influenced representatives from that region, and the preponderance of African-born slaves may well have added impetus to the movement for Christianization. At the same time, Charleston-area planters probably recognized that slaves and free blacks in and around the city had greater opportunities for independent organization than did slaves in other parts of the state.

In any case, the inland and Baptist victory of 1803 did not end the debate over the religious instruction of slaves. Planters, particularly in the low-country, continued to wonder whether slaves would draw from Christianity precisely the message they were taught by white preachers, and they re-mained suspicious that many ministers were secret abolitionists. In 1807, armed city guards attacked a Methodist meeting of slaves in Charleston even though it was presided over by a white preacher. Fifteen years later, as news spread of the Denmark Vesey plot, South Carolinians became con-cerned again that slaves would interpret the Christian message as a call for emancipation. With the rise of radical abolitionism in the North and grow-ing fear provoked by the Nat Turner rebellion in 1831, many planters were terrified that religious instruction was enabling slaves to read and thereby encouraging them to become acquainted with dangerous biblical passages and northern ideas. In 1834, following several unsuccessful attempts, the state legislature finally passed an act making it illegal to promote literacy among slaves. Again, backcountry representatives, less fearful of insurrec-tion, tended to oppose the measure.[42]

Although many South Carolinians remained uneasy about the effects of religious instruction on slaves, their general response was to follow Richard Furman, who, after the disclosure of the Vesey plot, urged planters to "take Measures for bringing them [the slaves] to a more full and just acquain-tance with" the Bible. Planters suppressed their Protestant heritage suffi-ciently to reject slave literacy, but they became increasingly committed to providing the slaves with oral instruction in Christianity. In a sense, the planters had no choice. Evangelical efforts in the quarters had been so successful that Christianity among slaves already had a life of its own. As the nineteenth century progressed, South Carolinians joined other south-erners in attempting to secure and justify their system by presenting slaves with a safe and self-serving version of Scripture. The South Carolina acts of 1800 and 1803, which together represented a compromise between inland

42. A. M. Chreitzberg, *Early Methodism in the Carolinas* (Nashville, Tenn., 1897), 97; William W. Freehling, *Prelude to Civil War: The Nullification Controversy in South Carolina, 1816–1836* (New York, 1966), 72–76, 334–335; Loveland, *Southern Evangelicals,* 193–194.

and coastal representatives, signaled a trend that characterized American slavery in the nineteenth century: on the one hand, a tightening of legal restrictions on manumission and, on the other, an effort by masters to justify slavery and ensure its stability by adopting a code of moral and religious stewardship.[43]

By the late eighteenth century, that code censored "excessive" punishment of slaves, and even so prominent a figure as John Ewing Colhoun was not immune to criticism. In 1798, Colhoun's Pendleton County overseer attempted to assuage certain "false and malicious" rumors that had been damaging to the reputation of his employer. At a trial of slaves accused of plotting Colhoun's murder, the overseer insisted that "the report of his [Colhoun's] having cruelly whipped or punished" a runaway was "utterly false and without foundation." The overseer had, according to his own testimony, found the runaway and given such punishment as he "thought he deserved and judged proper." He admitted that the slave in question died soon thereafter, but he insisted that the beating had consisted of no more than "6 or 8 sticks with a switch" administered "for the fellows obstinacy in refusing to put on his cloaths." Apparently Colhoun had been asleep through the whole episode, and the overseer pronounced the rumors of Colhoun's brutality as "injustice and cruelty" and "unfounded slander."[44]

In Kershaw District, about ten years later, a similar incident revealed the prevalence of comparable public standards of planter behavior. John, the son of Joseph Kershaw, testified that an overseer on his sister's plantation did "most wantonly, unjustly and cruelly . . . inflict upon a negro man Slave named Will . . . many cuts, bruises and wounds, with a species of whip made of hard untanned leather . . . in such an improper manner and with such force that the said negro man Will languished under the pressure of the said bruises and wounds in great torment." The slave died soon after the punishment, and Kershaw had no doubt that the overseer had "sought occasion to create a difference with the said slave . . . in order that he might have a plea for inflicting so severe and fatal a punishment." That wanton murder of slaves was disadvantageous to masters from a narrow economic standpoint does not diminish the outrage of grand jurors from Kershaw, who responded to the incident by declaring that the existing laws were "entirely inadequate to prevent the too prevailing crime of murdering ne-

43. Davis, *Problem of Slavery*, 208–209; Eugene D. Genovese, *Roll, Jordan Roll: The World the Slaves Made* (New York, 1974), 51, 186–193.

44. Trial of Slaves Accused of Attempted Murder of Their Master, 1798, John Ewing Colhoun Papers, SCL.

groes whereby our land is becoming stained with Blood and the pages of our Records crowded with instances of unexpiated murder."[45]

vi

If Furman and other slaveholding ministers defined the boundaries of an evangelical faith that was acceptable to planters, we must turn to the predominantly yeoman evangelical communities of the upcountry to comprehend the foundation and limits of the proslavery Christian consensus. Particularly useful for purposes here are the minutes of two formerly New Light Baptist churches. Newberry's Bush River Baptist Church had been founded by the Separate preacher Philip Mulkey before the Revolution, and the Padget's Creek Baptist Church in Union County (later District) was formerly ministered by Thomas Norris. The majority of adult male members were, at least until 1810, nonslaveholders, and none of those who did own slaves held more than fifteen. The surviving minutes date from the last two decades of the eighteenth century, after the incorporation of New Light churches into the network of Regular Baptist associations, but they take us closer than anything else to what more prosperous Baptists saw as the most dangerously egalitarian tendencies of backcountry evangelicalism.[46]

White men played the dominant role in both the Bush River and Padget's Creek Baptist communities. Fifty-four percent of the white membership in each church through 1804 was male, and men were instrumental in initiating family members into their respective churches. At Bush River, there were twenty-five cases from 1799 through 1803 in which male and female family members experienced conversion at different times, and, of these, men led their families in the order of conversion on fifteen occasions. Among Padget's Creek church members, during the same years, there were nineteen cases in which men apparently initiated the conversion of their families, compared to only seven cases in which the first family member to convert was a woman. In both Baptist communities, all of the deacons and elders were white men, as were the committees that periodically considered disciplinary cases. Even when women were the subjects of investigation, men conducted the inquiries. Although women occasionally brought com-

45. Deposition of John Kershaw, Apr. 1, 1808, Presentments of the Grand Jury of Kershaw, Nov. 1808, Thomas J. Kirkland Papers, SCL.
46. Bush River Baptist Church, Journal, 1792–1923, SCL microfilm; Padget's Creek Baptist Church, Book, I, Nov. 22, 1784–July 15, 1837, SCL transcript and microfilm.

plaints against male church members, they were never appointed as exhorters.[47]

Churches were, for the most part, composed of family groups. Ninety surnames account for all the 238 white converts who belonged to the Bush River Baptist Church from 1792 through 1804, and 124 surnames account for the 324 white men and women who belonged to the Padget's Creek Baptist Church from 1794 through 1804. Membership reflected the tendency of kin to settle adjoining or neighboring lands. Both churches included a number of extended kin groups. Thus, 13 members of the Pitts family experienced conversion and joined the Bush River church during the revival, and the Greer and Prince families gave the Padget's Creek church 11 and 12 converts, respectively.[48]

It was within this context that the Bush River and Padget's Creek Baptist communities accepted black members, free and slave, with apparent lack of fanfare. The majority of black converts were slaves held by church members. Eleven slaves and one free black man joined the Bush River Baptist Church during the first decade of the nineteenth century. Of these, three women and two men belonged to the church members Thomas Eastland and his wife, Hezekiah. All of the other converted slaves belonged to church members as well. Thirty slaves joined the Padget's Creek church during the same period, and, of these, at least twenty-one belonged to church members.[49]

Frequent disciplinary cases involving drunkenness open a window into the religious culture of South Carolina's upcountry yeomen and their vision of family order. In marked contrast to the northeastern evangelicals, who sparked the temperance crusade in the antebellum North, these southern Baptists censured members only for drinking "too much." Rather than holding each other to a standard of total abstinence, they objected to drinking when it threatened to interfere with family or community order. The Methodist minister James Jenkins testified to the prevailing attitude toward alcohol consumption when, in 1797, he attempted to enforce a standard of

47. Names of church members through 1804, in Townsend, *S.C. Baptists*, 164 n–166 n, 249 n–250 n; Bush River Baptist Church, Journal; Padget's Creek Baptist Church, Book, I. For an extensive exploration of the ways in which lowcountry yeoman churches represented and regulated gender relationships, see McCurry, "Defense of Their World."

48. Townsend, *S.C. Baptists*, 164 n–166 n, 249 n–250 n; Bush River Baptist Church, Journal; Padget's Creek Baptist Church, Book, I.

49. Slaves admitted to church membership are identified in Bush River Baptist Church, Journal, Aug. 22, Sept. 11, 18, 25, 1802, May 7, June 26, Aug. 6, 1803, Nov. 12, 1808, May 13, 1809, 20–21, 22–24, 40; Padget's Creek Baptist Church, Book, Mar. 15, Aug. 16, Sept. 2, Oct. 18, Dec. 20, 1800, July 18, 1801, July 16, 20, Aug. 13, 18, Sept. 17, Dec. 17, 25, 26, 1802, I, 32–33, 34, 37–39.

restraint among Methodists of the upcountry Saluda Circuit. Jenkins took it upon himself to "reprove the practice of distilling," but he found the people to whom he preached "so offended" that they gave him "only eight dollars" for his ministerial labors.[50]

In their concern for the maintenance of order within and among households, church members gave particular attention to the prevention of ruptures between husbands and wives. The Padget's Creek Baptist Church cited James Willard and his wife, Winnie, for "fighting each other," but it was unable to prevent a split. Thomas Barlow of the Bush River Baptist Church also met with censure for disorderly behavior. He was excluded from fellowship for "drunkenness and profanely swearing and for abusing his wife [and] for presenting a gun at his wife's brother threatening to shoot him." Couples who lived together out of wedlock were also subject to exclusion. Bush River members charged Henry Butler "for having a disorderly base woman living in his house greatly to the dishonor of religion and against the Peace of his children." When Butler refused to "put her away," he came under censure. Adultery and premarital sex were grounds for dismissal of women and men alike, and members of the Padget's Creek church tried to prevent such occurrences in advance. They were thus able to find Rebekah Addenton guilty for having countenanced "a Married Man in her house with her Daughter," and they censured Sister Charity Alexander for "very unseemly behaviour with a Young Man." Male church members were not immune to comparable charges of misconduct. After confessing that "he was guilty of the sin of adultery and that he had told a wilful falsehood to hide his sin," David Johnson was excluded from the Bush River church.[51]

The sheer frequency of disciplinary cases involving accusations of sexual misconduct among the converted should caution us against attributing bourgeois standards of self-discipline to upcountry evangelicals. The Baptists of Bush River and Padget's Creek located order not so much in a notion of disciplined individual character or passionless womanhood as in a

50. [Jenkins], *Experience, Labours, and Sufferings*, 74. For cases involving drunkenness, see Bush River Baptist Church, Journal, Oct. 7, 1803, Mar. 23, 1805, 24, 29; Padget's Creek Baptist Church, Book, Feb. 18, 1804, July 31, 1805, Dec. 20, 1806, Jan. 14, 1809, I, 45, 49, 54, 59. For a discussion of the bourgeois notion of disciplined character and its expression in the temperance movement of the antebellum North, see Paul E. Johnson, *A Shopkeeper's Millennium: Society and Revivals in Rochester, New York, 1815–1837* (New York, 1978); Ronald G. Walters, *American Reformers, 1815–1860* (New York, 1978), esp. 123–143. See also Eric Foner, *Politics and Ideology in the Age of the Civil War* (New York, 1980), esp. 15–33.

51. Padget's Creek Baptist Church, Book, July 23, 1803, Aug. 20, Sept. 16, 1803, July 20, 1805, I, 42, 43, 49; Bush River Baptist Church, Journal, Apr. 9, 1796, Feb. 12, 1803, Aug. 10, 1805, 11, 22, 31.

vision of the well-ordered family. Church members took sexuality among women as well as men for granted. They sought to protect family order by confining sexual relations to marriage, but they were not holding each other to a new standard of inner restraint.[52]

Baptists were sufficiently serious about their Christianity to apply their standards of marital union to slaves, but they were also careful to protect the discretionary power of masters. As early as 1788, the Charleston Association responded to a query from an inland church by observing that slaves were not "entitled to the privileges of freemen by the law of the land" and that therefore "the customary mode" of marriage was unnecessary, but the association went on to sanction slave family unions by ruling that, if slaves "cohabit without entering into obligations to each other, according to the usual mode among negroes, it is fornication." Thus members of the Padget's Creek Baptist Church were able to exclude "Foster's Negroe Fan for the sin of adultery," and the Baptists of Bush River excluded "Hardin's Andrew" for the same transgression. There were, however, no cases at either church in which members disciplined masters for failing to protect familial connections among slaves. The Reverend John Waller gave clear expression to the limits of Baptist concern for family life in the quarters. At his death in 1801, Waller owned twenty slaves. He urged his children to "rule the slaves . . . with mercy and give them what is equal and Right and not part man and wife among them," but only "if they can prevent it."[53]

Baptists appointed black exhorters, probably because the denomination sought slave converts, but such appointments did not signal power within the church. Black as well as white exhorters were subject to scrutiny, and church members periodically restricted those who violated acceptable boundaries of behavior. Precisely why the Bush River church decided that a free black man named Moses Gift had "no call to the work of preaching or exhortation" remains unclear, but members did not hesitate to exclude him from fellowship when he disobeyed their ruling. In May 1804, the upcountry Baptist church at Cedar Spring went so far as to permit a slave named

---

52. The organic vision of social order and sexuality revealed in these upcountry yeoman churches bears some resemblance to that of New England Puritans whose religious world represented the social relations of a nonslaveholding household economy. See Edmund S. Morgan, *The Puritan Family: Religion and Domestic Relations in Seventeenth-Century New England* (Boston, 1944). For an exploration of the sexual morality associated with the evangelical revival in the antebellum North, see Mary P. Ryan, *Cradle of the Middle Class: The Family in Oneida County, New York, 1790–1865* (New York, 1981), 117–165.

53. Charleston Association, Minutes, Oct. 27, 1788, in *Minutes of the Association*, 1788, 2; Padget's Creek Baptist Church, Book, June 15, 1806, I, 49; will of John Waller, Dec. 11, 1801, County Wills, WPA Trans., Abbeville County, I, 300.

Titus to "sing, pray and exhort in public, and appoint meetings in the vicinity of the church." Members were careful, however, to declare that "all his acting to be in Subordination to his master, and that his master council him in particular cases as his prudence may dictate." Apparently church members suspected Titus of transgressions, for they suspended him in November.[54] Upcountry Baptists could sanction the use of black exhorters, free and slave, not because they regarded slaves as equals in the church, but because they assumed that Christianity, properly understood and enforced, would strengthen the unequal relationship between master and slaves.

In short, membership in these predominantly yeoman churches may have brought slaves a measure of protection, but it did not give them any formal mechanism for limiting the prerogative of their masters. Black men were, along with all women, excluded from positions as ministers, deacons, elders, and committeemen. That slaves in the Bush River and Padget's Creek churches brought no charges against any of the white members gives ample testimony to their lack of power. Finally, while the churches found it necessary, on several occasions, to discipline slaves, they left their standard of Christian stewardship entirely to the individual conscience of slaveholding members.

Given their concern for the protection of slaveholders' patriarchal power, it was no coincidence that both the Bush River and Padget's Creek churches devoted more attention to the regulation of order among households than within them. Members were particularly concerned about the restraint of covetousness, and, along with Baptists throughout the upcountry, they held their exchange agreements to a Christian standard. Thus the Bush River Baptist Church heard a charge against Brother James Pitts "for overreaching a man in trading and refusing to disannull the bargain (which appeared to be necessary in order to do justice) without compensation being made to him." The church found this behavior "entirely unjust," and, when Pitts continued to "justify his conduct in taking a sum of money for a nice bargain," he was excluded from fellowship. Other upcountry Baptist communities made comparable efforts to enforce a Christian economy. The covenant of the Church of Christ at Poplar Springs in Laurens declared that members would not engage in "extortion in the Sale of any Commodity; but to follow the Rated Medium in such a manner; as to answer the dictates of a well Informed Judgement." They promised to "comply with the golden Rule: Exhibited in Gods word; to do to others; as we would wish to be done by, in change of Circumstance." Archibald Fowler of the Brushy Creek

---

54. Townsend, *S.C. Baptists*, 258; Bush River Baptist Church, Journal, Oct. 11, 1794, Oct. 10, 1795, 10, 11.

Baptist Church in Greenville met with charges of "extortion" for paying only one dollar to a Mrs. Cole for three chairs. The church also charged Fowler with "unchristianity for saying that if a man owed him and could not pay when due, that he would take a mortgage of his land." Members of the upcountry Big Creek Baptist Church in Anderson decided that those who sold corn at one dollar per bushel might still "be held in fellowship," but several months later they demonstrated a willingness to enforce their collective sense of a fair price. When their "Brother Johnson" brought a complaint against "Brother Hand for failing to do his work according to promis and also for charging him too high," the members found in Johnson's favor. To the query, "What is extortion?" the committee of Pendleton's Shoal Creek Baptist Church responded, "To recve more for any artickel than its Rail value."[55]

The vision of a Christian economy that emerges from these records grew out of a society in which local exchange relationships were generally direct and personal, carried on between neighbors and kin.[56] These upcountry Baptists assumed that covetousness, like the inclination to adultery, drunkenness, idleness, and fighting, were and would remain human failings, but they also believed that churches, like loving families, could restrain those sinful tendencies. It is significant that church members refused to notice or intervene when worldly concerns interfered with the acknowledged obligations of masters to slaves, but, within mutually understood limits, they struggled to incorporate the rampant acquisitiveness unleashed by the cotton boom into a network of personal and familial exchange.

Although members of the Bush River and Padget's Creek Baptist communities were consistent in protecting the power of masters over slaves, differences between their respective church hierarchies suggest that the relationship between planters and yeomen remained a contested terrain. The Bush River church was more or less consistent in appointing slaveholders as deacons, and slaveholders also appear to have played a disproportionately active role as members of committees of inquiry. At the Padget's Creek

---

55. Bush River Baptist Church, Journal, Sept. 7, Oct. 12, 1805, I, 31; Baptist Church of Christ at Poplar Springs, Minutes, 1794–1937, July 14, 1794, 2, SCL transcript; Brushy Creek Baptist Church, Minutes, 1794–1927, Mar. 20, 1802, 13, SCL transcript; Big Creek Baptist Church, Minutes, Aug. 1, 1807, May 30, Oct. 4, 1808, Feb. 4, 1809, SCL; Townsend, *S.C. Baptists*, 234.

56. For a discussion of the culture of local exchange created by Georgia's upcountry yeomen, see Steven Hahn, *The Roots of Southern Populism: Yeoman Farmers and the Transformation of The Georgia Upcountry, 1850–1890* (New York, 1983), esp. 50–85.

church, on the other hand, members of the church hierarchy were drawn primarily from the ranks of nonslaveholders.[57]

On at least two occasions before 1810, prosperous slaveholders of the Padget's Creek Baptist Church became the objects of disciplinary action meted out by less prosperous men. One of these cases involved Woodson Rountree, who owned at least nine slaves at the time of his conversion in 1802. He was excluded from fellowship four years later when the church deemed him "very disorderly" and noted his refusal to attend meetings. For reasons that remain unclear, the members also excluded Thomas Blossengame from fellowship and then readmitted him thereto. As the owner of fifteen slaves, Blossengame may well have been the wealthiest member of the Padget's Creek church. Such cases held a complex class meaning. On the one hand, they worked to legitimize the position of slaveholders. By holding prosperous members to a standard of Christian behavior, the Padget's Creek church was acknowledging an underlying compatibility between social inequality and spiritual community. At the same time, members were revealing a marked unwillingness to grant unconditional respect to their wealthier brethren. The church essentially demanded that Blossengame, who was probably related to a state senator from Union District, accommodate to the yeoman community.[58]

Uniting the broad spectrum of disciplinary cases was the expectation that

57. Thomas Davis and James Teague, appointed deacons at the Bush River Baptist Church, held seven and five slaves, respectively. Providence Williams, who was active on committees of inquiry, held five slaves. Joseph Johnson, also a deacon, may have been a slaveholder, but there were also nonslaveholders in Newberry County with that name. Richard Shackleford, a deacon or elder in the Bush River church, was listed on the census of 1800 as a minister and the owner of eleven slaves in Laurens County. Jacob King, also an elder or deacon at Bush River, held five slaves. Joseph Nix, Benjamin Nix, Nathan Langston, David Floyd, Hosea Ray, all appointed as deacons by the Padget's Creek Baptist Church, were nonslaveholders. Slaveholding yeomen were a minority in the church hierarchy. William Wilbanks, Jr., owner of six slaves, was an elder, but his appointment as deacon met with opposition. Thomas Greer, owner of six slaves, was a frequent member of committees of inquiry at the Padget's Creek church. Bush River Baptist Church, Journal, Apr. 5, Sept. 8, 1798, Mar. 13, 1802, Mar. 23, 1805, Aug. 29, 1807, I, 14, 19, 29, 37; Padget's Creek Baptist Church, Book, Sept. 14, 1793, May 10, Nov. 8, 1794, Feb. 10, 1798, May 9, 1802, Sept. 16, 1803, Apr. 14, 1810, 23, 24, 25, 30, 37, 43, 62; Federal Population Census, South Carolina, 1800.

58. Padget's Creek Baptist Church, Book, June 18, July 20, 1802, Feb. 14, Mar. 15, 1806, I, 37–38, 51; Federal Population Census, South Carolina, 1800. Blossengame, who appears on the South Carolina census of 1800 as Thomas Blasingame, was probably related to John Blassingame, who represented Greenville District in the South Carolina House of Representatives, and Union District in the South Carolina Senate. Edgar *et al.*, eds., *Biographical Directory of the House*, III, 74–75.

those placed under investigation demonstrate the requisite acknowledgment of guilt and assume the appropriate attitude of humility before their respective churches. In other words, backcountry Baptists expected from each other, as a condition of church membership, a willing acceptance of church discipline. With the possible exception of cases involving adultery, church members tended to forgive sinners who admitted their "fault," but they generally excluded men and women who appeared unrepentant. Church members accepted as inevitable the sinfulness of human nature but sought to contain it within their respective spiritual communities. Thus Wiot Wood and his wife were excommunicated when, after being cited for "living disorderly together," they refused to attend the Padget's Creek Baptist Church "according to citement." When the church cited James and Winnie Willard for fighting, James acknowledged his "fault" and won reacceptance, while Winnie "disappear'd" and was excommunicated. James Hollis won forgiveness when he "confess'd drinking too much," as did David Murrell, who "confess'd his fault" after being found guilty of fighting. On the other hand, Rebekah Coat of the Bush River Baptist Church "confessed she had drunk rather too much, but endeavored as much as possible to hide her crimes." It was because, upon further investigation, she spoke "an additional falsehood . . . in saying before God she was clear of the charge" that church members decided to exclude her from fellowship.[59]

Although these yeoman churches embodied an organic vision of social and spiritual order, members did not adopt a submissive attitude toward church hierarchy. Throughout the winter of 1793, the Padget's Creek Baptist Church considered a disciplinary case involving their own minister, Frederick Crowder. The minutes do not reveal the nature of the alleged transgression, but church members deemed the minister's "fall" sufficiently serious to merit exclusion. Crowder, who apparently fled to Georgia, continued to press for readmission, but he was not accepted back into the church until the winter of 1796. William Wilbanks, Jr., owner of six slaves and the son of a leading member of the church, met with serious opposition when, in December 1800, the membership considered whether he was "a fit person to put to the work of a Deacon."[60]

The Reverend William Capers gave revealing testimony to the unwillingness of backcountry yeomen to adopt a submissive attitude toward men

59. Padget's Creek Baptist Church, Book, Mar. 15, 1793, Aug. 27, Sept. 16, 1803, Feb. 18, 1804, Dec. 16, 1805, I, 22, 43, 45, 50; Bush River Baptist Church, Journal, Mar. 23, June 8, 1805, 29–30.

60. Padget's Creek Baptist Church, Book, Feb. 16, Mar. 15, 28, 1793, June 6, 1794, May 9, 1795, July 12, 1795, Dec. 10, 1796, Dec. 20, 1800, I, 22, 24, 25, 26, 28, 33; Federal Population Census, South Carolina, 1800.

who identified themselves as spiritual or social leaders. As a nineteen-year-old preacher whose ties to the planter class were probably all too apparent, Capers had considerable difficulty winning respect from his audiences. Years later, he wrote at some length about a particularly tumultuous meeting held in Lancaster Court House in 1809. The interruption came while he was in the midst of saying "something about" a passage in which "Balaam said unto Balak, 'Lo, I am come unto thee: have I now any power at all to say anything?' " One man in the audience thought that Capers did not have the power and said so. The man stepped forward and cursed "with a loud, angry voice." Apparently he had his own ideas about preaching and told Capers to "quit that gibberish" and return to the text. "Now, Mr.," said the man, "Jist give me them thar books, and you'll see." Everyone seemed to find this "exceeding funny, and of course the titter was renewed with increase."[61]

vii

From the point of view of South Carolina's leading ministers, the path to the "reform of mankind" must have seemed a rocky one. Yeomen were not always duly respectful of their spiritual leaders and social superiors, and church men and women frequently fell victim to the temptation of excessive drink and adultery. All too often, Christian planters failed to meet their own standard of stewardship, and converted slaves continued to give evidence of recalcitrance and misunderstanding. Religion did not put an end to covetousness even among the converted, and scoffers continued to plague camp meetings.

Nonetheless, as slavery spread through the backcountry, religion did exert a powerful influence that strengthened the position of planters generally. Although evangelicalism became a vehicle for the expression of persistent tensions between yeomen and planters, it also upheld the foundation of planter power. Ministers did their best to define slavery as an extension of God-given inequalities, and backcountry churches accommodated their familial vision of social order to the distinctive concerns of slave masters. In this sense, backcountry evangelicalism paralleled the democratic-republican political assumptions that prevailed in the same region. It could express powerful anti-elitist sentiments while locating slavery among the unequal familial relationships that yeomen as well as planters took for granted.

Evangelicalism, even as it developed in the Old South, was no more essentially or necessarily supportive of slavery than it was intrinsically anti-

61. Wightman, *Life of Capers*, 109–110.

slavery or egalitarian. Richard Furman and other slaveholding Baptists revealed, through their careful negotiations with the New Lights, a keen sensitivity to threatening potentialities within their own faith. The very existence of James Gilleland and his small group of antislavery Presbyterians indicates that backcountry evangelicals were capable of distinguishing slavery from other forms of household dependency. That most of the region's yeoman majority saw no such distinction testifies not only to their growing involvement in slavery but to the complex accommodations and identifications that gave backcountry planters their distinctive political character.

Conclusion:
The Limits of Unification

In 1808 South Carolina was poised to withstand the democratizing pressures that transformed other southern state constitutions during the Jacksonian era. The new system of apportionment kept political power squarely in the hands of Black Belt representatives, and an expanding slave-plantation system was reducing the sources of sectional tension. During the preceding decades, backcountry political leaders had forged ties to their coastal counterparts, and, by the second decade of the nineteenth century, the two groups were beginning to merge.

The state constitutional reform of 1808 revealed the willingness of planters throughout the state to safeguard slavery by limiting political equality among citizens, but it remained for a younger generation of South Carolinians to develop a proslavery argument and to articulate a theory of politics that was compatible with the interests of planters generally. Not until the second quarter of the nineteenth century, when northern politicians and reformers began to identify democracy and equality with free labor, did spokesmen for the planter class feel it necessary to articulate their own vision of a slaveholders' republic.

In fact, elements of that distinctive proslavery vision had long been apparent, signaling tensions that were to persist among southern spokesmen of the antebellum decades. On the one hand, the lowcountry Federalists Henry William Desaussure and Timothy Ford were among the first of those proslavery intellectuals who publicly identified the interests of planters with a baldly inegalitarian conception of the polity. During subsequent decades, intellectual spokesmen for the planter class—those who were unbeholden to wide constituencies—reified social and political hierarchy by describing the slaveholders' republic as a family writ large. At the same time, backcountry leaders, constrained by their complex relationship to yeoman constituencies, anticipated an alternative tendency among southern political leaders. Their democratic-republican ideology, which linked yeomen and planters as a fraternity of independent producers and property holders, emerged as a powerful voice in South Carolina and persisted, in various guises, throughout the antebellum South.[1]

There were significant points of contact between the openly hierarchical and democratic-republican versions of the proslavery argument. From the outset, proslavery spokesmen of all stripes presumed a world in which household dependents, excluded from political participation, existed in some degree of subordination to the men who entered the political arena as citizens. That construction of social order identified yeomen with planters by emphasizing their joint position as independent household heads. By the antebellum decades, southern spokesmen from all regions were also insisting that slavery was itself the guarantor of yeoman independence. Proslavery spokesmen differed concerning the acceptable extent of political equality among citizens, but they shared in the effort to locate slavery within a broader network of unequal familial relationships, and together they argued that slavery protected free men from the degradation of dependence on the marketplace.[2]

The democratic-republican rhetoric that came to predominate among southern political leaders did not make yeomen the locus of power and authority. The story of South Carolina's backcountry should caution against confusing political language with social relationships.[3] Pressure

1. On the proslavery argument, see Eugene D. Genovese, *The World the Slaveholders Made: Two Essays in Interpretation* (New York, 1969), 118–244; Drew Gilpin Faust, "A Southern Stewardship: The Intellectual and the Proslavery Argument," *American Quarterly*, XXXI (1979), 63–80; Faust, ed., *The Ideology of Slavery: Proslavery Thought in the Antebellum South, 1830–1860* (Baton Rouge, La., 1981); Faust, *James Henry Hammond and the Old South: A Design for Mastery* (Baton Rouge, La., 1982). On the link between Federalism and proslavery thought, see Larry E. Tise, *Proslavery: A History of the Defense of Slavery in America, 1701-1840* (Athens, Ga., 1987).

2. Eugene D. Genovese, "Yeomen Farmers in a Slaveholders' Democracy," *Agricultural History*, XLIX (1975), 331–342; Steven Hahn, *The Roots of Southern Populism: Yeoman Farmers and the Transformation of the Georgia Upcountry, 1850–1890* (New York, 1983), 86–91; Stephanie McCurry, "Defense of Their World: Class, Gender, and the Yeomanry of the South Carolina Lowcountry, 1820–1861" (Ph.D. diss., State University of New York, Binghamton, 1988).

3. For classic depictions of the Old South as a yeoman or white man's democracy, see Fletcher Melvin Green, *Democracy in the Old South and Other Essays*, ed. J. Isaac Copeland (Nashville, Tenn., 1969), esp. 65–86; Fletcher M. Green, *Constitutional Development in the South Atlantic States, 1776–1860: A Study in the Evolution of Democracy* (Chapel Hill, N.C., 1930); George M. Frederickson, *The Black Image in the White Mind: The Debate on Afro-American Character and Destiny* (New York, 1971). For an important reformulation of this position, see Lacy K. Ford, Jr., "Social Origins of a New

from the yeomanry gave shape to the political ideology articulated by many state representatives, but it did not place yeomen in the dominant political position. Backcountry planters agreed to a state constitution that protected the prerogatives of wealth, and the bonds of interdependency that mediated local political practices gave the balance of power to planters.

Not until the Civil War did the contradictions inherent in southern society begin to explode. The exigencies of war exposed tensions between the planters' dependence on social rank and political inequality and the yeomen's vision of fraternity among citizens. In a sense, coastal Federalists had been correct. Ultimately, resentment of planter privilege and commitment to the preservation of local and individual liberties prompted resistance to the Confederate government and weakened the planters in their struggle for regional independence.[4]

Nonetheless, backcountry political leaders of the eighteenth and early nineteenth centuries, together with their sympathizers on the coast, succeeded in formulating a democratic-republican vision that simultaneously sanctioned slavery, contained persisting tensions between yeomen and planters, and provided the ideological foundation for South Carolina's political unification. Backcountry leaders bowed to principles of political equality and made ostentatious demonstrations of deference to the yeomanry, but they were democrats only within narrowly defined limits. They saw slavery as a legitimate extension of household dependency and expected planters to wield influence beyond their numbers. Those assumptions, shaped by a deepening commitment to slavery, enabled a colony rent with sectional conflict to emerge, by the first decade of the nineteenth century, with the South's most unified and politically powerful statewide leadership.

South Carolina: The Upcountry in the Nineteenth Century" (Ph.D. diss., University of South Carolina, 1983). Where Ford sees yeoman dominance in a democratic political process, I see planters maintaining power and authority through their accommodations (sometimes grudging) to the yeomanry. Much of Ford's own rich evidence actually points to the persistence of the sort of unequal, patron-client relationships that mediated political practices in the post-Revolutionary backcountry.

4. On tensions between yeomen and planters on the eve of secession and during the Civil War, see Michael P. Johnson, *Toward a Patriarchal Republic: The Secession of Georgia* (Baton Rouge, La., 1977); Hahn, *Roots of Southern Populism*, 116–133; Bell I. Wiley, *The Life of Johnny Reb: The Common Soldier of the Confederacy* (New York, 1943); Steven E. Ambrose, "Yeoman Discontent in the Confederacy," *Civil War History*, VIII (1962), 259–268.

Appendix 1.
South Carolina Parishes, Districts, and Counties, 1767–1808

Judicial Districts

South Carolina's Circuit Court Act, which won approval by the crown in 1769, divided the colony into seven circuit court districts:

Lowcountry: Georgetown, Charleston, Beaufort
Backcountry: Cheraws, Camden, Orangeburg, Ninety Six

Before the establishment of circuit courts, all of South Carolina's judicial administration was centralized in Charleston.

The state legislature, in 1785, passed an act for the establishment of county courts within each of the existing judicial districts. Although the act created county divisions in the lowcountry, it did not require lowcountry districts to set up county courts. County government never took firm root in the lowcountry, where parish organization was firmly entrenched and where many residents enjoyed relatively easy access to Charleston. In the backcountry, however, counties became an important locus of administration. Backcountry districts were identified as follows:

Cheraws: Chesterfield, Marlboro, Darlington
Camden: Clarendon, Claremont, Richland, Lancaster, Kershaw (created in 1791), Salem (created in 1791), Fairfield, Chester, York
Orangeburg: Winton, Orange, Lewisburg, Lexington
Ninety Six: Edgefield, Newberry, Union, Abbeville, Laurens, Spartanburg, Pendleton (created in 1789), Greenville (created in 1786)

The legislature established two new backcountry court districts in 1791. Washington District encompassed Greenville and Pendleton counties, and Pinckney District encompassed York and Chester counties.

In 1800, the legislature abolished the county courts and created district courts in their place. (The new system was presided over by traveling state judges.) The five coastal court districts were Beaufort, Colleton, Charleston, Georgetown, and Marion. Claremont, Clarendon, and Salem counties were combined to form the middlecountry district of Sumter, and Barnwell

District was formed from part of the old circuit court district of Orange-burg. Throughout the rest of the backcountry, existing counties simply became court districts.

Election Districts

In 1767, the twenty parishes of the established Anglican church were serving as South Carolina election districts, and other administrative and judicial offices were centralized in Charleston. Only the vast and vaguely defined parish of St. Mark, created in 1757, was located in the backcountry. The following year, the crown approved the establishment of two additional backcountry parishes, St. Mathew and St. David.

The state constitutions of 1776 and 1778 designated existing coastal parishes as election districts but modified and expanded backcountry districts as follows:

1. District between Savannah River and North Fork of Edisto (middle-country)
2. St. Mathew Parish (middlecountry)
3. Orange Parish (created in 1778 out of St. Mathew Parish, middle-country)
4. District Eastward of Wateree River (spanned the middle and upcountry)
5. St. David Parish (middlecountry)
6. Saxe Gotha District (middlecountry)
7. District between Broad and Catawba Rivers (spanned the middle and upcountry)
8. Lower District between the Broad and Saluda Rivers (upcountry)
9. Ninety Six District (the upcountry election district of Ninety Six included only Abbeville and Edgefield counties; it was, in other words, only a section of the circuit court district with the same name)
10. Upper Spartan District (upcountry)
11. Little River District (created in 1778 out of the Upper Spartan District, upcountry)
12. New Acquisition District (upcountry)
13. Cherokee Indian Lands (upcountry, unrepresented)

The State Constitution of 1790 continued to designate existing coastal parishes as election districts, but it made an important modification by subdividing the lowcountry election districts of Prince Fredrick and Prince George Parish, Winyah into Williamsburg, Liberty, Kingston, and Prince George Parish, Winyah districts.

Under the State Constitution of 1790, backcountry districts were redefined. With the exception of Winton District, Orange Parish, and St. Mathew Parish, the new system of backcountry election districting corresponded to county divisions:

1. The District between Savannah River and North Fork of Edisto became Winton District (middlecountry).
2. St. Mathew Parish was unchanged.
3. Orange Parish was unchanged.
4. The District Eastward of Wateree River became Clarendon District (middlecountry), Claremont District (middlecountry), Kershaw District (included middle and upcountry areas), and Lancaster (upcountry).
5. St. David Parish became Darlington District (middlecountry), Marlboro District (middlecountry), and Chesterfield District (middlecountry)
6. Saxe Gotha District was unchanged.
7. The District between the Broad and Catawba Rivers became Richland District (middlecountry), Fairfield District (upcountry), and Chester District (upcountry).
8. The Lower District between the Broad and Saluda Rivers became Newberry District (upcountry).
9. Ninety Six District became Edgefield District (spanned the middlecountry and the upcountry) and Abbeville District (upcountry).
10. The Upper Spartan District became Union District (upcountry) and Spartan District (upcountry).
11. The Little River District became Laurens District (upcountry).
12. The New Acquisition became York District (upcountry).
13. The Cherokee Indian Lands became Pendleton District (upcountry).

Sources: Walter B. Edgar *et al.*, eds., *Biographical Directory of the South Carolina House of Representatives* (Columbia, S.C., 1974–1984), I, 46–47, 164–166, 226–227; Thomas Cooper and David J. McCord, eds., *The Statutes at Large of South Carolina* (Columbia, S.C., 1836–1841), VII, 211–242, 293–300; Richard Maxwell Brown, *The South Carolina Regulators* (Cambridge, Mass., 1963), 96–111; "Formation of Counties in South Carolina," SCDAH, Typescript.

Appendix 2.
Landholdings of People Accused of Crimes, 1767–1775

Name	Crime as listed in court record
Accused criminals without warrants or deeds to land	
1. Christopher Allen	horse stealing
2. Joseph Armstrong	horse stealing
3. James Arts	
4. Thomas Avery	
5. Constantine Bombazine	horse stealing
6. Arthur Bowers	horse stealing
7. Valentine Brasil (Brasswell)	
8. James Cain	house robbery
9. Michael Carrol	larceny
10. Jesse Carter	
11. John Cod	larceny
12. Nicholas Cole	larceny
13. Matthias Collins	larceny
14. John Connaway	larceny
15. William Courtney	larceny
16. David Cozart	horse stealing
17. Thomas Daly	felony
18. Henry Dayer	felony
19. Matthew Dempsey	larceny
20. Winslow Driggers	
21. Thomas Floyd	
22. Robert Foster	larceny
23. Jeremiah Fulsom	
24. Edward Gibson	
25. Henry Granger	horse stealing
26. Obdiah Greenage	

27. Dempsey Griffith . . . . horse stealing, stealing a
    Negro
28. Jesse Hambersam
29. Fred Harper . . . . horse stealing
30. Timothy Harrison . . . . stealing
31. George Heyward
32. Charles Higden
33. Daniel Higden
34. Hugh Hinds . . . . horse stealing, house
    robbery, murder
35. Jacob Hock . . . . larceny
36. William Hoddy
37. Absolom Hooper . . . . felony, murder
38. James Hooper . . . . suspicion of felony, murder
39. Robert Hurdle . . . . larceny
40. William Hutto
41. Edmund James . . . . stealing Negroes
42. James Kay
43. Jacob Malheree . . . . larceny
44. William Malloy
45. James Marlow
46. Christopher Marr
47. Daniel Mylander (Nylander) . . . . larceny
48. James Nowland . . . . house robbery
49. John Nowland . . . . larceny
50. William Nowland . . . . larceny
51. Benjamin Ogden
52. John Ogden
53. Emanuel Osterman . . . . felony
54. Thomas Parrington . . . . felony
55. Robert Prine . . . . killing of steer
56. Benjamin Reeves . . . . larceny
57. Isaac Reeves . . . . highway robbery, horse
    stealing
58. Solomon Rivers
59. Noah Roundtree . . . . house robbery
60. Samuel Schaw . . . . larceny
61. George Seacought
62. Richard Seymore
63. Thomas Seymore
64. William Sherlock . . . . larceny

65. Arthur Sikes (Sykes)
66. Solomon Sikes (Sykes)
67. Salathiel Sinnenon
68. Levi Sparkman (Lupier) . . . . horse stealing, house robbery
69. James Spikes
70. Levi Starn . . . . house robbery
71. Sylvester Stokes
72. Connor Sullivan . . . . stealing
73. Jeremiah Tilly . . . . horse stealing
74. William Toatwine . . . . horse stealing
75. William Trapnell . . . . horse stealing
76. Joseph Trull . . . . horse stealing
77. Timothy Tyrell
78. John Velasky . . . . horse stealing
79. Salthouse Weatherly . . . . larceny
80. Ebenezer Wells
81. Noel Williams
82. Thomas Woolfingtown . . . . larceny
83. James Yates . . . . larceny

Accused criminals with plats or deeds to land

1. John Baker . . . . larceny
2. John Sullivan Berry . . . . horse stealing
3. George Black
4. John Boyle . . . . larceny
5. George Burns
6. James Burns . . . . larceny
7. John Burns . . . . horse stealing
8. James Cain . . . . house robbery
9. John Cain . . . . suspicion of a felony
10. John Cameron . . . . larceny
11. Daniel Campbell . . . . larceny
12. Thomas Campbell . . . . horse stealing
13. James Clark . . . . larceny
14. Thomas Clark . . . . larceny
15. John Cornelius . . . . horse stealing
16. Anthony Duesto (Distow, Distoe)

17. John Eager . . . . larceny
18. John Field . . . . stealing
19. William French . . . . horse stealing
20. James Gray
21. Thomas Gray
22. William Griffin . . . . stealing a Negro, forgery
23. Joseph Hancock . . . . felony
24. Ezekiel Harlin . . . . suspicion of robbery
25. Jacob Hoffman . . . . robbery
26. John Hogan
27. Joseph Hogg . . . . horse stealing
28. Thomas Hooper . . . . horse stealing
29. William Howell . . . . horse stealing
30. Patrick Hughes . . . . larceny
31. James Hunter . . . . larceny
32. Benjamin Hutto
33. Martin Johnson . . . . horse stealing
34. John Kennely . . . . stealing
35. Nimrod Kilcrease . . . . house robbery
36. Sabastian King
37. Henry Lightman . . . . horse stealing
38. John Lowry . . . . larceny
39. Edward Lynch . . . . horse stealing
40. John Lynn . . . . horse stealing
41. James McClenachan . . . . stealing a Negro
42. Alexander McCulloch . . . . larceny
43. John Mcgregor . . . . horse stealing
44. Redmon McMahan (land grant
    to Edmund McMahan, 1765)
45. James McWhir . . . . larceny
46. James Moon
47. Thomas Moon
48. Henry Pooner (Poozer) . . . . felony
49. Thomas Powell . . . . burglary
50. Isaac Reeves . . . . horse stealing
51. Thomas Reeves . . . . larceny
52. Hardy Rice
53. John Roly (plat to John Role, 1738) . . . horse stealing
54. Arnold Russell . . . . house robbery
55. Abraham Shelly . . . . felony
56. Thomas Spell

57. John Sprout . . . . robbery
58. Benjamin Spurlock
59. Ebenezer Starn . . . . house robbery
60. Daniel Sullivan . . . . stealing
61. Henry Summerall . . . . horse stealing
62. Charles Tais . . . . larceny
63. John Tilly . . . . horse stealing
64. James Tyrell
65. George Underwood
66. John Walker . . . . horse stealing
67. Thomas Webb . . . . larceny
68. Patrick Welsh . . . . stealing hogs
69. Benjamin West . . . . stealing a Negro
70. Thomas Whitehead . . . . horse stealing
71. John Wood . . . . horse stealing

Accused criminals whose names appear on plats held by others

1. George Frick
2. Roger Martin
3. Drury Morris . . . . house robbery
4. Richard Rottenbury

Criminals accused of banditry during the Regulation who acquired their first plat or deed to land after 1769

1. James Ashworth
2. Ephraim Jones
3. John Mackilroy
4. Patrick Morris
5. Dennis Nowland . . . . horse stealing
6. Richard Rottenbury
7. Absolam Tilly . . . . horse stealing
8. Hezekiah Tyrell

Women accused of crimes (landholdings could not be identified)

1. Mary Coll . . . . felony
2. Rachel Davis . . . . larceny
3. Lydia Davis . . . . larceny

4. Ann Dawson . . . . horse stealing
5. Jean Gallway . . . . larceny
6. Sarah Gowais . . . . larceny
7. Catherine Hood . . . . larceny
8. Sarah Kelly . . . . larceny
9. Mary Myers . . . . horse stealing
10. Francis Patty . . . . burglary
11. Margaret Reily . . . . larceny
12. Margaret Robertson . . . . felony

Note: The above lists include people accused of crimes in newspaper reports and/or convicted of crimes in court. The lists exclude accused criminals found not guilty, those who could be reasonably identified as lowcountry residents, and those whose names were too common to be traced. Those whose crime is not specified were identified in newspaper accounts, the South Carolina Council Journal, the South Carolina House of Assembly Journal, or the records of pardons listed in the Miscellaneous Records of the South Carolina Department of Archives and History.

Sources: Charleston Court of General Sessions, Journal, 1769–1776, SCDAH; South Carolina House of Assembly Journal, Nov. 11, 1767, Feb. 15, 28, Apr. 9, 1770, SCDAH; South Carolina Council Journal, May 30, 31, June 16, 1768, Feb. 22, 1769, Feb. 28, 1770, SCDAH; *South-Carolina Gazette; and Country Journal* (Charleston), Apr. 3, 14, June 9, July 28, Oct. 20, 1767; *South-Carolina and American General Gazette* (Charleston), Apr. 3, Aug. 21, June 5, Nov. 13, 1767, Feb. 19, June 10, 1768, Feb. 27, Nov. 2, 1769; *South-Carolina Gazette* (Charleston), Aug. 3, Oct. 6, 1767, Oct. 11, 1770, July 18, 1771, Nov. 26, Dec. 10, 1772; records of criminal pardons, Miscellaneous Records, MM, 85, 345, 365, 586–587, OO, 413, PP, 9; Richard Maxwell Brown, *The South Carolina Regulators* (Cambridge, Mass., 1963), 29–52.

Index

Platt, George, 29
Pledger, Philip, 67n, 69, 71
Plows: in inventories, 24–25
Plundering: by British, 100–104; by
    whigs, 102–103; of slaves, 107; after
    war, 117
Population: for backcountry, 9, 19–20;
    distribution of, circa 1765, 41; of free
    blacks, 71–72; and 1790 census, 221;
    rate of increase of, 250–254
Postal service, 206
Potatoes, 24
Powell, George Gabriel, 69, 71
Presbyterian churches: in piedmont, 42;
    ministry of, 276n; and revivals, 283
Presbyterians: loyalties of, 81; in Assem-
    bly, 155; and academies, 243; and slav-
    ery, 251, 273, 284
Presbyterian Synod of South Carolina,
    284
Prevost, Augustine, 99–100
Prince family, 294
Prince Frederick Parish, 113, 167
Prince George, Winyah, Parish, 113,
    265–266
Prince William Parish, 1, 74, 213
Prine, Robert, 62
Pringle, John Julius, 123–124
Privy Council, 74
Property: in Republicanism, 149, 214;
    and representation, 226–225
Proslavery argument, 270–272, 303–305.
    See also Baptists; Religion
Provincial congress, 82–83, 92
Public schools: 63, 68, 206, 239
Pugh, Evan, 66–67, 67n
Purrysburg, 11
Purse, William, 24–25

Quakers: in Wateree area, 13; Regulators
    among, 50; as loyalists, 81; and leaving
    state, 250–251, 275; and slavery,
    274–276; fear of, 276
Queensborough Township, 11

Rambo, Laurence, 187
Ramsay, David: on backcountry
    resentments, 90; on tories, 95–96; on
    British alienation of backcountry, 102;
    on black soldiers, 106; on effects of
    war, 109, 114; and slavery, 114, 217;
    on debt relief, 129; and constitutional
    convention, 143–144; on state govern-

ments, 165; on cotton, 249; on squat-
    ters, 249
Ramsay, Ephraim, 221
Ranger companies, 38, 68, 95, 116,
    118–119
Rawdon, Francis, 101
Ray, Hosea, 229n
Ray, James, 39n
Read, Jacob, 123–124, 174, 219–221,
    229
Read, William, 219–221
Redd, John, 137
Reese, Joseph, 43, 281
Reese, Thomas, 220, 269–271, 280–284
Reese, William, 122, 125
Regional distinctiveness, 4–5
Regional diversity in 1780s, 109–110
Regular Baptists. *See* Baptists
Regulator movement, 38–46, 51–56, 71,
    74
Regulators: described, 47–51; program
    of, 48, 63, 69, 80; and elections, 48;
    and petitioning Assembly, 48, 50;
    wealth of, 49, 61, 68; and religion, 50,
    66–67; as creditors, 50–51, 65; and
    hunters, 51–56, 64; and vagrants, 54;
    and bandits, 57–64; and North Caro-
    lina Regulators, 64–68; lowcountry
    view of, 67–70, 74–77, 80; and coastal
    authorities, 67–72, 74–77; and ranger
    companies, 68; pardons for, 69, 74;
    and racial boundaries, 69–72; opposi-
    tion to, in backcountry, 72; and election
    of candidates, 74; and Moderators, 74;
    reasons for success of, 77; in Revolu-
    tion, 79–81; as speculators, 187; persis-
    tent demands of, 239; in Mount Zion
    Society, 239
Religion: and family order, 5; in back-
    country, 42–46; among Regulators, 50,
    66; of representatives, 155; and social
    order, 269, 297–300; as proslavery,
    270, 291; and social hierarchy,
    270–271; and slaves, 294–297
Representation. *See* Apportionment
Representative Reform Association, 193,
    195–196, 221, 224, 228
Republican coalition, 6, 204, 212–217,
    237
Republicanism: regional diversity of, 5,
    159, 216; and loyalism, 81; defined,
    149–150; and slavery, 150; and aristoc-
    racy of talent, 158–159; and U.S. con-